MW01031082

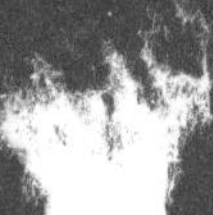

MICHAEL WALLIS

with SUZANNE FITZGERALD WALLIS ROBERT G. MCCUBBIN, *Picture Editor*

ABRAMS, NEW YORK

INTRODUCTION

For many, the words "Wild West" bring to mind the geography and lore of the trans-Mississippi United States during the late 1800s. Although it is true that the thirty-five years between the close of the Civil War and the end of the nineteenth century saw many of the best-known events, as well as the most romanticized individuals associated with the West, the real origins of Wild West culture began long before the Civil War, and the mythos of that era reached into the twentieth century.

An examination of the events between 1830 and 1930 provides a more complete picture of the Wild West, including the personalities, battles, treaties, innovations, and migrations that sprang from the call of Manifest Destiny. Before and throughout the Civil War, that drive would inspire the securing and exploitation of the western lands, the expansion of federal authority, and the nation's struggle to shift from an agrarian society to an industrialized power.

Finally, in the first three decades of the twentieth century, the last iconic figures of the Wild West would pass into history but remain firmly rooted in the imaginations of Americans and people around the world.

Many of the key elements contributing to the image of the Wild West are found in these pages. They include the famous and the infamous, courageous and despicable acts, legendary names and unsung heroes and heroines. An American icon in and of itself, the "Wild West" draws visitors from around the world who travel through this region of the United States in search of the adventures chronicled in books and films, played out by cowboys, Indians, outlaws, and heroes. In the eyes of visitors both foreign and domestic, the modern American West is still first and foremost the Wild West.

In many instances, we have chosen to include the language of the time period. For example, instead of the term "Native American," the word "Indian" is used in order to retain the authenticity and feel of the era. For better or for worse, during the century this book chronicles there was no such thing as political correctness in either word or deed.

When considering sources for the images needed to bring the stories here to life, Robert McCubbin—publisher emeritus of *True West* magazine and a founder of the Wild West History Association—was an obvious choice. Simply put, the Robert G. McCubbin Collection is unquestionably the premier private collection of American Old West photographs. Beyond the vast numbers of images covering every aspect of life in the West, Bob has assembled an impressive library containing thousands of books and publications. Most of the works are not only first editions, but many are rare and one-of-a-kind.

The team devoted countless hours to the demanding task of selecting the best candidates to convey the century of American history during which the concept of the "Wild West" was forged. The result is a compendium that flows chronologically from 1830 to 1930 with each day providing a concise text and accompanying images. The daily entries found at the top of the pages are generally not connected to the tale told by the main text and images, but constitute a separate running diary of incidents or events that actually happened on that specific date.

A landmark event or a particularly compelling personality may get fleshed out by more than one entry in these pages. Each stands on its own as a complete vignette, but for those readers who choose to go through the book in order from January 1 to December 31, an epic tale will unfold.

So saddle up, keep a sharp lookout for desperados, and enjoy the ride.

Michael and Suzanne Wallis
Tulsa, Oklahoma, 2010

JAN

1

1875 Doc Holliday has his first brush with the law. As the *Dallas Weekly Herald* reports: "Dr. Holliday and Mr. Austin, a saloon keeper, relieved the monotony of the noise of firecrackers by taking a couple of shots at each other yesterday afternoon. The cheerful note of the six-shooter is heard once more among us."

PAINTBRUSH HISTORIANS

In the summer of 1832, Philadelphia artist George Catlin lived among the Mandan tribe, a sedentary people dwelling in large villages along the upper Missouri River. The Mandans' first contact with white men was in 1738, and in 1804 the Lewis and Clark Expedition visited the area. Catlin—who wanted to portray "man, in the simplicity and loftiness of his nature"—arrived at a time when most eastern tribes were already confined to reservations. The Mandans were amazed by the portraitist's ability to capture their images on canvas and embraced him as a powerful medicine man. They sacrificed a dog in his honor and presented Catlin with a medicine staff and a rattle adorned with grizzly bear claws and bat's wings. In 1833, the Swiss artist Karl Bodmer followed in his footsteps and produced hundreds of works depicting daily life of Mandan and Hidatsa villages. Noted historian John C. Ewers credited Catlin and Bodmer for "establishing the Plains Indian in the minds of millions." In 1837, a trading vessel steaming up the Missouri from St. Louis brought with it a devastating smallpox epidemic that nearly wiped out the Mandan, Hidatsa, and Arikara tribes. The virus killed as many as twenty thousand Indians. Almost 90 percent of the Mandan tribe died, and today no full-blooded Mandans remain.

▶ George Catlin's painting of a Mandan village near the Missouri River in the 1830s.

"Ever since I can remember I have loved the Whites. I have lived With them even since I was a Boy. . . . I have Never called a White Man a Dog, but to day I do Pronounce them to be a set of Black hatred Dogs. They have deceived me, them that I always considered as Brothers has turned out to be My Worst Enemies."

—speech of the Mandan warrior Four Bears, July 30, 1837

JAN 2

1873 At Clear Creek Canyon, Arizona Territory, the Twenty-third Infantry confronts a party of hostile Indians. There are no casualties in the incident.

HORSEMEN OF THE GREAT PLAINS

The vast sea of grass bounded by the Mississippi River on the east and the foothills of the Rocky Mountains to the west nurtured the native tribes that would become the standard image of all American Indians. Although culturally diverse and each with their own language, these tribes—including Sioux, Comanche, Cheyenne, Arapaho, Blackfoot, Kiowa, Pawnee, and Crow—shared a common identity and came to be known as the Plains Indians. Many were nomadic hunters and warriors, whose way of life had been revolutionized by the horse, allowing them to pursue the vast herds of buffalo and also wage war more effectively.

My horse be swift in flight
Even like a bird;
My horse be swift in flight.
Bear me now in safety
Far from the enemy's arrows,
And you shall be rewarded
With streamers and ribbons red.

—Sioux warrior song

▲ Northern Plains warriors.

▶ An early engraving of Indians in combat. Most tribes were in constant warfare with each other.

JAN 3

1846 The term "Manifest Destiny" is used for the first time in Congress by Robert Winthrop of Massachusetts.

FUR TRADE

For most of the first half of the nineteenth century, hard-edged characters of every stripe roamed the American West in search of fur. During the heyday of the fur trade, as many as three thousand men trapped the streams that flowed across the Rocky Mountain watersheds. These rugged individuals were mostly looking for beaver, for many years the most profitable pelt due to its great demand for the making of felt hats. Trapping beaver proved to be relatively easy, but the trick was to get the fur to market without it falling prey to moths and mildew, and without the trapper losing his own hair in the process.

"After daylight disappeared I took a star for my guide. . . . It was near midnight when I laid down to rest. I had plenty of provisions, but could not eat. Water! Water was the object of my wishes. Travelling for two days in the hot burning sun without water is by no means a pleasant way of passing the time. I soon fell asleep and dreamed of bathing in the cool rivulets issuing from the snow-capped mountains. About an hour before day I was awakened by the howling of wolves, they having formed a complete circle within thirty paces of me and my horse. At the flashing of my pistol, however, they soon dispersed."

—Osborne Russell, Rocky Mountains fur hunter, 1834–43

▲ Alfred Jacob Miller's painting from life of a trapper in the 1830s. It is interesting to note that most of Miller's trappers do not have beards, as they are usually depicted today.

▶ This early engraving of a trapper, commonly called a "mountain man," shows him with his horse, packhorse, and all his gear in the wilderness.

JAN 4

1847 The U.S. government orders one thousand Walker revolvers from Samuel Colt for use in the Mexican War.

BUCKSKIN ADVENTURERS

From the early 1800s, after Meriwether Lewis and William Clark returned from their expedition to the Pacific Coast, and for the next four decades, large numbers of hunters and trappers pushed into the Rocky Mountains and beyond in search of beaver pelts and other valuable furs. These adventurous individuals were the progenitors of what became the myth of the American West. The West would not have gained its "wild" reputation without these colorful characters whose escapades became the stuff of legend, particularly among the populace who dwelled east of the Mississippi River. James Pierson Beckwourth was one such man. Born in Virginia in 1798, the son of a slave mother and an Irish overseer, Beckwourth roamed much of the West as a fur trapper, trader, horse thief, and scout from 1824 until his death in 1866. Although, like most of his peers, he was inclined to exaggerate his exploits often making it difficult to separate truth from fiction, the enigmatic Beckwourth became acquainted with legendary figures such as fellow trapper Jedediah Smith and also spent a winter on the Great Salt Lake with famed mountain man Jim Bridger. A striking mulatto clad in buckskin and wearing his hair plaited Indian-style, Beckwourth appeared at rough-and-tumble spring rendezvous, was made a member of the Crow tribe in 1828, and took part in both the 1847 Taos Rebellion and the 1849 California gold rush.

▲ A daguerreotype, the earliest form of photography, of James P. Beckwourth. This is one of the earliest photographs of a trapper or scout.

▶ This engraving of Beckwourth appeared in his biography, first published in 1856.

JAN 5

1874 A young Henry (McCarty) Antrim is in attendance at the opening of the first school in Silver City, New Mexico Territory. In later years, he would be known as "Billy the Kid."

RENDEZVOUS

Far removed from creature comforts and so-called civilization, mountain men had to be self-reliant in order to survive the perils of the wild. Starting in 1825 on Henry's Fork of the Green River and for many years to follow at various sites, they devised a summer rendezvous as a way to get their furs to market and buy supplies for the coming year. Such gatherings also gave the mountain men a chance to connect with other humans and let off some steam by fighting and fornicating. Some of the rowdiest and most memorable gatherings were staged at San Fernando de Taos, named for the nearby Taos Pueblo, situated on a sage-studded plain snug against the Sangre de Cristo Mountains. Taos became known for its annual fairs that had started long before the arrival of the Spanish when Comanches, Utes, Apaches, and other tribes camped near the pueblo. For many years, this huge jamboree also attracted great numbers of mountain men, Spanish and Mexican traders and merchants, bands of Indians, and soldiers eager to try their luck with the ladies and games of chance. Yarns were swapped, bold-faced lies told, and crusty souls fresh from the wilderness learned who had become president of the United States. There was ample time to barter and trade for horses, weapons, gunpowder and lead, twists of tobacco, jewelry, clothing, foodstuffs, good luck crystals, hostages, and slaves.

"It was a rich treat . . . to see the 'chivalry' of the various encampments engaged in contests of skill at running, jumping, wrestling, shooting with the rifle, and running horses. Here the free trappers were in all their glory, they considered themselves the 'cocks of the walk' and always carried the highest crests."

—Washington Irving, c. 1835

▲ The cover of a book about trapper Kit Carson, who participated in many rendezvous. Originally centered in what is now Wyoming, these gatherings later came to be held regularly in Taos, New Mexico Territory, where Carson settled.

▶ This engraving depicts a mountain man rendezvous, where trappers and Indians would trade and make merry.

Thos. Hogan

1912 New Mexico Territory becomes the forty-seventh state in the Union.

MEN OF THE MOUNTAINS

Of all the rugged trappers and explorers who roamed the Rocky Mountains during the first half of the nineteenth century, arguably the title "King of the Mountain Men" belonged to Jim Bridger. In 1822, he was a strapping lad of seventeen when he responded to an advertisement seeking enterprising men to "ascend the Missouri" and collect furs. Over the many years he spent trapping beaver, trading pelts, dealing with Indians, and scouting for the army, Bridger lived life to the fullest. He was one of the first white men to view the Great Salt Lake, wed and outlived three Indian wives, feuded with Brigham Young, and established Fort Bridger on Black's Fork of the Green River in Wyoming Territory. Bridger could not write his own name; yet, besides English he spoke Spanish, French, several Indian dialects, and was an expert at sign language. Often called by his nicknames "Old Gabe" and "Blanket Chief," the grizzled Bridger also came to be known as "Big Throat," either for a goiter under his jaw or his endless supply of tall tales. One of Bridger's friends was Jim Baker, only twenty-one when he was recruited by Old Gabe to join a trapping expedition. Baker also proved to be a skilled scout and guide, and over sixty years was said to have married six Indian women and fathered at least fourteen children. Baker fought in hand-to-hand combat with Blackfoot warriors, was adopted by the Shoshones, rustled horses from Spanish ranchers in California, killed a grizzly with a knife, and was quoted by Mark Twain and Theodore Roosevelt. He was mild and sensible when sober, but when drunk was said to become violent and frequently dangerous.

▲ Jim Baker, trapper and scout, in his old age.

▶ Jim Bridger, mountain man and scout, in his old age. Photography had not been invented when both Bridger and Baker were young.

JAN 7

1874 Vigilante Clay Allison kills gunman "Chunk" Colbert during the Colfax County War in New Mexico Territory.

SANTA FE TRAIL

Opened in 1821 by Missouri trader William Becknell, the storied Santa Fe Trail was the first international pathway connecting the Mexican province of New Mexico with the western frontier of the United States. For sixty years, countless traders, soldiers, settlers, and large caravans of freight wagons made the 780-mile journey from Westport on the Missouri River to Santa Fe. But by the early 1880s, the well-worn trail had become obsolete with the advent of the railroad. The most famous of all the Santa Fe traders was Josiah Gregg, who between 1831 and 1843 made twelve trips over the trail. In 1844, he shared many of those adventures in his classic account *Commerce of the Prairies: The Journal of a Santa Fe Trader*. The book had wide appeal in the United States and beyond and is still considered the cornerstone for all studies of the Santa Fe Trail.

"Five or six days after our arrival, the caravan at last hove in sight, and wagon after wagon was seen pouring down the last declivity at about a mile distance from [Santa Fe]. . . . It was truly a scene for the artist's pencil to revel in. Even the animals seemed to participate in the humor of their riders, who grew more and more merry and obstreperous as they descended towards the city. I doubt, in short, whether the first sight of the walls of Jerusalem were beheld by the crusaders with much more tumultuous and soul-enrapturing joy."

—Josiah Gregg, *Commerce of the Prairies*, 1844

▲ Other than the fear of Indian attacks, the most dreaded stretch of the Santa Fe Trail was negotiating the Raton Pass.

▶ A busy street in the Mexican settlement of Santa Fe, the destination of traders traveling the Santa Fe Trail from Missouri.

JAN 8

1877 Colonel Nelson A. Miles's Fifth and Twenty-second Infantry meet Crazy Horse's combined Sioux and Cheyenne force in the Battle of Wolf Mountain, fought along the Tongue River in Montana.

ADOBE CASTLE ON THE PLAINS

Born in St. Louis in 1809 and one of four sons of a Missouri Supreme Court Justice, William Bent became one of the leading figures on the western frontier. While just fifteen years old, Bent joined his older brother Charles on a fur-trapping expedition along the upper Arkansas River. A few years later, the Bent brothers took a wagon-load of trade goods down the Santa Fe Trail. They soon formed a business alliance with Ceran St. Vrain, which resulted in the building of a trading post that served as a second home for many of the most illustrious figures of the American West. Strategically located along the mountain branch of the Santa Fe Trail and the north bank of the Arkansas River in present-day southeastern Colorado, the massive adobe complex—eventually known as Bent's Fort—became a hub of mercantile trade and an important stopping point for Indians, soldiers, caravans, trappers, and gold-seekers. William Bent served as manager of Bent's Fort and also developed relationships with various Indian tribes, including a lifelong association with the Cheyenne. In 1835, Bent wed Owl Woman, daughter of a Cheyenne chief, and they raised four children before her death in 1847. Bent then married her sister Yellow Woman, with whom he had five more children. When Pawnees killed her, Bent took a third wife, a Métis woman of Blackfoot descent.

▲ William Bent.

▶ Bent's Fort, the well-fortified trading post on the Santa Fe Trail.

"At a distance [Bent's Fort] represents a handsome appearance, being castle-like with towers at its angles . . . the design . . . answering all purposes of protection, defense, and as a residence."

—George R. Gibson, U.S. soldier, 1846

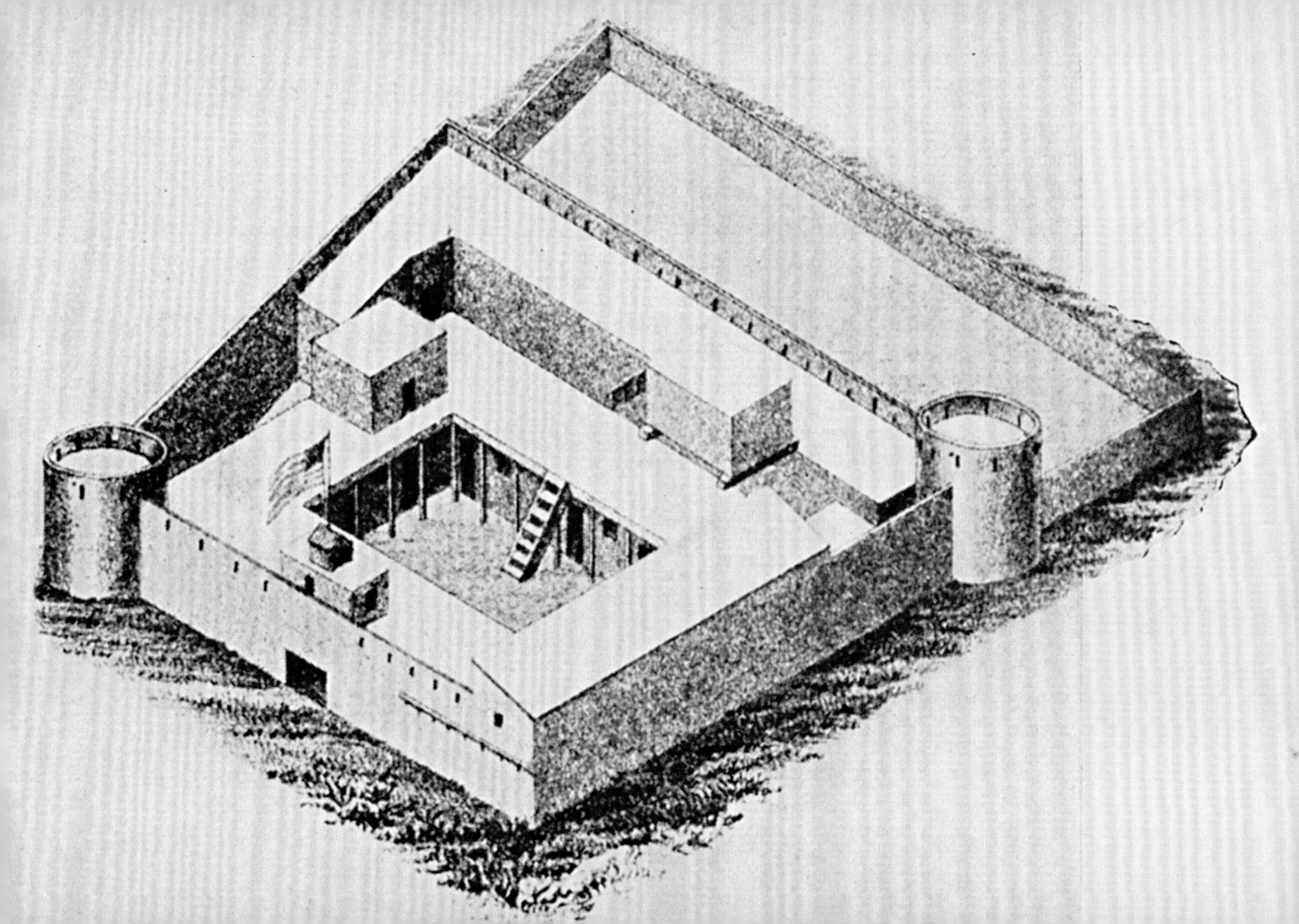

JAN 9

1879 At Fort Robinson, Nebraska, Cheyenne chief Dull Knife leads his group out of their barracks after four days without food. U.S. soldiers attack, shooting and clubbing to death fifty Cheyenne, most of whom are women and children.

CHEYENNE DOG SOLDIERS

Although not the largest Indian tribe, by the 1820s the Cheyenne had allied with the Arapahos and Lakotas and become the most dominant warrior force on the Great Plains. In the early 1830s, they divided into two branches, with the Southern Cheyenne choosing to hunt near the newly established Bent's Fort. In Cheyenne society the care and welfare of the family was the main priority. The clan and the tribe as a whole came next. According to tribal tradition, the women—who outnumbered the men because of constant warfare—ruled the camp and owned not only the tepees but also large numbers of horses. Most of the men belonged to one of six militaristic societies. The most elite of these were the Dog Soldiers, so named because of the buffalo skin sashes they carried to symbolically tie themselves to one spot in battle from which they would never retreat, even in the face of death. George Bent, the son of white trader William Bent and Owl Woman, a Southern Cheyenne, straddled both worlds but chose to become a Dog Soldier and took part in retaliatory raids on white settlements.

"Only head men and brave men could wear this sash. It is called a Dog Rope. On the end of it there is a sharp pin eight inches long. In a fight, these headmen were supposed to stick this pin in the ground and not run off. Anyone could pull this pin out and hand it to the owner. At the same time, the person pulling this pin must hit him with a whip to make him leave."

—George Bent, letter, 1904

▶ A Plains Indian tepee village.

JAN 10

1880 Billy the Kid kills Joe Grant in Bob Hargrave's saloon in Fort Sumner, New Mexico Territory.
1917 Buffalo Bill, man of the frontier and star of numerous Wild West shows, dies six weeks before his seventy-fourth birthday, in Denver, Colorado.

GRAND OLD POST

From 1834 until 1890 when the last troops took their leave, Fort Laramie stood guard between the Great Plains and the Rocky Mountains at the crossroads of America's westward expansion near the confluence of the Platte and Laramie rivers in Wyoming Territory. Originally called Fort William in honor of William Sublette, leader of the mountain men who established the outpost, the fort was sold to the American Fur Company in 1835 and six years later rebuilt as an adobe fortress. Renamed Fort John-on-the-Laramie, after fur company partner John Sarpy, most people simply called it Fort Laramie, and the name stuck. By 1849, after the fur trade declined, the U.S. Army took control and transformed it into a base of operations for the protection and supply of the growing numbers of westward-bound travelers traversing the Oregon Trail and other overland emigrant paths. For many years to come, the "Grand Old Post," as Fort Laramie was often called, served as a staging center for soldiers in campaigns against the Sioux, who became more antagonistic as the number of settlers entering their homeland soared.

▶ Fort Laramie, the last stop on the Overland Trail before the Rockies, 1849.

"Traveled about fifteen miles. Passed some trader's encampment, stopped a short time at noon, set three wagon tires, and encamped about two miles beyond Fort Laramie. During the day we passed the graves of three gold diggers, all from the state of Missouri, we believe. The wolves had disinterred one. . . . I visited the Fort the following morning, purchased twenty-eight pounds of bacon at ten cents per pound and carried the same on my back to camp, some two miles."

—journal of William I. Appleby, September 5, 1849

JAN 11

1912 The man responsible for the capture of Black Bart, detective Harry Morse, dies of natural causes in Oakland, California.

MONARCHS OF THE PLAINS

More than any other animal—including the mustang and Longhorn—the buffalo or bison symbolizes the American West. Nothing has ever matched the drama of an endless herd of these huge, shaggy beasts rumbling over a sea of grass. It is believed that what we now commonly call the American buffalo crossed over a land bridge that once connected Asia and North America. Through the centuries, the herds moved southward and at one time reached from Canada to Mexico and from the Pacific to the Atlantic. The largest herds, however, lived on the Great Plains and prairies between the Mississippi River and the Rocky Mountains. It is not known just how many buffalo once roamed the land, but by the start of the nineteenth century the smaller herds east of the Mississippi had vanished, killed off by the growing human population. In 1800, it was estimated there were as many as sixty million "Monarchs of the Plains" grazing in the West. Ninety years later, that number had been reduced to fewer than six hundred.

"You, O buffalo, are the earth! May we understand this!"

—Lakota Sun Dance prayer

▲ *Buffalo on the March: A Drawing from Eye-Witness Accounts* by bison expert Martin S. Garretson.

▶ A lithograph from the book *New Tracks in North America* by William A. Bell, 1869, depicting *A Herd of Buffalo in Western Kansas.*

JAN 12

1872 In North Platte, Nebraska, Buffalo Bill leads the Grand Duke Alexis of Russia on a buffalo hunt.
1915 The Henry Starr Gang robs two banks in Oklahoma—the First National Bank in Terlton and the Garber State Bank in Garber.

THE BOUNTY OF BUFFALO

The great herds of buffalo provided almost everything the Plains Indians needed for survival. Bison were not only a major food source, but their hides and bones were also used to create shelter, clothing, weapons, tools, utensils, and ceremonial objects. Every part of the buffalo was utilized—hide, hair, flesh, blood, bones, and internal organs. Buffalo hooves made the glue for attaching heads and feathers to arrow shafts. Even the stones from the gallbladder became an ingredient for medicine paint. Marrow from boiled bones was used for hair grease; ribs made good runners for sleds pulled by dogs; and dried dung fueled cooking fires. There can be no doubt why buffalo were held in such high regard by the Plains Indian tribes.

"Everything the Kiowas had came from the buffalo. Their tipis were made of buffalo hides, so were their clothes and moccasins. They ate buffalo meat. Their containers were made of hide, or, of bladders and stomachs. Most of all the buffalo were part of the Kiowa religion. . . . The buffalo were the life of the Kiowas."

—recollection of Old Lady Horse, a Kiowa woman, n.d.

▲ A "bull-boat" made of buffalo hide.

▶ Plains Indian women pegging out buffalo hides. Buffalo meat hangs to dry in the front of tepees made of buffalo hide.

JAN 13

1929 Wyatt Earp dies in Los Angeles, California, two months shy of his eightieth birthday.

BIG DOG HUNT

The heroic warrior wearing an eagle feather warbonnet, astride a speedy pony, in pursuit of a thundering herd of buffalo, personified the Plains Indians during the time after they acquired horses and before they lost their tribal sovereignty to the white man. These mounted horsemen became the romanticized image of all Indian people. When Indians first saw the horses of the Spanish conquistadors, they feared the strange four-legged creatures, but soon realized that like dogs, horses could serve men. Some tribes called a horse "Big Dog" or "Medicine Dog," while other tribes, such as the Comanches, called it a "God Dog." Once they began to use horses, Plains Indians no longer had to don wolf skins and stalk buffalo on foot or provoke a stampede over a cliff hoping the fall would either kill or cripple the buffalo. A mounted hunter armed with a lance and bow and arrows could ride a well-trained horse into a herd and kill enough buffalo in a single day to feed and clothe his family for a month.

▲ Buffalo stampeding over a cliff.

▶ Bow and arrows and spears were the original weapons the Indians used to hunt the buffalo.

JAN

14

1864 In Virginia City, Montana Territory, vigilantes hang five accused road agents: "Clubfoot" George Lane, Jack Gallagher, Frank Parish, Haze Lyon, and Boone Helm. A sixth outlaw, Bill Hunter, escapes, but is captured later and lynched on February 1.

THE RAVEN

Sam Houston, protégé of Andrew Jackson and hero of the 1814 Horseshoe Bend engagement with the Creeks, enjoyed success in politics until 1829 when his eleven-week marriage to a teenaged girl came to a sudden end. The emotionally depleted Houston abruptly resigned as the governor of Tennessee, dashed across the Mississippi to Indian Territory, and began living with the Cherokees, who had adopted him long before and named him "The Raven." He took a Cherokee wife and together they ran Wigwam Neosho, a trading post near Fort Gibson that became known as the "Hell Hole of the Southwest." Soon Houston began swilling the Monongahela whiskey, cognac, and rum he illegally traded and became known by a new name—Big Drunk. Years later, Houston started to acquire property south of the border. He brought back word of disgruntled Anglo colonists in Mexico who were preparing to stage an uprising and claim the state of Tejas as their own.

▶ Sam Houston.

"I do think within one year that it [Texas] will be a Sovereign State and within three years . . . will be separated from the Mexican Confederacy, and will remain so forever. . . . Texas, will be bound to look to herself, and to do for herself. . . . The course that I may pursue, you must rely upon it, shall be for the true interests of Texas."

—Sam Houston, letter to land speculator James Prentiss, April 24, 1834

JAN 15

1846 John C. Frémont's expedition arrives at Sutter Fort, California. Famous mountain man Kit Carson is lead scout for the group.
1896 Bill Doolin is captured by Deputy U.S. Marshal Bill Tilghman at Eureka Springs, Arkansas.

GONE TO TEXAS

During much of the nineteenth century, it was not uncommon to see the letters "G.T.T." painted or carved on the doorways of cabins in some parts of the country, especially the South. It was a sign that the occupants had packed up and "Gone to Texas." First seen in print in 1825, the expression became popular for people who had committed crimes, owed money, or just did not want to be found, and took off for Texas, the Mexican state that would become an American state in 1845. When bill collectors came looking for defaulters only to find an empty house, they knew those they hunted had taken "French leave"—another term used for evading creditors—and Gone to Texas. When the sheriff had no luck bringing in the accused, the lawman likely reported that the outlaw had Gone to Texas. When a banker rifled the vaults of his institution and made a getaway, he was Gone to Texas. And when a man found himself in a broken marriage, lost his job, and left to start fresh on the Mexican frontier, he, too, was Gone to Texas.

"There are now four vacancies in the senate of Missouri; that the legislature convenes in January next, and the acting Governor has failed to issue writs of election . . . Col. McGuire has resigned, Mr. Carr has removed from the State, Mr. Brown is at Santa Fe, in the service of the General Government, and Col. Palmer is said to have taken French leave and gone to Texas."

—*National Gazette and Literary Register*, December 29, 1825

▶ A daguerreotype of a Southern youth, perhaps contemplating going to Texas, as many did in the 1830s.

▶▶ A young cowboy, pleased and proud to have "Gone to Texas."

JAN 16

1903 President Theodore Roosevelt commutes Oklahoma bank robber Henry Starr's fifteen-year sentence, and he is released on a promise of good behavior.

LION OF THE WEST

David Crockett (he never signed his name Davy) was both authentic and contrived. It was only after seeing the play *The Lion of the West*, which featured a character based on Crockett named Nimrod Wildfire wearing an animal-skin hat, that Crockett took to wearing the ubiquitous coonskin cap to boost his public image. Wise in the ways of the wilderness, Crockett was most comfortable when deep in the woods on a hunt, yet he also held his own in the halls of Congress or with men of power and prestige in the fancy parlors of Philadelphia and New York. He fought under Andrew Jackson in the bloody Indian Wars, only to later become his bitter foe over the issue of removal of Indian tribes from their homelands. Crockett had only a few months of formal education, yet he read Ovid and "The Bard." He was a contradiction, always evolving on the stage of a nation in its adolescence. Crockett met his end during an exploratory trip in the then-Mexican state of Texas, but he spent most of his life in Tennessee and more than half of those forty-nine years in the east Tennessee of his birth. All too often, Crockett's two months in Texas at the end of his life garner more attention than his many years in his home state. David Crockett may have perished on March 6, 1836, in the final assault on the Alamo, but the mythical Davy Crockett did not die. He rode on.

▲ An early engraving of the distinguished David Crockett.

▶ Davy Crockett as he is imagined by many Americans.

Improved Edition. } **1842.** { Containing Real Stories.

CROCKETT ALMANAC

IMPROVED 1842

HARTWELL

Croome

Boston.

Printed and published by S. N. Dickinson, and for sale by T. Groom & Co., Boston; D. Felt & Co., Collins, Keese & Co., F. J. Huntington & Co., New York; Grigg & Elliot, and Thomas, Cowperthwait & Co., Philadelphia; Cushing & Brothers, Baltimore; Oliver Steele, Albany.

JAN 17

1863 Near Fort McLean, New Mexico Territory, Apache chief Mangas Coloradas is killed after being captured by a party of gold-seekers led by Joseph R. Walker. Before they could turn the chief over to the California Volunteers, Mangas Coloradas was shot while trying to escape after his guards burned his feet and legs with heated bayonets.

BLOODY BOWIE

James "Jim" Bowie, a Kentucky native, conjures images of his trademark knife, which he did not make himself but used with much proficiency in the infamous Sandbar Fight of 1827 on the banks of the Mississippi near Natchez. Following a duel on a stretch of river sand, the altercation quickly escalated into what one newspaper described as "a sanguinary affair." Bowie brandished his big knife, commissioned for him by his brother, Rezin, and proceeded to disembowel one man, savagely wound another, and chase the horrified survivors away. But there was more to Bowie than a big knife. Some years earlier, the Bowie brothers partnered with Jean Lafitte, the notorious privateer and cutthroat, to traffic the slaves he smuggled into Galveston Island and sold to plantation owners as if they were meat on the hoof. Besides making a fortune as a dealer in human cargo, Bowie also became a land speculator. He sold fraudulent claims in Arkansas Territory, masterminded a series of property swindles in Louisiana, and speculated land in Texas. Bowie liked Texas and saw there was an immense profit to be made in real estate. He learned Spanish, joined the Catholic Church, became a Mexican citizen, and married into one of San Antonio's prominent Tejano families. When his wife and two children died during a cholera epidemic, Bowie went into an alcoholic depression that lasted until his death in a sickbed at the siege of the Alamo.

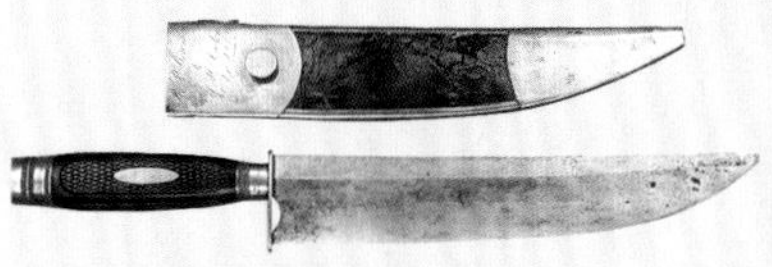

▲ The famous Bowie knife.

▶ The only generally accepted image of Jim Bowie, although it is also questioned.

JAN 18

1867 Frontier bandit Tiburcio Vásquez enters the California State Prison at San Quentin. He will remain there until June 4, 1869.

NAPOLEON OF THE WEST

To this day Antonio López de Santa Anna Perez de Lebron, the ruthless Mexican dictator, is most often portrayed as the devil incarnate, especially by Anglo-Texans. He has been called the "Napoleon of the West" or "Butcher of the Alamo," depending on the side of the border. "His Serene Highness," the moniker Santa Anna preferred, had a love-hate relationship with the Mexican citizens he governed sporadically for many years. "If I were God," he once said, "I would wish to be more." He survived a few expulsions, coup attempts, and exiles, as well as battles against the United States and France. The one-legged dictator, who lost his limb to a French cannonball at Vera Cruz in 1838, died alone, in poverty, and mostly forgotten on June 21, 1876, just days before another major egotist—George Armstrong Custer—got his comeuppance at the Little Bighorn River.

▶ A rare portrait, reverse-painted on encased glass, of Antonio López de Santa Anna as he looked at about the time he was in personal command of the Mexican forces fighting against the Texans in 1836.

GAL SANTA-ANNA

JAN

19

1847 In Taos, New Mexico Territory, Mexican residents revolt against white settlers. The conflict lasts eight days, during which time the American-appointed governor of New Mexico, Charles Bent, is assassinated.

1896 Upon being pardoned, Butch Cassidy is released from the Wyoming State Prison in Laramie after serving eighteen months of a two-year sentence.

REMEMBER THE ALAMO

By 1836, the mostly Southern-born white settlers of the Mexican state of Texas were on a collision course with the Mexican government. The two sides could no longer avoid the slavery issue. Mexico fully supported equality for its entire population, but many of the white immigrants wanted Texas to become an empire for slavery. The result of this impasse was the much-mythologized Siege of the Alamo, which ended on March 6, 1836, when Santa Anna's forces killed all the defenders. The oft-used battle cry "Remember the Alamo!"—employed just weeks later by Sam Houston to fire up his force when they captured General Santa Anna and defeated the Mexican army at San Jacinto—still reverberates through history and culture. For many Anglo-Texans, those three words conjure up embellished imagery of patriotic heroes, unabashed sacrifice, and love of liberty. Almost immediately, the last stand at the Alamo was compared to the resolve of the ancient Greek Spartans facing the Persian army at the Battle of Thermopylae. A newspaper editorial published just eighteen days after the fall of the Alamo read: "That event, so lamentable, and yet so glorious to Texas, is of such deep interest and excites so much our feelings that we shall never cease to celebrate it." The Alamo was transformed into the "Cradle of Texas Liberty" and a monument to the Anglo westward expansion that became known as Manifest Destiny.

▲ The Alamo as it appeared in the 1900s after it was modified and the now-familiar bell-shaped parapet was added to the top.

▶ The Alamo as it appeared after the battle in 1836.

rawn by Edwd. Everett — C.B. Graham Lithog

RUINS OF THE CHURCH OF THE ALAMO, SAN ANTONIO DE BEXAR.

Scale 10 Feet to an Inch

JAN 20

1867 In Virginia City, Nevada, beloved madam Julia Bulette is murdered for her jewelry and furs. French drifter John Millain is eventually arrested for the crime and sent to the gallows. Mark Twain is present for the hanging.

REPUBLIC OF TEXAS

Following the Mexican victory at the Alamo, a ragtag army of nine hundred rebellious Texans under the command of Sam Houston dealt Santa Anna and his troops a crushing defeat at San Jacinto. On the Mexican side, the sneak attack left 630 killed, 208 wounded, and 730 captured, including General Santa Anna himself. The battle took only eighteen minutes, but it would take many years for the newly independent Republic of Texas to become part of the United States. Despite the republic's first election in September 1836, when most of the fifty thousand Texans endorsed a constitution, elected Houston president (for the first of two terms), and voted by an overwhelming majority to seek annexation; statehood was blocked. Antislavery forces delayed the motion because Texas allowed trade in humans, one of the causes of conflict with the government of Mexico, which had outlawed the "peculiar institution." After almost a decade of political fighting, Texas became the twenty-eighth state—the so-called Lone Star State—in 1845. The controversial Mexican War soon followed.

▶ Sam Houston, president of the Republic of Texas.

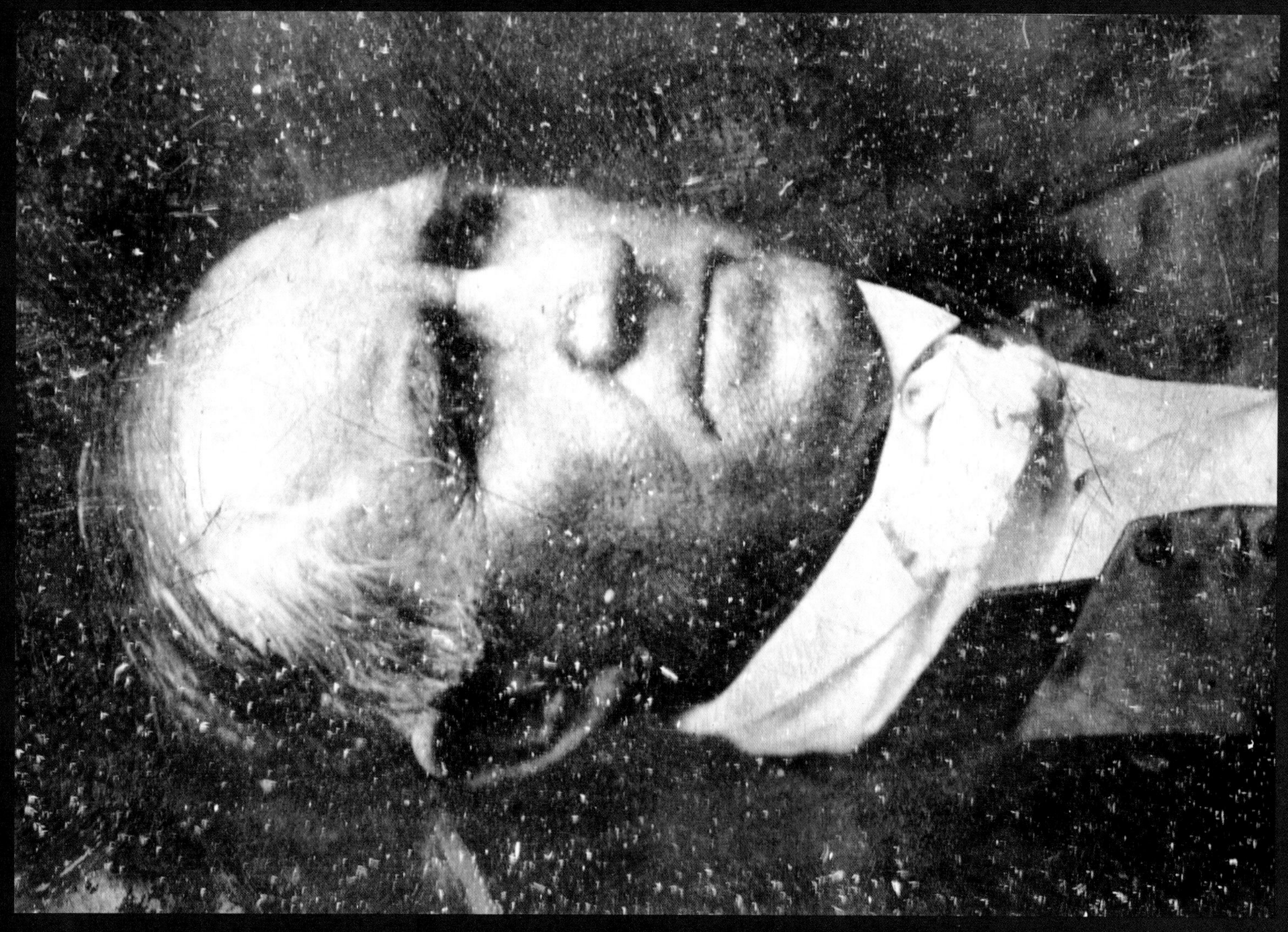

JAN 21

1860 Sam Houston submits a resolution of secession from the Union to the Texas legislature.

SAMUEL COLT'S EQUALIZER

During a sea voyage in 1830, sixteen-year-old Samuel L. Colt conceived the idea of a revolving firearm while watching the action of the ship's wheel. When he returned home to Connecticut, the youngster used the wooden model he had carved to woo investors and get a patent. On March 5, 1836—just one day before the Alamo fell during the rebellion in the Mexican state of Texas—Colt founded the firm that would become the oldest manufacturer of repeating firearms in the world. Although sales started off slow, Colt doggedly peddled handguns to early Texas Rangers battling Comanche warriors and Mexican irregulars. With the start of the Mexican War in 1846, the federal government purchased large quantities of Colt's weapons and resurrected his floundering enterprise. On the frontier, the revolver allowed a man to keep his hands free while he drank or tended to chores. More important, for the first time in history, a man could kill critters or his fellows in rapid succession. A popular saying of the time was "God created men; Colonel Colt made them equal."

"Treat them well and they will treat your enemies badly. They are always worth what they cost—in the Far West much more, almost a legal tender! If you buy a Colt's Rifle or Pistol, you feel certain you have one true friend, with six hearts in his body, who can always be relied on."

—early Colt advertisement

▲ Samuel L. Colt, inventor and manufacturer of the multi-shot sidearm revolver.

▶ A young cowboy with his Colt.

JAN 22

1883 In Nevada, Wells Fargo agent Aaron "Hold-the-Fort" Ross becomes a hero when he survives repeated attempts by a group of five outlaws to rob an express car.

TRAIL OF TEARS

The passage of the infamous Indian Removal Act of 1830, championed by President Andrew Jackson, represented the peak of tribal displacement from the eastern United States. The seeds of removal sowed by Thomas Jefferson had taken root. The Cherokee Nation—Jackson's former ally—would reap the harvest. So would the Creeks, Choctaws, Chickasaws, and Seminoles, the other so-called Five Civilized Tribes, a pejorative term coined by white men. Jackson had hoped Indians residing on their homelands in the southeastern United States would obey the law and relocate to distant Indian Territory on their own. This was not to pass. Some tribes had assimilated into the white culture, including using slaves on their plantations, and believed that the federal government would not force them to leave. Tribal leaders followed protocol and tried negotiation and legal channels to solve the dilemma. Despite their best efforts, and a Supreme Court decision upholding their rights, Jackson chose to forcibly uproot the tribes. In October 1838, the first organized contingent of one thousand Cherokees began the twelve-hundred-mile forced march westward escorted by soldiers with fixed bayonets. Many more Cherokees followed, and altogether at least four thousand died in detention camps along the way. First called "the trail where they cried," the journey is now best remembered as the Trail of Tears.

▶ A painting of the Trail of Tears by Robert Lindneux, 1942, Woolaroc Museum, Bartlesville, Oklahoma.

"We are now about to take our leave and kind farewell to our native land, the country that the great spirit gave our Fathers, we are on the eve of leaving that country that gave us birth . . . it is with sorrow that we are forced by the authority of the white man to quit scenes of our childhood . . . we bid a final farewell to it and all we hold dear."

—George Hicks, Cherokee leader on the Trail of Tears, 1838

Robt. Lindneux
1942 ©

JAN 23

1894 The Doolin Gang robs the Farmers and Citizens Bank in Pawnee, Indian Territory.

COMANCHE MOON

When the Comanches acquired horses in the late seventeenth century, they gained an advantage that defined their entire way of life. They became nomadic horsemen of the plains, conducting warfare from horseback and following the great buffalo herds that provided the tribe's lifeblood. Eventually the Comanches migrated south and became a formidable force in Texas where they had greater access to the mustangs of the Southwest as well as the horses of the growing Anglo population. Raids—many of which extended far into Mexico—to steal horses and take captives usually took place during the full moon when the warriors could ride by moonlight.

"One time Jack Brown and the men of the settlement were after some Indians who had stolen a number of their horses. While his wife and three small children were at home, the Indians stole Mrs. Brown's favorite pony that she kept in a log barn behind the houses. They took him upon a hill, built a fire and roasted him. They danced around the fire and ate the meat. When the moon went down they left."

—from early account of life in San Saba County, Texas, c. 1870

"It was the custom of the Comanches to leave their camps and ride into San Saba and the counties east just at the time the moon would be getting full. Then, when the moon was full, they would return to their homes, frequently killing settlers as they went taking with them horses and other property."

—diary of cowboy James D. Rainwater, 1871

▲ Comanches.

▶ A Comanche warrior.

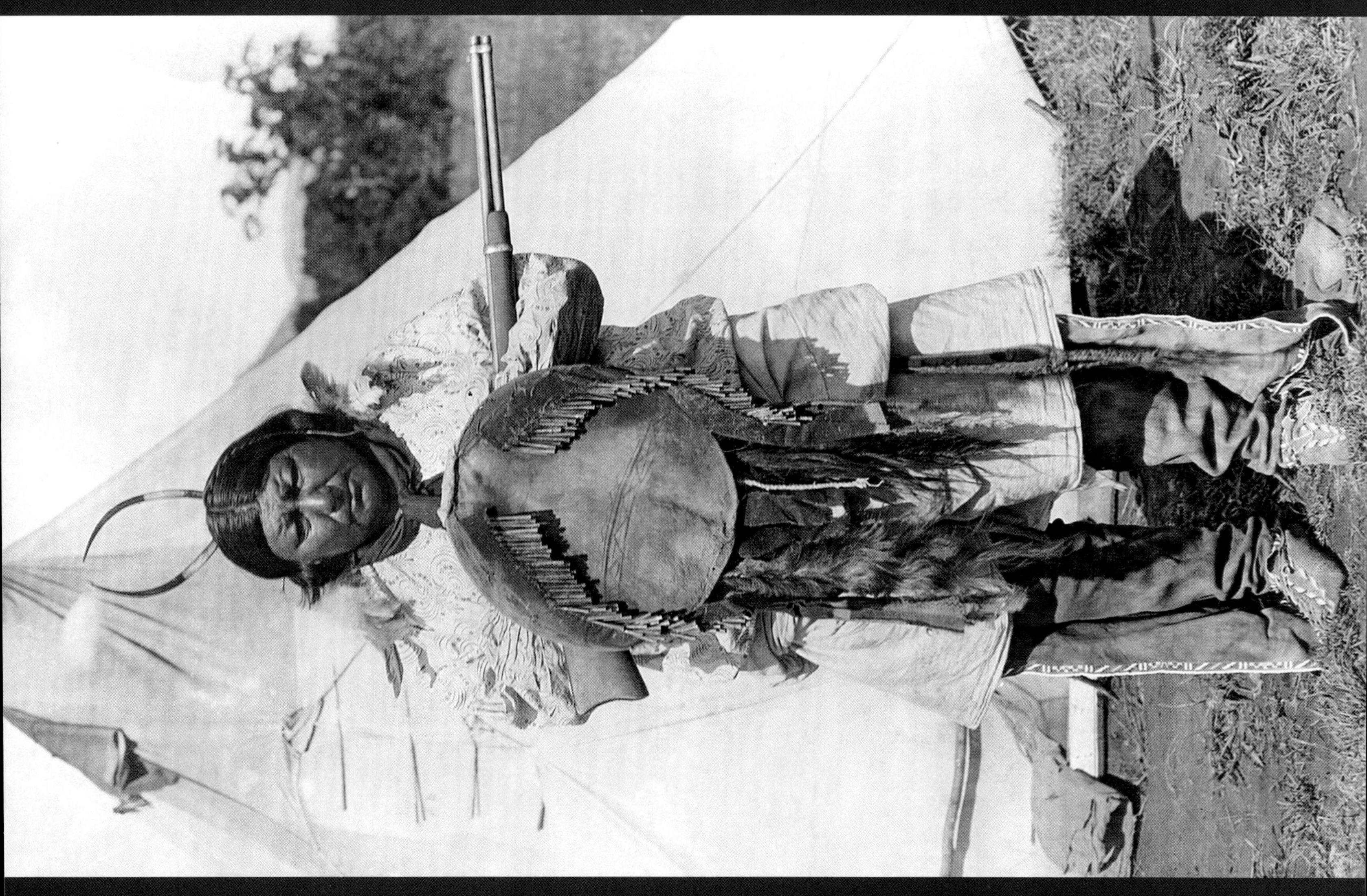

JAN 24

1848 James W. Marshall discovers a small nugget of gold at Sutter's Mill on the American River in California, marking the beginning of the California gold rush.

1876 In Sweetwater (later Mobeetie), Texas, Bat Masterson is shot in the pelvis by a soldier during a gunfight over the affections of a woman. The soldier dies during the exchange and a stray bullet kills the girl. Masterson walks with a cane for the rest of his life.

HIGH PLAINS DRIFTERS

For almost two centuries, mounted Mexican hunters—colorfully dressed and sometimes riding bareback—prowled the Southern plains in pursuit of bison herds. Called Ciboleros, from *cibolo*, the Spanish word for buffalo, these hunters rode in groups on fleet ponies trained to run in tandem with the quarry. They shot buffalo until they ran out of ammunition and then used short razor-sharp lances to kill at close range. By the early 1830s, Ciboleros killed about twelve thousand bison each year in order to furnish meat and hides for the flourishing trail trade and for markets as distant as Mexico City, where buffalo tongues sold for two dollars apiece. The Ciboleros' skill at navigating the grassy plains and their trading relationship with Plains Indians directly inspired another distinct group known as Comancheros. These were primarily New Mexican natives who made their living trading with nomadic Plains Indians, chiefly the Comanches and Kiowas. Explorer Josiah Gregg coined the name Comanchero in his classic *Commerce of the Prairies*, published in 1844. Gregg wrote that Comancheros "are usually composed of the indigent and rude classes of the frontier villages, who collect together several times a year and launch upon the plains with a few trinkets and trumperies of all kinds." Although some historians defended the Comancheros, ample evidence exists of their dealing in stolen property and the ransoming of women and children abducted by Indian raiders.

▲ A pen-and-ink drawing by José Cisneros of a Comanchero.

▶ A hand-colored pen-and-ink drawing by José Cisneros of a Cibolero. Cisneros took great care in the authentic representation of the clothing and gear of the horsemen of the Southwest.

J. CISNEROS-67

JAN 25

1867 The first article about Wild Bill Hickok's exploits appears in an issue of *Harper's Weekly* magazine.

SUN DOG WARRIORS

▶ A young Kiowa man.

▶▶ Kiowa women.

Sometime in the eighteenth century, the Kiowas loaded their animal-hide tepees on travois pulled by dogs and left their homeland near the sources of the Yellowstone and Missouri rivers in present-day Montana. Migrating south to the Black Hills, they lived peaceably among the Crow Indians who taught them to ride horses, which the Kiowas called Sun Dogs, larger versions of their canine helpers. The Kiowas eventually followed the great bison herds and became one of the most feared of all the Plains Indian tribes. In 1790, they made peace with the Comanches and started an active trade in horses and captives with their former foes. The Kiowas became friendly with other Plains tribes but remained at odds with the white settlers despite signing their first treaty with the U.S. government in 1837. It was said that the Kiowa clan was the fiercest of all the tribes of the American West and killed more whites and Mexicans than any other tribe in proportion to their numbers. Between 1834 and 1846 alone, Kiowa and Comanche war parties, ranging in size from one hundred to one thousand warriors, made frequent raids deep into Mexico.

I have one love.
I have one love.
I have one love.
And he is far away,
On the warpath.
Eh-yeh, eh-yeh,
Lonely are the days and weary.

—Kiowa Wind Song

42
BE-LOW-CAZED.
(KIOWA.)

JAN 26

1882 Charles E. Bolton, better known as "Black Bart," robs a stagecoach traveling from Ukiah to Cloverdale, California.

TRAIL'S END

Throughout the 1800s, a steady flow of newcomers showed up on the dusty and teeming Santa Fe Plaza. Local merchants mingled with traders from El Camino Real (the trail winding northward from the old colonial capital of Mexico City) and freighters who, starting in 1821, traversed the Santa Fe Trail. Many traveled back and forth on the trade route between the ancient city and Missouri, but others remained in Santa Fe. They made themselves at home in a land that in some ways had changed little since the arrival of the conquistadors. The Spaniards had come with a cross in one hand and a sword in the other, forcing both on the tribal people living along the Rio Grande. A wealth of stories sprang up about the plaza being the site for bullfights, public floggings and executions, gun battles, political rallies, and fiestas. Running the full length of the square's north side was El Palacio, the Palace of the Governors, an adobe structure built in 1609–10 and used continuously as a seat of government. Justice was meted out in the old adobe palace and sometimes ears severed from slain Indians adorned the outside walls.

▲ A photograph of a street in Santa Fe, c. 1860s.

▶ A wagon train on the Santa Fe Trail coming in sight of their long-awaited destination, the small New Mexican settlement of Santa Fe.

"The festoons of Indian ears were made up of several strings of dried ears of Indians killed by parties sent out by the government against the savages, who were paid a certain sum for each head. In Chihuahua, a great exhibition was made with the entire scalps of Indians which they had killed by proxy. At Santa Fe only the ears were exhibited or retained."

—R. E. Twitchell, *The Leading Facts of New Mexican History*, 1912

JAN 27

1861 Fourteen-year-old Feliz Tellez Ward is kidnapped by Apache Indians near Sonoita, Arizona Territory, setting off a twenty-year war with Chief Cochise. Feliz is raised by the Apaches and later becomes a scout, assuming the name Mickey Free.
1922 Outlaw Al Spencer escapes from the Oklahoma State Penitentiary in McAlester.

SCALP HUNTER

Beginning in the 1830s, one of the most profitable enterprises in the Southwest and Mexico was the human scalp industry. In Mexico alone, between 1835 and 1885, the government—weary of marauding Apaches and Comanches—paid private armies to provide protection. Mostly Forty-niners in need of grubstake money or former Texas Rangers, these mercenaries hunted down and killed as many Indians as possible, including women and children. Of course, the bounty paid for a scalp depended on the victim's age and sex. Generally that meant one hundred dollars for a warrior's scalp, fifty dollars for a squaw's scalp, and twenty-five dollars for all children less than fourteen years of age. James Kirker, a native of Ireland known as the "King of the Scalpers," was the most notorious and brutal of his kind. He was also the most successful at his trade. Kirker was known to work for both sides, taking Mexican as well as Indian scalps. It was said he became so skilled at his trade that even his few friends feared he would remove their topknot. An absolutely fearless and accomplished horseman, Kirker led his gang of Delaware and Shawnee Indian followers on many scalp-hunting expeditions he irreverently referred to as "barbering."

▶ Scalp hunter James Kirker.

▶▶ Tintype of a scalp-hunting frontiersman.

JAN 28

1887 Two outlaws rob a Southern Pacific passenger train outside of Tucson, Arizona. The perpetrators make off with twenty thousand dollars in Arizona's first recorded train robbery.

THE FORGOTTEN PEOPLE

The Métis people—the mixed offspring of European fur traders and Indian women—developed their own distinctive society and traditions in their homeland in Canada and the northern United States. Skilled hunters and horsemen, the Métis played a vital role in the success of the western fur trade by acting as scouts, guides, interpreters, and trappers. They also helped to establish improved trading relationships and bridge cultural gaps thanks to their understanding of different customs and languages. The Métis followed the great buffalo herds and were known for making moccasins, jerky, and pemmican—dried buffalo meat that was a staple among traders and trappers. The buffalo hunts were led by elected officers and governed by a set of strictly enforced rules known as "the law of the prairie." Often referred to as "children of the fur trade," in later years Métis were also called the "Forgotten People," because they were not accepted by many whites nor considered to be Indians. Despite being ignored by most American West history books, the Métis Nation endured.

"It was truly a happy life that these people were living. The camp was in the midst of the buffalo herds and they hunted and worked hard during the day but when night came they danced and sang the old French songs, until the late hours, arranged for many and diverse horse races for the following day, then slept the sleep of people who have no cares for the moment."

—Eli Gardipee, describing a Métis camp in Montana, 1868

▶ An extremely rare daguerreotype of a mixed-blood frontiersman, most likely Métis, with knife and tomahawk.

JAN **29**

1861 Kansas becomes the nation's thirty-fourth state.
1863 California Volunteers under Colonel Patrick Connor massacre 368 Shoshone Indians, including women and children, near present-day Preston, Idaho.

THE PARIS OF THE WILDERNESS

Founded as a Spanish presidio in the eighteenth century, San Antonio evolved during the 1800s into a bustling city where enterprising Texas cattlemen gathered millions of wild Longhorns that had proliferated from stock left by the conquistadors. Known across the Southwest as "the gay capital of the mesquite and chapparal [sic]" and "the Paris of the wilderness," San Antonio offered a wide variety of diversions, all of which could turn even the most forthright cowboy's head. There were cockfights, fiestas, and gambling lairs galore. Strumpets sold their favors from cribs and bordellos scattered throughout the city. On the plazas, town boys trapped wild pigeons; gangs of rats bold enough to fight dogs and kill cats hunted their next meal; and the odor of fresh manure mixed with the aroma of roasting goat. The Plaza de Armas was one of the most popular gathering places in the city. Once a drill ground for Spanish troops, the military plaza dated back to the eighteenth century. After Texas won its independence in 1836, it became a commercial and entertainment center and remained a hub of activity for another fifty years. Every evening, citizens came there to trade gossip and peruse the open-air booths. Under the glow of lanterns, the city's famous "chili queens" ladled out bowls brimming with pungent chili con carne, made of fiery peppers and chunks of tough Longhorn meat, cooked for hours in huge iron kettles over mesquite fires.

▲ The San Antonio Military Plaza.

▶ A drawing of the San Antonio River, c. 1868.

SAN ANTONIO DE BEXAR.
1848

JAN 30

1878 A posse led by Bat Masterson arrests "Dirty Dave" Rudabaugh and Edgar West near Kinsley, Kansas, on suspicion of train robbery.

LOS DIABLOS TEJANOS

Considered the oldest law enforcement agency in the United States, the Texas Rangers formed in the early 1820s, when Stephen F. Austin put out a call for ten men "to act as rangers for the common defense" against Indian attacks and criminals. In 1835, the first Rangers became more organized and grew in numbers after Texas won its independence from Mexico. Those early lawmen waged an all-out war against Indian tribes and gained a reputation for brutality when dealing with Mexicans, who gave them the name *los diablos Tejanos*—the Texas devils. A common saying was that a Ranger could "ride like a Mexican, trail like an Indian, shoot like a Tennessean, and fight like the devil." Two Tennessee natives—Ben and Henry McCulloch—fit that description to a tee. Ben and his younger brother, Henry, grew up in Tennessee where they became good friends with the legendary frontiersman David Crockett. When Crockett was voted out of Congress and decided to look into new ventures in Texas, the McCulloch boys soon followed. Their lives were saved when a combination of being tardy and coming down with the measles prevented them from joining Crockett at the Alamo. They did take part in the battles that followed, though, and earned reputations as fierce fighters against the Comanche. Both brothers joined the Rangers and, along with such Ranger immortals as John "Rip" Ford and John Coffee "Jack" Hays, earned their place in the Valhalla of Lone Star heroes.

Free as the breeze
Swift as a mustang
Tough as a cactus

—motto inscribed on Ben McCulloch's Colt pistol

▶ Henry McCulloch, brother of Ben and also an early Texas Ranger.

▶▶ Early Texas Ranger Ben McCulloch.

JAN 31

1874 The James Gang robs the Little Rock Express train in Gads Hill, Missouri.

MANIFEST DESTINY

The jingoistic term "Manifest Destiny" became a popular rallying cry with mid-nineteenth-century politicians who believed that the United States had a divine mandate to expand from "sea to shining sea." John L. O'Sullivan, editor for *The United States Magazine and Democratic Review*, coined the phrase in his 1845 editorial advocating the annexation of the Republic of Texas and total control of the Oregon Territory, which had been the object of an ongoing boundary dispute between the United States and Great Britain. This concept became the driving force responsible for changing the face of American history as the federal government encouraged residents in the crowded East to move west. There they would find rich natural resources, vast farm and rangelands, timber forests, and untapped mineral riches. By 1846, the concept of Manifest Destiny had galvanized proponents of expansionism and pro-slavery Southern planters eager to expand their domain. Despite opposition from many Americans, including Henry David Thoreau and Congressman Abraham Lincoln, the land-hungry President James Polk provoked a two-year war with Mexico in order to gain control of much of the land in the West.

▲ Wagon train on the long trail west.

▶ Indians watching an approaching wagon train.

"We are a restless people, prone to encroachment, impatient of the ordinary laws of progress. . . . We boast of our rapid growth, forgetting that, throughout nature, noble growths are slow . . . the Indians have melted before the white man, and the mixed, degraded race of Mexico must melt before the Anglo-Saxon, . . . We talk of accomplishing our destiny. So did the late conqueror of Europe (Napoleon)."

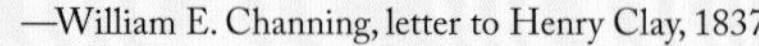

—William E. Channing, letter to Henry Clay, 1837

FEB 1

1901 Butch Cassidy, the Sundance Kid, and Etta Place rent a room at 254 North Twelfth Street in New York City, before booking passage to Argentina.

WESTWARD HO!

The summer of 1846, Francis Parkman, a twenty-three-year-old Harvard Law School graduate from a wealthy Boston family, set out on a two-month trek that he described as "a tour of curiosity and amusement to the Rocky Mountains." Destined to become one of the nation's preeminent historians, Parkman spent much of his time with a band of Oglala Sioux. As a result of this experience, in 1849 Parkman published his adventures in *The Oregon Trail: Sketches of Prairie and Rocky-Mountain Life*. This work—despite the misleading title since Parkman's excursion took him along only the first third of the Oregon Trail—inspired many people to move westward and also had a profound impact on views of Indians for generations of readers. With a sense of national entitlement and a belief that the land was theirs for the taking—regardless of the Indian tribes who dwelled there—thousands of white settlers shouting "Westward ho!" struck out to grab the land they considered their natural due.

▲ The first edition of Francis Parkman's book, originally titled *The California & Oregon Trail.*

▶ The deluxe leather edition of Parkman's book with the shortened title, *The Oregon Trail.*

"Great changes are at hand in that region. With the stream of emigration to Oregon and California, the buffalo will dwindle away, and the large wandering communities who depend on them for support must be broken and scattered. The Indians will soon be corrupted by the example of whites, abased by whisky, and overawed by military posts; so that with a few years the traveler may pass in tolerable security through their country. Its danger and its charm will have disappeared together."

—Francis Parkman, *The Oregon Trail*, 1849

THE
OREGON
TRAIL
FRANCIS PARKMAN

FEB 2

1848 The Treaty of Guadalupe Hidalgo is signed just north of Mexico City, ending the war between the United States and Mexico. The treaty's terms cede parts of the future states of Colorado, New Mexico, Arizona, and Wyoming to the United States as well as the whole of California, Nevada, and Utah.

THE GREAT PATHFINDER

Despite being born the illegitimate son of a Virginia socialite, John Charles Frémont's dashing good looks and ability to forge strategic connections helped him go far. In 1838, as a newly appointed army officer, Lieutenant Frémont showed his skill at surveying and mapmaking, while at the same time wooing Jessie Benton, the teenaged daughter of Thomas Hart Benton, a powerhouse in the U.S. Senate for thirty years and the champion of Manifest Destiny. Initially opposed to the marriage, Benton quickly recognized Frémont's potential and pushed through congressional appropriations to fund his son-in-law's survey expeditions of the Oregon Trail, Oregon Territory, and the Great Basin and Sierra Mountains of California. Frémont encountered Kit Carson on a Missouri River steamboat in 1842 and made the frontiersman his chief guide. Considered one of the greatest explorers of California and the West, Frémont was dubbed "The Great Pathfinder" by the press. He took part in the Mexican War, was arrested by General Stephen W. Kearny and court-martialed for mutiny (sentence commuted by President James Polk), served as one of the first two senators from California, and, though unsuccessful, was the first presidential candidate of the newly formed Republican Party in 1856. In later years, Frémont lost his fortune due to poor business decisions and was supported by his wife's writing. He died in New York in 1890, the same year that the American West he had helped open was declared closed.

▲ "The Great Pathfinder," John C. Frémont.

▶ Frémont's memoirs, with contributions by his wife, Jessie Benton Frémont.

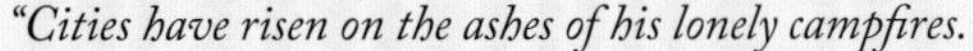

"Cities have risen on the ashes of his lonely campfires."

—Jessie Benton Frémont, writing of her husband, 1887

MEMOIRS OF MY LIFE

by JOHN CHARLES FRÉMONT

WITH A SKETCH OF THE LIFE OF SENATOR BENTON

BY JESSIE BENTON FRÉMONT

POUR LE MERITE

OREGON

FEB 3

1860 The first Pony Express rider departs St. Joseph, Missouri, for Sacramento, California. He would arrive ten days later.
1889 Belle Starr is shot dead in Indian Territory by an unknown person two days before her forty-first birthday.

KIT CARSON

In his own lifetime, Kit Carson—a consummate frontier scout—became a household name forever guaranteed a prominent place in the popular imagination. Born on Christmas Eve, 1809, in Kentucky, Christopher Houston "Kit" Carson grew up in Missouri, and at age fourteen was apprenticed to a saddlemaker. In 1826, Carson ran away and joined a Santa Fe Trail caravan headed west. He gained a reputation as a skilled woodsman and guide whose adventures on trapping and scouting expeditions and prowess as a hunter at Bent's Fort became fodder for countless dime novelists. The missionary Samuel Parker encountered Carson and in 1838 published his exploits, the first mention of Carson in a book. His first two wives were Arapaho and Cheyenne women, but during the time he guided John Frémont's expeditions, Carson met and in 1843 married María Josefa Jaramillo, the daughter of a prominent and well-connected Taos family. Josefa's sister was the wife of Charles Bent. Josefa was but fifteen and Carson twice her age. As a wedding gift, Kit gave his young bride a rambling adobe house, not far from the plaza in Taos, where they lived for many years and where the beloved Josefa died from complications while delivering their seventh child.

▶ A young Kit Carson.

▶▶ Kit married María Josefa Jaramillo of Taos, New Mexico.

"It was the prettiest fight I ever saw. The Indians stood their ground for some time. I would often see a white man on one side of a rock and an Indian on the other side, not ten feet apart, each dodging and trying to get the first shot. We finally routed them, taking several scalps."

—Kit Carson describing a fight with the Blackfoot, 1837

1889 Harry Longabaugh is pardoned by Governor Thomas Moonlight after serving all but one day of an eighteen-month jail sentence in Sundance, Wyoming. After this he becomes known as the Sundance Kid.

BUCKSKIN PALADIN

The daring frontiersman Alexis Godey, born in St. Louis of French parents, entered the Rocky Mountain fur trade when he could barely shave. By his seventeenth birthday in 1835, the young man had journeyed far and wide and was trapping with the likes of Jim Bridger and Kit Carson, who became one of Godey's closest friends. Both men joined three of John Frémont's expeditions and, along with guide Dick Owens, received high praise for their diligence and courage. To hear Frémont tell it, Godey, Carson, and Owens could have served as field marshals in Napoleon's army. Godey had several Indian wives before marrying María Antonia Coronel, from a pioneer California family. For many years, Godey maintained a sheep ranch near Bakersfield, California. It was there he was laid to rest after visiting a Los Angeles circus where he "got too close to a lion and was scratched severely, dying from blood poisoning."

▶ A rare photograph of Alexis Godey, after he moved to California.

▶▶ María Antonia Coronel, who became Godey's wife.

FEB 5

1848 Myra Maebelle Shirley, better known as the outlaw Belle Starr, is born in Carthage, Missouri.

FATHER OF THE U.S. CAVALRY

At the outset of the U.S. war with Mexico in 1846, Colonel Stephen Watts Kearny was promoted to brigadier general and designated commander of the Army of the West. A veteran officer who began his career as an infantry lieutenant in the War of 1812, Kearny made his mark when he transformed a regiment of dragoons—mounted infantry who fought dismounted—into a cavalry unit. The U.S. Cavalry grew out of this regiment, earning Kearny the moniker "Father of the United States Cavalry." A month after the start of the war with Mexico, General Kearny's force of sixteen hundred troops departed Fort Leavenworth, Kansas, and marched down the Santa Fe Trail. On August 18, the Army of the West entered the provincial capital of Santa Fe, where they met no opposition and took control of the city without firing a shot. Kearny was named military governor. He declared New Mexico a U.S. territory and worked with local leaders to assure a smooth transition. In only one month, Kearny implemented a legal code and organized a new civil government. Continuing on to California with a greatly reduced force, Kearny met Kit Carson who was returning from California with a message from John Frémont, prematurely reporting that California had already been taken by American troops. In light of this news, Kearny sent even more of his men back to Santa Fe and proceeded on, only to encounter resistance and narrowly defeat enemy cavalry at the Battle of San Pasqual, where Kearny himself was wounded. By January 1847, the combined American forces had taken control of San Diego and Los Angeles.

▶ Stephen Watts Kearny, commander of the Army of the West in the Mexican War.

▶▶ Kit Carson played an important role in the conquest of New Mexico.

1873 In Indian Territory, two bands of Choctaw warriors capture sixteen men of their tribe who are suspected of horse thievery. They later shoot and kill six of the outlaw leaders.

LA TULES

A notorious woman who smoked hand-rolled *cigarritos* and had amassed a fortune at her popular gambling house, Doña Tules, or simply La Tules, was a major power broker in Santa Fe at the time the United States acquired New Mexico. Born in Mexico as María Gertrudis Barceló, she came to New Mexico Territory as a child. After marrying Manuel Antonio Sisneros in 1823, she broke with custom by keeping her maiden name and retaining the right to make contracts and hold her own property. Two years later, the couple moved to a mining camp to operate a saloon and gambling house. By the 1830s, she and her husband had relocated the operation to Santa Fe, where La Tules gained her reputation as a woman of independent means whose behavior shocked Anglo visitors from back East. Susan Shelby Magoffin, writing in her Santa Fe Trail diary in 1846, described La Tules as "a stately dame of a certain age, the possessor of . . . that shrewd sense and fascinating manner necessary to allure the wayward, inexperienced youth to the hall of final ruin." La Tules sided with the Americans during the Mexican War. After General Stephen Kearny marched into Santa Fe and a rumor spread that he did not have the funds to pay his troops, La Tules came to the rescue and offered a loan. When she died in 1852, La Tules bequeathed three houses, livestock, and cash to family members and gave substantial amounts of money to the church and city officials for charitable use.

▲ A crude sketch of Doña Tules, 1854.

▶ A novelist's more flattering illustration of Doña Tules.

DOÑA LONA

A STORY of TAOS and SANTA FÉ

FEB 7

1880 Three men accused of murder are lynched on the infamous "Hanging Windmill" in Las Vegas, New Mexico Territory, by town Marshal Joe Carson.

▲▲ Charles Bent, first territorial governor of New Mexico, was killed in the Taos Rebellion.

▲ Bent's wife, María Ignacia Bent (the sister of Kit Carson's wife), escaped death during the 1847 rebellion.

▶ A sketch of Taos, c. 1830s.

TURBULENT TAOS

By 1835, Charles Bent, of trading post fame, had settled in Taos and married María Ignacia Jaramillo, a well-to-do widow with whom he fathered five children. Thanks to his wife's good standing in the community, Bent prospered as a merchant and gained influence throughout the region. Yet not everyone thought so highly of him. His arrogance and condescending view of the Hispanic population surfaced in correspondences to American associates. "They have no opinion of their own," Bent wrote. "They are entirely governed by the powers that be and without exception the most servile people that can be imagined. . . . The Mexican character is made up of stupidity, obstinacy, ignorance, duplicity, and vanity." This attitude, coupled with Bent's practice of awarding interest to friends in land grants, contributed to his demise. The stage was set in 1846, when General Stephen Kearny conquered New Mexico and appointed Bent as the new territorial governor. Despite the seemingly peaceful takeover, many New Mexicans deeply resented the invasion and loss of sovereignty. Bent's continuing feud with a powerful Taos family and general fear of land seizures led to the Taos Rebellion of January 1847 and an attack on Bent's family home, during which he was scalped alive and then decapitated. His wife, her sister (wife of Kit Carson), and the children escaped by cutting a hole through an adobe wall with a large spoon and a poker. That spring, the ringleaders and several participants were tried and hanged.

FEB 8

1897 Outlaw Fleming Parker is captured while attempting to rob the Atlantic and Pacific Railroad at Peach Springs, Arizona.

BIG FOOT

When William Alexander Anderson Wallace was born in Virginia in 1817, weighing in at thirteen pounds, the midwife said that he could kick harder and yell louder than any baby she ever saw. He grew to be six feet, two inches tall, two hundred forty pounds, with oversized feet—earning him the moniker "Big Foot." In 1836, when Wallace learned of the deaths of a brother and a cousin in the Battle of Goliad in Texas, his Scot-Irish blood boiled. In a flash, he was "Gone to Texas" to settle the score and, in his own words, "take pay out of the Mexicans." Big Foot made it to Texas after the Battle of San Jacinto. He fought Comanche raiders and during a punitive expedition into Mexico he was taken prisoner. After his release, Big Foot joined the Texas Rangers, serving under John Coffee Hays during the Mexican War and later in campaigns against Indians and border outlaws. When he was not busy fighting and telling tales, Big Foot drove a mail coach on the dangerous route connecting San Antonio and El Paso. He also earned a living chasing runaway slaves with his pack of snarling hounds. Big Foot never married and read the Bible daily. He died in 1899 in Bigfoot, a town named for him. Laid to rest in Austin, the epitaph on his tombstone reads:

BIG FOOT WALLACE
HERE LIES HE WHO SPENT HIS
MANHOOD DEFENDING THE HOMES
OF
TEXAS
BRAVE HONEST AND FAITHFUL

▲ A photo of Wallace, and his big feet, taken in his old age.

▶ Big Foot Wallace was propelled into fame by this 1872 book.

"BIG FOOT WALLACE."—Frontispiece.

THE ADVENTURES

OF

BIG-FOOT WALLACE,

THE TEXAS RANGER AND HUNTER.

BY

JOHN C. DUVAL,

AUTHOR OF "JACK DOBELL; OR, A BOY'S ADVENTURES IN TEXAS;" "THE YOUNG EXPLORERS; OR, BOY-LIFE IN TEXAS," ETC.

With Portrait and Engravings.

SECOND EDITION.

PHILADELPHIA:
CLAXTON, REMSEN & HAFFELFINGER,
819 & 821 MARKET STREET.
MACON, GA.: J. W. BURKE & CO.
1872.

FEB 9

1880 The "Hanging Windmill" of Las Vegas, New Mexico Territory, is torn down due to mischievous children hanging their dogs from the gallows.

EMPIRE BUILDER

As the relentless leader of a historic migration to Utah and president of the Mormon Church for more than thirty years, Brigham Young was both praised for many accomplishments and damned for a multitude of transgressions. Young was proof of a widely held notion that converts tend to be more devout and zealous than those who grow up in a faith. Born into a poor Vermont farm family in 1801, Young was a skilled craftsman when, at the age of twenty-one, he and his wife moved to western New York, where he joined the Methodist Church and became a preacher. Then, in 1830, Young experienced an epiphany after reading the *Book of Mormon* written by Joseph Smith, prophet of what was to become the Church of Jesus Christ of Latter-day Saints. Two years later, the converted Young was baptized and ordained an apostle. For several years, he devoted his life to mission work in Canada and England. Back in the United States, Young stood by Smith as his second-in-command while they guided their growing flock in a series of moves to avoid the persecution of hostile gentiles, or non-Mormons. When Smith and his brother were murdered by a mob in 1844, Young assumed command of the church and led the faithful on a westward exodus that only ended when they reached a high desert promised land in what would become Utah. According to Mormon tradition, on June 24, 1847, Brigham Young first gazed upon the Salt Lake Valley and declared, "This is the place."

▶ Brigham Young.

FEB 10

1878 A Dodge City posse, searching for the perpetrators of the January 27 train robbery in Kinsley, Kansas, rides out for west Texas. The men return after twelve days with no suspects in custody.

SQUAW MAN

Brigham Young and John Young Nelson, the frontiersman who for forty dollars a month guided Mormons across the prairies and plains to the Great Salt Lake, had something in common—wives. The difference being that Young, as a polygamist, was married to many women at the same time. He wed as many as fifty-six women, including several widows of Joseph Smith. Nelson had many wives himself, although one at a time, and always chose Indian women, something Young would have found reprehensible. In the parlance of the time, Nelson was a "squaw man," the name given to white men who married into a tribe and adopted the traditions of his wife's people. To some, squaw man was another way of saying "turned Injun" or "gone native." Nelson was just a boy when he ran away from home and signed on with some traders headed west. When they encountered a band of Sioux, Nelson was so attracted to their culture that he stayed with the Indians. They eventually adopted Nelson, giving him the name Cha-Sha-Sha-O-Pogeo or "Redwood Fill the Pipe," since he was fond of mixing red willow powder with tobacco. Nelson's succession of Indian wives provided the language skills and insight that made him invaluable in trading transactions and as an interpreter while scouting for the army.

▲ John Young Nelson traveled with Buffalo Bill's Wild West with his Indian wife and their children.

▶ Painting of a mountain man with his dogs, packhorse, and Indian wife following with a travois.

FEB 11

1856 The first supply of camels for the Texas Camel Corps arrives in Indianola, Texas. Secretary of War Jefferson Davis created the Camel Corps in order to test their efficiency as pack animals in the southwestern desert.

GOLD!

"Boys I believe I have found a gold mine!" With those words, James W. Marshall, a carpenter building a sawmill for John Sutter on the American River in California, triggered an avalanche of events that would shape the social and economic future of the American West. In an instant, the entire world caught gold fever. By the end of 1849, almost one hundred thousand "Forty-niners" flocked to California. Many of them struck out on new overland routes, and others arrived at bustling seaports. Very few of them struck it rich though, and that included John Sutter. All of his ranch workers quit to pan for their own fortune, and his property was overrun with gold-seekers who devoured his cattle. Sutter ended up flat broke.

"The blacksmith dropped his hammer, the carpenter his plane, the mason his trowel, the farmer his sickle, the baker his loaf, the tapster his bottle. All were off to the mines, some on horses, some on carts, and some on crutches, and one went on a litter."

—Walton Colton, mayor of Monterey, California, 1848

"There probably never occurred, in all history, a more wonderful combination of circumstances than that of which the present condition of California has grown. It is a phenomenon the likes of which can never happen again, since there is no part of the world in which it is possible."

—Bayard Taylor, *New York Tribune* correspondent, 1849

▲ An ambrotype of a California Forty-niner.

▶ Pioneers panning for gold.

FEB 12

1836 General Santa Anna leads a force of six thousand soldiers across the Rio Grande into the Mexican state of Texas en route to the Alamo to suppress a rebellion.

SEEING THE ELEPHANT

No phrase epitomized the California gold rush more than "seeing the elephant." For the Forty-niners, the idea of laying eyes on such an exotic beast symbolized an exciting adventure of a lifetime. The elephant represented fame and fortune. Those headed west announced they were "off to see the elephant." The many who came back empty-handed said they had "seen the elephant," or "seen the elephant's tail." The catchphrase often appeared in diaries and letters, and newspapers published cartoons depicting an elephant chased by miners. In 1848, *Seeing the Elephant*, a musical comedy ridiculing the gold rush, opened in New York. By the spring of 1850, it reached San Francisco and, appropriately, was billed alongside two traveling circuses.

"We are told that the Elephant is waiting, ready to receive us. . . . If he shows fight or attempts to stop us on our progress to the golden land, we shall attack him with sword and spear."

—James D. Lyon, en route to California, 1849

"All hands are up early anxious to see the path that leads to the elephant."

—John Clark, Missourian bound for California, 1852

▲ California miners extracting gold from the river.

▶ California miners "seeing the elephant."

FEB

13

1866 Jesse James holds up the Clay County Savings Association in Liberty, Missouri. It is the first daylight bank robbery in U.S. history.

EL DORADO

During the heady gold rush years, the population of California swelled. Whole towns emptied as the citizens flocked to the goldfields. Entire crews jumped ship in San Francisco to have a go of it. Some newspapers even had to cease publication when the whole staff left to become miners. "Such a medley as were never thrown together in the world before," wrote prospector A. J. McCall in 1850. "Cities sprang up in a night." Yet even though the gold rush continued after California joined the United States in 1850, it became increasingly difficult to find payable amounts. The days of panning for gold did not last. New and improved mining methods came along, and before long many prospectors took jobs with large concerns and searched for the treasure locked in underground streams and quartz deposits.

▶ Mine in the California gold country.

"There was no place of deposit for money, and the men living in the house dropped into the habit of leaving their dust with me for safe keeping. Many a night have I shut my oven door on two milk-pans filled high with bags of gold dust, and I have often slept with my mattress literally lined with the precious metal. At one time I must have had more than two hundred thousand dollars lying unprotected in my bedroom, and it never entered my head that it might be stolen."

—memoirs of Luzena Stanley Wilson, n.d.

FEB 14

1905 In Argentina, two unidentified Americans rob the Banco de Tarapaca y Argentino in Rio Gallegos and get away with twenty thousand pesos. Butch Cassidy and the Sundance Kid are forced out of the country on suspicion of executing the robbery.

GOLDEN GATE

In 1846, John C. Frémont dubbed the entrance to San Francisco Bay "Chrysopylae," or "Golden Gate." It was a fortuitous choice. In only a few years, San Francisco would be transformed from a sleepy village to a boomtown and center of commerce and finance. For the first time in America's history, a poor person could become wealthy overnight. In those flush times—when clouds of gold dust flew and yellow nuggets were there for the taking—the "City by the Bay" was the place to be for those who struck it rich. In a single year, the population of San Francisco increased from one thousand to twenty-five thousand, making it the West's first full-fledged city. When the gold rush began, only 2 percent of those bound for the "land of milk and honey" were female. By 1857, women accounted for half of the pilgrims on the westbound wagon trains. They worked alongside men in the goldfields, ran boardinghouses, and dealt cards. Others turned to prostitution, which, next to gambling, was the most lucrative trade. Some made enough money to integrate into polite society and find respectable husbands. When men could afford it, they sent for their wives and sweethearts. It might have been a man's world, but plenty of women also "saw the elephant."

▶ A California woman elegantly dressed.

▶▶ A daguerreotype of a Spanish lady in San Francisco.

FEB 15

1900 After attempting to rob a train at Fairbank, Arizona Territory, near the town of Tombstone, outlaws "Three-Fingered" Jack Dunlap, Bravo Juan Yoas, and the Owens brothers are foiled by lawman Jeff Milton, even after he is shot in the arm.

HUMAN CANVAS

In 1851, thirteen-year-old Olive Oatman and her Mormon family were bound for California on the Gila River in what would become Arizona when Yavapai Indians attacked. Olive's father, her pregnant mother, and three of her siblings were killed. Her brother Lorenzo was badly wounded and left for dead, but survived. Olive and her seven-year-old sister, Mary Ann, were taken as slaves. They lived with the Yavapais for a year during which time the girls were forced to do menial chores and routinely beaten. When a band of Mojave Indians visited the camp, they traded some horses, vegetables, and blankets for the pair of white girls and brought them to their village on the Colorado River. The Mojave chief's daughter adopted the sisters and treated them as her own children. Like the Mojaves, both girls were tattooed on their chins with a distinctive blue cactus–ink symbol as part of a puberty ritual. Tattooing was a common practice in the tribe, and according to tradition, the spirit of a Mojave who died without facial tattoos was doomed to enter a rat hole for life. Mary Ann, however, grew frail, and in 1854, at the age of ten, she died during a famine. In 1856, white authorities located Olive in the Mojave village and obtained her release. Her reunion at Fort Yuma with her brother Lorenzo made front-page news across the nation. In 1857, a minister named Royal B. Stratton wrote a highly sensationalized bestselling book about the Oatman sisters. Olive went on the lecture circuit, married, adopted an infant daughter, and quietly lived out her life in Texas.

▲ Olive Oatman, after her release from her Indian captors.

▶ Fanny Kelly's narrative about her life as a captive with the Sioux. She was but one of many white youngsters taken prisoner by various Indian tribes throughout the 1800s.

Respectfully
Fanny Kelly

NARRATIVE

OF

MY CAPTIVITY

AMONG THE

SIOUX INDIANS.

BY

FANNY KELLY.

WITH A BRIEF ACCOUNT OF GENERAL SULLY'S INDIAN EXPEDITION IN 1864, BEARING UPON EVENTS OCCURRING IN MY CAPTIVITY.

CINCINNATI:
WILSTACH, BALDWIN & CO., PRINTERS,
No. 143 Race Street,
1871.

FEB 16

1877 Following California and Oregon's lead, Montana Territory passes a law that sanctions a three-hundred-dollar bounty on any perpetrator of a stagecoach or train robbery.

ALERT AND FAITHFUL

During the last half of the nineteenth century, Wells Fargo & Co. was the most powerful and well-known business in the American West. Organized in 1852 in New York, Wells Fargo opened a San Francisco office later that same year and immediately began speeding gold shipments to mining offices and banks. The red-and-yellow Wells Fargo six-horse stagecoaches bouncing across the plains became one of the iconic symbols of the Wild West. True to the motto—"Alert and Faithful"—the company hired tough and dependable shotgun-toting guards to ride beside the stage driver and keep an eagle eye out for pesky bandits or renegade Indians. Beneath the driver's feet rested the sturdy wooden (later iron) padlocked strongboxes crammed with gold dust, gold bars, legal tender, checks, mail, and documents. By 1857, most of the forty-three million dollars in gold taken from California mines has been carried by a Wells Fargo coach. Though most commonly used for gold and silver, the express company would transport just about anything—a fire engine pumper, brides from back East to love-starved miners, soldiers en route to new posts, the first shipment of ice to Los Angeles, and perishable foodstuffs such as oysters and butter to the mining camps.

▲ A Wells Fargo strongbox, which held the gold and silver.

▶ From their beginning, Wells Fargo stages were targeted by both Indians and outlaws.

WELLS FARGO & CO. EXPRESS

FEB 17

1909 Geronimo, the famous Apache warrior and occasional participant in Wild West shows, dies of pneumonia at Fort Sill at the age of eighty, still a prisoner of war.

THE FIVE JOAQUINS

The dashing Joaquin Murieta (sometimes spelled Murrieta or Murietta) came to California in 1849 to seek his fortune in the goldfields. But soon he turned to a life of crime to avenge the brutal acts supposedly committed against himself and his wife. Murieta and his lieutenant, Manuel García, best known as "Three-Fingered Jack," led a band of brigands that included Joaquin Valenzuela, Joaquin Botellier, Joaquin Ocomorenia, and Joaquin Carrillo. Dubbed by the authorities as the "Five Joaquins," the gang was said to have been responsible for most of the robberies, murders, and cattle rustling in the Sierra Nevada region between 1850 and 1853. Their crime spree led to the creation of the California State Rangers, led by Captain Harry Love, a former Texas Ranger. On July 25, 1853, Love and his men confronted the gang, and in the ensuing shootout Murieta and Three-Fingered Jack were killed. To prove their kills, the Rangers supposedly sliced off one of Garcia's hands and severed Murieta's head. The grisly trophies were preserved in whiskey and later placed in jars of alcohol for exhibition purposes.

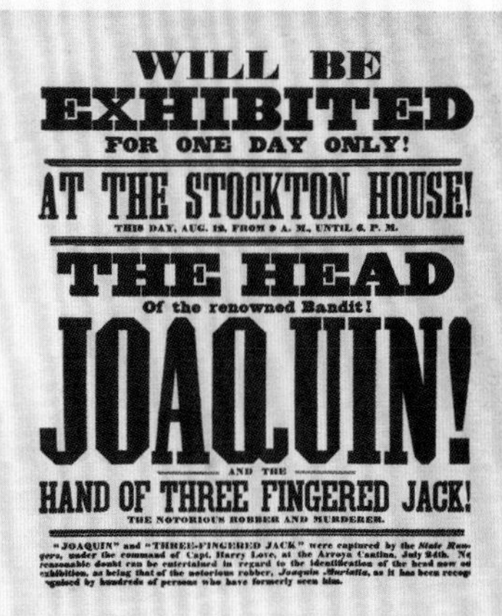

▲ Murieta's severed head was a popular attraction of the day.

▶ There are no known photographs of Joaquin Murieta. This rendering was likely drawn using his severed head as a model.

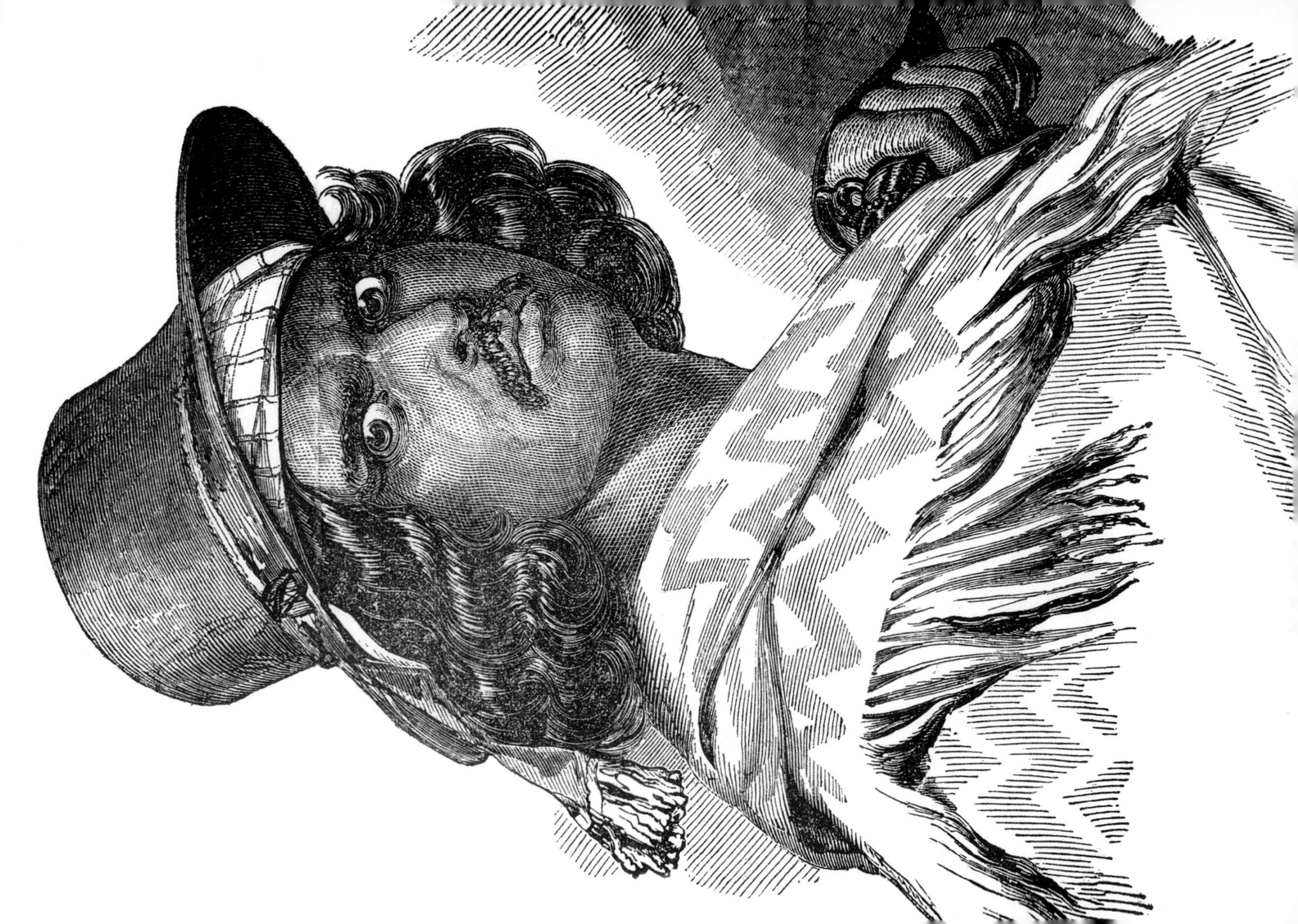

FEB **18**

1878 Billy the Kid's employer, New Mexico rancher John Henry Tunstall, is killed by members of the Murphy-Dolan Gang. This marks the beginning of the Lincoln County War.
1921 Henry Starr robs the People's National Bank of Harrison, Arkansas, but is shot while making his getaway. This is the first time an automobile, rather than a horse, is used in a bank heist. Starr dies four days later.

ROBIN HOOD OF EL DORADO

Described as a brutal cutthroat and vicious bandit by some and a noble patriot and champion of the oppressed by others, in death Joaquin Murieta—"the mountain robber"—became the most legendary figure of the 1850s Gold Rush era. Even in death, it was difficult to separate fact from fiction when it came to Murieta, whose pickled head soon began making the rounds of mining camps and exhibitions throughout California and surrounding territories. Pulp writers and yarn spinners built his legend. In 1854, John Rollin Ridge, a San Francisco journalist writing under the nom de plume "Yellow Bird," published a fictional account of Joaquin Murieta's life that portrayed him as a Robin Hood–style folk hero who robbed moneyed people to help the poor and downtrodden. Several other books followed, and reportedly it was Murieta who inspired in part the fictional character of Zorro, the masked swordsman. Despite skeptics who claimed the head in the jar was not Murieta, the trophy that earned Captain Love his reward was acquired for the Pacific Museum of Anatomy and Science in San Francisco. It remained on display for forty years among Egyptian mummies and the "amazing Cyclops child," before being destroyed in the devastating 1906 earthquake and fire.

▶ One of the first books to make bandit Joaquin Murieta a legendary figure.

▶▶ Murieta became a folk hero to Spanish-speaking Californians through books like this one.

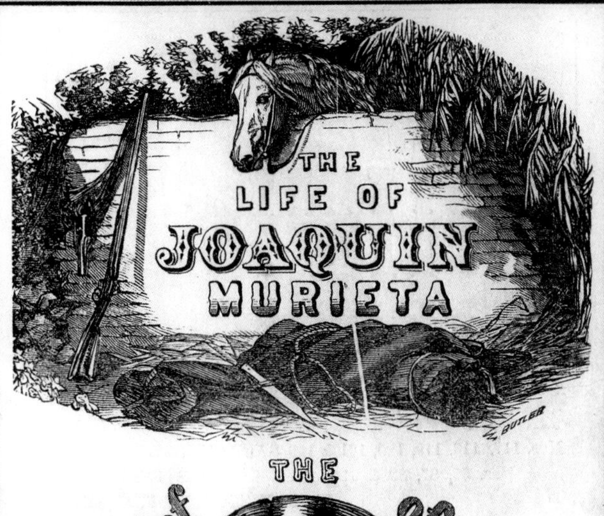

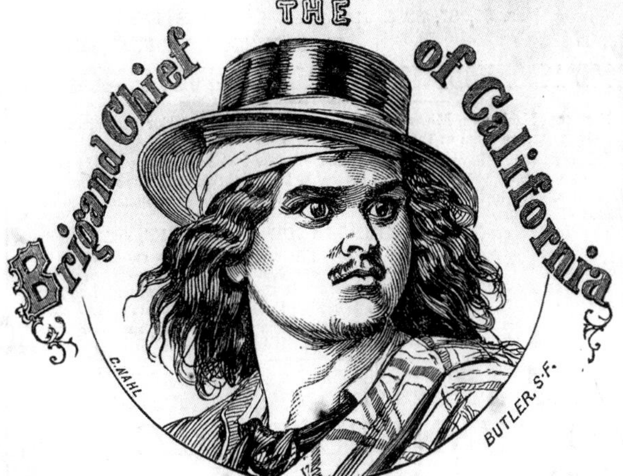

THE
LIFE OF
JOAQUIN
MURIETA
BUTLER
THE
Brigand Chief of California
C. NAHL
BUTLER. S.F.
BUTLER & CO.
PUBLISHERS OF THE "CALIFORNIA POLICE GAZETTE,"
SAN FRANCISCO.

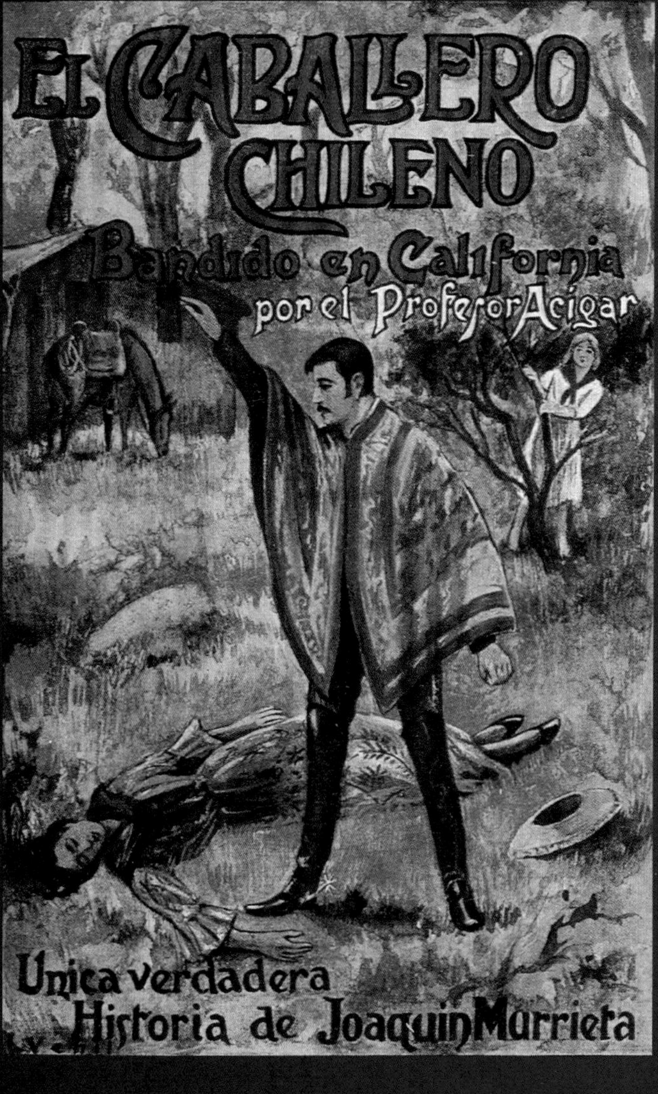
EL CABALLERO CHILENO
Bandido en California
por el Profesor Acigar
Unica verdadera
Historia de Joaquin Murrieta

FEB 19

1846 In Austin, Texas, a ceremony takes place to officially mark the change in status of the area, from the Republic of Texas to the state of Texas.

GAUDY LIAR

In 1856, the appearance of the action-packed *Life and Adventures of James P. Beckwourth, Mountaineer, Scout, and Pioneer, and Chief of the Crow Nation of Indians* offered the first published account of the escapades of a black man in the American West. In the goldfields of California, Beckwourth dictated his rousing life story to T. D. Bonner, an itinerant justice of the peace, journalist, and temperance advocate with a drinking problem. The book was an immediate success. It was released in England later that same year, followed by a second U.S. printing and a French edition in 1860. While much of the public eagerly devoured the tales of high adventure among the Indians, others, in that time of blatant racism, dismissed the book as the musings of a "mongrel of mixed blood." Critics pointed out that among his fellow mountain men, Beckwourth was jokingly referred to as a "gaudy liar." But later historians, such as the acclaimed Bernard DeVoto, reassessed Beckwourth and found that much of what he described actually happened. They also pointed out that to be a "gaudy liar" among mountain men was actually a compliment, since exaggerated tale spinning was a skill as valued as marksmanship and tracking. Beckwourth's autobiography remains the best account of several Indian tribes in the first thirty years of the nineteenth century.

"This man Jim P. Beckwourth met with plenty adventure in his lifetime, and Mr. T. D. Bonner his biographer is a fine writer and tells an interesting storey [sic], yet this mulatto negro is without doubt the biggest lier [sic] that ever lived."

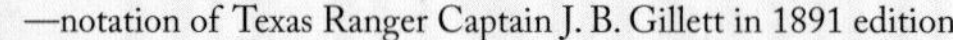

—notation of Texas Ranger Captain J. B. Gillett in 1891 edition

▲ James Beckwourth.

▶ This copy of Beckwourth's book, published in 1856, was annotated by retired Texas Ranger James B. Gillett, with notes by each of Beckwourth's lies and exaggerations.

LIFE AND
ADVENTURES
OF
JAMES P.
BECKWOURTH

FEB 20

1903 Retired outlaws Frank James and Cole Younger buy the "Buckskin Bill Wild West Show," but their new venture only lasts one season.

DESTROYING ANGEL

Convinced that by leaving his hair uncut he would be invincible like the Old Testament Samson, Orrin Porter Rockwell was as controversial as any character in the American West. Rockwell stopped trimming his locks based on the words of Joseph Smith, the founder of the Church of Jesus Christ of Latter-day Saints. "I prophesy, in the name of the Lord," Smith told him, "that you—Orrin Porter Rockwell—so long as ye shall remain loyal and true to thy faith, need fear no enemy. Cut not thy hair and no bullet or blade can harm thee." For many years, Rockwell acted as the personal bodyguard for Smith and then Brigham Young as the Mormons established themselves in Utah. Rockwell—called "the Destroying Angel" and "the Terror of the Plains"—was accused of as many as one hundred cold-blooded murders, mostly on command from church leaders. His weapons of choice were either a dagger or a Colt pistol that Rockwell referred to as "three pounds of Black Death." It was said that "His gun never missed; his knife was never dull." Rockwell waylaid some travelers for their money, but he also murdered fellow Saints who dared speak out against the church. "I never killed anyone who didn't need killing," he once told a crowd. In his role as enforcer, Rockwell became so confident that he generously gave his famous long hair to a wigmaker for a widow who had gone bald from typhoid fever. When author Fitz Hugh Ludlow visited Salt Lake City and met Rockwell, he wrote that he "found him one of the pleasantest murderers I ever met."

▶ Orrin Porter Rockwell, controversial gunman for Brigham Young and known as "the Destroying Angel."

FEB 21

1896 Judge Roy Bean, known as the "Law West of the Pecos," sets up a World Championship boxing match at Langtry, Texas, between Irishman Peter Maher and "The Freckled Wonder" Bob Fitzsimmons, skirting a ban on professional prizefighting in Texas by setting the match on a sandbar in the middle of the Rio Grande.

MOUNTAIN MEADOWS MASSACRE

In September 1857, one of the most shameful events in the annals of the Old West took place at a mountain pass in southwest Utah Territory named Mountain Meadows. Sparked by fear, paranoia, and a growing resentment of gentiles, a combined force of Mormon militia and their Paiute Indian allies attacked a wagon train of about 140 Arkansas and Missouri emigrants bound for California. After the initial assault and a siege lasting several days, the attackers, using the ruse of a white flag of truce, entered the camp and slaughtered about 120 men, women, and children. Seventeen children under eight years old were allowed to live and given to Mormon families. The Church of Jesus Christ of Latter-day Saints denied any role in the massacre for many years. Finally in 1875, public pressure forced the prosecution of one of the militia leaders, John D. Lee. After two trials, Lee was convicted. On March 23, 1877, he was taken back to Mountain Meadows for his execution. While a firing squad took their positions, Lee rose from his seat on his own coffin and gave some final remarks, mostly claims that the church to which he had devoted his life had wronged him. Before the fatal shots were fired, Lee requested that the firing squad "shoot the balls through my heart! Don't let them mangle my body." He left nineteen widows and sixty-four children.

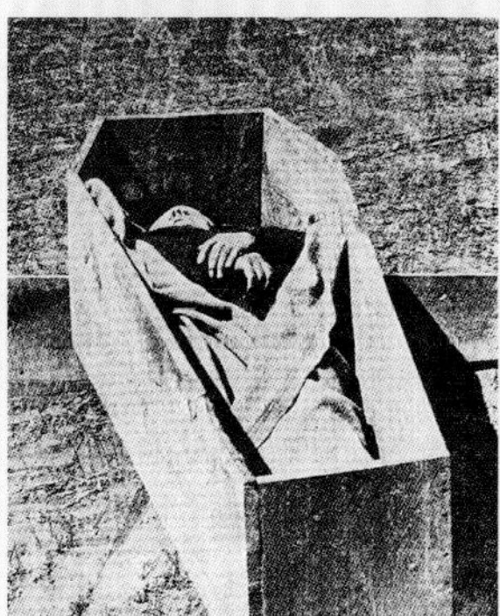

▲▲ John D. Lee, Mormon militia leader in the 1857 Mountain Meadows Massacre.

▲ Lee's body after his execution by firing squad at the site of the massacre, 1877.

▶ Lee calmly sitting on his coffin at left just before his execution, 1877.

"I have but little to say this morning. Of course I feel that I am at the brink of eternity, and the solemnities of eternity should rest upon my mind at the present. . . . I am ready to die. I trust in God. I have no fear. Death has no terror."

—John D. Lee, at his execution, March 23, 1877

FEB 22

1878 The Sam Bass Gang robs the Houston and Texas Central Express train in Allen, Texas.

THE OVERLAND STAGE

Thanks in large part to such entrepreneurs as Ben Holladay and John Butterfield, the arduous journey from the Mississippi to the Pacific was greatly improved by the growth of competing stagecoach lines. Holladay—"Stagecoach King of the West"—employed thousands of men and owned twenty thousand freight wagons and stages during his heyday. Beginning in 1858, the Butterfield Overland Mail Service carried the U.S. mail and legions of passengers by stagecoach from St. Louis to California, covering the challenging 2,800-mile journey in twenty-five days. This meant that the Butterfield drivers had to urge their horse teams to move at breakneck speeds, averaging 120 miles per day across open country where occasional bandit and hostile Indian attacks were not unknown.

"All the traveler needs to render himself comfortable is a pair of blankets, a revolver or knife (just as he fancies), an overcoat, some wine to mix with the water (which is not of the sweetest quality), and three or four dollars worth of provisions. . . . Arms are not furnished the passengers by the Company. Were I to make the trip again, I would take the stoutest suit of clothes I could get, with a strong loose pair of boots."

—special correspondent, *San Francisco Evening Bulletin*, 1858

YOU WILL BE TRAVELING THROUGH INDIAN COUNTRY AND THE SAFETY OF YOUR PERSON CANNOT BE VOUCHSAFED BY ANYONE BUT GOD

—John Butterfield's warning poster

▲ The primary destination of the Overland Stage was the gold country of California.

▶ The Denver Holladay Overland Mail office and a stagecoach.

HOLLADAY OVERLAND MAIL & EX-PRESS CO.

FEB 23

1836 Sam Houston and Cherokee chief Bowles sign a treaty allotting certain lands in Texas exclusively for Indian use. However, after the war with Mexico, Texas lawmakers fail to ratify the treaty.

IRON PANTS

One of those who struck it rich during the California gold rush was Levi Strauss, a Bavarian immigrant tailor who arrived in bustling San Francisco in 1853 and opened a wholesale dry goods firm under his own name. Soon Strauss was supplying stores all over California and the West with clothing for miners and settlers. Strauss's firm grew and prospered throughout the 1860s, but gained even more notoriety thanks to one of its customers, Jacob Davis of Reno, Nevada. Davis found a way to improve workpants by using duck fabric as durable as canvas and placing metal rivets at the base of the button fly and in the pocket corners. In need of capital and a business partner, he joined with Strauss, and in 1873 they patented and began to manufacture versatile "waist overalls." Eventually they started using sturdy denim fabric and copper rivets, and their blue jeans—much later simply called Levi's—became popular across the West and eventually around the world.

▶ A miner wearing Levi's, late 1850s.

▶▶ A cowboy in Levi's, 1870s.

EVERY PAIR GUARANTEED
ONLY THE VERY BEST MATERIALS USED IN THEIR MANUFACTURE
THE DENIM WHICH IS SOFT AS COTTON

—from an early Levi-Strauss & Co. advertisement

FEB 24

1911 An entertainment feature in a trade magazine called *Film Fancies* declares "the world has gone wild over the 101 Bison Pictures," early Westerns shot on the 101 Ranch in Oklahoma Territory.

PIKES PEAK OR BUST

By the spring of 1859, driven by reports of the first significant gold find in the Rocky Mountains, as many as one hundred thousand hopeful miners and prospectors swarmed what would become Colorado, all of them part of the greatest gold rush in North American history. The treasure seekers—called Fifty-niners—often scrawled the slogan "Pikes Peak or Bust" across the wagon canvas, even though the richest deposits of gold were to the north of the mountain named for explorer Zebulon Pike. Bold newspaper headlines and exaggerated stories chronicling the discovery spurred on the Pikes Peak rush, and as a result, at least half of those embarking on the quest never even reached the Rockies. Many of them were poorly equipped for the trek and either starved, became ill, got lost, or fell prey to Indians. Soon wagons were headed back East with the words on the canvases changed to "Busted, by God."

▲ A mining operation during the boom in Colorado.

▶ The mining boomtown of Black Hawk, Colorado.

"It was a mad, furious race for wealth, in which many men lost their identity almost, and toiled and wrestled, and lived a fierce, riotous, wearing, fearfully excited life; forgetting home and kindred; abandoning old, steady habits; acquiring restlessness, craving for stimulant, unscrupulousness, hardihood, impulsive generosity, and lavish ways."

—Pikes Peak prospector's reminisces, c. 1860

MEAT MARKET

FEB 25

1836 Samuel L. Colt receives the patent for his Colt .45 revolver.

COMSTOCK LODE

About the same time that the Pikes Peak rush was on, the Comstock Lode was discovered in the Washoe Mountains of what was soon to become Nevada Territory. Those who benefited called the find history's greatest bonanza in gold and silver. Over the years, the Comstock yielded more than four hundred million dollars in gold and silver, helped finance the Civil War, and convinced Abraham Lincoln to make the territory a state in 1864. The glut of mining riches also turned the boomtown of Virginia City into the most important settlement between San Francisco and Denver. At its zenith, Virginia City boasted thirty thousand citizens, many of them former prospectors who had become filthy rich and built lavish mansions filled with furniture and art imported from Europe and Asia. The roses of vice stayed busy in a thriving red-light district, known locally as Sporting Row. Fashionably dressed gents carried one-thousand-dollar watches, attended Shakespeare plays, dined on champagne and caviar delivered on ice by Wells Fargo, and used toothpicks made of gold.

▶ An ambrotype of a high-stakes card game, c. 1850s.

FEB 26

1846 William F. "Buffalo Bill" Cody is born in Leclaire, Iowa Territory.

ROGUE OF THE RIO GRANDE

The legend of Juan Nepomuceno Cortina began in 1859 when he happened upon a Mexican man being pistol-whipped by the marshal of Brownsville, Texas. The outraged Cortina demanded that the Anglo lawman stop, and when he refused, Cortina shot him in the shoulder. He then pulled the badly beaten man onto his horse, and they galloped off to Cortina's ranch. Two months later, Cortina led an armed force into Brownsville to free some Mexicans he believed to have been unfairly jailed. Shouting "Death to the gringos!" Cortina ordered his men to raise the Mexican flag before they left. For the next six months, what came to be called Cortina's War raged. While Cortina continued his raids, a force of Texas Rangers often indiscriminately attacked any Mexican they came upon. The Mexican government dispatched some troops to join the Anglos, but Cortina and his followers defeated the allied forces. Soon the U.S. Army jumped in the fray, and bested the insurgents in late 1859. Hailed as a hero by the Mexican people on both sides of the border, Cortina retreated into Mexico. In the 1860s, he battled pro-Confederate forces in south Texas, fought under Benito Juárez against the French intervention, and was made a general in the Mexican army.

▶ Juan Nepomuceno Cortina, who waged a war against the American forces in south Texas.

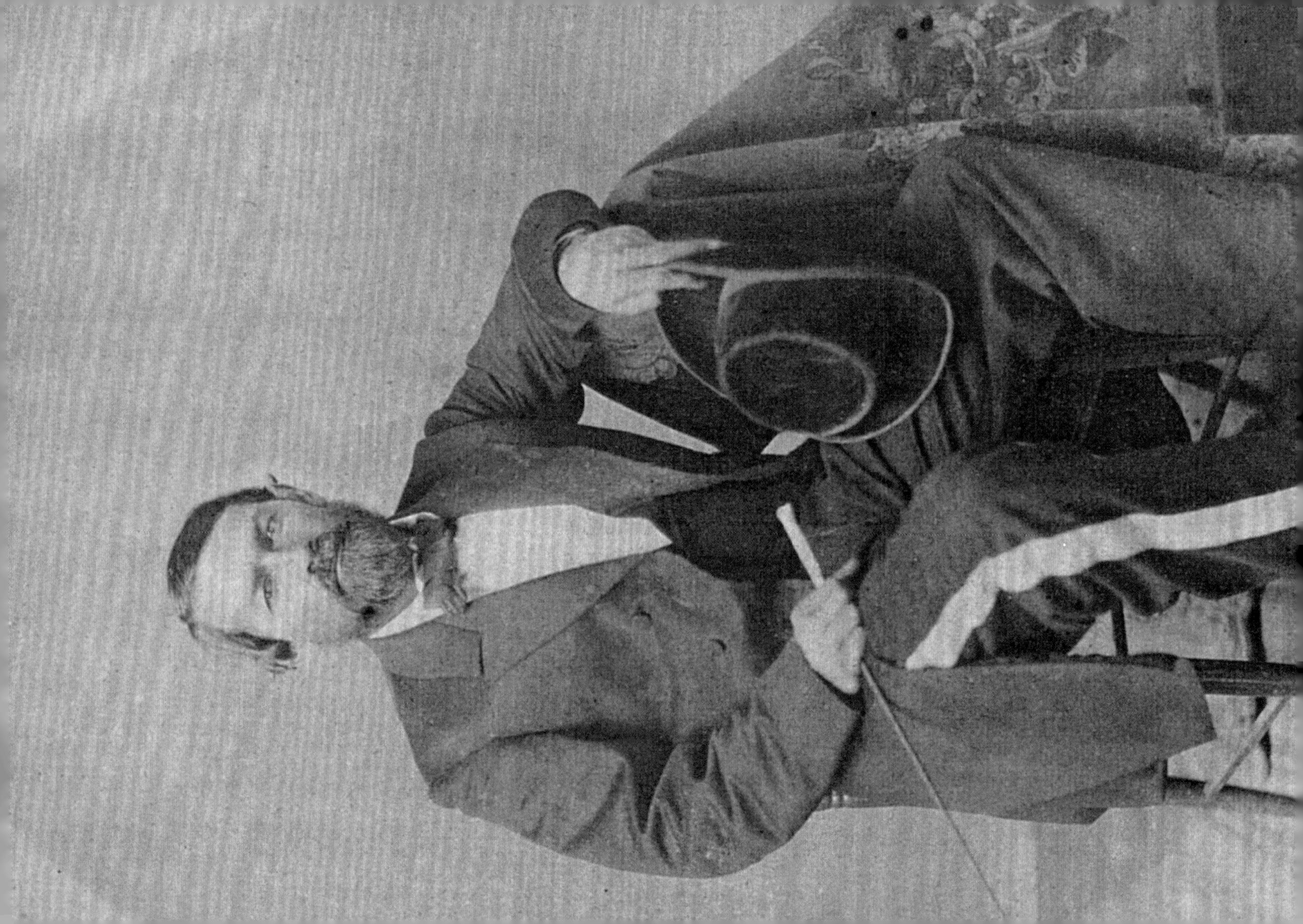

FEB

27

1887 Henry Longabaugh (later the Sundance Kid) steals a horse, saddle outfit, and pistol from employees of the Triple V Ranch in Sundance, Wyoming.

LOLA MONTEZ

Just after the California gold rush peaked, the exotic beauty Lola Montez, no doubt attracted by the abundance of newfound wealth, captivated San Francisco dandies, shocked their prim ladies, and endured the taunts of rowdy miners. Her original name was Marie Dolores Eliza Rosanna Gilbert, but the Irish native adopted the stage sobriquet Lola Montez, became a dancer, and had a series of romantic trysts with Franz Liszt, Victor Hugo, Frederic Chopin, and George Sand. She also served as the confidante and mistress of King Ludwig of Bavaria, a scandalous relationship that contributed to his abdication and also sent the banished Lola packing. During a tour of the United States, Lola arrived in California in 1853 and stayed for two years. She quickly became known for performing her famously suggestive "Tarantula Dance," a provocative ballet in which Lola pretended to become entangled in a spider's web and discovered spiders hiding in the folds of her flowing gown. As she waved her arms, leaped in the air, and vigorously shook her clothing, revealing her petticoats, the audiences sat spellbound. Lola threw lavish parties; gave dance lessons to Lotta Crabtree, a miner's daughter who went on to become a celebrated star of the American stage; and was frequently seen in the company of her pet cinnamon bear. At the dock in 1855, Lola broke into tears as she departed San Francisco bound for Australia. A local newspaper editorial praised her as a "noble-hearted and generous lady" whose "many good acts so won the esteem of our citizens."

▲ An older Lola Montez, perhaps in the California gold town of Nevada City.

▶ Lola Montez at the height of her stage performance career.

"Whatever Lola Wants, Lola Gets"

—song inspired by life of Lola Montez from *Damn Yankees*, 1955

FEB

28

1881 In Santa Fe, New Mexico Territory, Sheriff Romulo Martinez discovers an escape tunnel in Billy the Kid's jail cell and places him in solitary confinement.

DON JUAN OF THE THOMPSON

Mariano Medina, born in Taos in 1812 and one of the last of the authentic mountain men, made his name as a trapper, hide trader, and part-time bounty hunter in the 1830s. But Medina's most valuable contribution to history came in 1858 as the first settler in the rugged Big Thompson River Valley, near present-day Loveland, Colorado. Medina—who had scouted for John Frémont and counted as friends Jim Bridger, Kit Carson, and the Bent brothers—first established a ferrying enterprise, charging as much as fifty dollars in gold for a raft ride across the Big Thompson. He expanded his operations by building a toll bridge and a trading post that most travelers knew as Marianne's Crossing. It became a popular stopping place and for many years the only way to cross the roaring river. It was said Mariano had a flexible toll rate, charging some only twenty-five cents on busy days but as much as one hundred dollars when business was slow. Medina gained the nickname "Don Juan of the Thompson" due to his courtly manners, flashing smile, and colorful dress, which charmed the ladies. According to one writer, the news of Medina's death in 1878 "echoed throughout the Rocky Mountain empire like the mournful sound of distant thunder." The old mountain man was eulogized on the front pages of many newspapers.

▶ Mariano Medina, a Mexican mountain man, scout, and friend of Kit Carson.

"This remarkable man seems to have had no affection for any but his own relatives, his horse, and his rifle."

—Frank K. Smith, *Fort Collins Express*, 1894

MAR 1

1877 Jack McCall is hanged in Yankton, Dakota Territory, for the murder of Wild Bill Hickok.

THE JEHUS OF THE PLAINS

Some of the boldest characters to emerge from the American West were the intrepid stagecoach drivers. These rugged individuals, admired for their ability to handle a team of horses, propelled their stages over rough terrain frequented by brigands or hostile Indians. Although mostly men took up the profession, some women proved to be just as capable of handling horses with a whip—a reinsman's most prized possession. Drivers were given nicknames such as "Whip," "Charlie," or the popular "Jehu" (*Gee-who*), taken from a hard-driving charioteer from the Old Testament. Weather permitting, the seat next to the Jehu was the most desireable, but it was always reserved for a person selected by the driver.

"I think I should be compelled to nominate the stage-drivers, as being on the whole the most lofty, arrogant, reserved and superior class of being on the coast—that class that inspired me with the most terror and reverence."

—Reverend Henry Bellows, on a stage trip to California, 1864

"The best seat in a stage is the one next to the driver. If the team runs away—sit still and take your chances. If you jump, nine out of ten times you will get hurt. Don't smoke a strong pipe in the coach—spit on the leeward side. Don't sweat or lop over neighbors when sleeping. Never shoot on the road as the noise might frighten the horses. Don't discuss politics or religion. Don't point out where murders have been committed especially if there are women passengers. Don't grease your hair, because travel is dusty."

—tips for stagecoach riders, *Omaha Herald*, 1877

▲ An unknown stage driver.

▶ Advertisement for stage travel into the gold country of California.

OVERLAND MAIL ROUTE

TO CALIFORNIA.

Through in Six Days to Sacramento!

CONNECTING WITH THE DAILY STAGES

To all the Interior Mining Towns in Northern California and Southern Oregon.
Ticketed through from PORTLAND, by the

OREGON LINE OF STAGE COACHES!

And the Rail Road from Oroville to Sacramento,

Passing through Oregon City, Salem, Albany, Corvallis, Eugene City, Oakland, Winchester, Roseburg, Canyonville, Jacksonville, and in California— Yreka, Trinity Centre, Shasta, Red Bluff, Tehama, Chico, Oroville, Marysville to SACRAMENTO.

TRAVELERS AVOID RISK of OCEAN TRAVEL

Pass through the HEART OF OREGON—the Valleys of Rogue River, Umpqua and Willamette.

portion of the Pacific Slope embraces the most BEAUTIFUL and attractive, as well as of the BOLD GRAND and PICTUERESQUE SCENERY on the Continent. The highest snow-capped mountains, (Mt HOOD Mt SHASTA and others,) deepest ravines and most beautiful valleys.

Stages stop over one night at JACKSONVILLE and YREKA, for passengers to rest. Passengers will be permitted to lay over at any point, and resume their seats at pleasure, any time within one month.

FARE THROUGH, FIFTY DOLLARS.

Ticket Office at Arrigoni's Hotel, Portland.

H. W CORBETT & Co.,

Proprietors Oregon Stage Line.

PORTLAND, July 19, 1866

MAR 2

1930 Clyde Barrow (of Bonnie and Clyde fame) is arrested in Waco, Texas, and charged with several area burglaries and car thefts.

LONG DAY'S JOURNEY

Whether transporting people or freight, every party moving West required plenty of pauses to refresh and replenish. Bullwhackers, the men and sometimes women who walked alongside the freight wagons cracking bullwhips to keep the yoked oxen moving, made camp every evening to feed, water, and rest both themselves and their beasts. Likewise, stagecoaches on the long run across the West made periodic stops along the way for fresh horses and to give comfort to the weary passengers. At the swing stations, usually about a dozen miles apart, the coaches pulled in only long enough to hitch up a fresh team of horses. Every forty or fifty miles were home stations where drivers changed out and passengers had a half hour or so to relieve themselves and gobble some food. These ramshackle stations were manned by a couple of attendants who cared for the teams and hunted local game to put food on the table. Vittles usually varied in quality from poor to awful.

"The station keeper up-ended a disk of last week's bread, of the shape and size of an old-time cheese. . . . He sliced off a piece of bacon for each man, but only the experienced old hands made out to eat it, for it was condemned army bacon . . . the stage company had bought it cheap. . . . Then he poured for us a beverage which he called 'Slumgullion'. . . . It really pretended to be tea, but there was too much dish-rag, and sand, and old bacon-rind in it to deceive the intelligent traveler."

—Mark Twain, *Roughing It*, 1872

▲▲ Brown's Hotel at Fort Laramie, Wyoming, 1868.

▲ A bullwhacker with his whip, c. 1850s.

▶ A female bullwhacker in the Black Hills with her freight wagons and oxen teams.

MAR 3

1853 Congress approves the start of a railroad survey extending from the Mississippi River to the Pacific Ocean.
1924 Frank "Jelly" Nash is convicted of the assault of a mail custodian and sentenced to twenty-five years in the prison at Leavenworth, Kansas.

CAPTAIN JACK

Folks who knew Joseph "Jack" Slade considered him tough but fair, hardworking, and loyal to friends—that is if he was not drinking whiskey. A few tastes of strong drink turned Jack ornery and often violent. In 1858, Slade—called Captain Jack after several years spent as a captain of wagon trains moving freight over the Oregon Trail—hired on as a division chief for the Overland Stage Company. While supervising the many swing stations along the route, Slade earned a reputation as a no-nonsense manager, not opposed to enforcing the rules. It came as no surprise when he turned sour toward Jules Beni, the devious and unsavory stationmaster at Julesburg, perched on the border of Colorado and Nebraska. After one of their arguments, Beni grabbed his revolver and shot the unarmed Slade several times and then fired both barrels of a shotgun into the crumpled body. Miraculously, Slade survived, and in 1861, two years after the shooting, he got his revenge. According to popular legend, Slade caught up with Beni, tied him to a corral fence, and then spent hours sipping whiskey and periodically shooting his captive. Finally, Slade delivered a fatal shot and then sliced off Beni's ears as mementos. Over the next few years, Slade's increased alcohol intake made him such a nuisance that he ended up the guest of honor at a vigilante hanging in Montana. His grieving widow claimed the corpse and had it placed in a zinc-lined coffin filled with whiskey.

▲ The only generally accepted image of Jack Slade.

▶ A stage station like Jack Slade managed on the Overland Oregon Trail.

Stage Station on
Overland Route

1879 New Mexico Territorial Governor Lew Wallace makes a list of thirty-six desperados he wants arrested in Lincoln County. "Texas John" Slaughter is number one on the list; Billy the Kid is number fourteen.

1905 President Theodore Roosevelt takes the oath of office and watches Tom Mix ride with the Cowboy Brigade in the inaugural parade.

ORPHANS PREFERRED

WANTED
Young skinny wiry fellows not over eighteen.
Must be expert riders willing to risk death daily.
Orphans preferred. Wages $25 per week.

—Pony Express advertisement, 1860

▶ A daguerreotype of a frontiersman, possibly a Pony Express rider.

For only nineteen months, starting on April 3, 1860, daring Pony Express riders delivered mail between Saint Joseph, Missouri, and Sacramento, California. Their speedy maneuvers out on the open plains stirred anyone who caught a glimpse of one of the young riders going hell-bent for leather. Organized by Russell, Majors & Waddell, an overland freight and coach line service, the Pony Express boasted a crew of bold messengers, who in only ten days galloped across 1,966 miles of plains, mountains, and deserts to deliver the U.S. mail. When a young man was hired, the company issued him a leather-bound bible and required him to sign an oath that read:

I hereby swear, before the great and living God, that during my engagement, and while I am an employee of Russell, Majors & Waddell, I will, under no circumstances, use profane language; that I will drink no intoxicating liquors; that I will not quarrel or fight with any other employee of this firm; and that in every respect, I will conduct myself honestly, faithful to my duties, and so direct my acts to win the confidence of my employers. So help me God.

1876 Gunfighter and scout Wild Bill Hickok marries circus owner Agnes Lake Thatcher in Cheyenne, Wyoming Territory.

PONY BOYS

During the brief time the Pony Express was in business, the riders endured the extreme elements and other perils while carrying almost thirty-five thousand pieces of mail and earning only one hundred to one hundred fifty dollars per month, plus room and board. To keep their burden light, the riders usually carried nothing more than a trusty Colt revolver or two, and a knife. They kept their precious cargo—between forty and ninety letters—wrapped in oiled silk and crammed inside the pockets of a leather saddle cover, called a *mochila* (Spanish for "knapsack"). It was slung over the saddle and easily removed when the riders changed mounts at relay stations every fifteen miles along their path. Remarkably, only one pony boy was ever killed and one mail sack lost.

▶ Changing horses at a Pony Express station.

"When I arrived at Cold Springs to my horror I found that the station had been attacked by Indians, the keeper killed, and all the horses taken away. I decided in a moment what course to pursue—I would go on. I watered my horse, having ridden him thirty miles on time, he was pretty tired, and started for Sand Springs, thirty-seven miles away. It was growing dark, and my road lay through heavy sagebrush, high enough to conceal a horse. I kept a bright lookout and closely watched every motion of my poor pony's ears, which is a signal for danger in an Indian country. I was prepared for a fight, but the stillness of the night and the howling of the wolves and coyotes made cold chills run through me at times."

—Robert Haslam, Pony Express rider in Nevada, May 1861

1836 After days of intense fighting with Santa Anna's army, Colonel William Barret Travis's outfit fails, and the Alamo falls. Popular figures Jim Bowie and David Crockett lose their lives in the incident, although whether Crockett was killed in the heat of battle or executed after the fact is a matter of dispute.

PIONEER MADONNAS

"Thoughts stray back to the comfortable homes we left behind and the question arises, is this a good move? The wagon train is divided. Some want to turn back; others favor going on. A decision is reached at noon; the train is to move on."

—diary memories of Lucy A. Die, 1878

"Out in the midst of level stretches of prairie even to cook and eat the very limited variety that the table affords is a task that makes heavy demands upon the weary woman with her family to care for, the garden-patch to cultivate, the cows to milk, and the plow-handles to hold in the intervals. Yet she accomplishes it all—and more."

—*The Outlook*, January 6, 1894

▲ A young pioneer woman.

▶ A cover of an 1870s book, on which a female pioneer defends her home and children from a band of attacking Indians.

PIONEER LIFE AND FRONTIER ADVENTURE
ARMSTRONG & CO. LITH BOSTON

MAR 7

1848 After the discovery of gold on his property, John Augustus Sutter, once one of California's richest men, complains in his journals about hired hands abandoning their work to mine gold. As a result of the gold rush, Sutter loses all of his wealth and dies a poor man.
1929 Charles "Pretty Boy" Floyd is released from prison in Jefferson City, Missouri, after serving the majority of a five-year sentence.

PRAIRIE SCHOONER

Between 1841 and the late 1860s, more than four hundred thousand emigrants made the two-thousand-mile overland journey from what was then the western edge of the United States (marked by the Mississippi River) to the new lands opening in the far West. Despite the idealized images of wagon trains depicted by countless artists, writers, and filmmakers, there was nothing even remotely romantic about those arduous journeys. Early emigrants took to the trails in Conestoga wagons, named for the Pennsylvania valley where they were first built. These wagons were typically about ten feet long and four feet wide and had metal hoops over which the canvas covering was stretched. Everything a family needed, or thought they needed, was crammed into the wagon, leaving little room for passengers. Old folks, infants, and the disabled squeezed inside, but most others made the long journey on foot. After the California gold rush, travelers began to use smaller wagons popularly called "prairie schooners," because from afar their white canvas tops resembled sailing ships. Landlocked voyagers, who grew anxious and more homesick with each passing mile, sang an old Missouri River chantey to lift their spirits. One of America's most recognizable folk tunes, it spoke of the Shenandoah Valley in Virginia. For the lonely traveler headed to unknown lands, the song became a hymn.

Oh, Shenandoah, I long to hear you,
Away, you rolling river!
Oh, Shenandoah, I long to hear you,
Away, I'm bound away,
'Cross the wide Missouri.

▶ The interior of a covered wagon packed for the long journey west.

1930 Bonnie Parker smuggles a gun inside the McLennan County, Texas, jail in order to help Clyde Barrow escape.

CIRCLE THE WAGONS

Every day on the emigrant trail began and ended in a circle. Each morning, sentinels fired their rifles to wake the camp. Soon, cook fires were going, horses were saddled, and the teams of oxen picketed inside the circle of wagons were yoked for another day's toil. At evening, the wagons were again arranged in a circle with the front wheels of each up against the rear wheels of the preceding wagon. This formed a corral to keep the animals from straying and also act as a barricade in case of Indian attack. In reality, Indians were not the biggest danger on the trail. Indian assaults on wagon trains only increased in later years as more and more settlers pushed into their lands. Some adventuresome souls even hoped Indians would attack just to provide a diversion during the monotonous and grueling trip. Wagon accidents and lightning strikes took many lives. Other causes of death were accidental shootings, drownings at river crossings, and diseases—especially cholera, for which there was no cure.

"The tire became loose on a wheel of the next to the last wagon in a freight train, the men stopped to tighten it, while the rest of the train moved on, not thinking of danger, and was out of sight in a few minutes. An hour later some of the men came back to see what kept them. They were there—dead and scalped—horses gone, and wagons on fire. The Indians had taken all the freight they could use, piled wood under the wagons, and set it on fire."

—diary of Sarah Raymond, July 16, 1865

▲ Circling the wagons for protection from Indian attacks.

▶ A rendering of an Indian attack on a wagon party.

1878 In a running gun battle, Tunstall's Regulators (including Billy the Kid) capture two men suspected of killing John Tunstall. The accused murderers, Frank Baker and Billy Morton, are killed during the return to Lincoln, New Mexico Territory.
1916 Mexican revolutionary leader Pancho Villa raids Columbus, New Mexico.

THE PROMISED LAND

In the twenty-five years following the Civil War, more land was broken by plowshares than during the previous 250 years. Great numbers of people moved to the West thanks to the Homestead Act of 1862, which authorized Congress to open public lands. The government promised 160 acres of land to any citizen who filed a claim, paid a modest fee, and agreed to work the land for five years. A westward tide of war veterans, farmers, former slaves, and dreamers swept across the plains and prairies to claim their piece of the Promised Land. They built dugouts or cut hunks of sod from the unplowed prairie to build homes. By the close of the century, the sodbusters and dirt farmers had filed about six hundred thousand claims for more than eighty million acres of western land.

▲ Homesteaders, most likely in Kansas or Nebraska.

▶ A homesteader family with their children, dog, team of horses, cow, and sod home built into the side of a hill.

MAR 10

1864 Gunfighter Jack Slade is hanged by vigilantes in Virginia City, Montana Territory.

JAMES BUTLER HICKOK

James Butler Hickok would not see his fortieth birthday, yet in his lifetime he became one of the foremost contributors to America's "Wild West" image. Hickok was born May 27, 1837, in Homer (later known as Troy Grove), a prairie village in La Salle County, Illinois. James was one of seven children whose parents—native Vermonters William Alonzo Hickok and Polly Butler Hickok—moved from New York State to Illinois and eventually settled in Homer. William opened the town's first general merchandise store, a short-lived venture that he was forced to close due to the financial panic of 1837. He then began working for area farmers, and his four boys did what they could to help. Young James earned a reputation as a deadeye shot capable of putting plenty of game on the supper table. He also learned about risk-taking from his parents, who were abolitionists, helping escaped slaves dodge bounty hunters and flee north. Following the death of his father in 1852, James grew restless and, like so many others, looked to the West. In 1856, he struck out for Kansas Territory to claim some land and become a farmer. His desire to spend his days behind a plow quickly fizzled, so for a time Hickok rode with the vigilantes of the Free State Army, engaging in skirmishes with the proslavery Border Ruffians from Missouri. By 1858, Hickok was elected as one of four constables in Monticello Township, Kansas Territory. It was his first law enforcement job and a post he held only briefly before the pull of the frontier took him farther west.

▶ One of the earliest photographs of James Butler Hickok.

MAR 11

1884 Notorious characters Ben Thompson and King Fisher are shot dead in San Antonio, Texas.

ROCK CREEK STATION

By the spring of 1861, James Hickok had gained some experience as a teamster working for the freighting company Jones & Cartwright, when he signed on with their competitor—Russell, Majors & Waddell, stage operators and owners of the Pony Express. They sent Hickok to Nebraska Territory to work as a stock tender at the Rock Creek Station, a relay stop and supply center. Hickok and David McCanles, former owner of the stage stop who lived nearby, took an instant dislike to each other, due in part to their shared affections for McCanles's longtime mistress. On July 12, 1861, the tension came to a head. McCanles stopped by the station to collect some money owed to him, and an argument erupted with the stationmaster. In what some later called a massacre, Hickok shot and killed McCanles and two other men. In the coming years, fabricated accounts of what transpired at the relay stop claimed that after being shot multiple times himself, Hickok single-handedly killed ten men in vicious hand-to-hand combat. In fact, Hickok emerged from the fracas unscathed. He and two fellow employees were arrested for murder, but the charges were dropped. This incident marked the beginning of Hickok's reputation as a shootist and folk legend. Some also began calling Hickok either William or Bill, possibly because of his nickname "Duck Bill," which poked fun at his distinctive aquiline nose and protruding lips.

▲ An artist's rendering of Wild Bill's fight with the McCanles Gang, featured in one of the earliest books about Hickok.

▶ Rock Creek Station in southeastern Nebraska Territory.

MAR 12

1912 Ben Kilpatrick, the last active member of the Wild Bunch, attempts to rob a Southern Pacific Train near Sanderson, Texas, and is killed.

SINGING WIRES

Although the mail delivery service was fast and efficient, even the Almighty could not have kept the Pony Express alive. After losing more than two hundred thousand dollars during a scant nineteen months, Russell, Majors & Waddell had to discontinue the service. Most of the riders were not surprised. After all, they had seen an easier form of message delivery going up as they had delivered progress reports to work crews erecting transcontinental telegraph poles. On October 26, 1861, just two days after the singing wires linked the nation, the Pony Express officially ceased operations.

▶ A sketch depicting the construction of the telegraph line across the plains, with a Pony Express rider waving as he passes, and Indians watching from the hilltop.

"Our little friend, the Pony, is to run no more. 'Stop it' is the order that has been issued by those in authority. Farewell and forever, thou staunch, wilderness-overcoming, swift-footed messenger! . . . Rest upon your honors; be satisfied with them: your destiny has been fulfilled—a new and higher power has superseded you. Nothing that has blood and sinews was able to overcome your energy and ardor. . . . Rest then, in peace, for thou hast run thy race, thou has followed thy course, thou hast done the work that was given thee to do."

—*Sacramento Bee*, October 26, 1861

MAR 13

1908 Henry Starr and his gang rob the bank at Tyro, Kansas, and then flee to Oklahoma.

THE MINNESOTA MASSACRE

In August 1862, as the Civil War raged, what became known as the Great Sioux Uprising began on the Minnesota frontier. A failed 1852 treaty between the U.S. government and the Santee (a part of the Sioux Nation) sparked the six-week revolt. The treaty required the Santee to surrender twenty-four million acres of their traditional hunting grounds and relocate to a narrow reservation along the upper Minnesota River. As compensation for this tremendous loss, the Santee collected a sizable lump sum of money and assurances of goods and cash annuities in the future. Over the next eleven years, the Indians were cheated by unscrupulous white traders and merchants, while the promised payments from the government failed to arrive. By 1862, after a horrific winter that brought them to the brink of starvation, the desperate Santee burst from the reservation and went on a killing spree that resulted in the deaths of more than 450 white settlers. After U.S. troops quelled the rebellion, 303 Indian prisoners were convicted and sentenced to death. President Lincoln commuted most of the executions, but on December 26, 1862, in Mankato, Minnesota, thirty-eight Santee Sioux were marched to a huge scaffold and hanged simultaneously. It was said to be the largest mass execution in U.S. history. Within several months, more than seventeen hundred Santees were forced from Minnesota to reservation lands in South Dakota and Nebraska.

▲ Refugees from the Minnesota Massacre, 1862.

▶ A depiction of the mass hanging of the Santee Sioux in Mankato, Minnesota, on December 26, 1862.

MAR 14

1868 At Dunder and Blitzen Creek, Oregon, the First and Eighth Cavalries engage a Paiute band. Twelve Indians are killed in the battle.

TIGERS OF THE HUMAN SPECIES

Often the last word heard by Anglo and Mexican settlers on the southwestern frontier was the warning cry, "Apaches!" A collective name for several culturally related groups, the Apaches were determined to protect their ancestral lands in the deserts and mountains of the Southwest. Their principles of warfare were part of a tribal social organization that focused on raiding and fighting against any and all intruders. As more Americans began moving into Apache country after the end of the Mexican War, warriors kept up their raids south of the border, but also increased hostilities along the Santa Fe Trail and the Butterfield Overland mail route. During the 1850s and 1860s, bands of Apaches—unsurpassed at guerrilla warfare—emerged from hiding for hit-and-run attacks. While still a junior army officer, future general George Crook called the Apaches the "tigers of the human species."

▶ An Apache warrior.

▶▶ An Apache woman with various earthenware vessels.

MAR 15

1887 An employee of the Triple V Ranch rides into Sundance, Wyoming, to report stolen property. It is the first recorded crime of the Sundance Kid.
1919 Henry Starr is paroled from Oklahoma State Penitentiary at McAlester and goes into the movie business, producing and playing himself in *A Debtor to the Law*.

LIKE FATHER, LIKE SON

The formidable Chiricahua Apache leader Cochise not only resisted westward expansion of white settlers into the American Southwest, but was a bitter enemy of all Mexicans, leading raiding parties into Chihuahua and Sonora as early as 1832. He continued to make a name for himself as a warrior when he was taken captive by Mexican troops and then exchanged for a dozen Mexican prisoners. When still a young warrior, Cochise married the daughter of Mangas Coloradas, a noted chief until 1863 when, under a flag of truce at a peace conference, he was taken captive and murdered by American soldiers. In 1861, when a rancher blamed Cochise and his band for stealing his cattle and kidnapping his eleven-year-old stepson, U.S. troops intervened. Cochise vehemently denied taking part in the raid and told the authorities another band of Indians was responsible. Warfare soon followed and persisted until 1867, resulting in many deaths on both sides. Cochise was captured in 1871, but escaped and continued to lead the resistance against both Americans and Mexicans. In 1874, he died of cancer on reservation lands and, as he requested, his body was secretly buried in his old mountain hideout. Cochise left two sons: Taza, who assumed the role of chief until his own death from pneumonia in 1876, and Naiche, who became the last chief of the free Chiricahua. Naiche resisted his people's removal to the San Carlos Apache reservation and rode with the famous Geronimo on raids of Mexican and American settlements. By the mid-1880s, Naiche and the Apaches had surrendered. He was imprisoned for several years before enlisting as a scout for the U.S. Army at Fort Sill, Oklahoma Territory.

▶ An engraving of Apache war chief Cochise, of whom there is no known photograph.

▶▶ Naiche, the younger son of Cochise and the last chief of the free Chiricahua.

MAR 16

1903 In Langtry, Texas, Judge Roy Bean, known as the "Law West of the Pecos," dies in the midst of a drinking binge.

THE BOY GENERAL

Born in 1839, George Armstrong Custer—son of a blacksmith in New Rumley, Ohio—is one of the most mythologized figures in the American West, and one of the most controversial. Though he won a congressional appointment to West Point in 1857, Cadet Custer did not shine at academics nor earn any medals for deportment. The only thing he really excelled at was horsemanship. He came close to expulsion several times, and when his class graduated a year early in June 1861 because of the onset of the Civil War, Custer ranked dead last in a pool of thirty-four. Assigned to the cavalry, the new lieutenant first saw action at the Battle of Bull Run. In 1862, while at his half-sister's home in Monroe to recuperate from an illness, Custer met Elizabeth Bacon, a young woman who would become his biggest champion. Promoted to captain, the flamboyant Custer impressed the top brass with his bravado and dash on the battlefield. In 1863—just days before he distinguished himself at Gettysburg—he was promoted to brigadier general and, at twenty-three years of age, became the youngest general in the Union army. The next year, back in Michigan recovering from a shrapnel wound, Custer won over the Bacon family and married Elizabeth, or Libbie as she was known. Dubbed "The Boy General" by the press, Custer continued to turn heads and ended up having a dozen horses shot out from under him. In gratitude for Custer's help in forcing the retreat of Robert E. Lee's army, General Philip Henry Sheridan purchased the Appomattox surrender table as a gift for Custer and Libbie.

▶ George Armstrong Custer, relaxing on the ground with a dog. This photograph was taken during the Civil War, before Custer's engagements in the Indian wars.

MAR 17

1879 Governor Lew Wallace meets with Billy the Kid in Lincoln, New Mexico Territory, to discuss the possibility of a pardon for his willingness to testify against the killers of Huston Chapman. The Kid appears at the meeting with a Winchester in one hand and a revolver in the other.

1896 After being sentenced by Judge Isaac Parker, outlaw Cherokee Bill is hanged at Fort Smith, Arkansas.

UNDER THE BLACK FLAG

The catalyst for a criminal dynasty that lasted more than seventy years and the basis for many popular outlaw legends of the Old West was a former Ohio schoolteacher—William Clarke Quantrill. During the Civil War, Quantrill led a band of mostly teenaged farm boys on a rampage of hatred and murder through Union border strongholds in Kansas and Missouri. They rode under Quantrill's standard—an ominous black flag intended to show that no quarter would be given. Quantrill and his crew of guerrilla fighters left a trail of lawlessness and death cloaked in the guise of patriotism and social redress. In the postwar years, many of his young riders formed feared outlaw gangs such as those organized by the James and Younger brothers. On May 10, 1865, a month after General Lee's surrender, Quantrill was mortally wounded during a skirmish with Union troops on a Kentucky farm. At a military prison infirmary in Louisville, he converted to Catholicism and died at the age of twenty-seven. He bequeathed some of his money to a lady friend so she could finance a fancy house of ill repute in St. Louis and gave the rest to a priest for the purchase of a plot and headstone.

"But Quantrill and his men were no more bandits than the men on the other side. I've been to reunions of Quantrill's men two or three times. All they were trying to do was protect the property on the Missouri side of the line."

—President Harry S. Truman, n.d.

▶ William Clarke Quantrill.

▶▶ This photograph has been modified from the original to show Quantrill in a Confederate uniform. In another version, a mustache was added.

WILLIAM CLARKE QUANTRILL
THE GUERRILLA CHIEF

MAR 18

1882 Morgan Earp is shot and killed at Campbell and Hatch's Saloon in Tombstone, Arizona.

JAYHAWKERS AND REDLEGS

Pro-Confederate Missourians came to despise James Henry Lane, the first U.S. senator from the free state of Kansas and commander of a brigade of fifteen hundred Volunteers who led a rampage of terror and mayhem in the slave state of Missouri. Two bands of citizen scouts made up much of Lane's force—the Jayhawkers, named for a mythical bird, and the Redlegs, ruffians who wore maroon leggings made of pilfered sheepskin leather. Every bit as bloodthirsty as William Quantrill's raiders, on September 23, 1861, the Kansas Brigade descended on Osceola, Missouri. Houses and businesses were looted and burned, the bank robbed, and citizens executed in the courthouse square. When Lane and his men rode away, the town was a heap of smoldering ruins. Motivated by the Osceola attack, on August 21, 1863, Quantrill led a brazen raid on Lawrence, Kansas, an abolitionist stronghold and Lane's hometown. As dawn broke, Quantrill and 450 well-armed marauders riding under the black flag swept down on a sleeping Lawrence. The attack lasted four hours as Quantrill's men pillaged and burned houses and shops, leaving at least 150 townspeople dead in the streets. Lane escaped in his nightshirt and found cover in a cornfield, as gunfire and shouts of "Remember Osceola!" rang in his ears. Shaken by the war, Lane shot himself on July 1, 1866, and died ten days later.

▶ U.S. Senator James Henry Lane.

▶▶ General James Henry Lane, leader of the Kansas Jayhawkers.

"They even stole the clothes of my little dead grandson."

—Osceola resident, *New York Daily Times*, November 9, 1861

"Quantrill's massacre at Lawrence is almost enough to curdle the blood with horror."

—*New York Daily Times*, August 24, 1863

MAR 19

1875 Infamous outlaw Tiburcio Vásquez is hanged in front of a crowd of invited guests in San Jose, California. His final mortal word: "¡*Pronto*!" (Quick!)

BLOODY BILL

Terror swept central Missouri in the 1860s in the wake of William "Bloody Bill" Anderson. Described as even more ruthless than William Quantrill, Anderson "took to the brush" out of pure hatred of Union sympathizers. As he explained: "I have chosen guerrilla warfare to revenge myself for wrongs that I could not honorably revenge otherwise. I lived in Kansas when this war commenced. Because I would not fight the people of Missouri, my native state, the Yankees sought my life, but failed to get me. Revenged themselves by murdering my father, destroying all my property, and since that time murdered one of my sisters and kept the other two in jail for twelve months." A homicidal maniac with no regard for human life, Anderson often broke into tears and frothed at the mouth during battle. Just a month after Quantrill's bloody raid on Lawrence, Anderson and some followers attacked Centralia, Missouri. The guerrillas blockaded the railroad tracks and waited for the afternoon train. When it arrived, twenty-three unarmed Union soldiers on leave after the Battle of Atlanta were removed and told to strip off their uniforms. The soldiers were shot and their bodies mutilated and scalped. Only a few weeks later, Anderson met his end during a skirmish, when a .36 caliber ball tore through his head. Federal troops took Bloody Bill's body to nearby Richmond, Missouri, where a series of photographs were taken. That evening, soldiers buried the outlaw chieftain and proceeded to urinate on the unmarked grave.

▶ "Bloody Bill" Anderson.

▶▶ A photograph of Bloody Bill's body taken in Richmond, Missouri, soon after his death.

MAR 20

1882 Outlaw Frank Stilwell, one of the men suspected in the death of Morgan Earp, is killed in Tucson, Arizona Territory. Murder indictments are issued for Doc Holliday, Wyatt Earp, Warren Earp, Sherman McMasters, and John "Turkey Creek Jack" Johnson.

COLE YOUNGER

The seventh of fourteen children born to a respectable family near Lee's Summit, Missouri, Thomas Coleman Younger was only sixteen when he enlisted in the Confederate state guard. He fought at Carthage and then rode with the guerrilla raiders of William Quantrill. In 1862, Cole accepted a commission as a Confederate lieutenant after Kansas Jayhawkers killed his father, a Union sympathizer who owned slaves. Cole distinguished himself in various engagements, and after returning to Quantrill's ranks, he intervened to stop the execution of Stephen B. Elkins, his former teacher and a future U.S. senator. Younger took part in the siege of Lawrence, Kansas, and then fled to Texas and served under General Ben McCulloch. About this time, Cole supposedly encountered Myra Maebelle Shirley, the teenager who would later become Belle Starr and spread the unlikely story that her daughter, Pearl, was fathered by Cole. After the war ended in 1865, Younger was back in Missouri when an unsolved murder blamed on him and other sins from his past forced him into hiding. In 1866, Cole reached a turning point in his life when he ran into a former neighbor and pal from his times with Quantrill. His name was Frank James and he introduced Cole to his younger brother, Jesse. It was the beginning of a fateful relationship doomed from the start.

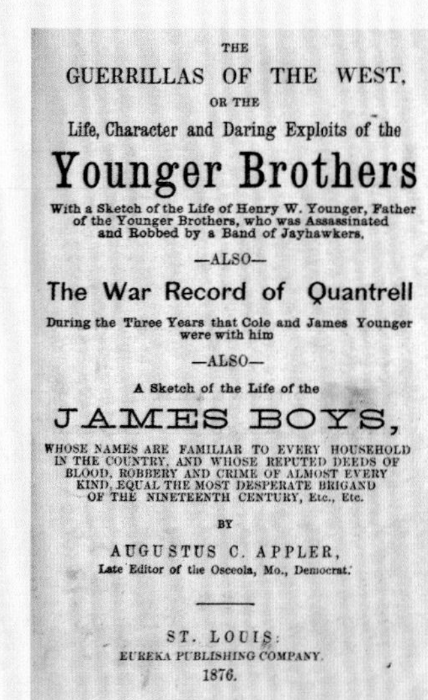

THE
GUERRILLAS OF THE WEST,
OR THE
Life, Character and Daring Exploits of the
Younger Brothers
With a Sketch of the Life of Henry W. Younger, Father of the Younger Brothers, who was Assassinated and Robbed by a Band of Jayhawkers.
—ALSO—
The War Record of Quantrell
During the Three Years that Cole and James Younger were with him
—ALSO—
A Sketch of the Life of the
JAMES BOYS,
WHOSE NAMES ARE FAMILIAR TO EVERY HOUSEHOLD IN THE COUNTRY, AND WHOSE REPUTED DEEDS OF BLOOD, ROBBERY AND CRIME OF ALMOST EVERY KIND, EQUAL THE MOST DESPERATE BRIGAND OF THE NINETEENTH CENTURY, Etc., Etc.
BY
AUGUSTUS C. APPLER,
Late Editor of the Osceola, Mo., Democrat.
ST. LOUIS:
EUREKA PUBLISHING COMPANY.
1876.

▲ A book on the Youngers published while they were still at-large and wanted for bank and train robbery, 1876.

▶ Cole Younger, during the Civil War.

MAR 21

1848 California businessman John Augustus Sutter of Sutter's Mill fame is threatened by a band of robbers near his compound in New Helvetia, California.

BAND OF BROTHERS

No single criminal left so deep an impression on American culture as Jesse Woodson James. Born in Missouri in 1847, Jesse and his older brother Alexander Franklin James, or Frank (born in 1843), grew up in an atmosphere of unrest in the turbulent years leading to the Civil War. Even before the war, the western counties of Missouri were already acquainted with the horrors of unbridled violence. Coming from a family of staunch Southern sympathizers, Frank, and later Jesse, took up arms and—like some of the Younger brothers—rode off to war as Confederate irregulars, known as bushwhackers. Frank and his friend Cole Younger were in the guerrilla band that raided Lawrence, Kansas, under the command of William Quantrill, remembered by Northerners as "the bloodiest man known to the annals of America." Jesse and Jim Younger rode with Bloody Bill Anderson at the massacre at Centralia, Missouri, and in other actions where they learned the tactics of advance scouting and surprise attack. The James and Younger brothers were among the most able students of Quantrill and Anderson and honed survival skills that would serve them well in their coming outlaw days.

"At night and when we were in camp we played like schoolboys. Some of the play was rough as football. The truth was we were nothing but great big boys anyhow."

—Frank James, c. 1903

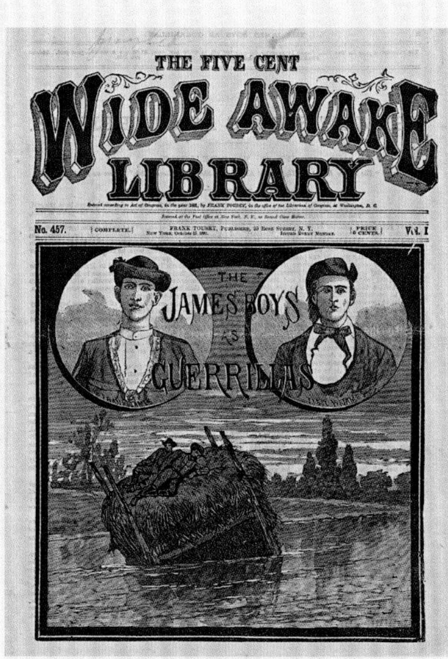

▲ A five-cent novel recounting the guerrilla days of Frank and Jesse James.

▶ Young Jesse James, at seventeen or eighteen years old, as one of Quantrill's guerrillas.

Jesse James, age 17 years

MAR

22

1881 Murderer "Big Nose" George Parrott is lynched by a mob in Rawlins, Wyoming Territory. The skin from his chest is made into a medicine bag and a pair of shoes.

FIRST DAYLIGHT BANK ROBBERY

On the afternoon of February 13, 1866, a gang of Missouri bushwhackers believed to have been led by Jesse and Frank James rode into the town of Liberty, Missouri, wearing long military overcoats and armed with Colt pistols. They dismounted in front of the Clay County Savings Association and entered the bank. With guns drawn, they "withdrew" fifteen thousand dollars in gold and silver coins and greenbacks and about forty-five thousand dollars in bonds. As the bandits made their escape, a student from William Jewell College named George Wymore got caught in their path and one of the outlaws pumped four bullets into the boy. He was dead before he hit the street. The crime made national headlines as the first daylight bank robbery recorded in American history. Jesse James vehemently denied any participation in the Liberty bank robbery. He even penned a letter of protest to the governor of Missouri. Nonetheless, the brazen crime placed the James Gang at the forefront of the public's consciousness. Soon James and his crew were worshipped as heroes by the economically disenfranchised and those still loyal to the ways of the Old South.

▲ Frank James, seated, and Jesse James, right, about the time they began their outlaw career. Standing on the left is former guerrilla Fletch Taylor.

▶ A reward notice posted following an 1867 bank robbery in Independence, Missouri, offering ten thousand dollars for the capture of two armed men, thought to be the James brothers.

$10,000

REWARD!!

About 4 o'clock P. M. of the

27th inst., the 1st National Bank of Independence, Mo. was entered by two armed men and robbed of about Twenty Thousand Dollars—belonging to the Bank, Stone, McCoy & Co., and special depositors; about $2,000 in gold and silver, and the remainder in Bank and Treasury notes.

THE

ABOVE REWARD

Will be paid for the arrest and delivery of the robbers and return of the money, or in the same proportion for any part of it.

P. ROBERTS, Pres't.
Wm. McCOY, Cash'r.
STONE, McCOY & Co.

Independence, Mo., Nov. 28, 1867.

MAR 23

1888 In Chihuahua, Mexico, lawman Bob Paul and Mexican police track and kill three members of the Larry Sheehan Gang who had recently robbed two trains in Arizona Territory.

THE GUNS THAT WON THE WEST

Although the Winchester Model 1873 rifle was nicknamed "The Gun that Won the West," several other weapons deserve at least a share of that title. Many hunters preferred a heavy Sharps rifle—the most popular buffalo gun and the epitome of American single-shot rifles. A common saying was, "Sharps made the West safe for Winchesters." Before the first Winchesters starting rolling off production lines, the Henry repeating rifle played a dominant role in the frontier days of the American West. Benjamin Tyler Henry patented his design for the first practical, lever-action, repeating rifle in 1860. His .44 caliber rimfire Henry was the forerunner of all the famous Winchesters to follow. The Henry appeared in 1862, and when production ended four years later, more than fourteen thousand rifles had been manufactured by New Haven Arms. The gun was widely distributed to Union soldiers, who fired the rifles at a rate of twenty-eight rounds per minute. That prompted a Confederate officer to famously remark, "It's a rifle that you could load on Sunday and shoot all week long." After the war, Oliver Winchester, owner of New Haven Arms, renamed his firm the Winchester Repeating Arms Company. The first Winchester model was ready in 1866. That rifle, as well as the classic Winchester 1873 and later models, developed from the Henry. It was because of the Henry that the name Winchester became synonymous with "rifle" throughout the West.

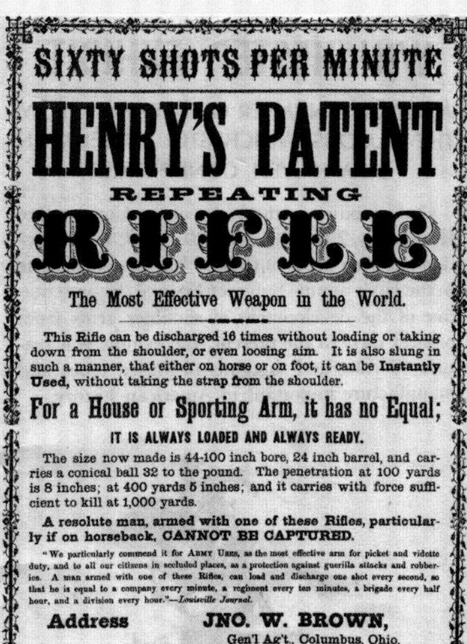

▲ An advertisement for the newly invented Henry repeating rifle.

▶ A cowboy proudly holding a Henry .44 caliber rifle.

MAR 24

1877 Sam Bass and four others attempt to rob the Deadwood stagecoach. The driver is killed during the robbery.

YELLOW BOY

Recognizing the superiority of the white men's weapons, Indians began acquiring guns from traders as early as the seventeenth century. Yet Indian hunters continued to use bows and arrows and seldom took guns on buffalo chases, mainly because it was too difficult to prime a cumbersome muzzleloader while astride a racing pony. That changed when breech-loading rifles appeared on the frontier. By the late 1860s, Plains Indians were using the lever-action repeating rifles quite effectively for both hunting and warfare. One of the rifles most preferred by the Indian hunters was the first one to bear the Winchester name—the Winchester 1866 lever-action rifle. Some Indians nicknamed it "Yellow Boy," because of the distinctive brass frame, while others called it "Many Shots," and decorated the wooden stock and butt with tacks. No matter what name it went by, the sturdy rifle was easy to handle and an asset to anyone on horseback. The popularity of the Yellow Boy and the other Winchesters that followed, especially the more powerful Model 1873, only increased over time. All of them proved to be equal opportunity weapons—common to both army troopers and the Indians they battled.

▲ The Winchester became a popular buffalo-hunting gun.

▶ The "Yellow Boy" greatly changed the way the Indians hunted buffalo.

MAR 25

1901 The Arizona Rangers are established in Phoenix, Arizona Territory.

HIDE HUNTERS

"The vast plains west of the Missouri River are covered with the decaying bones of thousands of slain buffaloes. Most of them have been slaughtered for the hide by professional hunters, while many have fallen victims to the sportsmen's rage for merely killing for the sake of killing. The first shot brings down a splendid animal, wounded purposely in a manner not to kill but to make him 'pump blood,' that is to say, to bleed profusely. Others of the herd gather around their wounded comrade, and appear to be too much stupefied to avoid danger by flight. The hunters kill as many as they can, until the survivors at last take flight and gallop off."

—*Harper's Magazine*, December 12, 1874

"Buffalo hunting was a business and not a sport. It required capital, management, and a lot of hard work. Magazine writers and others who claim that the killing of the buffalo was a national calamity and was accomplished by vandals simply expose their ignorance, and I resent such an unjust judgment upon us. . . . Any one of the families killed and homes destroyed by the Indians would have been worth more to Texas and to civilization than all the millions of buffalo that ever roamed from the Pecos River on the south to the Platte River on the north."

—Josiah Wright Mooar, 1933

▲ The most effective way to kill large numbers of buffalo was to "get a stand" downwind from the animals.

▶ A buffalo hunter with a Sharps rifle, which became the gun of choice because of its large caliber. However, it was too heavy to be useful on horseback.

MAR 26

1862 At Glorieta Pass near Santa Fe, New Mexico Territory, advance parties for the Union and Confederate armies meet. Two days later, the cornerstone battle of the New Mexico Campaign of the Civil War ends as the Union army forces the Confederates back into Texas.

SCALPING

More than a few hide hunters never collected their wages when they fell prey to Indian war parties angered by the white men's incredible slaughter of their primary food source. Instead of harvesting a bison hide, the warriors often took the hunter's own scalp as a prize. Torture of captured foes and the removal of scalps for trophies were not peculiar to Indians. Scalping had been employed by many cultures in Europe as far back as ancient Greece, although the more common practice was to display the severed heads of enemy combatants. Early settlers in America paid bounties for Indian scalps and other body parts. Some sources believe the origin of the word "redskin" lies in the collecting of bloody Indian scalps.

"Scalping, barbarous as it is, is reduced to an art among the Indians. The victor cuts a clean circle around the top of the head, so that the crown may form the center, and the diameter of the scalp exceed six inches; then, winding his fingers in the hair, he puts one foot on the neck of the prostrate foe, and with a vigorous pull tears the reeking scalp from the skull. To the dead, this, of course, would not be absolute cruelty; but it is too frequently the case that the process is performed and the scalp severed while the mangled victim lives; and there are instances where parties have recovered, and long survived the barbarous mutilation. Occasionally, a warrior is not satisfied with the part of the scalp taken, but bares the skull entirely, and carries away in triumph even the ears of the victim."

—Texas Ranger James Pike, 1865

▲ A painting of a white captive staked to the ground, while an Indian stands guard. This scenario is unlikely however, since Indians most often killed and scalped the white men and took only the women and children captive.

▶ A photograph of a scalped hunter discovered by a soldier and a scout on the plains near Fort Dodge, Kansas.

Soule

MAR 27

1915 Henry Starr and six others rob the Stroud State Bank and the First National Bank simultaneously in Stroud, Oklahoma. Starr is shot and captured by authorities.

DINEH

The name *Navajo* derives from the Spanish for "people with the big fields," but members of the tribe referred to themselves in their own language as the *Dineh*, meaning "the People." Cousins of the Apaches, the Navajos first acquired sheep—a significant part of their lifestyle—from the Spanish who also tried to enslave them. Traditionally the largest Indian tribe in the Southwest, the Navajos' early relations with the Anglo settlers were relatively peaceful but began to deteriorate around 1850 when a respected tribal leader was killed and the U.S. government began establishing forts in Navajo country. Subsequent treaties further reduced the tribe's land holdings. By the 1860s, under the leadership of Manuelito, a principal war chief, the Navajos engaged in several clashes with U.S. Cavalry. Both sides were blamed for massacres during raids and counterattacks. American authorities considered the Navajos to be one of the so-called wild tribes and ordered them to a reservation. Resistance led to the U.S. Army's policy of "total war" against the Dineh.

▲ The Navajos' Canyon de Chelly in northeast Arizona.

▶ Navajo hunting party.

1884 Five men convicted of the Bisbee Massacre—during which four people, including a pregnant woman were shot dead—are hanged simultaneously in Tombstone, Arizona Territory.

THE LONG WALK

In 1862, General James Carleton, the newly appointed commander of the U.S. Army in New Mexico Territory, turned his attention to what was referred to as the "Indian problem." To track Apaches and Navajos, Carleton chose the well-known scout Christopher "Kit" Carson. The dutiful Carson and five companies of New Mexico Volunteers arrived at the Mescalero Apaches' traditional hunting grounds with orders to kill as many Apache men as possible and round up the women and children. Carson waged a rigorous punitive campaign, and in less than three months crushed the Mescaleros. In January 1863, the 450 Apaches who had surrendered were herded more than 130 miles to Bosque Redondo, a grove of cottonwoods near an old trading post on the Pecos River. Soldiers from nearby Fort Sumner guarded the prisoners while Carson and his troops headed west to conduct a scorched earth campaign against the Navajos. Carson gave no quarter. His men laid waste to everything the Navajos needed for survival. The lands and the tribe were starved into submission. By the end of 1864, some ten thousand Navajo prisoners began a desperate 450-mile forced march from their sacred homeland to join the Apaches at Bosque Redondo. The journey came to be known as the "Long Walk." One in five Navajos died during the trek. Those who fell behind—the old, injured, and even pregnant women—were shot point-blank or abandoned. During the next four years, one-fourth of the Navajos died of disease or starvation. Eventually the War Department relented, and in 1868, under terms of peace, the Navajos were released and returned to their homeland.

▲ Kit Carson in military uniform.

▶ Navajo war chief Manuelito and Juanita, one of this wives.

1886 A few miles from Fort Bowie, Arizona Territory, Geronimo reconsiders his recent surrender to General George Crook and escapes with Naiche and twenty warriors.

MILE HIGH

▶ Cherry Creek overflowing in the western metropolis of Denver, Colorado, 1864.

Denver has been a thriving commercial hub ever since 1858, when gold was discovered at the confluence of Cherry Creek and the South Platte River. The gold boom soon ended, but many who struck it rich stayed and got even richer in later gold booms. During the 1860s, Denver was ravaged by fires, subject to Indian attacks, and threatened by invading Confederates. Then in 1864, the city was inundated with a flood described as "fierce as ten furies, terrible as hell" and "prancing with the violence of a fiery steed gone mad." Still, even that did not stop newcomers from flocking to the "Mile High City." Besides mineral wealth, there was another lure. Thousands of people with tuberculosis came to the Rocky Mountains in a quest for comfort and a cure in the dry mountain air. Wealthy "lungers," as tuberculars were known, took up residence at any number of the health resorts that popped up throughout the region. After buying 760 acres near Denver to winter his circus, flamboyant showman P. T. Barnum wisecracked, "People come here to die and they can't do it."

"A large number of Indians added to the harlequin appearance of the Denver streets. . . . There were men in every rig: hunters and trappers in buckskin clothing; men of the Plains with belts and revolvers, in great blue cloaks, relics of the war; teamsters in leather suits; horsemen in fur coats and caps and buffalo hide boots with the hair outside, and camping blankets behind their huge Mexican saddles; Broadway dandies in light kid gloves; rich English sporting tourists, clean, comely, and supercilious looking."

—Isabella L. Bird, *A Lady's Life in the Rocky Mountains*, 1879

COMMONWEALTH
D AND LIVERY STABLE
AMERICAN HOUSE

MAR 30

1855 Colonel Samuel Young leads a large contingent of Missourians into Kansas to illegally vote in favor of making Kansas a slave state.

SHOWDOWN

The 1865 Hickok-Tutt duel in Springfield, Missouri, became known as the first classic Old West showdown. In reality, few differences of opinion in the West were settled by the ritualistic face-to-face confrontation between armed parties on a dusty street. Even in the fleeting heyday of the storied Kansas cattle towns frequented by boisterous cowhands and charismatic shootists, few bona fide gun duels took place. When they did, those shootouts became the stuff of legends for generations of Americans yet unborn. Wild Bill Hickok's fame and illustrious name became indelibly imprinted on the public's consciousness in February 1867, when an article simply entitled "Wild Bill" appeared in *Harper's New Monthly Magazine*. Written by George Ward Nichols, the profile of Hickok not only greatly exaggerated his exploits, but was riddled with many inaccuracies and fabrications, such as: "Yes, Wild Bill with his own hands has killed hundreds of men. Of that I have not a doubt. He shoots to kill, as they say on the border." Even though the far-fetched article misspelled his surname as Hitchcock, the moniker "Wild Bill" was enough to perpetuate a "Wild West" legend that has never died.

▲ A sketch of Wild Bill, as he would have appeared around the time of his duel with Dave Tutt. This image comes from an early book about the scouts of the West.

▶ Wild Bill Hickok, with whiskers and fur cap.

WILD BILL

MAR

31

1895 Lawman James P. Masterson, brother of famed gunfighter Bat Masterson, dies of consumption in Guthrie, Oklahoma Territory.

MASSACRE AT SAND CREEK

Just after dawn on November 29, 1864, Colonel John M. Chivington led 650 Volunteers from the First and Third Colorado regiments in an attack on peaceful Cheyenne and Arapaho Indians camped beside Sand Creek in eastern Colorado Territory. Chivington—a former minister called the "Fighting Parson"—led the attack not only because he despised Indians, but also to further his political ambitions for when Colorado won statehood. He jumped at a chance to annihilate warring Indians who refused to sell their lands and move to reservations. While the Civil War raged on in the East, Chivington launched a campaign of indiscriminate attacks on Indian villages. Although he knew that Black Kettle, the chief of the Indians camped at Sand Creek, had surrendered and proudly flew both an American and a white flag of peace over his tepee, Chivington decided to strike. The Volunteers fell upon the sleeping camp with orders to take no prisoners, but to "Kill and scalp all, big and little, nits make lice." Four howitzers pounded the village and carbines blazed, as the stunned Indians fled in panic. A few, including Black Kettle and his wife, managed to escape. At least two hundred died, half of them women and children. Their corpses were mutilated and scalped. Chivington returned a conquering hero. He appeared onstage, regaling audiences with details of the slaughter and showing off the one hundred scalps he kept as reminders of his triumph. Not everyone, however, was in awe of the Fighting Parson. Although never charged, he faced three official investigations over the Sand Creek incident and withdrew from politics. He died of cancer in 1894, still protesting, "I stand by Sand Creek."

▲ John M. Chivington, leader of the massacre at Sand Creek.

▶ An engraving depicting the Sand Creek Massacre.

Kappes

APR 1

1878 Regulators kill Sheriff William J. Brady and deputy George H. Hindman during the Lincoln County War in New Mexico Territory. Billy the Kid is later convicted of the crime, although there is still doubt as to whether he was actually guilty.

STEEL TRACKS

When President Abraham Lincoln opened the West to settlers with the Homestead Act and the Pacific Railroad Act in 1862, a strong movement to span the Great Plains with twin steel rails began. In 1863, ground was broken for both legs of the railroad and soon two builders had their construction crews in place. The Central Pacific Co. was chosen to lay tracks eastward starting from Sacramento, California. From the East, the newly formed Union Pacific Co. chose Omaha, Nebraska, for the westward starting point. The U.S. government paid the railroad companies for every mile of track they laid, and the race was on.

▶ Laying rails and ties as the railroad raced west.

"We may now look forward with confidence to the day, not far distant, when the Pacific Coast will be bound to the Atlantic Coast by iron bonds that shall consolidate and strengthen the ties of nationality, and advance with giant strides the prosperity of the State and Country."

—California governor Leland Stanford, groundbreaking, January 8, 1863

"Come the gaugers, spikers, and bolters, and a lively time they make of it. It is a grand 'anvil chorus' . . . in triple time, three strokes to the spike, ten spikes to a rail, 400 rails to a mile, 1800 miles to San Francisco."

—W. A. Bell, journalist with the Union Pacific construction crew, c. 1866

APR 2

1878 The Sam Bass Gang robs the Texas and Pacific Railroad at Eagle Ford, Texas.

HELL ON WHEELS

Following the advancing rails linking the eastern and western United States, portable settlements called end-of-track towns sprang up along the construction line. The boomtowns served as supply centers and provided diversions for weary surveying, grading, and construction crews. Tents and flimsy buildings housed saloons, dance halls, gambling dens, and brothels. The violence and disorderly activity these places encouraged earned such towns the name "Hell on Wheels." As track building continued, populations declined and many of the temporary settlements vanished. Four times as many railroad workers met their end in "Hell on Wheels" towns than were killed in rail accidents. Some of the settlements, such as Cheyenne and Laramie, survived and prospered.

▶ As railroad construction moved, "Hell on Wheels" towns popped up to cater to the needs and desires of the workers.

"The wildest roughs from all parts of the country are congregated here, as one may see by glancing into numerous dance-houses and gambling halls—men who carry on the trade of robbery openly, and would not scruple to kill a man for ten dollars. . . . Strangers are beset and robbed, and honest traders leaving the city with their mule teams are often waylaid and rendered penniless at a moment's warning."

—Jim Chisholm, description of Cheyenne, 1868

"As the day advanced we beheld in the far distance what appeared to be a speck on the horizon. As we approached, it assumed the aspect of the white wings of motionless animals. They were the white tents of the embryo city of Cheyenne . . . the advance-guard of the army which shortly appeared and laid the foundation of the capital city of the new territory of Wyoming."

—John W. Clampitt, 1889

PACIFIC
HOTEL
SODA WATER
BAKERY
ECHO RESTAURANT
MEALS AT ALL HOURS

APR 3

1882 Robert Ford assassinates Jesse James in his Saint Joseph, Missouri, home. Robert and his brother Charley Ford conspired to kill James to collect the reward. Charged with first-degree murder, they are later granted pardons, but never see a dime of the reward money.

RED CLOUD'S WAR

Oglala Sioux chief Red Cloud became one of the most influential tribal leaders on the Great Plains during the nineteenth century. Almost all of his eighty-seven years were spent at war, either with other tribes or the U.S. Army. In 1866, Red Cloud led what came to be known as Red Cloud's War against the United States, in response to continued encroachment into Indian lands in the Powder River country of north-central Wyoming. White settlers wanted to control this land because it lay along the Bozeman Trail, the main access route to the Montana goldfields. Red Cloud's warriors won decisive victories over the U.S. Army that led to the Treaty at Fort Laramie in 1868, which created the Great Sioux Reservation, covering all of what became western South Dakota, including the Black Hills. Although the government did not adhere to the treaty, Red Cloud became the only Indian leader credited with winning a major war against the United States. Yet his achievements were not restricted to the battlefield. He was also a capable diplomat and statesman who tried his best to achieve a lasting peace.

"I only want to do that which is peaceful. . . . I came to Washington to see the Great Father in order to have peace and in order to have peace continue. . . . The Great Father showed me what the treaties were; he showed me all these points and showed me that the interpreters had deceived me. . . . We do not want riches, we do not ask for riches, but we want our children properly trained and brought up."

—Red Cloud, Cooper Union speech, New York, July 16, 1870

▲ Oglala Sioux chief Red Cloud.

▶ Chief Red Cloud with his bonnet and peace pipe.

APR 4

1868 Jesse Chisholm—scout, trader, and namesake of the Chisholm Trail—dies at Left Hand Spring near present-day Geary, Oklahoma, after eating rancid bear grease.

GATHERING OF EAGLES

The progression of the railroad caused problems for more than just the stagecoach and freight companies. It was also opposed by a significant sector of the population of the West—the American Indians. The various tribes greatly resented the intruders who violated their treaties with the U.S. government. Although both rail lines crossed Indian land, the Union Pacific drew the most wrath when construction crews entered areas that had long been held by Plains Indians, in particular the Northern Cheyenne and Sioux. War parties began raiding the moving camps that followed the construction crews and then increased their attacks when sharpshooters started to kill buffalo for hides and food. When not defending against Indians, the Union Pacific directors waged wars among themselves. Continued infighting for power and disagreements over engineering issues and the proposed route finally resulted in a showdown in July 1868 at Fort Sanders in Wyoming Territory. All the top railroad officials were in attendance, along with Ulysses S. Grant, campaigning in the West as a presidential candidate. It was only appropriate that Grant had a role in the parley since his campaign slogan was "Let us have peace." Grant came with distinguished guests, including William T. Sherman, Philip Henry Sheridan, and at least six other generals. Although not all the internal strife was put to rest at the meeting, the historic event was immortalized by noted photographer A. J. Russell, who took this memorable group picture of the distinguished participants.

▶ This gathering at Fort Sanders, Wyoming, in July 1868, includes Ulysses S. Grant (soon to become president), William T. Sherman, Philip Henry Sheridan, among other officers, soldiers, and railroad dignitaries.

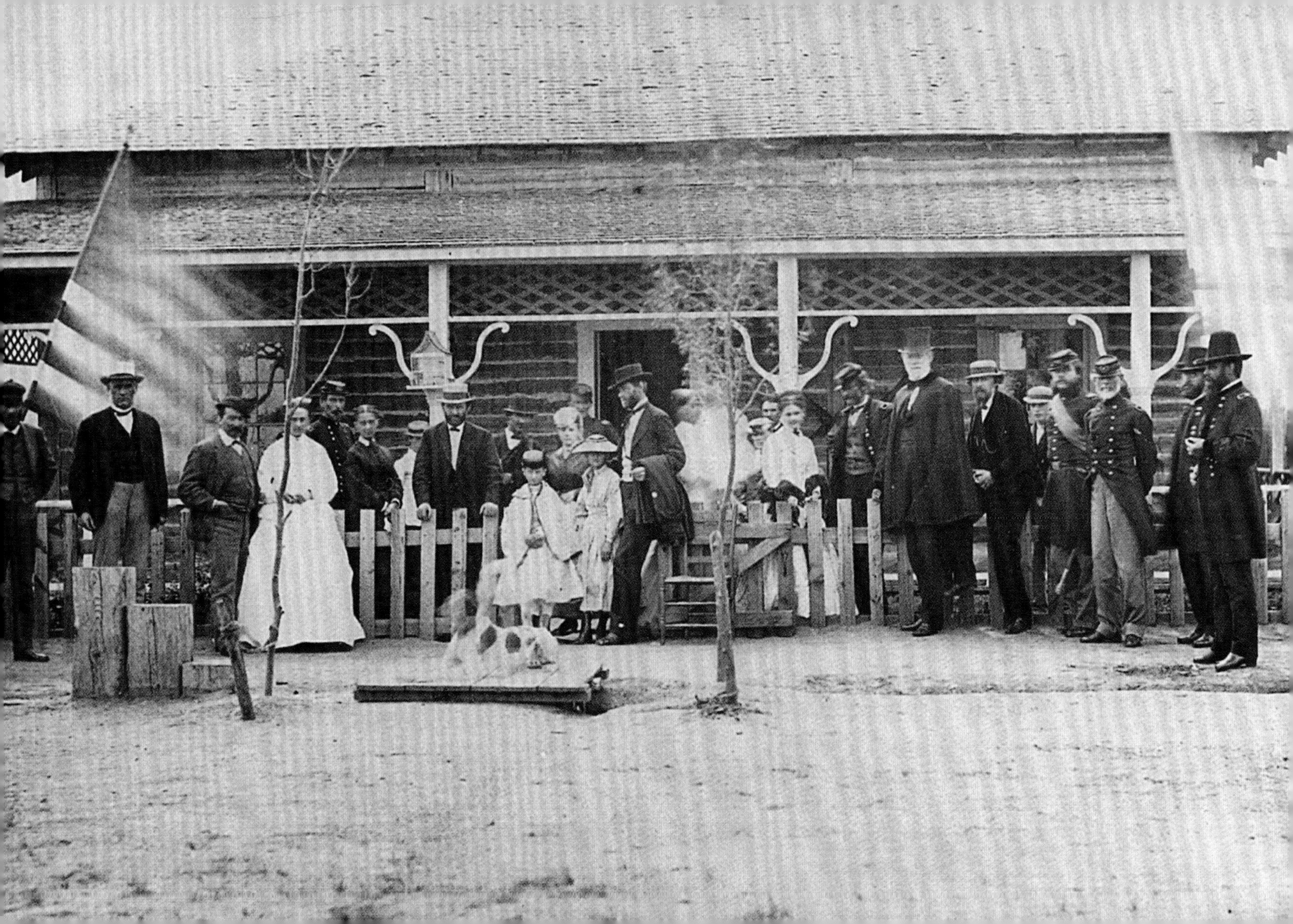

APR 5

1896 In El Paso, Texas, John Selman is killed in a shootout with U.S. Marshal George Scarborough in the Wigwam Saloon. Selman had killed Scarborough's friend, former Texas Ranger Bass Outlaw, in 1894 and gunfighter John Wesley Hardin the following year. Scarborough was mortally wounded in a gunfight on April 5, 1900, exactly four years to the day after killing Selman.

FOURTEEN MILE CITY

In 1863, a party of Crow warriors waylaid William Fairweather and some fellow fortune-seekers traveling through what became southwestern Montana. While taking cover in a gulch, the men discovered gold. They named the place Alder Gulch after the alder bushes lining the sides of the creek. Word of the find spread, and within ten days a throng of miners swarmed the site. In less than three months, the string of settlements that grew up along the gulch had become the "Fourteen Mile City." The largest of the instant towns, Virginia City, supported a population of ten thousand by 1864 and, just a year later, was named territorial capital. Between 1863 and 1865, Alder Gulch yielded about thirty million dollars in gold. Miners, homesteaders, and merchants continued to make their way to Virginia City into the early 1870s. They came either on the Bozeman Trail or aboard one of the many steamboats out of St. Louis, churning along the muddy Missouri River with passengers, general merchandise, and equipment for the gold rush towns in Montana. Like the overland trails, river travel had its own perils. In 1865, the steamboat *Bertrand* hit a snag on the Missouri and sank just north of Omaha.

▲ Steamships carried prospectors up the Missouri and Yellowstone rivers to the mines in Montana.

▶ Wagons and stages loaded with the goods of those heading to the gold mines.

APR 6

1886 In Newton, Kansas, an "anti-dude" club is formed and establishes fines for various infractions: five dollars for carrying a cane, ten dollars for wearing kid gloves and a plug hat, and twenty dollars for parting one's hair down the middle.

3-7-77

At the height of the Montana gold rush, a wave of lawlessness ignited one of the most violent episodes of vigilante justice in American history. In late 1863, twenty-four citizens secretly met in Virginia City and formed a Vigilance Committee, complete with bylaws. After swearing oaths of allegiance, the "Innocents," as they called themselves, swept through the mining camps. In just the first five weeks of 1864, the vigilantes hanged twenty-one men, including Henry Plummer, the newly elected sheriff of the town of Bannack. His executioners claimed Plummer was the ringleader of a murderous gang of road agents, an allegation that became the source of heated debate for years to come. Montana lore also attributes the numbers 3-7-77 to the vigilantes as a symbol for their cause. If those numbers were found painted on a tent or cabin door, the inhabitants knew to take their leave. Hanging victims might have the numbers carved into their corpses. There were several theories behind the 3-7-77. One was that the person at risk had 3 hours, 7 minutes, and 77 seconds to leave town. Others said the numbers were either the dimension of a standard grave, or meant that the suspected outlaw had to purchase a 3-dollar ticket on the 7 A.M. stage to make the 77-mile trip from Helena to Butte.

▶ This painting by N. C. Wyeth illustrates the vigilantes' determination to deal with the thieves, murderers, and troublemakers who inevitably came with the rush to the boomtowns.

APR 7

1898 Richard "Little Dick" West, a former member of the Doolin Gang, dies near Guthrie, Oklahoma Territory, after being ambushed by a posse led by Deputy U.S. Marshal Chris Madsen.

BETTER KNOWN AS X

John Xavier Beidler, a charter member and chief hangman of the Montana vigilante movement, was a lone wolf with a peculiar sense of gallows humor. Reminiscing about the hanging of Jack Slade in 1864, Beidler recalled that "my friend had fallen into the sleep of the innocents and snored like a band of Mormon wives." After the 1859 hanging of his close associate abolitionist John Brown, the diminutive Beidler went west, worked a variety of jobs, and arrived at Alder Gulch in 1863. Better known only by his middle initial "X," Beidler joined the Innocents, as the Montana vigilantes were called. "The people around and in Virginia [City] were at the time in an excited state of mind, and I concluded to quit prospecting for gold and prospect for human fiends," Beidler explained. On January 14, 1864, he presided at the execution of five road agents at Virginia City and continued to dispense his own brand of merciless justice on many other occasions. Beidler provided author Thomas J. Dinsdale, perhaps a vigilante himself, with much of the material used in *The Vigilantes of Montana*, his 1866 book written as a vindication of the controversial execution of Sheriff Henry Plummer. Following his stint with the Innocents, Beidler rode shotgun on stagecoaches and, as a reward for his services rendered as a hangman, was appointed deputy U.S. marshal. Beidler died in Helena, Montana, in 1890. His death certificate listed his occupation as "Public Benefactor."

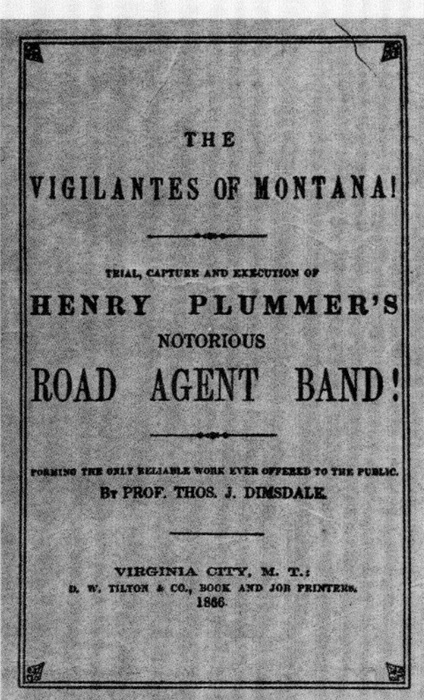

THE

VIGILANTES OF MONTANA!

TRIAL, CAPTURE AND EXECUTION OF

HENRY PLUMMER'S

NOTORIOUS

ROAD AGENT BAND!

FORMING THE ONLY RELIABLE WORK EVER OFFERED TO THE PUBLIC.

BY PROF. THOS. J. DIMSDALE

VIRGINIA CITY, M. T.:

D. W. TILTON & CO., BOOK AND JOB PRINTERS,

1866.

▲ This pamphlet written in defense of vigilantes was the first book printed in Montana Territory.

▶ John Xavier Beidler, one of the Montana vigilante leaders.

APR 8

1892 Outlaw Butch Cassidy is arrested for horse theft in Auburn, Wyoming. He is taken to a Fremont County jail in Lander where he posts bail and is set free.

HANGIN' TREE

"News arrived this P.M. of the attack of the stagecoach going east—by road agents. Four men killed, one missing. The road agents numbered about twenty. There is a mass meeting of the Vigilantes this evening."

—diary of James P. Miller, July 7, 1865

"Two men found 'hanging in the air' this morning up the gulch a little bit with a card on their backs on which were the words 'Hung by the Vigilance Committee for being road agents.'"

—diary of James P. Miller, September 27, 1865

▲ Lynching was the most popular method vigilantes used to deal with outlaws.

▶ A row of graves on a hilltop above Virginia City, Montana, marking the resting place of many of the victims of the vigilante justice.

APR 9

1878 In Dodge City, Kansas, lawman Ed Masterson, brother of famed lawman and gunfighter Bat Masterson, is shot and killed in the line of duty.
1892 Nate Champion and Nick Ray are killed by a posse of fifty hired gunmen on Champion's KC Ranch near Buffalo, Wyoming. This marks the beginning of the Johnson County War.

NECKTIE PARTY

Although many of the vigilante groups were more lawless than those they strung up—often without even the semblance of a trial—there were those varmints who needed to have their necks stretched. Throughout the American West of the late 1800s, no crime posed a greater risk than horse stealing. Those who depended on trusty mounts for their livelihood knew that the loss of a good horse could be devastating. Vigilante groups formed in some areas just to deal with the problem. A horse thief was an abomination, and anyone caught in the act or even suspected of such activity might end up "decorating a cottonwood," a popular expression for hanging. Sometimes it was easier to get away with cold-blooded murder than to make off with another man's horse.

▲ A lynching from a telephone pole in Tombstone, Arizona Territory, of a man a jury found innocent of the crime. A group of vigilantes disagreed with this verdict.

▶ A lynching in Laramie, Wyoming Territory. Lynchings often attracted a photographer and a crowd the following morning.

APR 10

1878 The Sam Bass Gang robs the Texas and Pacific Railroad at Mesquite, Texas, pulling in just $150 for their efforts.

WILD BILL

His given name was James Butler Hickok, but history would brand this former wagon boss, civilian army scout, and Union spy with shoulder-length auburn tresses and a drooping straw-colored mustache, with an unforgettable nickname—Wild Bill. The origin of his illustrious handle is unclear, but Hickok had picked up the catchy moniker by the end of the Civil War when he operated as a professional gambler out of Springfield, Missouri. Hickok left his mark on the town one summer evening when he and Dave Tutt, a gambling companion, clashed over a wager during a card game at the Lyon House. Tempers flared and harsh words were exchanged. The following evening—July 21, 1865—Hickok and Tutt met in the downtown square to duel. When they were about seventy-five yards apart, Hickok told Tutt not to come any closer. Tutt responded by drawing a pistol from the scabbard on his leg. He took aim and fired, but the shot missed its mark. Simultaneously, Hickok lifted his single-action Colt revolver, cocked back the hammer, steadied himself, and returned fire. His bullet struck true. Hickok turned himself in and was skillfully defended by John S. Phelps, later elected a Missouri governor. A jury acquitted Hickok on a reduced charge of manslaughter, and he was released, his standing as a shootist, or man-killer, secure for the rest of his stormy life. The first published reference to Hickok as Wild Bill appeared in a story about the duel published in the Springfield *Weekly Patriot* of July 27, 1865, when the paper noted that Hickok was "better known in Southwest Missouri as 'Wild Bill.'"

▲ Hickok, 1867.

▶ This *Harper's Magazine* article by George Ward Nichols propelled James Butler Hickok to fame as "Wild Bill."

HARPER'S
NEW MONTHLY MAGAZINE.

No. CCI.—FEBRUARY, 1867.—Vol. XXXIV.

WILD BILL.

SEVERAL months after the ending of the civil war I visited the city of Springfield in Southwest Missouri. Springfield is not a burgh of extensive dimensions, yet it is the largest in that part of the State, and all roads lead to it—which is one reason why it was the *point d'ap-*

George Ward Nichols.

APR 11

1873 General Edward R. S. Canby, commander of the U.S. Army's forces in the Pacific Northwest during the Indian Wars, is assassinated by Modocs at a peace conference during California's Modoc War. He is the only army general to die in the Indian Wars.

LITTLE RAVEN

Many Indians and even some whites believed that Little Raven, a principal chief of the Southern Arapaho, was a reasonable man and courageous leader, who would go to war only as a last resort. Little Raven mediated peace between his tribe and the Cheyenne and also tried to work with the U.S. government despite the frequent failures of the white men to comply with terms of treaties. Disillusioned and angry following the massacre of Indians at Sand Creek in 1864, Little Raven still counseled for peace. In 1867, he attended the parley held at the confluence of the Medicine River and Elm Creek in Kansas, where he and leaders from several other Plains tribes signed the Medicine Lodge Treaty. The gathering of thousands of Indians and U.S. soldiers at Medicine Lodge attracted newspaper correspondents from across the nation, including Henry M. Stanley, who would later search for Livingston in Africa. The series of treaties signed at Medicine Lodge failed to bring immediate peace, but under the terms of the agreement, the Southern Arapaho agreed to eventually relocate to a reservation between the Arkansas and Cimarron rivers in Indian Territory. "It will be a very hard thing to leave the country that God gave us," said Little Raven. "Our friends are buried there, and we hate to leave these grounds."

▶ Arapaho chief Little Raven worked hard for peace as one of the leaders who signed the Medicine Lodge Treaty, but had little long-term success.

APR 12

1875 Near Kearney, Missouri, the James brothers and Clell Miller kill local farmer Daniel Askew on the suspicion that he has been harboring a Pinkerton agent.

LONGHORNS

The Longhorn—an enduring symbol of the American frontier—was the toughest creature to emerge from the Lone Star State. One old-time cattleman declared: "The average Texas Longhorn was about as mean a creature as ever went on four legs, and rivaled in this respect some of the worst of his contemporaries that went on two; and, the longer he lived the meaner he became." The roots of the hybrid breed went back to the conquistadors who came to the New World with cattle that shared the blood of Spanish fighting bulls. These critters made their way to what became the Mexican state of Texas before 1700 and eventually mixed with other stock brought in by Anglo colonists. In the 1850s, Longhorns were trailed to markets in New Orleans and California. The 1860 census reported six hundred thousand people residing in Texas and four million head of cattle. During the Civil War, the half-wild herds wandering the open ranges increased to five million. In 1865, defeated Confederate soldiers returning to Texas found Longhorns free for the taking and a great demand for beef in northern markets. Longhorns were tough enough to withstand drought and blizzards, and, unlike buffalo, had no natural enemies. Even wolves were leery of tangling with a mother Longhorn protecting her newborn calf. Longhorns were so hardy that they were even known to gain weight along the long trails north.

▲ Buffalo discover a Longhorn in their midst.

▶ The domain of the buffalo eventually gave way to the Longhorns.

APR 13

1881 In Mesilla, New Mexico Territory, Judge Warren Bristol sentences Billy the Kid to hang in one month's time. The Kid escapes before the sentence can be carried out.

FATHER OF THE TEXAS PANHANDLE

In 1866, a former Texas Ranger and Confederate soldier named Charles Goodnight teamed up with Oliver Loving, and the two drove their first herd of feral Longhorns northward on what would become known as the Goodnight-Loving Trail. Before departing on that historic trek, Goodnight developed the first chuck wagon, a handy portable kitchen on wheels that greatly improved trail life for future drovers. The following year, after Loving was killed by a Comanche war party, Goodnight extended the busy cattle trail from New Mexico Territory to Colorado, and eventually Wyoming. Goodnight became enormously wealthy. In 1876, he partnered with financier John Adair and established the JA Ranch, a million-acre operation with one hundred thousand cattle of various breeds, near Palo Duro Canyon in the south Texas Panhandle. In addition to raising cattle, Goodnight established a herd of the endangered native buffalo, which hide hunters were decimating. He also crossbred cattle and buffalo into what he called "cattalo." In his later years, Goodnight—who never learned to read or write and at one time smoked fifty cigars a day—made an unwise investment in Mexican silver mines. He was forced to convey his ranch to a friend with the provision that Goodnight and his wife, Mary Anne, could stay there until they died. Goodnight became interested in filmmaking and spent his winters in Arizona, where he died in 1929, knowing that his small herd of buffalo had saved the entire species from virtual extinction.

▲ Charles Goodnight, frontiersman, scout, and one of the most powerful cattlemen in Texas.

▶ Goodnight loved the buffalo and worked to protect and preserve them.

APR 14

1878 Thirty Mexican marauders led by a white man split into three groups and plunder the town of Laredo, Texas. Twenty innocents, including women and children, lose their lives.

COWBOYS

Some historians claim the word "cow-boy" was first used in medieval Ireland to describe boys who tended cattle. Others say the name was bandied about in early America, when youngsters such as Daniel Boone and later David Crockett herded cows. Even so, only after the Civil War did the term "cowboy" come into common use. The heyday of the genuine cowboys was brief. It began in 1865, when Texans returned home after serving the Confederacy, poor in cash but rich in rangelands teeming with ubiquitous Longhorns. Prior to the war, those who had trailed cattle usually were known as drovers. In the late 1860s, Texas ranchers used the term "cowboy" as they gathered unbranded wild Longhorns during roundups at first called "cow hunts." By about 1870, ranchers hired youngsters, whom they generally referred to as cowboys, to herd cattle up the trails to northern railheads and markets. Some of them were only twelve to sixteen years old and hardly big enough to climb into a saddle. Not everyone approved of such work. "Parents, do not allow your boys to load themselves down with Mexican spurs, six shooters and pipes," warned a reporter for Texas's *Denton Monitor*. "Keep them off the prairies as professional cow hunters. There, in that occupation, who knows but they may forget that there is a distinction between 'mine' and 'thine'? Send them to school, teach them a trade, or keep them at home."

▶ Six cowboys from southern Arizona Territory.

▶▶ A working cowboy visits a photo studio wearing his gun and rig, c. 1870s.

APR 15

1881 Billy the Kid tells a reporter from the *Mesilla News*: "I expect to be lynched in going to Lincoln, [New Mexico Territory] . . . [and I] advise persons never to engage in killing."

THE CHISHOLM TRAIL

For most people, the name Chisholm brought to mind the famous cattle trail beaten out by millions of Texas Longhorns driven to Kansas railroad towns and northern markets in the first twenty-five years after the Civil War. The Chisholm name was so common that it often was used indiscriminately for all cattle trails out of Texas. The trail, expanded later from south Texas through Indian Territory to Abilene, Kansas, proved the most feasible route for cattle drivers looking for fresh water and good grazing for northbound herds. Ironically, the trail's namesake Jesse Chisholm was not a cattleman and more than likely never owned a single cow. Rather, he was known for building trading posts and creating wagon roads throughout Indian Territory as early as 1832. Chisholm died in Indian Territory in 1868. While visiting Arapaho friends, he unknowingly ate contaminated bear grease from a brass cooking pot. He was wrapped in a blanket and buffalo skin and buried on a low sand knoll overlooking the North Canadian River. Years later, some of his devotees erected a plain stone marker there with the inscription: "No One Ever Left His Home Cold or Hungry."

Come along, boys, and listen to my tale,
I'll tell you of my troubles on the old Chisholm Trail
Coma ti yi youpy, youpy ya, youpy ya!
Coma ti yi youpy, youpy ya!

—"The Old Chisholm Trail," a traditional cowboy song

▲ A Texas Longhorn with exceptionally long horns.

▶ A cattle boss keeps watch over his herd moving up a trail.

CMRussell

APR 16

1881 Bat Masterson returns to Dodge City, Kansas, at the request of his brother Jim. As Bat steps from the train, he encounters his brother's enemies and gunfire erupts. A man is killed in the ensuing gun battle and, as a result, the Mastersons are run out of town.

SHANGHAI PIERCE

Arguably the most flamboyant and iron-willed of the cattle empire builders was "Shanghai" Pierce. Born Abel Head Pierce in 1834 in Rhode Island to industrious, conservative parents, he left home at an early age when he grew tired of arguing with his straitlaced father. The free-spirited Pierce ended up in Texas, where he and his brother Jonathan enlisted in the Confederate army. In the Lone Star State, Pierce learned about cowboys and cattle and started going by Shanghai, which stuck for life. Several explanations have been given for how the colorful nickname came about, but six-feet-four-inch Pierce claimed it was because the large rowels, or wheels, on his custom-made spurs made him look like a fancy Shanghai rooster. Eager to make a fortune in the cattle business, Shanghai and his brother established a ranch near the Texas Gulf coast. Jonathan ran the operation while Shanghai and his cowboys built up substantial herds by "mavericking"—rounding up free-roving strays, branding them, and bringing them to market. Shanghai's exploits on the range took on mythic qualities. He was a skilled self-promoter and perhaps as big a braggart as ever emerged from Texas. Shanghai lived up to his colorful image as he gathered herds of moss-backed Longhorns called "sea lions" because of their swimming prowess. He left a lasting impression when riding into cattle camps accompanied by his black servant Neptune Holmes, whose pack mule was laden with enough gold coins to buy entire herds.

▶ Rowdy cattleman Abel "Shanghai" Pierce.

APR 17

1881 In El Paso, Texas, Marshal Dallas Stoudenmire and Doc Cummings shoot Bill Johnson after he attempts to bushwhack the marshal.

THE REAL McCOY

The crusty Scot-Cherokee trader Jesse Chisholm may have marked the famous trail that bore his name, but it was Joseph McCoy, a smart cattle buyer from Illinois, who made the Chisholm Trail the most successful cattle route in the West. McCoy knew the railroad companies planned to expand their freight operations, and he seized the opportunity to turn Abilene, Kansas, into a first-rate cattle market for the tens of thousands of Longhorns trailing northward out of Texas. McCoy erected stockyards, a bank, and hotel along the Union Pacific tracks and advertised Abilene as a major shipping center. Between 1867 and 1872, Abilene was the busiest cow town in Kansas as more than three million head of cattle were driven there along the Chisholm Trail. It was said that in 1871 as many as five thousand cowboys were paid trail wages in a single day. Soon other Kansas rail towns shared in the wealth as more routes opened. Joe McCoy had once boasted that he would bring two hundred thousand head to market in a decade, but he actually brought ten times that number in only four years, a feat which some believed led to the phrase, "It's the real McCoy!"

▲▲ Joseph McCoy, the man most responsible for turning Abilene, Kansas, into a market for millions of Texas Longhorns.

▲ A cattle car waiting to be loaded in Abilene.

▶ Loading Longhorns into the cattle cars in Abilene.

HICKS STOCK CAR
ED CATTLE CAR 3896

APR **18**

1875 At Fort Abraham Lincoln, Dakota Territory, a jailer helps Lakota chief Rain-in-the-Face escape the guardhouse. The Indian warrior later says, "The old soldier taught me some of the white people have hearts." Some believe that George Armstrong Custer arranged the escape to avoid a trial for which he had little evidence.

DROVERS

"The Texas cattle herder is a character, the likes of which can be found nowhere else on earth. Of course he is unlearned and illiterate, but with few wants and meager ambition. His diet is principally navy plug and whiskey and the occupation dearest to his heart is gambling. His dress consists of a flannel shirt with a handkerchief encircling his neck, butternut pants and a pair of long boots, in which are always the legs of his pants. His head is crowned by a sombrero, which is a Mexican hat with a high crown and a brim of enormous dimensions. He generally wears a revolver on each side of his person, which he will use with little hesitation on a man as on a wild animal. Such a character is dangerous and desperate and each one had generally killed his man."

—*The Topeka Commonwealth*, August 15, 1871

▲ The Drover's Cottage hotel in Abilene, Kansas.

▶ A tintype of drovers ready for the trail.

▶▶ A drover.

"I have never forgotten the feel of the saddle after a long day, the weight and pull of the old six-shooter, and what a blessing to cowmen was the old yellow slicker. Those were the days when men depended on friends to help if necessary. Days of hard work but good health; plain food but strong appetites, when people expected to work for a living and short hours and big pay was unknown."

—J. B. Pumphrey, Texas drover, n.d.

APR 19

1909 Hired killer James B. "Deacon Jim" Miller and the three ranchers who solicited his dubious services are lynched in Ada, Oklahoma. A photograph of the four men hanging in a livery stable remains an enduring image of frontier justice.

FORT DODGE

On St. Patrick's Day 1865, orders were issued to build Fort Dodge, a U.S. Army post on the Arkansas River just a few miles southeast of what would become Dodge City, Kansas. Erected on a site that had been used as a camping ground by wagon trains, the fort's main purpose was to protect railroad workers and travelers on the nearby Santa Fe Trail. It also served as a supply center and base of operations for troopers engaged with warring Plains Indian tribes. The first buildings and barracks were either adobe or sod dugouts, prone to flooding. Then shipments of lumber arrived, and soldiers also set to work quarrying stone for a hospital and officers' quarters, arduous labor that significantly boosted the desertion rate. Sanitation was poor, cholera and other diseases common, and Indian attacks frequent. The lone source of comfort was the Sutler's Store, the basic general mercantile operation found on every military post. All manner of items were sold there (mostly at excessive prices), and each evening whiskey was served from 6:30 to 9:00 P.M., with a three-drink limit. Apparently, the bartenders frequently lost count since drunkenness was a common offense and the guardhouse never lacked for occupants.

▶ A hand-colored engraving of the Sutler's Store at Fort Dodge, Kansas.

SUTLER'S STORE AT FORT DODGE, KANSAS.—[SKETCHED BY THEODORE R. DAVIS.] 1867

APR 20

1882 Outlaws Belle Starr and Sam Starr (her third husband) are arrested at Younger's Bend, Oklahoma, for stealing horses.

ADIOS, COMPADRES

Although much of his adventuresome life was spent fighting Indians, Kit Carson later became a sympathetic ally to the Utes and other tribes and devoted his last years to arguing on their behalf as the superintendent of Indian Affairs for Colorado Territory. After the Civil War, Carson was mustered out of the military and took up residence in Colorado where he ranched and assisted his many Ute Indian friends. In late 1867, Carson, despite failing health, personally escorted a party of Ute chiefs to Washington, D.C., to meet with President Andrew Johnson and other federal officials. Carson's delegation sought additional government assistance and also pressed for continued treaty negotiations. While he was back East, Carson also consulted with several physicians about his health problems. The strenuous trip took a toll on Carson. Soon after his return to Colorado, his wife, Josefa, died of complications from the difficult birth of their seventh child. Carson was devastated and lost the will to live. He made arrangements for his children and wrote his will. On May 23, 1868, exactly one month to the day of his wife's passing, Christopher "Kit" Carson uttered the words "Adios, compadres," and died at age fifty-nine from an abdominal aortic aneurysm at Fort Lyon, Colorado Territory. His legend continued to grow, thanks to scores of dime novels and books filled with exaggerated accounts of Carson's life on the frontier.

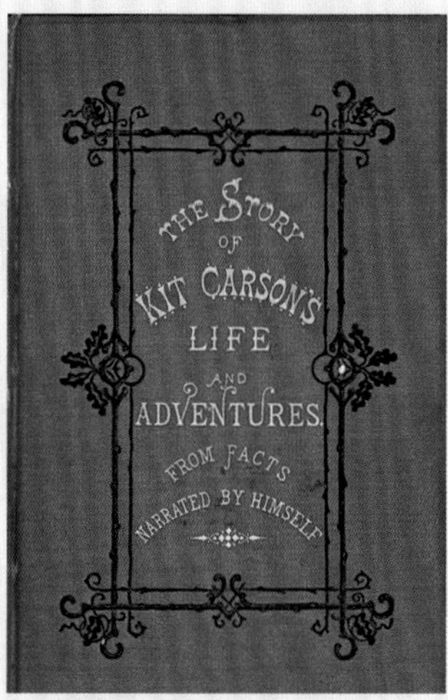

▲ At the time Carson visited Washington, this and other books had made him famous across the country.

▶ Kit Carson (seated left) and three dignitaries on the occasion of Carson's visit to Washington, D.C., 1867.

APR 21

1836 The battle cry "Remember the Alamo!" is used for the first time during the battle at the San Jacinto River. Santa Anna is captured shortly after the melee.

ISLAND OF PUTRID HORSE MEAT

In August of 1868, Major George Forsyth was ordered to pursue the Indians attacking homesteaders and railroad workers in Kansas Territory. Forsyth gathered fifty-one civilian scouts and frontiersmen and chose Lieutenant Frederick H. Beecher, a nephew of famous abolitionist minister Henry Ward Beecher, as his second-in-command. The civilians were paid a dollar a day plus thirty-five cents per day allowance for their horses. They were issued Spencer repeating carbines, Colt revolvers, and plenty of ammunition. On September 17, while camped on the Arickaree fork of the Republican River in present-day northeastern Colorado, Forsyth and his men were ambushed by hundreds of Northern Cheyenne, Sioux, and Arapaho warriors. The scouts scrambled to a sandbar covered with willows and dug in. During the weeklong siege that followed, half of the scouts and all of their horses were killed; Forsyth was badly wounded; and Lieutenant Beecher, whose name would later be used to commemorate the engagement, was shot dead. The survivors found cover behind their dead mounts, repelled several assaults, and killed many Indians, including the great Cheyenne warrior Roman Nose. Forsyth's men survived by drinking river water and eating rotting horseflesh. Noted scout Jack Stilwell saved the day when he managed to escape under cover of darkness to seek help at Fort Wallace. Due to Stilwell's action, on the eighth day, a relief column of cavalry arrived, and the Battle of Beecher Island was over.

"September 24th. All fresh horse meat gone. Tried to kill some wolves last night, but failed. The boys began to cut putrid horse meat. Made some soup tonight from putrefied horse meat. My God have you deserted us?"

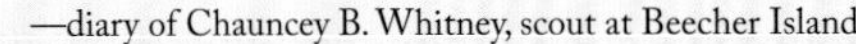

—diary of Chauncey B. Whitney, scout at Beecher Island

▲ Jack Stilwell, on the right, was a hero of the Beecher Island fight, having slipped through the Indians to bring aid to the trapped soldiers.

▶ A magazine sketch depicting the Battle of Beecher Island.

APR 22

1889 The Oklahoma land run begins after the federal government opens up Indian Territory for settlement.

WASHITA

He was just a soldier following orders. That's what Lieutenant Colonel George Armstrong Custer would later reply when asked about the events of November 27, 1868. The plains of western Indian Territory were blanketed in snow, and Custer's troopers from the Seventh Regiment of the U.S. Cavalry rose in the bitter cold before dawn. They waited in silence, forbidden to kindle fires for warmth or coffee, or walk around, or even stamp the chill out of their feet. Custer wanted no one from the sleeping Cheyenne village nearby to know of their presence. He conferred with his Osage scouts and whispered final instructions to his junior officers. The plan was to surround the camp of Black Kettle on the banks of the Washita River by splitting up the regiment of bluecoats, much as Custer would do eight years later at Little Bighorn. The sneak attack at Washita turned into a day of death and destruction, starting with Custer's orders for soldiers to get rid of the many dogs in the camp so they would not alert the sleeping Cheyenne. The dogs were muzzled with ropes and strangled or stabbed. One of Custer's favorite staghounds—Blucher—was spared.

"If the savage resists, civilization, with the Ten Commandments in one hand and the sword in the other, demands his immediate extermination."

—President Andrew Johnson, message to Congress, 1867

▲ Lt. Col. George Armstrong Custer in full uniform.

▶ Lt. Col. George Armstrong Custer standing behind his Osage Indian scouts after the Washita battle. What is said to be Custer's pet pelican is at right.

APR 23

1875 In northwestern Kansas, Little Bull and seventy-five Cheyenne followers en route to their home in the Black Hills are nearly wiped out by buffalo hunters and a cavalry company out of Fort Wallace.

CREEPING PANTHER

On a chilly November morning in 1868, four battalions of the Seventh Regiment, led by Lieutenant Colonel George Armstrong Custer, marched through the snow quiet as thieves and took the Indian village on the Washita River completely by surprise. Only when they approached the Cheyenne shelters did the army bandsmen put instruments to their lips and strike up "Garryowen," an old Irish drinking tune adopted by Custer as a march for his regiment. The strains of the stirring tune filled the air, and the wild charge was on. Eight hundred soldiers swept down on a village of about three hundred Cheyenne, mostly women and children. Accounts vary as to how many died that morning, but most believe at least one hundred Cheyenne, including Black Kettle and his wife Medicine Woman, were slaughtered. Custer lost about twenty troopers. One of them was Captain Louis Hamilton, grandson of the famed Alexander Hamilton, who was killed, some later said, by a young soldier who actually intended to shoot Custer but missed. The entire battle—although most historians now acknowledge it was a massacre—lasted only a few minutes. It took several hours to hunt down wounded Indians hiding in the snow-filled gullies. The soldiers burned the village and killed its herd of almost nine hundred ponies. From that morning on, Custer earned a new name among many Plains people. They began to call him *Ouchess*, or Creeping Panther.

"The only good Indians I ever saw were dead."

—General Philip Henry Sheridan, January 1869

▲ A crude monument at the Washita battle site, 1868.

▶ Cheyenne Indians captured at Washita. They have been identified as, left to right, Fat Bear, Big Head, and Dull Knife.

APR 24

1874 Jesse James marries first cousin Zerelda Mimms in Kearney, Missouri. Older brother Frank James elopes with Annie Ralston.

THE LUCK OF ROARING CAMP

At a time when the American West produced very little in the way of true literature, Bret Harte was a notable exception. A native of New York State, Harte published his first poem at age eleven. After arriving in California only seven years later, he began to churn out poems and short stories that by the late 1860s earned him the title "new prophet of American letters." Harte was a masterful storyteller whose colorful and often romanticized tales of gold rush miners, gamblers, and prostitutes made California famous. His stories, which seemed to come directly from the mining camps and gambling dens, convinced readers back East to board trains and see the West for themselves. Two of Harte's most memorable and entertaining short stories, "The Luck of Roaring Camp" and "The Outcasts of Poker Flat," appeared in the *Overland Monthly*, founded in 1868 with Harte as editor. These stories helped established Western American fiction and became the formula to follow for many future books and films depicting the West.

"The assemblage numbered about a hundred men. One or two of these were actual fugitives from justice, some were criminal, and all were reckless. Physically they exhibited no indication of their past lives and character. The greatest scamp had a Raphael face, with a profusion of blonde hair; Oakhurst, a gambler, had the melancholy air and intellectual abstraction of a Hamlet; the coolest and most courageous man was scarcely over five feet in height, with a soft voice and an embarrassed, timid manner."

—Bret Harte, "The Luck of Roaring Camp," 1868

▲ Bret Harte's classic story of the mining days in the West.

▶ Bret Harte.

APR 25

1903 G. W. Miller, one of the founders of the 101 Ranch, dies in a dugout on the Salt Fork River in the Cherokee Outlet territory of what is now Oklahoma.

GOLDEN SPIKE

On May 10, 1869, two locomotives—Union Pacific No. 119 and Central Pacific No. 60 (best known as the *Jupiter*)—drew so close their cowcatchers almost touched at Promontory Summit, Utah Territory. At long last, iron rails bridged the continent. As the "Wedding of the Rails" ceremony commenced and commemorative golden spikes were driven into place, a telegrapher at the scene tapped out the word "Done." Some witnesses declared it the nation's finest moment.

▶ The celebration of the completion of the transcontinental railroad at Promontory Summit, Utah Territory.

"I saw the Gold Spike driven at Promontory, Utah. . . . It was a hilarious occasion, everybody had all they wanted to drink all the time. . . . California furnished the Golden Spike. Governor Tuttle of Nevada furnished one of silver. . . . Stanford presented one of gold, silver and iron from Arizona. The last tie was California laurel. . . . When they came to the last spike, Governor Stanford, president of the Central Pacific, took the sledge and the first time he struck he missed the spike and hit the rail. What a howl went up! Irish, Chinese, Mexicans, and everybody yelled with delight. Everybody slapped everybody else on the back and yelled 'He missed it Yee!' The engineers blew their whistles and rang their bells. Then Stanford tried it again and tapped the spike and the telegraph operators had fixed their instruments so that the tap was reported in all the offices, east and west, and set bells to tapping in hundreds of towns and cities."

—Alexander Toponce, stage driver, 1869

APR 26

1901 "Black Jack" Ketchum is legally hanged at Clayton, New Mexico Territory. In the process, he is accidentally decapitated.

IRON HORSE HUNTS

"At this season of the year the herds of buffalo are moving southward, to reach the canyons which contain the grass they exist upon during the winter. Nearly every railroad train which leaves and arrives at Fort Hayes on the Kansas Pacific Railroad has its race with these herds of buffalo, and a most interesting and exciting scene is the result. The train is 'slowed' to a rate of speed about equal to that of the herd; the passengers get out fire-arms which are provided for the defense of the train against Indians, and open from the windows and platforms of the cars a fire that resembles a brisk skirmish. Frequently a young bull will turn at bay for a moment. His exhibition of courage is generally his death-warrant, for the whole fire of the train is turned upon him, either killing him or some member of the herd in his immediate vicinity."

—*Harper's Magazine*, December 14, 1867

"In the days of the first Pacific railroad, and before the herds had been driven back from the tracks, singular hunting parties were sometimes seen on the buffalo range. These hunters were capitalists connected with the newly constructed roads; and some of them now for the first time bestrode a horse, while few had ever used firearms. . . . Here all was mirth and jest and good fellowship, and the hunters lived in as much comfort as when at home. The killing of the buffalo was to them an excuse for their jolly outing amidst novel scenes."

—*Scribner's Magazine*, September 1892

▶ A migrating buffalo herd could take hours, or even days, to cross railroad tracks.

N.H.Trotter

APR 27

1877 In Rath City, Texas, buffalo hunter Tom Lumpkins is shot and killed by Limpy Jim Smith. Lumpkins's grave, the first in the town's Boot Hill cemetery, is marked with a buffalo skull.

CYNTHIA ANN PARKER

On May 19, 1836, a band of Indians attacked Parker's Fort on the fringes of the Comanche frontier in the newly formed Republic of Texas. In the skirmish that followed, five Texans were killed and five others were taken captive, including nine-year-old Cynthia Ann Parker and her younger brother John. The little girl would become one of the most renowned Indian captives in the history of the West. Both of the Parker children quickly adjusted to the Comanche culture. John became a warrior and took part in several raids, while Cynthia Ann lived as a Comanche for almost twenty-five years. She eventually married Chief Peta Nocona and bore him two sons and a daughter. Their first-born son Quanah became the last great war chief of the Comanches. In 1860, Texas Rangers led by Captain Sul Ross swept down on a Comanche village, killing many inhabitants and taking others captive, including the long-lost Cynthia Ann and her two-year-old daughter, Prairie Flower. They were returned to Parker family members, but her many years living with the tribe had changed Cynthia Ann irrevocably. She had nothing in common with her white relatives and begged to be returned to her Indian family. Her escape attempts failed, and when her daughter died of influenza in 1864, Cynthia Ann lost all hope. Broken in spirit and bitter at her enforced captivity, she starved herself to death. It was not until forty-six years later that Quanah Parker was able to bring the remains of his beloved mother and his baby sister from Texas to Oklahoma. He dedicated a great feast to honor the memory of his mother, who lived and died as a Comanche.

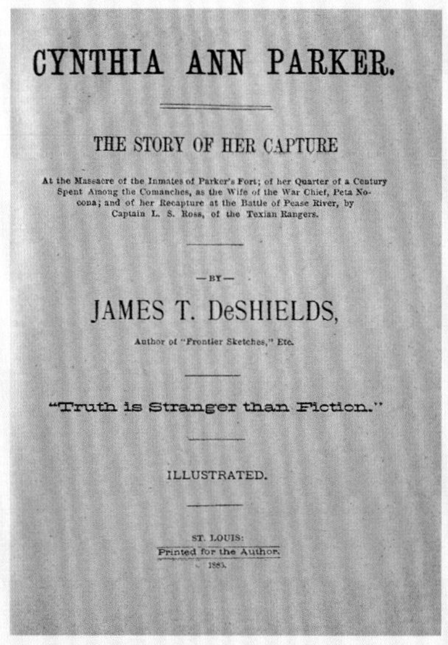

CYNTHIA ANN PARKER.

THE STORY OF HER CAPTURE

At the Massacre of the Inmates of Parker's Fort; of her Quarter of a Century Spent Among the Comanches, as the Wife of the War Chief, Peta Nocona; and of her Recapture at the Battle of Pease River, by Captain L. S. Ross, of the Texian Rangers.

—BY—

JAMES T. DeSHIELDS,

Author of "Frontier Sketches," Etc.

"Truth is Stranger than Fiction."

ILLUSTRATED.

ST. LOUIS:
Printed for the Author.
1886.

▲ The first book to tell the story of Cynthia Ann Parker's capture and life among the Indians, published in 1886.

▶ Cynthia Ann Parker, mother of Quanah, with her baby daughter Prairie Flower.

Cynthia Ann Parker and her baby
"Prairie Flower,"
Mother and sister of Chief
Quanah Parker.
Just after her re-capture in 1860.

APR 28

1881 After being transferred to Lincoln, New Mexico Territory, following his murder trial, Billy the Kid kills Sheriff Pat Garrett's deputies James Bell and Bob Ollinger and makes his escape.

BUFFALO BILL

William Frederick Cody inspired and promoted the romanticized image of the Wild West by transforming his own experience into an enduring national myth. Born on the Iowa prairie in 1846, at the age of seven Cody moved with his family to Kansas Territory, and his father died when the boy was just eleven. Like some other youngsters at that time, he quit school to work for a freight company and then as a mounted messenger. Cody later claimed that during his brief stint with the Pony Express he completed one ride of 322 miles—the third longest in the service. In the early years of the Civil War, Cody operated with the Jayhawkers until 1864 when he enlisted in the Union army and served as a teamster with the Seventh Kansas Volunteer Cavalry. After the war, Cody found a bride in St. Louis in 1866 and began to work as a scout and guide. In 1867, Kansas Pacific Railroad contractors hired him to hunt buffalo needed to feed the construction hands. Cody's contract stipulated that for five hundred dollars a month the expert marksman must shoot at least a dozen buffalo a day. He picked up his soon-to-be legendary .50 caliber Springfield rifle "Lucretia Borgia," mounted his favorite buffalo horse, Brigham (named for Brigham Young), and rode off in search of buffalo. They were not difficult to find. Cody boasted that he killed 4,280 buffalo over eighteen months (another dubious claim since his contract was only for eight months). Nonetheless, Cody was undisputedly an impressive sharpshooter and, by late 1867, had won the name "Buffalo Bill."

▲ William F. Cody.

▶ Young scout William F. Cody.

APR 29

1872 The James-Younger Gang robs the Deposit Bank at Columbia, Kentucky.

NED BUNTLINE

Writer Edward Zane Carroll Judson helped to form the American public's image of the West by shamelessly blending equal helpings of myth and reality. He accomplished this alchemy and reached a wide and eager audience by churning out a raft of sensational dime novels and staging thrilling theatrical productions. Each one was a vivid reconstruction very loosely based on events most accepted as fact. Somewhat of a contradiction, the notorious womanizer and drunk made a living from time to time by delivering fiery temperance lectures, but, like P. T. Barnum, the rascal had his thumb on the pulse of America. Born in upstate New York in 1823, Judson ran away to sea as a boy and served in the U.S. Navy. He finagled a midshipman's commission after saving the crew of a capsized ship in New York's East River. His first stories were published in *Knickerbocker Magazine* under his preferred pen name of Ned Buntline, the handle he used for the rest of his life. In the 1840s and 1850s, Buntline survived many adventures and close calls, most of them of his own making, and continued to write, even during the Civil War. But his glory days came after the war, when Buntline crossed paths with William Cody. It was Ned Buntline who transformed the flamboyant buffalo hunter into "Buffalo Bill," who changed the way generations of Americans would view the West.

▲ Buntline introduced William F. Cody to the world as "Buffalo Bill."

▶ Edward Zane Carroll Judson wrote under the name Ned Buntline and portrayed a frontier scout onstage.

APR 30

1871 Near Camp Grant, Arizona Territory, the Tucson Commission of Public Safety along with a number of Mexicans and Papago Indians slaughter peaceful Pinal and Apache Indians while they sleep. Approximately one hundred women and children are killed in what is now called the Camp Grant Massacre.

FRAMING THE WEST

Photographers began documenting the landscape and the people of the American West just as U.S. expansion into the region got underway in the 1840s. It could be said that both the West and photography came of age at the same time. Early photographic images not only documented the history of the frontier, but also became an important medium in shaping how Americans and others viewed the Trans-Mississippi frontier. Photographers witnessed the settling of the West, recorded nature's curiosities and wonders, and offered a glimpse into the nation's future. Many photographs were reproduced as lithographic illustrations in government reports and popular illustrated publications such as *Harper's New Monthly Magazine*. By the 1860s, photographers were lugging their cumbersome cameras and large glass plates across prairies and rivers and up mountains to reach cattle towns, mining camps, Indian villages, and the most remote locales. They endured danger, hardship, and faced death in order to capture accurate images of the Western experience.

▲ This studio portrait of George Bill, a photographer with the Fisk Expedition to Montana, shows that frontier photographers had to carry guns as well as cameras.

▶ Photographer George Bill's boat, loaded with his equipment, in a cove of the Missouri River. Photographers' equipment was cumbersome and fragile and had to be carried to remote places in inventive ways.

ILLINGWORTH & BILL,
PHOTOGRAPHERS
MONTANA
EXPEDITION.

1

1852 Martha Jane Cannary, later known as "Calamity Jane," is born in Princeton, Missouri.

BEAR RIVER

Thomas James "Bear River" Smith was raised to a life of keeping the peace and knocking heads in New York City where he became a professional boxer and policeman. After accidentally shooting a fourteen-year-old boy, Smith was exonerated but resigned and headed west. He became a teamster at Bear River City, Wyoming, but his experience as a lawman helped him to become the first city marshal of Abilene, Kansas, in June 1870. His salary of one hundred fifty dollars per month was supplemented by a two-dollar bonus when persons he arrested were convicted. Within two months, Smith was earning two hundred twenty-five dollars a month. Smith gained a reputation for subduing assailants with his fists rather than his gun. However, on November 2, 1870, Smith's life came to an abrupt end. He was attempting to arrest an accused murderer, Andrew McConnell, when McConnell shot him. Although fatally injured, Smith was able to wound the gunman. McConnell's coconspirator in the original crime, Moses Miles, then struck Smith with his gun, grabbed an ax, and nearly chopped Smith's head off. McConnell was sentenced to twelve years in the penitentiary, and Miles received a sixteen-year sentence. President Dwight D. Eisenhower considered Smith a personal hero, and whenever he visited his boyhood home, he paid his respects at Smith's grave.

"According to the legends of my hometown [Smith] was anything but dull. . . . While he almost never carried a pistol he . . . subdued the lawless by force of his personality and his tremendous capability as an athlete. One blow of his fist was apparently enough to knock out the ordinary 'tough' cowboy."

—President Dwight D. Eisenhower

▲ Thomas "Bear River" Smith, the first city marshal of Abilene, Kansas.

▶ Thomas Smith acquired the name "Bear River" as a teamster in the wild end-of-tracks town of Bear River City, Wyoming.

R R RESTAURANT
LIQUORS

1895 Near Ingalls, Oklahoma Territory, brothers Jim, Dal, and Bill Dunn shoot and kill outlaws Charley Pierce and George "Bitter Creek" Newcomb in order to collect the five-thousand-dollar bounty on each man.

BLOOD FEUD

Spawned by the horrors of the Civil War, the Sutton-Taylor feud erupted in the late 1860s Reconstruction-era Texas, where misplaced machismo, irrational behavior, and a propensity for violence became an acceptable way of life. William Sutton, a DeWitt County deputy sheriff, and the only Sutton actually involved in the hostilities, headed the Sutton side. The conflict started in 1868 when Sutton killed some kinsman of Creed Taylor, patriarch of that clan, although Creed's brother Pitkin led the Taylor alliance. What followed was a bloodbath of murder, chaos, retaliation, and terror that left many dead and scarred victims on both sides. Considered the longest and most vicious blood feud in the state's history, this ongoing battle was actually far more complicated than the surface suggested: In reality what began as a family quarrel over cattle evolved into a vendetta pitting unreconstructed Confederate sympathizers against what many Texans viewed as a radical Republican government and corrupt state police force mostly composed of former slaves and Yankee carpetbaggers. Despite the intervention of Texas Rangers led by Captain Leander McNelly, the so-called feud and the legal actions that followed lasted more than twenty years. In the end neither side could claim victory, and there were some who could not say why the conflict started in the first place.

▲ The patriarch of the Taylor family, Creed Taylor, a rugged Texas pioneer.

▶ Armed members of the Taylor clan at their Creed Taylor Spring home in Texas.

MAY 3

1904 Mulhall's Wild West Show opens on the grounds of the St. Louis Fair Association during the World's Fair Exposition.

OLD WEST EMPEROR

In a span of twenty years, Lucien Bonaparte Maxwell rose from a frontier trapper and scout to the largest individual property owner in the history of the United States when he acquired a 1,714,765-acre land grant in northeastern New Mexico Territory—more than three times the size of Rhode Island. When he first came west as a young man, Maxwell and his new friend Kit Carson signed on with John C. Frémont's 1841 surveying expeditions. Three years later in Taos, the shrewd Maxwell wed fifteen-year-old Luz Beaubien, one of the six daughters of Carlos Beaubien, a prominent landowner. Maxwell became involved with the management of the land grant and acquired land of his own. After his father-in-law died in 1864, Maxwell bought out other family members and partners and became the sole owner of what he named the Maxwell Land Grant. He built a huge adobe house, complete with a gambling room and dance hall, in the Santa Fe Trail town of Cimarron, a lively settlement that attracted cowboys, gamblers, ladies of questionable virtue, mountain men, and an abundance of outlaws. New Mexico's *Las Vegas Gazette* once reported: "Everything is quiet in Cimarron. Nobody has been killed in three days." Cimarron lost some of its spark in the 1880s when the Santa Fe Trail gave way to the railroad, but by then Maxwell was long gone. He had sold all his interests in 1870 for $750,000 and moved to the demilitarized Fort Sumner. He turned over his affairs to his son, Pete, and spent the profits from the land sale. Maxwell died in 1875, just fifty-six years old and penniless.

▲ Lucien Maxwell (seated left), friend of Kit Carson and heir to the huge Maxwell Land Grant in New Mexico.

▶ The town of Cimarron, with Maxwell's mansion in the center background.

1865 In the Buena Vista Valley of Nevada, Paiute Indians raid the Cunningham Ranch and make off with all the cattle and horses. On the following day, a posse from Unionville recovers ninety-four head of cattle, but never finds the stolen horses.

THE COLFAX COUNTY WAR

In the early 1870s, the syndicate that purchased the enormous Maxwell Land Grant in Colfax County, New Mexico Territory, served eviction notices on settlers, miners, and small ranchers with the full blessing of the powers-that-be in Santa Fe. When that had little effect, pastures were burned, cattle were stolen, public officials were threatened, and ranches were raided and pillaged. No one was safe. In September 1875, a Methodist preacher who spoke out against the landowners was found dead in a remote canyon with two bullets in his back. Yet both sides in what was called the Colfax County War were guilty of violent acts. In Cimarron, already known for lawlessness, the locals formed the Colfax County Ring and recruited Clay Allison, a psychotic self-described shootist, to lead vigilantes into battle against the gunslingers riding for the Santa Fe puppet-masters. Allison, a former Ku Klux Klan member with a clubfoot, was once described as "hell turned loose," especially if he had a snoot full of liquor. Before and after the Colfax County War, Allison built up a staggering record of violence. Besides numerous shootouts, Allison hosted a few necktie parties, including one where he decapitated the corpse and stuck the head on a pole in a Cimarron saloon. Following a meal in a Texas eatery, Allison shot a fellow diner and reportedly said, "I didn't want to send a man to hell on an empty stomach." Ironically, Allison's own end did not come by way of a gun or a noose. In 1887, while under the influence in Pecos, Texas, he fell from a freight wagon, struck his head on a wheel, and died within the hour.

▲ A young Clay Allison.

▶ A rare copy of a book about Clay Allison's life in the West.

CLAY ALLISON
OF
THE WASHITA

FIRST A COW MAN AND THEN AN EXTINGUISHER
OF BAD MEN

—

RECOLLECTIONS
OF
COLORADO, NEW MEXICO AND THE
TEXAS PANHANDLE

REMINISCENCES OF A '79ER

—

TO MY FRIENDS IN THE ENCHANTING EAST
TO *Mis Compadres* IN THE FASCINATING WEST

COMPLIMENTS OF
O. S. CLARK,
ATTICA, INDIANA.

MAY 5

1877 Sitting Bull leads his people into Canada, which he calls "Grandmother's Land" in a reference to Queen Victoria.

ORATOR OF THE PLAINS

Like many other warriors in the Kiowa tribe, Satanta—also known as White Bear—had a hatred for Texans, considering them to be a race apart from other white Americans. Although he signed the 1867 Medicine Lodge Treaty, he continued to lead war parties on white settlements. After his arrest by General William Tecumseh Sherman, Satanta was tried and sentenced to hang. Later he was granted a pardon and released. When he led yet another raid, he was sent to Fort Sill where, in 1878, rather than submit he took his own life by diving through a second-story window of the prison hospital.

"I do not want to settle down in the houses you would build for us. I love to roam over the wild prairie. There I am free and happy. . . . I have heard that you intend to settle us on a reservation near the mountains. When we settle down, we grow pale and die. A long time ago this land belonged to our fathers; but when I go up the river I see camps of soldiers on its banks. These soldiers cut down my timber; they kill my buffalo; and when I see that, my heart feels like bursting; I feel sorry."

—White Bear, Medicine Lodge Council, 1867

▶ Satanta with bow and arrow and his peace medal.

MAY 6

1877 Lakota Sioux warrior Crazy Horse and nine hundred followers, having been promised a reservation, surrender to officials at the Red Cloud Agency near Fort Robinson in Nebraska.

SITTING BEAR

Satank, or Sitting Bear, was a fearsome Kiowa medicine man and tribal leader who belonged to the Koitsenko (*Ko-eet-senko*), the most elite warrior society limited to only the ten bravest warriors of the tribe. He led many raids against other tribes as well as the white settlers and soldiers he first encountered in the 1840s. Like Satanta and other Kiowa warriors, Satank signed the Medicine Lodge Treaty in 1867, but kept up his warring ways. This was especially the case after his favorite son was killed in Texas in 1870. An inconsolable Satank rode to Texas, collected his son's bones, and carried them with him until his own death a year later. He was arrested for taking part in a series of massacres and raids, but as he was being taken to trial, Satank managed to tear away some flesh from his wrist and work his hand free of the shackles. As he sang his death song, he drew a knife hidden in his clothing and stabbed a guard. He grabbed the man's carbine and turned to defend himself, but was cut down by rifle fire from the other guards. He was left on the side of the road to die, and some Tonkawa scouts took his scalp. Eventually, his remains were buried at the Fort Sill cemetery where Santanta was later interred after his suicide.

▶ Kiowa chief Satank, or Sitting Bear.

"I don't look at Satank's picture after dark. He might come and roost on the bed post."

—one of the unknown soldiers who shot Satank

MAY 7

1929 Charles "Pretty Boy" Floyd, destined to become the FBI's most wanted fugitive, is released from custody in Kansas City, Kansas, after being held on a vagrancy charge.

WILD BILL'S LAST FIGHT

In April 1871, the folks in Abilene found a marshal to fill the boots of Tom "Bear River" Smith. The one-hundred-fifty-dollar-per-month salary went to a gunslinger with the reputation of a mankiller—Wild Bill Hickok. For the first six months on the job, Hickok hardly ever drew his pair of reliable Navy Colts. The real trouble came at the end of cattle season when Abilene was filled with drovers, anxious to part with some cash before making the long ride home. Most of them were Texans, including many who had fought for the Stars and Bars and had little respect for a Yankee lawman such as Hickok. On the evening of October 5, 1871, Marshal Hickok made his rounds, settling disputes between drunks and warning cowboys against carrying guns. When he responded to a gunshot outside the Alamo Saloon, Hickok encountered Phil Coe, a gambler and former saloon owner, celebrating with some fellow Texans. Coe and Hickok didn't exactly see eye-to-eye, most likely due to their mutual admiration for the same harlot. Coe, gun in hand, was miming a potshot he had taken at a dog, when suddenly he pulled a second gun and fired at Hickok. Both shots missed their mark, so Hickok quickly got off two shots of his own that struck Coe in the stomach. When Hickok heard someone rushing him from behind, he whirled and fired again, killing the former jailer—and his own good friend—Michael Williams. On December 13, the town council fired Hickok and his deputies. The double killing in Kansas was Hickok's last gunfight and ended his career as a lawman.

▶ Wild Bill Hickok.

▶▶ Wild Bill Hickok while city marshal of Abilene, Kansas.

1871 Wyatt Earp is indicted for horse stealing in Van Buren, Arkansas. Earp jumps bail and flees to Kansas.

A PREACHER'S SON

John Wesley Hardin—born in Texas and named after the founder of the faith by his Methodist preacher father—became one of the most prolific killers in the Old West. In 1868, he was fifteen years old when he killed his first man—a former slave whom Hardin claimed he shot in self-defense. He was charged with murder, went into hiding, and before the year was out had ambushed and killed three soldiers attempting to apprehend him. More killings followed and Hardin was wanted by the law, so in 1871 his relatives persuaded him to join a cattle drive headed to Kansas. Along the trail, Hardin reportedly added more victims to his growing tally before reaching Abilene in June 1871, where he befriended the town marshal—Wild Bill Hickok. While in Abilene, Hardin stayed at the American House Hotel, the scene of his most legendary murder. When the snoring of a guest in the next room kept Hardin awake, he supposedly fired two shots through the wall to quiet him. The first shot was high, but a second shot found its mark and silenced the snorer forever. "I believed," Hardin later wrote, "that if Wild Bill found me in a defenseless condition, he would take no explanation, but would kill me to add to his reputation." Hardin leaped from the second-story window to the street and made his escape back to Texas. He never set foot in Abilene again. Years later, Hardin claimed that the hotel shooting had been greatly exaggerated. "They tell lies about me," Hardin complained. "They say I killed six or seven men for snoring. Well, it ain't true. I only killed one man for snoring."

▲ A sketch depicting Hardin's hurried exit from his room in the American House Hotel in Abilene, Kansas. This drawing appeared in his book, published many years after the incident.

▶ A tintype of John Wesley Hardin taken in Abilene, Kansas, 1871.

MAY 9

1891 The Dalton Gang robs the Santa Fe train in Wharton, Indian Territory (now Perry, Oklahoma).

LITTLE PHIL

Considered merciless by both the soldiers in his command and the Indian warriors they fought, General Philip Henry Sheridan waged a total war that ultimately broke the will of the Plains tribes, forcing them onto government reservations. Like his fellow army generals in the Indian campaigns, Sheridan gained invaluable experience during the Civil War, where the diminutive officer (5'5") was nicknamed "Little Phil." Employing tactics he had successfully used against the Confederates, Sheridan called for surprise attacks on Plains Indians while they were in winter camps. Seemingly unconcerned about the probable high number of noncombatant casualties, Sheridan told his subordinates that "if a village is attacked and women and children killed, the responsibility is not with the soldiers but with the people whose crimes necessitated the attack." One of his first successes came when Lieutenant Colonel George Armstrong Custer massacred Black Kettle's sleeping Cheyenne village on the Washita River. After succeeding General William T. Sherman as commander of the Department of the Missouri, Sheridan organized and led a campaign in the Texas Panhandle that proved to be the largest action against the Kiowas, Comanches, and other Southern Plains tribes.

▲ General Philip Henry Sheridan.

▶ Generals of the Indian wars in conference. From left to right: Wesley Merritt, Philip Henry Sheridan, George Crook, James Forsyth, and George Armstrong Custer.

MAY 10

1869 At Promontory Summit, Utah, the Central Pacific and Union Pacific lines are joined to form the first transcontinental railroad in the United States.
1875 Judge Isaac Parker, known as the "Hanging Judge," opens his first term of court in Fort Smith, Arkansas.

RED RIVER WAR

During the summer of 1874, the U.S. Army conducted the Red River War, a series of as many as twenty running battles fought in the Texas Panhandle. General Philip Henry Sheridan, the architect of the war, bragged that it was "the most successful of any Indian campaign in this country since its settlement by the whites." The uprisings that led to the war stemmed from the U.S. Army's failure to enforce the provisions of the Medicine Lodge Treaty banning whites from entering Indian lands. Buffalo hunters wiped out herds on the reservations, and government-issued rations proved insufficient, placing the tribes in a desperate situation. One of Sheridan's rising stars in the conflict that followed was Colonel Ranald Slidell Mackenzie. In contrast to George Armstrong Custer, who finished dead last in his West Point class, Mackenzie earned top marks. But like Custer, Mackenzie briefly served as one of the "boy generals" during the Civil War. Due to his sterling war record, Mackenzie was given command of the Fourth Cavalry, the army outfit that fought in the Red River War's most epic battles. Mackenzie was opposed by the famed Comanche chief Quanah Parker, a son of war chief Peta Nocona and Cynthia Ann Parker, the celebrated white captive who raised the boy to respect his Indian heritage.

▶ Colonel Ranald S. Mackenzie.

▶▶ Comanche chief Quanah Parker.

MAY 11

1889 Near Cedar Springs, Arizona Territory, a U.S. Army paymaster wagon is attacked. This incident becomes known as the "Wham Robbery" after paymaster Major J. W. Wham.

SCOUTS OF THE PRAIRIE

"There's the man you're looking for." That's what Frank North, commander of the Pawnee scouts, said to Ned Buntline while pointing at William F. "Buffalo Bill" Cody. It was July 1869 at Fort McPherson, Nebraska, on the banks of the North Platte River. Buntline was on tour, delivering his temperance lectures and, as always, on the lookout for fodder for his dime novels. Although he did not invent the frontier hero's famous sobriquet, after that first encounter Buntline knocked out four books about Buffalo Bill, as well as a short story, "Buffalo Bill, the King of the Border Men," which was turned into a play. In 1872, Buntline was inspired to write the drama—supposedly in less than four hours and with some liquid inspiration—in his room at Chicago's Palmer House. He also convinced Cody to quit his post as scout for the Fifth Cavalry, and appear onstage in *The Scouts of the Prairie*, a melodrama in which Cody would play himself. Although Cody blew several lines and was terrified during his first few performances, he was an overnight success with proven marquee value.

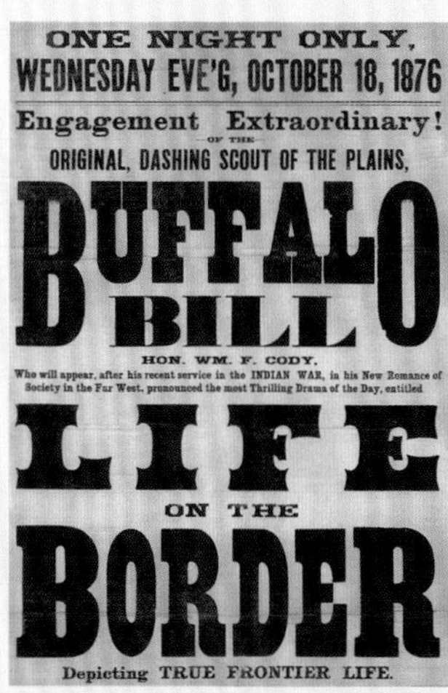

▲ A poster for one of Buffalo Bill's stage appearances.

▶ Ned Buntline dressed to appear onstage with Buffalo Bill.

MAY 12

1848 The California gold rush begins in earnest when newspaperman Sam Brannan runs through San Francisco waving bottled gold dust in the air and shouting, "Gold, gold, gold from the American River!"

TEXAS JACK OMOHUNDRO

In December 1872, *The Scouts of the Prairie* opened in Chicago, with Buffalo Bill Cody and Texas Jack Omohundro, Cody's pal and a legendary army scout, starring as themselves. Buntline also cast himself in the play and enticed a talented Italian actress, Giuseppina Morlacchi, to accept the role of the Indian maiden called Dove Eye. Buntline recruited a dozen tramps off the streets, dressed them in costumes, and splashed war paint on them to portray the "genuine Pawnee chiefs" promised in the advance billing. "Texas Jack," whose given name was John Burwell Omohundro, had served as a Confederate cavalry scout and after the war moved to Texas where he picked up his more colorful name. He found work as an army scout and became acquainted with Cody and Wild Bill Hickok. Without knowing it, Buntline invented the archetypal cowboy by casting Texas Jack, the first performer to ever use a lariat onstage. At the close of the first season of the play, Cody and Texas Jack, who eventually married his leading lady, broke their ties with Buntline and formed their own troupe, working together until 1875.

▲ A rare poster advertising Texas Jack's show.

▶ "Texas Jack" Omohundro, a genuine scout in the West, joined Buffalo Bill onstage and later had his own show.

MAY 13

1874 California outlaw Tiburcio Vásquez is discovered in his hideout in Alison Canyon, near present-day Hollywood. He surrenders after being wounded by George Beers, a former camel driver in the Army Camel Corps.

SCOUTS OF THE PLAINS

Following the success of Buntline's *Scouts of the Prairie*, Buffalo Bill and Texas Jack simply changed one word and renamed their drama for the 1873–74 season *Scouts of the Plains*. The big news, however, was the addition of another noted frontiersman to the cast—Wild Bill Hickok. Cody later related how they persuaded Hickok to join the show. "Thinking that Wild Bill would be quite an acquisition to the troupe, we wrote him at Springfield, Missouri, offering him a large salary if he would play with us that winter. He was doing nothing at the time, and we thought that he would like to take a trip through the States, as he had never been east. Wild Bill accepted our offer, and came on to New York, though he told us from the start that we could never make an actor out of him." Buffalo Bill should have listened. Instead of taking his role seriously, Hickok preferred to fire blank rounds near the legs of frightened extras. According to Cody, Hickok "had a fine stage appearance and was a handsome fellow, and possessed a good strong voice, yet when he went upon the stage before an audience, it was almost impossible for him to utter a word. He insisted that we were making a set of fools of ourselves, and that we were the laughing-stock of the people." In March 1874, Hickok had had enough and quit the show in Rochester, New York. As a parting gift, Cody and Omohundro each gave him five hundred dollars and a pair of .44 caliber revolvers. They bid him good-bye, and Hickok returned to where he was most comfortable—the West.

▲ A poster for Wild Bill's stage show.

▶ Wild Bill Hickok joined Buffalo Bill's stage show for a short time and had this handsome photograph taken in New York City.

MAY 14

1870 A Butterfield stagecoach arriving at the settlement of Kit Carson, Colorado, brings news of thirty killed by hostile Indians. Just the day before, the Indians had attacked a nearby Kansas Pacific construction crew, killing eleven, wounding nineteen, and driving off five hundred head of livestock.

ROUGHING IT

Published in 1872, Mark Twain's autobiographical novel and travelogue, *Roughing It*, followed his wanderings on the frontier during the years 1861–67. The book sold seventy-five thousand copies the first year of its publication and helped create a template for future writing about the American West. Readers became acquainted with the desperados, prospectors, stage drivers, lawmen, and vagabonds who populated the mining camps and boomtowns. Twain provided a vivid portrait of such memorable figures as Mormon leader Brigham Young and the dangerous Jack Slade in a work that was toasted as "wild, preposterous invention and sublime exaggeration."

"Fort Yuma is probably the hottest place on earth. The thermometer stays at one hundred and twenty in the shade there all the time—except when it varies and goes higher. It is a U.S. military post, and its occupants get so used to the terrific heat that they suffer without it. There is a tradition . . . that a very, very wicked soldier died there, once, and of course, went straight to the hottest corner of perdition—and the next day he telegraphed back for his blankets."

—Mark Twain, *Roughing It*

"The best known names in the Territory of Nevada were those belonging to these long-tailed heroes of the revolver. . . . They were brave, reckless men and traveled with their lives in their hands. To give them their due, they did their killing principally among themselves. . . . They killed each other on slight provocation, and hoped and expected to be killed themselves."

—Mark Twain, *Roughing It*

THE MINER'S DREAM.

▲ A sketch of a miner's dream in Mark Twain's *Roughing It*.

▶ The cover of Mark Twain's *Roughing It*, published in 1872.

ROUGHING IT

BY MARK TWAIN

A rollicking yet illuminating picture of the overland pioneer days when the frontiersmen were obliged to be humorists in order to survive the rigors and dangers of those rude times

MAY 15

1882 In Denver, Colorado, shootist Doc Holliday is arrested by a con man claiming to be an officer of the law.

1925 General Nelson A. Miles, famed Indian fighter, dies of a heart attack while attending a circus in Washington, D.C.

COW TOWNS

"I have been in a good many towns but Newton is the fastest one I have ever seen. Here you see young girls not over sixteen drinking whisky, smoking cigars, cursing and swearing until one almost looses [sic] the respect they should have for the weaker sex. I heard one of their townsmen say he didn't believe there were a dozen virtuous women in town. This speaks well for a town claiming 1,500 inhabitants. He further told me if I had any money that I would not be safe with it here. It is a common impression that they have a man every morning for breakfast."

—description of Newton, Kansas, *Wichita Tribune*, August 24, 1871

▲ Ellsworth, Kansas, a cow town at the end of the cattle trail from Texas.

▶ The Kansas cow town of Newton, 1872.

"Billy Brooks, marshal of Newton, formerly a stage driver between that point and Wichita, was shot three times on Sunday night last, in an attempt to arrest a couple of Texas men. As near as we can get at the facts, the Texans were on a spree, and, as a consequence, making it hot for pedestrians."

—*Wichita City Eagle*, June 14, 1872

"The coroner's inquest over the body of 'Happy Jack' decided that John Morco came to his death from the effects of two bullet wounds, discharged from a six-shooter in the hands of Charles Brown, a police officer of the city of Ellsworth, in self defence [sic], while in discharge of his duty, and was justified in the act."

—*Ellsworth Reporter*, September 11, 1873

Newton, Kans. 1872.
SALOON
A.F. HORNER STORAGE AND

MAY 16

1842 The first organized wagon train on the Oregon Trail departs Elm Grove, Missouri, for Oregon Territory.

MODOC WAR

The Modoc War, sometimes called the Lava Beds War, was the last of the Indian Wars in California and Oregon. The conflict began in 1852 when Modoc warriors attacked a wagon train and killed sixty-five white settlers. In retaliation, forty-one Modocs were slaughtered at a peace parley, and hostilities continued until 1864 when a treaty was signed. It stipulated that the Modocs give up their lands to white newcomers and move to the Klamath reservation in Oregon. Unwilling to live with the Klamaths, their traditional enemies, the Modocs fled the reservation twice before an inevitable final confrontation in 1870. Led by Keintpoos, or Captain Jack as the white soldiers called him, a band of resolute Modocs established a stronghold in the vast lava beds of their homeland. Fighting between the Modocs and army troopers took many lives, and weeks of negotiations followed. During one of the peace commission meetings, other Modocs convinced Captain Jack that if the white leaders were dead the soldiers would retreat. On Good Friday, April 11, 1873, Captain Jack and his warriors murdered General Edward R. S. Canby and other negotiators, the only instance that an army general died in the Indian Wars. But instead of leaving, the army laid siege to the Modoc stronghold. Indian-fighter Donald McKay, son of a white fur trader and a Cayuse Indian mother, played a key role in scouting for the U.S. Army. One by one, Captain Jack's followers surrendered, and finally he gave himself up. Captain Jack and several other Modocs were tried for murder, found guilty, and hanged on October 3, 1873.

▶ Captain Jack, who led the Modoc Indians in the Lava Beds War.

▶▶ Pa-Ka-We-Na, "The Mighty Hunter," otherwise known as Donald McKay, the noted scout of the Modoc War.

MAY 17

1867 In the midst of a scurvy epidemic at his camp near Fort Hays, Kansas, Lieutenant Colonel George Armstrong Custer humiliates several troops by shaving half of their heads and marching them around the camp. This punishment was for their leaving the camp to buy canned fruit, despite not missing any duties or roll calls and returning within forty-five minutes.

COLT PEACEMAKER

Prior to the Mexican War, the national murder weapons of choice had been the knife or bludgeon. However, Samuel Colt's handgun changed all that. By the end of the Civil War, largely owing to the huge surplus of firearms and the technological improvements that made them cheaper and easier to use, guns became the most common killing device in America. The weapon that became the symbol of American individuality in the West was not the rifle, but the pistol. On the 1870s frontier, the six-shooter figured prominently in some of the more lasting myths of the Old West. In reality, most people chose a rifle, carbine, or shotgun for hunting or personal defense. Long guns were more accurate at great distances and easier to control than the six-shooter, which was more effective at close range. The steady rise of the gun culture, or six-shooter mystique, throughout the West coined catchy expressions, such as "There's more law in a Colt six gun than in all the law books." Carried by lawmakers and lawbreakers alike, the six-shooter became known as "Judge Colt and his jury of six," "the gun that won the West," and "the great equalizer." Colt's revolver turned out to be the most popular handgun for both the military and civilians in the West with one of the favored models being the 1873 Single Action Army, ironically dubbed the "Peacemaker." This is arguably the most famous firearm ever made and certainly one of those mythologized in the annals of Western history.

▶ Scout "White Eye" Anderson, left, with his Colt Peacemaker.

▶▶ An unidentified cowboy proudly displaying his Peacemaker.

MAY 18

1871 Chief Owl Prophet decides not to attack a lightly guarded army ambulance as it crosses the Salt Creek Prairie in Texas, opting instead to wait for an approaching wagon train. Unbeknownst to Owl Prophet, Commanding General William T. Sherman was on board the ambulance.

DEVIL'S ROPE

When barbed wire first appeared in the 1870s, it was often called "devil's rope," a derogatory name used by religious groups and others concerned that the sharp steel barbs cut and injured too many cattle, horses, and men. Drovers and cattlemen cursed barbed wire because they hated seeing the wide-open ranges fenced. The wire boundaries were restrictive and made cowboys feel more like dirt farmers than range riders. Barbed-wire fences prevented cowboys and their herds from entering open grazing pastures and getting to water, forcing herders to spend more time on foot opening gates, and a frequent saying around cow camps was that a man on foot was no man at all. Patented in 1874 by Illinois farmer Joseph Glidden, barbed wire made large-scale farming possible but closed the open range. Along with windmills and trains, the advent of barbed wire was responsible for the taming of the West. Throughout the late 1800s, trail riders liked to sing this catchy ditty:

They say that heaven is a free range land,
Good-bye, Good-bye, O fare you well;
But it's barbed wire fence for the devil's hatband
And barbed wire blankets down in hell.

▲ A Western novel cover illustration in which a cowboy fires his gun at the hated barbed wire.

▶ Masked fence-cutters at work.

MAY 19

1894 A shotgun messenger kills a lone bandit near Angel's Camp, California. Reportedly, this is the last stage robber killed in California.

THE HORRELL WAR

An episode of frontier violence, the Horrell War broke out in 1873. The conflict began when the five felonious Horrell brothers and a pack of their renegade followers fled a series of cold-blooded murders in their home state of Texas and sought refuge in Lincoln County, New Mexico Territory. Almost immediately after the Horrell Gang's arrival, the inherent animosity and tension between the racist Texans and the local Hispanic community turned to bloodshed. The result was an all-out race war, in which the Horrells seemed bent on ruthlessly exterminating any "greasers," their derogatory name for Hispanics, who got in their way. On December 20, 1873, the Horrell Gang rode into the town of Lincoln with guns blazing and broke into a wedding celebration in an old dance hall. Four citizens were shot and killed, and two others wounded. Among the victims was Isidro Patron, the father of Lincoln County clerk Juan Patron, who fled to Santa Fe to seek help from Territorial Governor Marsh Giddings. The slaughter of the wedding guests led to more acts of revenge and terror. The rampaging Texans even shot and killed an Anglo deputy sheriff in front of his home simply because he had a Mexican wife. Nervous locals formed a vigilante committee. A plea for help even reached President Ulysses S. Grant, but no federal intervention came. As the conflict intensified, many of the local Anglos soured on the Horrells. By the end of 1874, the troublesome clan and their followers had returned to Texas, but in their wake, they left a pattern of armed violence and discord that would persist in the county for years.

▶ Lincoln, New Mexico, a one-street town with a violent history set in a beautiful mountain valley, mid-1880s.

MAY 20

1862 President Abraham Lincoln signs the Homestead Act into law.
1864 In Denver, Colorado Territory, Cherry Creek floods, destroying much of the town and leaving twenty dead.

HENRY MCCARTY

Born in 1859 to an Irish famine widow in New York City, Henry McCarty was the given name of a legendary figure forever known as Billy the Kid. But McCarty's true life, as nomadic as a wandering tumbleweed, began in New Mexico Territory. It was in the ancient city of Santa Fe that the first indisputable documentation of Henry McCarty was recorded. The precise date was March 1, 1873, when, after eight years of courtship and frequent cohabitation, William H. Antrim and Henry's mother Catherine McCarty at last wed. The simple ceremony took place in the First Presbyterian Church with the Reverend David F. McFarland officiating. Among the five official witnesses were Catherine's two sons—Joseph, or Josie, and his brother, Henry. Catherine had moved her family west after a Wichita doctor diagnosed her with tuberculosis and advised her to relocate to a warmer and drier climate. She and Antrim packed up the boys and first moved to Denver for a short time and then came to New Mexico Territory. After only about two months in Santa Fe, the family moved south to Silver City, thought to be an ideal high desert haven for the ailing Catherine, in the foothills of the Pinos Altos Mountains. Antrim, an itinerant miner, also had heard about recent silver strikes and was anxious to try his hand in the mines. When they departed Santa Fe, both Henry and his brother had dropped the name McCarty and assumed the surname of the man who married their mother. It would not be young Henry Antrim's last name change.

▲ San Francisco Street in Santa Fe, mid-1870s, around the time of the arrival of the young boy who would become known as "Billy the Kid."

▶ The Santa Fe, New Mexico, Presbyterian church, where young Henry McCarty's mother married William Antrim.

MAY 21

1856 A posse of one thousand proslavery Southerners surrounds the antislavery settlement of Lawrence, Kansas, and raids the downtown district. Newspaper offices, the Free-State Hotel, and several other businesses are destroyed. One man is killed by a stone falling from the burning hotel.

RANGERS RIDE AGAIN

Although a regiment of Rangers offered some protection on the Texas frontier during the Civil War, most of the Rangers were part of the Confederate army and did what they could to scout for Indians, deserters, and Yankee sympathizers. After the war, the legislature authorized new companies of Texas Rangers, but the funding measure failed. During much of the Reconstruction era, a highly controversial and unpopular state police force, including former slaves, handled Texas law enforcement. That federally controlled force was disbanded in 1873. The next year, however, seventy-five thousand dollars was appropriated to organize six companies of seventy-five Rangers each. This allowed newly elected Governor Richard Coke and state lawmakers to recommission the Rangers, ushering in a new era for the relentless force of men still called "Los Diablos Tejanos" by many Hispanics.

▶ A Texas Ranger by the name of Jenkins. He was sometimes called "Buffalo Bill," though of no relation to the more-famous William F. "Buffalo Bill" Cody.

▶▶ Two young Texas Rangers, early 1870s.

MAY 22

1868 The Reno Gang hits the northbound Jefferson, Madison, and Indianapolis train at Marshfield south of Seymour, Indiana, swiping approximately $96,000 in government bonds.

BUCKING THE TIGER

By the early 1870s, the droves of miners and settlers attracted to the New Mexico Territory boomtown of Silver City kept three shifts of bartenders busy round-the-clock quenching the thirst of patrons of saloons such as the Blue Goose and the Red Onion, or the more elegant Orleans Club opened by Joseph Dyer on Main Street. Dyer, who called himself "the eminent mixologist," bragged that his establishment was the ideal haunt for "all those who hanker after the good things of this life . . . and that the belligerent portion of the community can find a particularly rampant specimen of the Feline species, usually denominated the 'TIGER,' ready to engage them at all times." Greenhorns, unschooled in the gambling arts, may have thought the "TIGER" of Dyer's newspaper advertisement was a blatant tribute to the female companions provided for high rollers, but that was not so. It was actually a reference to faro—a popular card game in the nineteenth-century West that derived its name from the Egyptian pharaohs depicted on the cards. The game was also known as Tiger because an image of a Bengal tiger was painted on the dealer's faro box. Those playing this game of chance were said to "buck" or "twist the tiger." In the mining town of Leadville, Colorado, faro was the main draw at most of the one hundred gambling dens along State Street, which led to its nickname of Tiger Alley.

▶ This painting, modeled from an actual photograph, was titled "Bucking the Tiger" and used as a whiskey ad.

Bucking the Tiger
Cyrus Noble
old goods
$25 AND $50 FOR
$100 CHANGE IN
CYRUS NOBLE WHISKEY

1868 Kit Carson dies of an abdominal hemorrhage at Fort Lyon, Colorado Territory.

WES HARDIN'S BIRTHDAY PARTY

Mankiller John Wesley Hardin already boasted a staggering body count by the time he turned twenty-one on May 26, 1874. He marked the occasion in Comanche, Texas, where on that day his trio of fine racehorses all came up winners, earning young Hardin three thousand dollars in cash, a small herd of cattle, a wagon, and more than a dozen saddle broncs. That evening, Hardin, who preferred whiskey to cake, continued the celebration by making the rounds of Comanche's many saloons. When he reached Jack Wright's establishment, however, there was trouble. Soon after Hardin ordered a drink, Deputy Sheriff Charles Webb from nearby Brown County strolled through the swinging door. Webb had previously expressed his intention to bring Hardin down for all of his killings and other transgressions. At first, it appeared that nothing was amiss as the two men moved toward the bar to have a friendly swig, but then Webb suddenly went for his gun. Hardin, quick as a cat, wheeled and fired at the same time, shooting Webb in the face. As he fell mortally wounded, some of Hardin's pals shot Webb twice more to make sure he would not be getting back up. Webb's bullet only grazed Hardin who had to leave his birthday winnings behind and beat a hasty retreat from a mob outraged at the killing of a lawman. Hardin's brother and two cousins were lynched as a result of the shootout, and Hardin became a fugitive, escaping to Florida with a four-thousand-dollar bounty on his head.

▲ A tintype of John Wesley Hardin at about the age of eighteen.

▶ A sketch from Hardin's autobiography, published in 1896.

BLACKSMITH SHOP
DRY GOODS
CIRCUS

MAY 24

1856 In retaliation for the Lawrence raid three days earlier, John Brown, a radical abolitionist, leads a nighttime attack on a proslavery settlement along Pottawatomie Creek in Kansas, killing five men.

ADOBE WALLS

In 1874, a shootout at a buffalo hunter's camp in the Texas Panhandle occurred that came to be known as the Second Battle of Adobe Walls. On November 26 ten years earlier, Christopher "Kit" Carson and a party of mounted soldiers and friendly Indian scouts found cover there while fighting Kiowa warriors. After that scuffle, the ruins of the old adobe fort remained deserted until March 1874, when some Dodge City merchants arrived. They established a trading post to cater to the growing number of buffalo hunters who had decimated the herds in Kansas and were moving southward where buffalo were still plentiful. This further encroachment on Indian hunting grounds led to the Second Battle of Adobe Walls on June 27, 1874, when an alliance of various Plains tribes led by Comanche chief Quanah Parker assaulted the settlement. At the time, there were only twenty-eight hunters and one woman inside the compound. Yet despite being greatly outnumbered, the white defenders withstood the attack and the siege that followed thanks to their superior firepower. Many Indian warriors were killed or wounded, but only four white men died, including one who accidentally shot himself. Two of the defenders were the still-unknown Bat Masterson and a sharpshooter named Billy Dixon. On the third day of the siege, fame would catch up with Dixon when he supposedly killed an Indian with a shot from his Sharps rifle fired from almost a mile away. Dixon always said the feat was greatly exaggerated and that the distance was "not far from three-fourths of a mile." A rescue party arrived after a few days, but by then the Indian force had dispersed.

▲▲ Wild Horse, one of the Comanche chiefs in the Second Battle of Adobe Walls.

▲ Bat Masterson participated in the battle in 1874, having come to Texas to hunt buffalo.

▶ A sketch of the Second Battle of Adobe Walls from the cover of Billy Dixon's book.

1881 In Galeyville, Arizona Territory, a drunken William "Curly Bill" Brocious is shot by a cowboy cohort after an argument. The bullet passes through his neck and out his cheek, but he survives the attack.

BUFFALO WALLOW FIGHT

Plainsman Billy Dixon, the crack long shot said to have picked off an Indian at just under a mile at Adobe Walls, quit hide hunting after that battle and signed on as an army scout for Colonel Nelson A. Miles. On September 12, 1874, Dixon departed Miles's Texas headquarters along with fellow scout Amos Chapman and four cavalry troopers carrying dispatches to Camp Supply in Indian Territory. Two days later, as they neared the south bank of the Washita River, they were surrounded by a combined band of at least 125 hostile Kiowas and Comanches. Seeing no immediate cover, Dixon and the others dismounted and began a desperate fight for their lives. One soldier was killed immediately, and the horses ran off carrying all their supplies and canteens. Dixon, slightly wounded, managed to get the others to the cover of a wallow, a depression in the ground created when buffalo roll in the dust. Lying in the wallow and taking deadly aim, they kept the Indians at bay. Eventually all six of the survivors were wounded. A cold rainstorm quenched the besieged men's thirst and then almost drowned them when the wallow filled with water. At nightfall the Indians disappeared, and soon a relief column of U.S. Cavalry came to the rescue of the beleaguered men. For his bravery, Dixon and all the others were presented with the Medal of Honor. Dixon's and Chapman's medals were later revoked because they were civilian scouts, but Dixon refused to surrender what he felt he had justly earned. He kept it close to him for the rest of his life.

▲ Billy Dixon, a buffalo hunter who fought in the Second Battle of Adobe Walls, would later face the Comanches again in what became known as the Buffalo Wallow Fight.

▶ A western Kansas buffalo wallow, similar to the one used by Billy Dixon.

MAY **26**

1874 Gunfighter John Wesley Hardin engages in a shootout with Deputy Sheriff Charles Webb on his twenty-first birthday in Comanche County, Texas. Hardin, Jim Taylor, and Bill Dixon escape.

BLACK HILLS GOLD

"The expedition of General Custer, which entered the Black Hills proper—those of Dakota—in 1874, confirmed the reports of gold finds, and thereafter a wall of fire, not to mention a wall of Indians, could not stop the encroachments of that terrible white race . . . every man who lacked fortune, and who would rather be scalped than remain poor, saw in the mission of the Black Hills, El Dorado."

—John F. Finnerty, 1890

"In the main, the Indians adhered to the conditions of the treaty, but unfortunately the government could not, or did not, comply with its part of the compact. Between the years 1869–75 the pressure of advancing civilization was great upon all sides. The hunters, prospectors, miners, and settlers were trespassing upon the lands granted to the Indians."

—General Nelson A. Miles, 1896

"Are the Indians entitled to the Black Hills, and to defend their possession by war and bloodshed if necessary? Certainly not! The government of the United States has the power to make an ass of itself at any time, but it has neither the right nor the power to transform the American people into asses forever."

—Edwin A. Curley, *Guide to the Black Hills*, 1877

▲▲ A poster advertising stage travel to reach the goldfields of the Black Hills.

▲ A Black Hills prospector guarding his mine and camp.

▶ A drawing illustrating the exciting rush to the Black Hills.

STAGE LINE TO

MAY 27

1831 Trapper Jedediah Smith is mortally wounded by a war party of Comanches near the Cimarron River in what is now southwest Kansas. Although he lay dying, Smith managed to kill the war party's chief with his last shot.

DEADWOOD

"I have had leisure today to view the town, or as much thereof as the mud will permit. And writing of mud, you people that are back in the states that are prone to growl at your commissioners and officials generally, should you chance to discover a layer or two of filth upon the streets, you would be speechless could you stand upon one of Deadwood's boulevards. . . . Stages come in loaded down, and report hundreds of pilgrims en route on foot and in private vehicles. Every hotel and boarding house is constantly crowded to the utmost, and nightly turn away scores of applicants for accommodations. . . . A single game of poker drew into sight $1,200 in dust last evening, and continued until nine this morning. In the same room several faro games and other devices for gambling purposes were surrounded with apparently happy crowds. They bet, win, and lose with the utmost nonchalance."

—*Chicago Times*, "Deadwood in the Spring of 1877"

▶ The mining boomtown of Deadwood in the Black Hills of Dakota Territory.

ROATH
Herrmann & Treber.
SALE LIQUOR DEALERS
St Louis Lager Beer
DENTIST
BANK
STEBBINS, POST & CO.
JOB PRINTING
RED BIRD
WYOMING STORE
SHINGLE

MAY 28

1830 President Andrew Jackson signs the Indian Removal Act, marking the beginning of the decline of southeastern native culture and the forced migration of thousands of Indians.
1916 Iron Tail, a Lakota Sioux who fought with Sitting Bull at the Battle of Little Bighorn, dies in Fort Wayne, Indiana.

THE FRONTIER BATTALION

By 1874, the reestablished Texas Rangers had divided into two commands—the Special Forces under Captain Leander McNelly and the Frontier Battalion led by Major John B. Jones. The Special Forces were sent to the Mexican border to pursue cattle thieves and bandits and deal with white vigilantes committing outrages against the innocent Hispanic citizens of Texas. Meanwhile, the Frontier Battalion stayed on the move from the Big Bend country to deep in the heart of the state. Company D, the most high-profile of the half-dozen companies under Major Jones's command, had the distinction of losing more Rangers than any other outfit during the twenty-five-year lifespan of the Frontier Battalion. At a time when the racial divide was vast, the whites-only Rangers clashed with the Buffalo Soldiers, black troopers posted throughout West Texas. There also were allegations that the Company D boys tended to kill any armed Indian they encountered, including the "friendlies." Still, they fought a large number of "hostiles," especially Comanches and Kiowas. One such action was described thus in the 1874 *Austin Daily Statesman*: "The boys brought some fresh scalps with them and they report that Scott Cooley, who was fired at and run into camp, not only cut a wounded Indian's throat, but stripped a large piece of skin from his back, saying he would make a quirt out of it." Not long after Cooley collected these bloody souvenirs, he quit Company D and turned outlaw. For two years, his Rangers friends reluctantly chased him until Cooley died of brain fever in 1876.

▲ Company F of the Texas Ranger Frontier Battalion.

▶ Company D of the Texas Ranger Frontier Battalion in camp during a scouting mission.

MAY 29

1848 *The Californian* announces that it must suspend publication because of staff leaving to search for gold: "The whole country from San Francisco to Los Angeles, and from the seashore to the base of the Sierra Nevadas, resounds with the sordid cry of gold, GOLD, GOLD!, while the field is left half planted, the house half built, and everything neglected but the manufacture of shovels and pickaxes."

KENO CORNER

During the 1870s, Wichita, Kansas, was a rough-and-tumble place surrounded by a sea of grass that had long been the domain of Indians, buffalo hunters, and fur traders. It was not a milieu for the faint of heart. High crimes and misdemeanors were commonplace, particularly at the intersection of Main and Douglas. Better known as Keno Corner, after the popular game of chance, this locale became known as the wildest spot in Wichita. Here, large numbers of Texas drovers taking a break from the rigors of the cattle trail congregated to gamble, carouse, and swill hard liquor from sunrise to midnight. To attract customers to the gambling dens, a brass band on a two-story platform serenaded visitors. However, the music did little to soothe, as chaos and violence inevitably erupted.

"The streets clanged with the noisy spurs of Texas cow boys [sic] and Mexican ranchmen, while the crowds that marched along the resounding sidewalks, were as motley as could be seen at any one spot in America. Texan sombreros and leather leggings; brigandish-looking velvet jackets, with bright buttons, close together, of the Mexicans, buckskin garments of the frontiersmen, and the highly-colored blanket; representatives from a half dozen different tribes of Indians, were familiar sights on the streets."

—William G. Cutler, 1882

▲ Wyatt Earp first became a Kansas lawman in Wichita, before moving on to Dodge City.

▶ Wichita, Kansas, one of the more prosperous cow towns.

YORK STORE.

MAY

30

1899 Pearl Hart and her lover Joe Boot hold up the Benson-Globe stagecoach in Arizona Territory and get away with $431.

WE NEVER SLEEP

By the mid-1870s, desperate Midwestern bankers had grown weary of Jesse James and his gang's antics. They hired Allan Pinkerton, the detective dubbed "The Eye" by the criminals he tracked, to take care of the James problem. A Scottish immigrant who had come to the United States as a young man to avoid arrest for his political activities, Pinkerton worked his way up through the police ranks and became a favorite of Abraham Lincoln when he uncovered a plot to assassinate the president. During the Civil War, Pinkerton headed the Secret Service and gathered intelligence for the Union. In the years following the war, he gained a name as a henchman for big-business interest when he helped to break up mining strikes in Pennsylvania. He was a scourge of labor unions, and the methods used by his men were ethically questionable. Pinkerton was as relentless as a terrier, and so were those who served under him, including his two sons, Robert and William. The motto of their agency said it all: "We Never Sleep." The Pinkertons and their small army of crack detectives, despised by the stalwart former Confederates of the border states, were determined to snare James, break up his gang, and shatter the outlaw's myth of invincibility.

▶ Allan Pinkerton.

▶▶ The sons of Allan Pinkerton—Robert (left) and William (right)—in the field.

▼ The famous logo of the Pinkerton National Detective Agency, which was the origin of the term "private eye."

STILL

1867 At Bluff Ranch, Kansas, the Thirty-seventh Infantry clashes with Indians, and two enlisted men lose their lives.

JAMES FARM BOMBING

From the very start, the Pinkerton agents assigned to track the James brothers found the going difficult. Residents of Clay County, Missouri, sided with Frank and Jesse, offering them protection from the snooping detectives. Those citizens who did not sympathize with the outlaws remained quiet out of fear. At least three Pinkertons were murdered during the course of the investigation. Finally, in 1875, a group of special agents and some local constables surrounded the Jameses' family homestead under cover of darkness. They were convinced Jesse was inside. Two illumination devices were tossed through a window of the farmhouse. One of the flares exploded and showered the room with iron shrapnel. Neither Jesse nor Frank was present, but other family members were there. Zerelda Samuel, the James boys' mother, had her right arm shattered so badly that it had to be amputated at the elbow. Flying shrapnel killed Jesse's nine-year-old half-brother, Archie Samuel. Press coverage was immediate and overwhelmingly in support of the James family. The Pinkertons were denounced and lambasted. There were heated political debates and investigations into the incident. A grand jury indicted several men for murder. More cries for amnesty for the James brothers followed. So did bank and train robberies in Missouri, Kentucky, and Iowa.

▲ The James homestead many years after it was bombed by the Pinkertons.

▶ Frank and Jesse James's mother, Zerelda Samuel. The sleeve of her dress hides the amputated lower right arm, lost due to injuries sustained in the bombing.

JUN 1

1892 The Dalton Gang robs the Santa Fe Railroad at Red Rock Station, Oklahoma Territory.

SHARPSHOOTERS

After the Civil War ended, thousands of survivors from both sides—trained to kill and hardened by the acts of cruelty they had witnessed or committed—came home with their guns along with their nightmares. Some soldiers were permitted to keep their firearms; others held on to them illegally. Homicide and suicide rates soared, and the rise in felonies was blamed on the war. Many veterans headed west to find gainful employment and explore new opportunities. A number of these men, especially those who had served in sharpshooter companies and were already proficient with the Sharps rifle, were hired as professional hunters on the buffalo-killing fields of the Great Plains. The Sharps was the ideal buffalo gun. Weighing almost sixteen pounds with a thirty-inch octagonal barrel, the rifle absorbed much of its recoil. A Sharps "Big 50," or 50-caliber, could kill at half a mile and was very accurate at a range of five hundred yards or less. Hunters particularly liked the weapons that had been converted to cartridge-fire guns. In no time, hunters were shooting down hundreds of buffalo a day from long distances, prompting the saying that the Sharps Big 50 was "the gun that shoots today and kills tomorrow." Wolf and coyote populations soared as they feasted on the thousands of carcasses that littered the plains and prairies.

▶ A woman poses with a large-caliber, heavy, octagonal-barrel Sharps rifle in Tombstone, Arizona.

▶▶ A hunter with his Sharps rifle.

JUN 2

1875 Quanah Parker leads the Comanche Indians onto their new reservation in Indian Territory (now Oklahoma).
1899 The Wild Bunch robs the United Pacific's Overland Flyer at Wilcox, Wyoming.

THE HANGING JUDGE

For many years, a common saying about Indian Territory was: "There is no God west of St. Louis and no law west of Fort Smith." No God, perhaps, but finally a judge did come. For twenty-one years, from 1875 to 1896, Isaac C. Parker, a stern Methodist from St. Joseph, Missouri, served as federal judge of the Western District of Arkansas. He represented the law west of Fort Smith and held exclusive jurisdiction over the sixty thousand people and almost seventy-five thousand square miles of Indian Territory. Parker was just thirty-six years old in 1875 when he arrived in Fort Smith, wielding his gavel and dispensing justice. For openers, he rounded up more than two hundred marshals armed only with tin badges, Colts, and courage. These deputy U.S. marshals rode out through a territory roughly the size of New England in search of the worst of the killers and robbers. Any culprits caught operating in Indian Territory and the surrounding states were hauled back to Parker's dungeons and courtroom at Fort Smith, which became known as "Hell on the Border." During the years he served on the bench at Fort Smith, Judge Parker heard 13,500 cases. More than nine thousand defendants pleaded guilty or were convicted. But despite the best efforts of "Hanging Judge" Parker and his hired gunmen, frontier life remained dangerous.

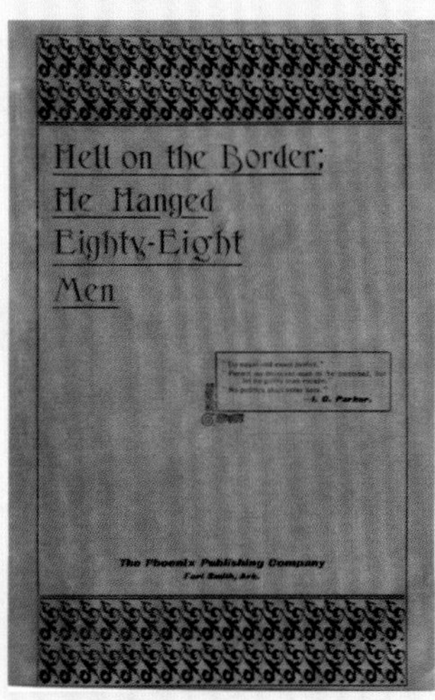

▲ *Hell on the Border*, published in 1898, presented most of the facts, and much of the fiction, surrounding "Hanging Judge" Parker's court.

▶ Judge Isaac C. Parker.

JUN 3

1833 The territories west of Missouri are officially named Indian Country.

THE MEN WHO RODE FOR PARKER

The two hundred deputy marshals Judge Isaac C. Parker appointed to ride herd over Indian Territory had their work cut out for them each time they crossed the Arkansas River with arrest warrants. "Bring them in alive or dead," was the standing order, but the officers usually tried to return with live prisoners in order to collect the mileage expenses and fees due them. Deputies received a flat payment of two dollars a head for every criminal brought in alive. They also depended on rewards offered for the most sought-after felons. Not all those who rode for Parker were angels. Several had been outlaws themselves or would later resort to a life of crime. Parker was obliged to swallow hard and permit some rascals to represent him in the field. All that mattered to the judge was that his men were tough and stood their ground. Parker could not abide a coward. At least one-third of Parker's total force of lawmen died in the line of duty. One of the many killed was Frank Dalton, a highly respected deputy who served Parker for three years until whiskey runners killed him in 1887. After his passing, Frank's younger brothers Grat and Bob Dalton became deputy U.S. marshals for the federal courts in Fort Smith and Wichita. Emmett Dalton, the youngest of the boys, often rode in their posse just a few years before the band of brothers switched sides and formed an outlaw gang. Other courageous deputies who took the oath to serve Parker and his court included Paden Tolbert, Zeke Proctor, David Rusk, Willard Ayers, and Dave Layman. Along with such top guns as Bass Reeves and Heck Thomas, these overworked and underpaid lawmen were collectively known as "The Men Who Rode for Parker."

▲ Heck Thomas (seated left) was one of the most effective of the deputies who rode for Parker.

▶ A deputy marshal "Oath of Office" instating Paden Tolbert, who later led the officers who killed the Cherokee outlaw Ned Christie. This document is signed by Judge Parker.

OATH OF OFFICE.

I, Paden Tolbert, do solemnly swear that I will faithfully execute all lawful precepts, directed to the Marshal of the United States for the Western District of Arkansas, under the authority of the United States, and true returns make and in all things well and truly, and without malice or partiality, perform the duties of Deputy Marshal of the Western District of Arkansas during my continuance in said office, and take only my lawful fees, so help me God.

Paden Tolbert [S. S.]

Sworn to and subscribed before me this 2nd day of Jan 1895

I. C. Parker

Judge U S Dist Court ~~Clerk.~~
West Dist Ark

JUN 4

1870 After being sworn in as marshal of Abilene, Kansas, Tom "Bear River" Smith drops "Big Hank" with his bare hands. The next day, he does the same to "Wyoming Frank."

GATES OF HELL

"Hanging Judge" Isaac C. Parker sentenced a total of 160 criminals to die on the gallows, dubbed the "Gates of Hell." This was the domain of Parker's dour executioner, George Maledon. After Parker declared, "I sentence you to be hanged by the neck until dead," the condemned would be fitted for a "necktie" by Maledon, known far and wide as the "Prince of Hangmen." Many of them were pardoned, had their sentence commuted, or else "beat the hangman" by dying in prison before the ultimate sentence could be carried out. Some attempted to escape and were shot down by Maledon, who was as skilled with a rifle as he was with a noose. Of the seventy-nine criminals who were actually hanged, sixty of them swung at the end of one of Maledon's handwoven hemp ropes. Maledon took great pride in his work. His deep-set eyes and long whiskers became a familiar sight on the streets of Fort Smith, where he usually carried a basket that contained one of his prized ropes, each one oil-soaked to prevent the hangman's knot, with its thirteen wraps, from slipping. This ensured a quick death for the black-hooded convicts. When he finally retired as a hangman in 1894, Maledon toured country towns and cities with one of his treasured ropes and lectured about the lives and consequent deaths of the culprits he had executed. "I never hanged a man who came back to have the job done over," Maledon often quipped. "The ghosts of men hanged at Fort Smith never hang around the gibbet."

▲ George Maledon, Judge Parker's hangman.

▶ Maledon displaying his handwoven hemp ropes and photos of those he hanged.

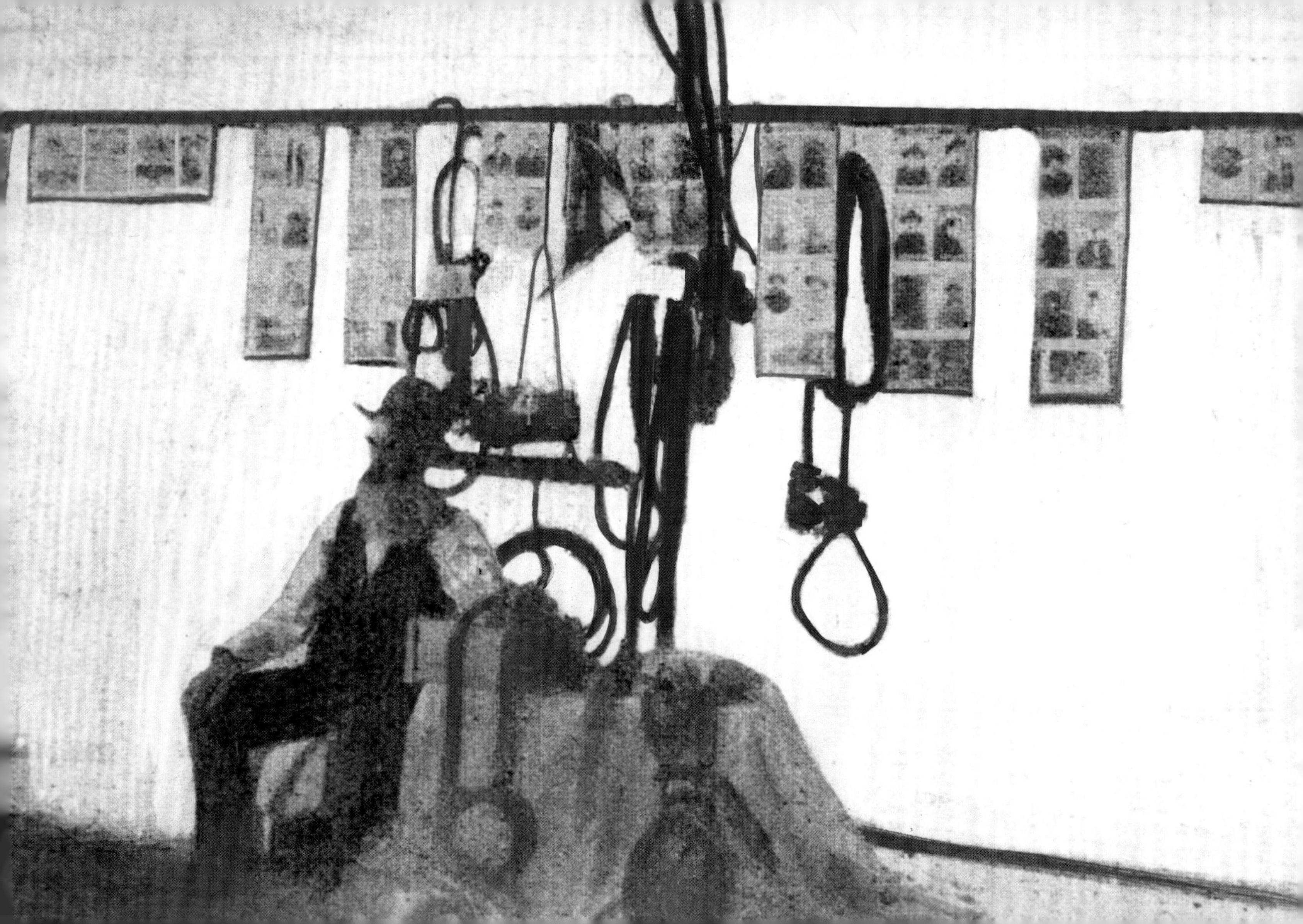

JUN 5

1883 Wyatt Earp, Bat Masterson, Charlie Bassett, and several others pose for the famous "Peace Commission" photo in Dodge City, Kansas.

INDIAN TERRITORY

In the years just after the Civil War, the thieves, killers, rapists, and robbers who found refuge in Indian Territory regularly made raids on trains, banks, stagecoaches, and even homesteads in neighboring states. Horses and cattle stolen from Texas ranches and hogs and cows snatched off Missouri farms were driven into Indian Territory and sold to unscrupulous livestock dealers who never questioned bogus bills-of-sale or improper brand registrations. Many renegades and outcasts found sanctuary there and made the territory their stomping ground. Their main occupation was staying alive, but there was also time to nurse wounds, divide loot, and plan future wrongdoing. It was a criminal's paradise and a legal and jurisdictional nightmare. One newspaper said that Indian Territory was "the rendezvous of the vile and wicked from everywhere." Law-abiding Indian Territory citizens were not immune to the outrages. Neither the companies of Indian light-horsemen guarding the borders nor the Chickasaw and Choctaw vigilantes could quell the rising tide of lawbreakers who flocked to hideouts in the Indian Nations. Tribal courts took no notice of horse thieves, prostitutes, whiskey peddlers, and bushwhackers pouring into lands where there were no courts for whites. Many of the very few peace officers in the territory had once been outlaws. A very thin line separated good and evil. Indian Territory became known as the consummate robber's roost, and its sinister reputation spread across the country.

▶ A tintype of a Cherokee holding a small knife with a gold-tinted handle.

▶▶ A tintype of two Cherokees in Indian Territory. The man on the left has a holstered pistol.

JUN 6

1877 Bat Masterson is arrested in Dodge City, Kansas, and fined twenty-five dollars on the charge of hooliganism.

BASS REEVES

One of the most feared deputy U.S. marshals in Indian Territory during his thirty-two years of service, Bass Reeves was born a slave and died a hero. Reeves, the first black federal lawman commissioned west of the Mississippi, had fled Texas as a fugitive slave during the Civil War. He settled in Indian Territory and in 1875 was hired to ride for Judge Isaac C. Parker, when the "Hanging Judge" first took the bench in Fort Smith, Arkansas. Reeves became fluent in Creek and several other Indian languages and was a master of disguise, a talent he often employed when pursuing criminals. He also was ambidextrous and could shoot a pistol with great accuracy using either hand. At a time when unconcealed racism was widespread, the physically imposing Reeves won the respect of his fellow deputies and even some of the outlaws he tracked down and brought to justice. He reportedly apprehended the largest number of fugitives of any of Parker's lawmen, pursuing such infamous outlaws as Ned Christie and Belle Starr, who turned herself in after learning that Reeves had a warrant for her arrest. Reeves sported fourteen notches on his six-gun, but despite having many close calls of his own, he was never wounded. He was, however, wrongly charged with murder in the accidental shooting of his camp cook, but won an acquittal. In 1902, the aging lawman arrested his own son for the murder of his wife, and the young man was sent to the federal prison in Leavenworth, Kansas. In Reeves's book, no one was above the law.

▲ Bass Reeves, one of Judge Parker's most active and reliable deputies.

▶ A commission for deputy marshal of the Western District of Arkansas, Judge Parker's jurisdiction.

UNITED STATES DISTRICT COURT

Know All Men By These Presents:

THAT I, GEO. J. CRUMP, *Marshal of the United States for the Western District of Arkansas, reposing special trust and confidence in* Heck Thomas *of* Guthrie Okl. Ter. *in said District have constituted and appointed and by these presents do constitute and appoint him, the said* Heck Thomas

DEPUTY MARSHAL OF THE UNITED STATES FOR THE WESTERN DISTRICT OF ARKANSAS,

UNDER ME, THE SAID MARSHAL.

AND I DO HEREBY GRANT UNTO HIM, The said Heck Thomas *full power and authority as my Deputy Marshal throughout the said District to use and exercise the said office of Deputy Marshal according to the laws and custom of the United States relative to and regulating the office of Deputy Marshal, during my term of office, unless he shall sooner be legally discharged therefrom.*

And I do fully authorize and empower him, my said Deputy Marshal, to execute any and all legal precepts and duties that might of right be required of me as Marshal, as aforesaid. And I do further declare all his official acts valid, as if done by myself.

In testimony Whereof, I have hereunto set my hand and seal, this 10 *day of* Jan

*A. D. 189*3 *at Fort Smith, in Western District of Arkansas.*

George J. Crump (Seal.)

Marshal of the United Stated for the Western District of Arkansas.

ATTEST: Stephen Wheeler

Clerk U. S Court, Western District of Arkansas.

By J. M. Dodge D.C.

WESTERN DIST. OF ARKANSAS

JUN 7

1904 Outlaw Harvey "Kid Curry" Logan and two others rob the Denver and Rio Grande train near Parachute, Colorado.

CALAMITY JANE

She was born Martha Jane Cannary at Princeton, Missouri, in 1852. When still a girl, she moved west with her family and was orphaned before she reached her teens. After that, with notable exceptions, everything else about one of the frontier's most curious characters remains a matter of conjecture—including how she got her handle of Calamity Jane. As with most every aspect of her life, Jane herself had a few ideas about her nickname's origin. Most of them came from her purported adventures as an army scout, which could never be officially documented. Some historians have suggested the name actually came from Jane's service nursing ill soldiers in General George Crook's encampment in 1876, or later when she helped victims of the smallpox epidemic that ravaged Deadwood. "I have always believed she got the name of 'Calamity,' because she was always present to help in times of disaster," explained Mary Borglum, who during her fourteen years in South Dakota while her husband, Gutzon, created the presidential sculptures at Mount Rushmore developed a keen interest in Calamity Jane's life. Although it made for another good story, Jane probably was called Calamity before she served as a frontier Florence Nightingale. Many of her claims are dubious, including that she was a stagecoach driver, Pony Express rider, and served with George Custer. The accounts of her being a camp follower, bullwhacker, and a prostitute are more likely. Still, the words of Borglum have a ring of truth: "There is an old cabin in the Black Hills of South Dakota, converted into a restaurant. Over the mantelpiece hangs Calamity Jane's old rifle. I have often sat looking at it. I am not an authority on firearms, but there is something clean and long-limbed and graceful about that rifle which to me typifies Calamity Jane."

▶ One of the earliest photographs of Calamity Jane. She is dressed as a scout.

▶▶ Calamity Jane, dressed as a lady.

JUN 8

1892 Bob Ford is shot and killed in his tent saloon by Edward O. Kelly in Creede, Colorado.
1894 Notorious outlaw and leader of the Dalton Gang, Bill Dalton is killed while resisting arrest in Ardmore, Oklahoma.
1904 As lawmen close in, a wounded Harvey "Kid Curry" Logan commits suicide rather than be captured near Rifle, Colorado.

HAYS CITY

Throughout the 1870s, scores of homicides occurred in Hays City, Kansas, site of the original Boot Hill, which would become a common name for cemeteries in the West. One of the most discussed bursts of violence took place in 1870, shortly after Wild Bill Hickok was defeated for reelection as Ellis County sheriff. It began when Hickok dropped by Paddy Walsh's saloon and was accosted by two drunken soldiers from nearby Fort Hays. One of the pair, Jeremiah Lonergan, had been in a dispute with Hickok in the past. The other soldier, John Kile, was a Medal of Honor recipient who deserted and then reenlisted in the Seventh Cavalry. Hickok was visiting with the bartender when the soldiers made their move. Lonergan wrapped his arms around Hickok and pulled him to the floor. Kile yanked out a pistol and stuck it in Hickok's ear, but the weapon misfired. Meanwhile Hickok was able to draw one of his pistols and shoot both men. Lonergan recovered from his wounds, returned to active duty, and was killed in another brawl. Kile died the next day and, because he had not been on duty but in a drunken row, no further action was taken. For many years, a famous photograph showing two dead soldiers sprawled on a Hays City boardwalk was said to be of Hickok's shooting victims, an obvious mistake since he killed only one soldier inside the saloon. It was later determined that the dead men were two other cavalrymen—Peter Welsh and George Summer, killed by fellow trooper David Roberts on September 6, 1873. Gradually, such shootings diminished. Hays City quieted down and dropped "City" from its name. Still, during the 1870s, as one resident so aptly put it: "Hays City by lamplight was remarkably lively, but not very moral."

▲ Wild Bill Hickok was blamed for the 1873 shooting, shown here, but had no part in it.

▶ Dead soldiers on the boardwalk outside a saloon in Hays City, Kansas. A small boy peeks around the corner of the building.

JUN 9

1902 Outlaw Harry Tracy kills three guards and escapes Oregon State Penitentiary in Salem, Oregon.

BUFFALO SOLDIERS

In 1866, the U.S. Congress established a peacetime army and created four new cavalry regiments that included two "colored" regiments. Four new black infantry units were also established. Most of the first recruits were veterans of all-black Civil War units as well as recently freed slaves. Because blacks were not allowed to rise above the rank of sergeant, only white officers commanded all of the new units. By 1867, the first of these black outfits were sent to the West to fight Indians as well as protect settlers and railroad crews. It was about this time that the troops acquired the famous moniker of "Buffalo Soldiers." Although the exact origins of the name remain obscure, it is believed that the Indians saw a similarity between the hair of the black soldiers and that of the buffalo. The buffalo was the most revered animal in the Indian culture, so the term as applied to the soldiers was thought to show respect. Troopers of the Tenth Cavalry were so proud of the title that the image of a buffalo became the most prominent feature of the regimental crest. Like other black citizens of that time, the soldiers were subjected to blatant racism and discrimination on every level. They were supplied with inferior cavalry mounts, issued substandard rations and equipment, and not always welcomed in the towns near their posts. Still the Buffalo Soldiers compiled an impressive record, and eighteen of their ranks were awarded the Congressional Medal of Honor for deeds of valor between 1866 and 1898.

▲ Buffalo Soldiers in camp.

▶ Buffalo Soldiers of the Twenty-fifth Infantry, Fort Snelling, Minnesota.

JUN 10

1896 Sam and Tom Ketchum loot a store and post office in Liberty, New Mexico Territory.

GONE ON THE SCOUT

By 1875, young Henry Antrim, still several years away from picking up the famous moniker of Billy the Kid, was a fifteen-year-old kid on his own. The year before, his beloved mother, Catherine, had lost her struggle with tuberculosis and died. Her husband William Antrim did little or nothing to support and comfort Henry and his brother, Josie. Left to his own devices, Henry—who had some schooling and became proficient in Spanish—lived by his wits doing odd jobs and dealing cards. He also placed his trust in some older rascals with dubious reputations. He was arrested for holding goods that had been stolen by a criminal mentor. Sheriff Harvey Whitehill, whose children played with Henry, hoped to teach the youngster a lesson by placing him in a jail cell only to face what he called a "storm of protest" from his wife. She told Whitehill to fetch Henry and bring him home for a proper breakfast. When he returned to the jail, Whitehill found that Henry had made a daring escape by climbing through the chimney to freedom. Now he was a fugitive running from the law, or in the lingo of that time and place, he was "among the willows, on the dodge, gone on the scout." Henry had danced over that thin line separating the lawful and lawless, and he never quite found his way back to the other side.

"I did all I could for the orphaned boy. After all, he was somebody's son and a boy that didn't need to go wrong."

—Sheriff Harvey Whitehill, 1902

▶ An oxen-drawn freight wagon on the muddy main street of Silver City, New Mexico Territory, about the time the young Henry Antrim was going to school (and jail) there.

JUN 11

1905 Geronimo comes to the Millers' 101 Ranch in Oklahoma Territory and hunts his first buffalo, although it is billed as his last buffalo hunt. The event becomes a field day for the press as Geronimo skins the buffalo after the kill and poses for pictures.

THE CALIFORNIA BANDIT

After the legendary Joaquin Murieta, suave and cunning Tiburcio Vásquez was the most notorious frontier bandit that California ever produced. Born into a respectable Monterrey family in 1835, Vásquez associated with known toughs and criminals at an early age. At nineteen, his twenty-three-year outlaw career began when he stabbed a constable to death during a fandango brawl. Vásquez joined a gang of desperados and in 1857 found himself at San Quentin prison convicted of stealing horses. Two years later, he escaped and returned to his outlaw ways, but was quickly apprehended and returned to prison. Released in 1863, Vásquez committed a string of stagecoach robberies and raids throughout central and southern California. During a bungled armed robbery in Mendocino in 1867, he was captured and briefly incarcerated at San Quentin for a third time. Vásquez was released in 1869 and then badly wounded two years later in a gun battle, but by late summer had recovered enough to rob another stagecoach. Although a posse killed two of his accomplices and wounded Vásquez, he safely reached his hideout in the rugged canyons north of Los Angeles. Governor Newton Booth's offer of one thousand dollars in reward money for Vásquez continued to increase in hefty increments until it reached six thousand dollars. By 1873, when Vásquez and his gang returned to the San Joaquin Valley, raided the town of Kingston, and carried out more robberies, the reward had jumped to fifteen thousand dollars, dead or alive. While considered a Robin Hood–style brigand by some Hispanic citizens, Vásquez was demonized by many of the Anglos residing in the region, and mothers were known to warn misbehaving children, "Hush, or Vásquez will get you!"

▲ A paperback account of the life of Vásquez.

▶ Tiburcio Vásquez.

1901 Suspected horse thief Gregorio Cortez shoots and kills Sheriff W. T. "Brack" Morris ten miles south of Kennedy, Texas.

"¡PRONTO!"

The crime spree of Tiburcio Vásquez finally ended in May 1874 in the Arroyo Seco area of Los Angeles. One of his gang members, jealous because Vásquez was romancing his wife, went to authorities to report the location of the gang's hideout in Alison Canyon. When the lawmen stormed the adobe house, Vásquez leaped out a back window and ran for his horse. A sheriff's deputy fired at the fleeing outlaw and missed, but George Beers, a reporter for the *San Francisco Chronicle* who had tagged along, leveled his shotgun and brought down Vásquez with a load of buckshot to the legs. Beers later wrote *Vasquez, or, The Hunted Bandit of the San Joaquin*, a detailed story of the outlaw's checkered life. While awaiting trial in the jail at San Jose, the famous outlaw received crowds of visitors, mostly women admirers. He accommodated all of them, answering questions and signing autographs. At the end of a speedy trial, Vásquez was found guilty on two murder charges and sentenced to hang. Shortly before the execution was carried out, he dictated a statement that said in part, "A spirit of hatred and revenge took possession of me. I had numerous fights in defense of what I believed to be my rights and those of my countrymen. . . . I believed we were unjustly deprived of the social rights that belonged to us." On the gallows, Vásquez—fully prepared to die—showed no fear. As a priest mumbled a prayer, the condemned man simply said, "¡*Pronto*!" The hangman complied.

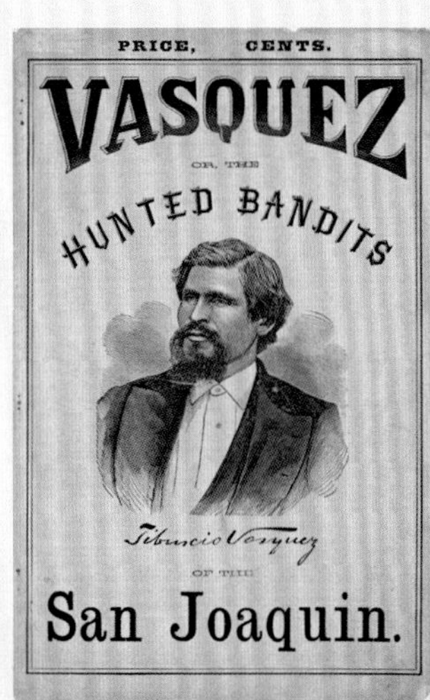

▲ This book describes Vásquez's execution as well as his life of crime.

▶ Vásquez, photographed shortly after his capture and while awaiting trial in San Jose, California.

JUN 13

1868 At Twenty-five Yard Creek, Montana Territory, the Thirteenth Infantry and a group of Indian scouts engage in battle with hostile Indians, killing three.

MONEGAW SPRINGS SHOOTOUT

Following the January 31, 1874, robbery of a train at Gads Hill, Missouri, the Pinkerton National Detective Agency was hired to capture the culprits: the James-Younger Gang, comprised mostly of brothers from both families. Led by Jesse James and Cole Younger, the outlaws continued to prey on banks, trains, and stagecoaches in several states. On March 11, John W. Whicher, a crack Pinkerton agent hunting gang members, was shot and killed near Independence, Missouri. Pinkerton agents John Boyle and Louis J. Lull were dispatched to investigate the killing. On March 17, just a week after the murder, the two detectives were riding the back roads near Monegaw Springs, a popular spa resort area with sandstone caves that offered criminals safe haven, accompanied by St. Clair County deputy sheriff Edwin Daniels. Posing as cattle buyers, the three men questioned local citizens, and soon word spread that strangers were snooping around. When brothers John and Jim Younger, with guns brandished, suddenly rode up on the three lawmen, a shootout ensued. John Younger—already wanted for murdering two deputies in Texas in 1871—fired his double-barrel shotgun, fatally wounding Deputy Daniels. Agent Lull was shot, but before tumbling from his horse, squeezed off a round that struck John in the neck, killing him instantly. Lull died a few days later after giving testimony at a coroner's inquest. Jim Younger made a getaway and, after laying low for a bit, returned to his outlaw ways. Outraged by the killings at Monegaw Springs, Missouri legislators appropriated ten thousand dollars for a force of armed secret agents to join in the war against outlaws spawned in their state. No quarter would be given on either side.

▲ The log cabin where the dying Captain Lull was taken after the Monegaw Springs shootout.

▶ John Younger.

▶▶ Deputy sheriff Edwin Daniels, killed in the gunfight with John and Jim Younger.

1854 Nat Love, one of the most famous black cowboys, is born a slave in Davidson County, Tennessee.

THE BLOODY BENDERS

In the 1870s, the Benders, an outwardly quiet family operating an inn on the Osage Trail in southeastern Kansas, became the nation's first recorded serial killers. News of the mass murderers flashed across the land when it was discovered that many hapless travelers had met their end at the family's "prairie slaughterhouse." The Bender family, who first appeared in Kansas in 1871, consisted of John; his wife whom everyone called Ma; a dim-witted son named John Jr.; and a fair-haired daughter, the beautiful Kate, known for her powers as a medium. She appeared in small Kansas towns to give public séances as "Professor Miss Kate Bender." Kate would lure male callers to the family home where they would be seated on a bench with their backs snug against a canvas curtain. As Kate worked her spell, her father or brother would sneak behind the curtain and smash the suitor's head in with a sledgehammer. Bodies were stripped of any valuables, dropped through a trapdoor to the cellar, and later buried on the property, usually in the orchard. After eighteen months of disappearances, including that of a prominent doctor, suspicion began to focus on the Benders, but it was too late. The family vanished just before authorities uncovered the grisly remains of at least a dozen people, including a little girl who had been buried alive. Thousands of sightseers visited the Bender property—called "Hell's Acre"—even after the inn was demolished in 1889. Rumors persisted for another fifty years about the whereabouts of the diabolical Benders, who, as it turned out, were not even related except through the blood of their victims.

▲ The cover of this book illustrates the method Kate Bender and her brother and father used to kill their victims.

▶ A montage of photographs taken at the Bender cabin during the search for victims' bodies.

VIEWS OF THE BENDER RESIDENCE.

PHOTOGRAPHED BY C. R. CAMBLE, PARSONS, KANSAS.

JUN 15

1876 Sitting Bull holds a three-day Sun Dance on Montana's Rosebud River, attracting fifteen thousand Indians. During a ceremony, Sitting Bull has a vision of soldiers attacking the camp and falling dead like grasshoppers.

THE CANNIBAL OF SLUMGULLION PASS

Alferd Packer earned a sinister place in the folklore of the West as a result of his acquired taste for human flesh. A shoemaker by occupation, in November 1873 Packer signed on as a guide to lead a party of twenty-one men from Utah to the gold-fields of Colorado Territory. The party lost most of its supplies at a river crossing and was snowbound at a camp near present-day Montrose, Colorado. When the remaining food ran out and they had boiled and eaten their moccasins, Packer and five of his charges struck out in the snowdrifts and below-zero temperatures to find help. On April 16, 1874, when Packer finally made it to Los Pinos Indian Agency, he was alone and had obviously gained weight. After some questioning, he claimed he had killed the others for self-preservation and lived off their flesh until the spring thaw. The remains of the bodies were found at the foot of Slumgullion Pass at a site that became known as Cannibal Plateau. Packer was tossed into a dungeon, but quickly escaped. He was apprehended eight years later in Wyoming, returned to Colorado for trial, found guilty, and sentenced to death. Packer spent several years behind bars before having his conviction overturned on a technicality. A second trial in 1886 sent him back to prison to serve forty years. In 1901, Packer was paroled thanks to the influence of the owners of the *Denver Post*, who wanted to tour him as a sideshow act with a circus. That deal fell through and the "Cannibal of Slumgullion Pass" lived quietly and apparently well nourished on an orthodox diet until his death in 1907.

▶ A frivolous card for the "Packer Club," formed eighty years after the crime.

PACKER CLUB

AL PACKER

26 COLO. 306 57 PAC. 1087
TIMBER LINE PAGE 37

"They was siven Dimmycrats in Hinsdale County, but you, yah voracious, man-eatin' son of a bitch, yah eat five of thim!"

I agrees to eliminat five *Nu Deal* Dimmycrats witch makes me a mimber of th' *PACKER CLUB of COLORADO*

____

SIGN HERE

CHARTER MEMBERS: RALPH CARR, GENE FOWLER, HERNDON DAVIS, FRED MAZZULLA

JUN 16

1906 President Theodore Roosevelt signs an act of Congress that combines Indian Territory and Oklahoma Territory into the single state of Oklahoma.

CENTENNIAL

The United States marked its one-hundredth birthday in 1876. To commemorate the anniversary, a Centennial Exposition was held in Philadelphia, featuring a variety of attractions such as Alexander Graham Bell's revolutionary telephone, the first Remington typewriter, and George Washington's false teeth. Crowds munched on hot popcorn and enjoyed exotic bananas packaged in tinfoil that cost a whole dime while they gawked at a display—sponsored by the Smithsonian Institution and the Department of the Interior—that featured Indian "curiosities." After visiting the exhibit, the respected intellectual William Dean Howells declared: "The red man, as he appears in effigy and in photographs in this collection, is a hideous demon." Yet the Centennial would be marked in more ways than by the perpetuation of the belief in white supremacy in Philadelphia. On June 25, for example, near the banks of the Greasy Grass River, Montana Territory, a force of Lakota and Northern Cheyenne warriors annihilated the controversial Lieutenant Colonel George Armstrong Custer and 261 men of the Seventh Cavalry. On Independence Day, the telegraph reporting the shocking news arrived at the celebration in Philadelphia where generals William T. Sherman and Philip Henry Sheridan read it in stunned disbelief. Just weeks later, on August 2, Wild Bill Hickok was gunned down from behind at a poker table in Deadwood, Dakota Territory. Finally, on September 7, the James-Younger Gang was shot to pieces during a bank robbery in Northfield, Minnesota. These three distinct events impacted the nation greatly and remain some of the most enduring stories of the American West. The Gilded Age had just begun, but already some of its shine had been lost. Manifest Destiny be damned. It was still a Wild West.

While the country's Centennial was celebrated in Philadelphia, three major events in the annals of the Wild West occurred in 1876:

▲ The Younger Brothers robbed the bank in Northfield, Minnesota.

▶ Wild Bill Hickok was assassinated in Deadwood.

▶▶ General George Armstrong Custer died at the Little Bighorn.

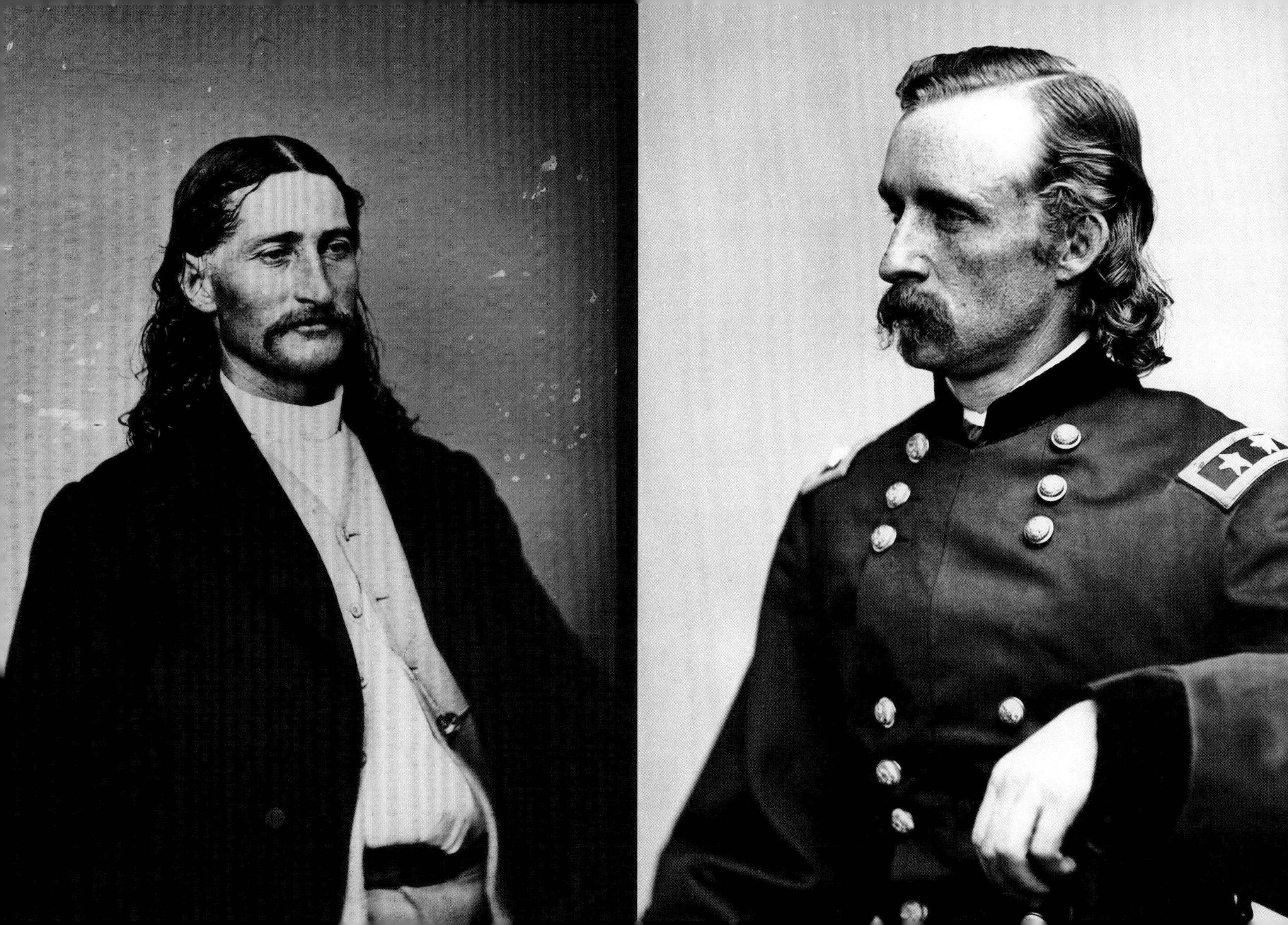

JUN 17

1901 Stage robber Bill Miner, known as the Grey Fox, is released after serving twenty years in the prison at San Quentin, California.

THE CUSTERS

George Armstrong Custer and his devoted wife, Elizabeth, or Libbie, captured the public's imagination and by the 1870s became the nation's most famous frontier couple. From the time of their marriage in 1864, Libbie used her charm and social connections to advance her husband's army career and bolster the self-styled "Custer Myth." Libbie followed Custer to various duty stations, starting after the Civil War when they were posted to Texas. Although Libbie found most Texans violent and rash, she prized the handsome serapes she found there and used them to decorate the family quarters at forts where the couple later lived. Like his sister-in-law whom he adored, Tom Custer was devoted to his older brother Armstrong, as he and Libbie called him. A hero of the Civil War and the first man in history to win two Medals of Honor, the charming and hard-drinking Tom never married but, as Libbie explained, he "honored and liked women extremely." Tom accompanied his brother and Libbie to Texas and served with George until both died at the Battle of Little Bighorn. After her husband's death, Libbie, who lived until 1933, spent the rest of her long life diligently working to preserve the memory and protect the reputation of both her husband and her wayward brother-in-law.

▲ The beautiful Elizabeth "Libbie" Custer.

▶ General George Armstrong Custer (seated) with his wife, Elizabeth, and his brother Tom.

JUN

18

1904 During an appearance of his Wild West show in St. Louis, Zack Mulhall opens fire during an argument with employee Rank Reed, leaving three bystanders wounded. The incident makes national headlines and is featured as a front-page story in the *New York Times*.

MY LIFE ON THE PLAINS

Prior to his fateful confrontation at Little Bighorn in 1876, George Armstrong Custer wrote a firsthand account of his experiences with the Seventh Cavalry in *My Life on the Plains*, first published serially in *The Galaxy* beginning in 1872. The book came out in 1874.

"Stripped of the beautiful romance with which we have been so long willing to envelop him, transferred from the inviting pages of the novelist to the localities where we are compelled to meet with him, in his native village, on the war path, and when raiding upon our frontier settlements and lines of travel, the Indian forfeits his claim to the appellation of the noble red man. We see him as he is, and, so far as all knowledge goes, as he ever has been, a savage in every sense of the word . . . one whose cruel and ferocious nature far exceeds that of any wild beast of the desert."

—*My Life on the Plains*, chapter 1

▲ Custer's *My Life on the Plains* first appeared in *The Galaxy* magazine. Shown here is the cover of the book published in 1874.

▶ George Armstrong Custer.

"As I pen these lines I am in the midst of scenes of bustle and busy preparation attendant upon the organization and equipment of a large party for an important exploring expedition, on which I shall start before these pages reach the publishers' hands. During my absence I expect to visit a region of country as yet unseen by human eyes, except those of the Indian. . . . Bidding adieu to civilization for the next few months, I also now take leave of my readers, who, I trust, in accompanying me through my retrospect, have been enabled to gain a true insight into a cavalryman's Life on The Plains."

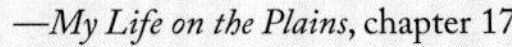

—*My Life on the Plains*, chapter 17

JUN 19

1867 Near Stein Mountain, Oregon, Indian scouts skirmish with another band of Indians. Twelve are killed in the confrontation.

CUSTER'S FOLLY

Truth was in woefully short supply from the moment the nation learned the news of what at the time was called "Custer's Last Stand." Many myths persist about what really transpired on June 25, 1876, when more than 250 soldiers from the U.S. Army's Seventh Cavalry, led by Lieutenant Colonel Custer, perished in Montana Territory. Many army officers and much of the public refused to believe that a large force of Indians could have destroyed the invincible Custer, still perceived as a hero who could not have been responsible for the biggest fiasco in the nation's military history. As the numbers of dead and wounded were tallied, many sought to blame someone other than the glorious Custer. The most convenient scapegoat became Major Marcus Albert Reno, the officer in command of the only unit to survive the battle. Reno's critics pointed to his defensive action after his attack on Sitting Bull's camp was repulsed. They also claimed he was a coward who held the defensive position while Custer and his troops were being slaughtered. In 1879, a military court of inquiry officially cleared Reno of charges of cowardice, but soon after he faced court-martial on several other counts, including drunkenness, and was dismissed from the army. At the time of his death in 1889, Reno was largely held in contempt and considered a disgrace to his uniform. In 1967, however, an army board of review reexamined the records and reversed the judgment against Reno. His general discharge was changed to honorable, and his remains from an unmarked grave were reinterred with honors in the Little Bighorn cemetery near the men he had led.

▶ One of three photographs taken of Custer in April 1876 in New York, three months before his death at Little Bighorn. Note that his hair was cut short.

▶▶ Major Marcus Albert Reno, who shouldered much of the blame, deserved or not, for Custer's defeat at Little Bighorn.

JUN **20**

1876 After being reviewed by General Alfred Terry, the Seventh Cavalry led by George Armstrong Custer begins marching toward the Little Bighorn River as the band plays "Garryowen." Scouts inform Custer that two thousand to four thousand warriors are camped on the Little Bighorn.

GREASY GRASS

On June 25, 1876, George Armstrong Custer and the U.S. Army's Seventh Cavalry went to battle against a large combined Sioux and Cheyenne army that proved to be superior to their enemy in every possible way. As the war chiefs saw it, they had everything to lose. Custer and his troopers were invaders intent on taking their homeland in violation of a treaty signed in 1868. One of the most-often depicted episodes in American history, the battle on the banks of Greasy Grass Creek, a ninety-mile-long river rising in the mountains of Wyoming and flowing north to the Bighorn River in Montana, became the subject of literature, paintings, and films. No photographs exist of what transpired that hot afternoon as the two sides locked in deadly combat. The whites called it the Battle of Little Bighorn, but to the Sioux the engagement became known as *Pe-hin* (Head-hair) *Hanska* (Long) *Ktepi* (Killed), or "the fight in which Long-hair was killed," referring to the thirty-six-year-old Custer, who usually wore his hair at shoulder-length. But on the day of the battle, that was not the case. Just before he and his troopers departed Fort Abraham Lincoln for their rendezvous with death, Custer had had his reddish-gold locks cropped short. Later, old soldiers mused that Custer was like the biblical Samson—his famous long hair had been the source of his strength. When he had his hair cut off, Custer's luck ran out.

▲▶ Custer Hill. These photographs were taken in 1913 by Rodman Wanamaker. The monuments are placed in the approximate locations where the soldiers' remains were found. The cross marks the spot where Custer fell. The Indians are the surviving Crow scouts who had accompanied Custer.

Copyrighted — Rinehart, Omaha

The Custer Battlefield — near Crow Agency, Mont.

JUN 21

1876 Santa Anna, known as the "Napoleon of the West" and the "Butcher of the Alamo," dies alone and mostly forgotten in Mexico.

SOLE SURVIVOR

All who stood with Custer on what became known as Custer Hill perished at the Battle of Little Bighorn. Besides Lieutenant Colonel Custer, found with three bullet wounds to his body, others from his family died that day. The body of Captain Tom Custer, commander of Troop C, was found not far from his famous brother. Boston Custer, another brother and a guest on the expedition, also died on Custer Hill, as did Custer's young nephew Arthur Reed, just a boy who came along as a herder. Although all humans with the Seventh Cavalry died, there were animal survivors—as many as one hundred army horses. The Sioux and Cheyenne warriors confiscated cavalry mounts that were still fit, but one badly wounded horse was left to die. Named Comanche, the buckskin gelding—found two days after the battle with seven serious wounds—was standing next to the body of Captain Myles Keogh, the officer who rode him into combat. Weak and barely able to walk, Comanche was placed in a sling and shipped by steamer to Fort Lincoln. Once he was nursed back to health and news of his survival got out, Comanche became the most famous horse in the West. Orders were given that he should never be ridden again, and he was made "Second Commanding Officer" of the Seventh Cavalry. Stabled at Fort Riley, Kansas, where he had the run of the grounds, Comanche occasionally led regimental parades and acquired a taste for beer. He died at age twenty-nine in 1891. A taxidermist stuffed him, and after being displayed at the 1893 Columbian Exposition in Chicago, the brave Comanche still stands wearing his cavalry blanket and saddle in a glass case at the University of Kansas Natural History Museum.

▶ Comanche, famed as the "only survivor" from the Seventh Cavalry.

JUN 22

1901 After a massive manhunt, outlaw Gregorio Cortez is captured in Gonzalez County, Texas.

CRAZY HORSE

Little is known about Oglala Sioux chief Crazy Horse, one of the leaders of the great Sioux-Cheyenne Uprising of 1876–77, which reached its high point with the destruction of George Armstrong Custer and more than 250 troopers of the Seventh Cavalry at Little Bighorn. There has never been agreement on the precise year or location of his birth. Like the Apache leader Cochise, no known photograph exists of Crazy Horse. There are drawings and sketches based on eyewitness descriptions, but those are inconsistent. Several people have tried passing off period tintypes as Crazy Horse, but none have been authenticated. According to his descendants, all this is with good reason. "He didn't trust the white man; he stayed away from any cameraman," explained Don Red Thunder, great-grandson of Crazy Horse. "There were no photos of him taken." Crazy Horse took part in several massacres, ambushes, and battles leading up the Little Bighorn victory. His final fight began in early 1877 when he and his warriors took on the U.S. Cavalry at Wolf Mountain in Montana Territory. The hostilities dragged into the spring, and he realized his people were starving and weak, so on May 6, he surrendered to officials at the Red Cloud Agency near Camp Robinson in Nebraska. This great warrior, who many Indians believed could not be killed by a white man's bullet, met his end by being stabbed to death by a guard's bayonet. His body was given to his elderly parents. The final resting place of Crazy Horse, just like many of the details of his life, remains unknown.

▶ There is no known photograph of Crazy Horse. This crude sketch was said to have been drawn using eyewitness descriptions, although accounts varied greatly.

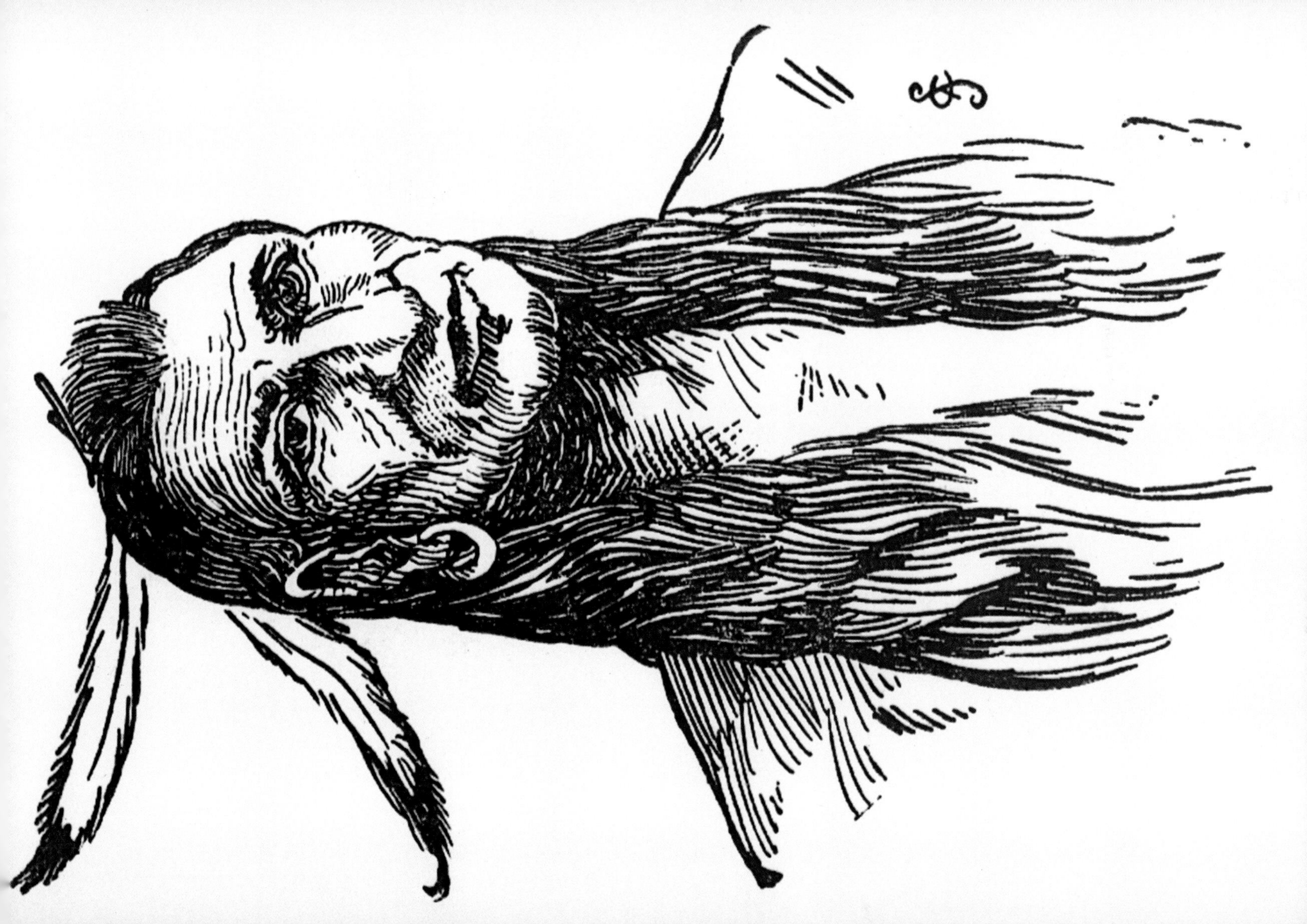

JUN 23

1883 Charles E. "Black Bart" Bolton robs a stagecoach four miles outside of Jackson, California.

SITTING BULL

Contrary to popular belief, the Sioux medicine man Sitting Bull did not fight at Little Bighorn. Others such as Crazy Horse and Gall were the war chiefs who led the Indian combatants to triumph against the Seventh Cavalry. Yet even though Sitting Bull did not fire a shot, count coup, or take a scalp on June 25, 1876, he knew before the battle even started that the forces he had helped gather would be victorious. Earlier that month, at his camp on Rosebud Creek in Montana Territory, Sitting Bull led Lakotas, Cheyenne, and Arapahos in the annual Sun Dance ceremony. During the ritual, Sitting Bull, revered for his exceptional spiritual powers, had a vision. When he emerged from his trance, he talked of seeing dead soldiers falling like grasshoppers from the sky into the Lakota camp. Inspired by the vision, Crazy Horse set out with five hundred warriors and on June 17 forced troops under General George Crook to beat a quick retreat. In celebration, the Lakotas moved their camp to the valley of the Little Bighorn and were joined by three thousand more Indians who left the reservation to follow Sitting Bull. The stage was set for Custer's untimely arrival only a few short days later. Sitting Bull continued to make medicine and calmly waited for his dream to come true.

▶ This photograph of Sitting Bull is one of the earliest of many of the famous Sioux medicine man.

▶▶ Sitting Bull, probably during his brief tour with Buffalo Bill's Wild West, c. 1885.

JUN 24

1837 The steamboat *St. Peters* brings smallpox to Dakota Territory. Its introduction into Native American populations during the nineteenth century results in widespread disease and death.
1927 Outlaw and bank robber Matt Kimes is captured in Flagstaff, Arizona.

GALL AND RAIN-IN-THE-FACE

Two of the most important Sioux warriors at the Battle of Little Bighorn were Gall and Rain-in-the-Face. Called "The Fighting Cock of the Sioux" by U.S. soldiers, Gall became a noted warrior as a youth and quickly rose in the tribal ranks. Like Sitting Bull, he resisted all efforts by the U.S. government to open the sacred Black Hills to white gold-seekers. Gall, who helped coordinate the efforts against the Seventh Cavalry at Little Bighorn, mounted a furious assault after his wife and three children were killed by Arikara scouts during the initial attack on the Indian camp led by Major Marcus Reno. "We took no prisoners," Gall recalled. "Our hearts were bad, and we cut and shot them all to pieces." Rain-in-the-Face was never recognized as a Sioux chief, but gained fame as a capable warrior. He was given his name as a boy after war paint and blood streaked his face during a hard fight in a rainstorm. During the Little Bighorn melee, Rain-in-the-Face was said to have cut out and eaten Tom Custer's heart, a tall tale made popular by Henry Wadsworth Longfellow in his poem, "The Revenge of Rain-in-the-Face." Many Indians also boasted that Rain-in-the-Face killed George Custer. However, as an old man on the Standing Rock Reservation, Rain-in-the-Face denied killing either Custer.

▶ Sioux chief Gall.

▶▶ Rain-in-the-Face, who was said to have killed both Tom and George Custer. He denied both accounts.

JUN 25

1876 Lieutenant Colonel George Armstrong Custer sends his Seventh Cavalry into the center of the single largest conglomeration of Sioux and Cheyenne warriors ever assembled. Outnumbered three to one, Custer's unit is decimated by the Indian warriors in the Battle of Little Bighorn.

CURLY AND LONESOME CHARLEY

Two memorable scouts who rode for the U.S. Seventh Cavalry Regiment were a Crow Indian called Curly and a battle-hardened veteran named Charley Reynolds. Of the pair, Curly was the rookie. Although he had been part of several war parties against the Sioux, he had only enlisted as an Indian Scout in April of 1876, less than three months before the Battle of Little Bighorn. Curly was one of the Crows tapped to lead the Little Bighorn expedition, along with Hairy Moccasin, Half-Yellow Face, Goes-Ahead, White-Man-Runs-Him, and White Swan. Curly was not directly involved in the battle, but was able to observe the action from distant vantage points. Reporters and hack writers, seemingly oblivious to the other Crow Scouts who returned safely, hailed Curly as the only survivor of Custer's Last Stand. But Curly always insisted that he was not part of the action, just an eyewitness to the carnage. Chief Scout Charley Reynolds, however, was in the thick of it. A seasoned buffalo hunter, trader, and scout, the reserved Reynolds was called Lonesome Charley. Reynolds had a premonition the night before the battle. That morning, he gave away all of his personal items to soldiers, and as the troops moved toward the Little Bighorn, Reynolds, who never drank, asked one of the interpreters for a gulp of whiskey. Riding into battle with Major Marcus Reno's detachment, Reynolds was killed that afternoon.

▶ Scout Charley Reynolds, who was killed in the Little Bighorn valley.

▶▶ Crow scout Curly, who viewed the fall of Custer and his men from a distance.

JUN 26

1876 Lieutenant James H. Bradley is the first to learn of Custer's death and defeat from Crow scouts Hairy Moccasin, Goes-Ahead, and White-Man-Runs-Him. The scouts had been dismissed before the battle.

CUSTER'S LAST FIGHT

Probably the best known of the many paintings of Little Bighorn is *Custer's Last Fight*, which was painted on a canvas tent fly by Cassilly Adams. The artist completed the piece in 1886 after interviewing various Indians who had witnessed the event, including the Crow scout Curly. The painting was hanging in a St. Louis saloon when it came to the attention of Adolphus Busch, the beer magnate. In 1890, he acquired the work and commissioned Otto Becker to copy it for use as a lithograph. The original Adams painting was presented to the Seventh Cavalry in 1895. It was destroyed in a fire at the officer's club at Fort Bliss, in El Paso, Texas, on June 13, 1946, not quite seventy years after the battle took place. Stacks of Becker's lithograph copies were distributed by Anheuser-Busch. Many of them were displayed on tavern walls where for years to come patrons toasted the memory of the mythical Custer. The famous barroom poster influenced the staging of such filmmakers as John Ford, who often framed his more memorable movie scenes as if they were oil paintings.

▶ *Custer's Last Fight* by Cassilly Adams, 1886.

CUSTER'S LAST FIGHT.

The Original Painting has been Presented to the Seventh Regiment U.S. Cavalry

BY **ANHEUSER BUSCH BREWING ASSOCIATION,**

ST LOUIS, MO. U.S.A.

JUN 27

1874 In present-day Hutchinson County, Texas, the Second Battle of Adobe Walls takes place between a group of twenty-eight buffalo hunters and a force of three hundred Comanche warriors led by Quanah Parker.

MIXED-BLOOD SCOUTS

Seasoned frontier scout and interpreter Johnnie "Big Leggins" Bruguier was born of a French father and Sioux mother and educated by the Christian Brothers in St. Louis. On December 15, 1875, Bruguier tried to stop a brawl involving his brother and in the process killed a man. He fled to the Black Hills and lived in Sitting Bull's lodge for two months, acting as the medicine man's interpreter. Bruguier then was asked to scout for General Nelson Miles, who agreed to intercede for him if authorities tried to question him concerning the brawl fatality. Bruguier was eventually tried for murder and acquitted. He worked for Miles from late 1876 until 1881, when he returned to Dakota with the Sioux bands that surrendered. After the Battle of Little Bighorn, there were unproven accusations that while scouting for the U.S. Army, Bruguier acted as a sort of double agent reporting to his Sioux friends on the whereabouts of cavalry units in the territory. In 1890, Bruguier again served as Miles's personal interpreter and died the following year from a blow to the head administered by an unknown assailant wielding a wagon wrench. Like Bruguier, interpreter Frank Grouard also was a mixed-blood pony scout; he had a Mormon missionary father and a Polynesian mother. Grouard lived with the Sioux for six years and became well acquainted with Sitting Bull and Crazy Horse, relationships that served him in good stead while scouting for General George Crook in the 1876 campaign. The next year, he was instrumental in persuading Crazy Horse to surrender and come to the reservation where the Sioux leader was later killed.

▶ Frank Grouard, whose long career as a frontier scout was told in a 545-page book published in 1894.

▶▶ Frontier scout and interpreter Johnnie Bruguier.

JUN 28

1897 Kid Curry, the Sundance Kid, and others rob the Butte County Bank in Belle Forche, South Dakota.

YELLOWSTONE KELLY

Blessed with matinee idol good looks and a passion for adventure, Luther Sage Kelly, familiarly known on the frontier as Yellowstone Kelly, cut a dashing figure as an army scout and guide during a career that spanned more than forty years. After serving in the Civil War, Kelly earned his nickname scouting for the army on the Yellowstone River during the Northern Plains Indian Wars of the 1870s and 1880s. While serving as chief scout for General Nelson Miles from 1876 to 1878, Kelly took part in campaigns against the Cheyenne as well as Sioux warriors led by Sitting Bull. According to Miles: "Yellowstone Kelly was of a good family, well educated and fond of good books, as quiet and gentle as he was brave, as kind and generous as he was forceful, a great hunter and an expert rifleman; he explored that extensive northwest country years before serious hostilities occurred and acquired a knowledge of its topography, climate and resources that was extremely helpful." Kelly also saw action against Chief Joseph and the Nez Perce in Montana and in the 1880 Ute conflict in Colorado. He almost always carried a long breech-loading Springfield rifle covered from muzzle to stock with the skin of a bull snake. It was said that he "was as likely to quote Shakespeare as skin a beaver." General Miles, who wrote the introduction for Kelly's memoirs published in 1926, two years before the old scout died, recalled their first encounter: "He had recently killed a large bear and cut off one of its huge paws, and upon this he inscribed his name and sent it to my tent, as he had no cards at the time."

▶ Luther S. "Yellowstone" Kelly.

▶▶ A later photograph of Yellowstone Kelly.

JUN 29

1857 At Solomon's Fork on the Kansas River in Kansas Territory, Lieutenant J. E. B. Stuart is wounded in a fight with Cheyenne Indians. Within a few years, Stuart will become famous as a cavalry general in the Confederate army.

THE SALT WAR

In the autumn of 1877, a dispute known as the Salt War erupted at San Elizario, a settlement near El Paso on the Texas-Mexico border. The violence was the culmination of an ongoing disagreement caused by Anglo attempts to take control of mining rights to the valuable salt flats east of El Paso. The extensive flats were considered communal property, available as a salt source to all, particularly the many Hispanics who had enjoyed free harvest of the life-sustaining salt since the mid-1700s. Some pilgrims pushing handcarts traveled the hundred miles from El Paso across arroyos and sand hills to collect salt. Several villages depended on the salt trade for sustenance. They were all outraged when the self-styled Salt Ring, a collection of contemptible Anglo politicians and lawyers, tried to acquire title to the salt deposits for their own profit. When mobs of angry Hispanic residents responded with firepower, retaliation from the Anglos was swift. The feud resulted in the looting of San Elizario and death and destruction on both sides. A force of Texas Rangers led by Lieutenant J. B. Tays headed to San Elizario, and later an all-black troop of the Ninth Cavalry arrived on the scene. Citizen posses entered the melee and besieged the Rangers and soldiers. El Paso Sheriff Charles Kerber put out a call to New Mexico Territory for help, and criminal mastermind John Kinney responded. He came with one hundred well-armed men and laid waste to the area, murdering indiscriminately. Kinney's riders were so cruel that even the Rangers, hardly known for compassion, stayed clear of them. When the dust from the Salt War cleared, everyone had to start paying for salt.

▲ John Kinney, a hired gun from New Mexico Territory.

▶ Sheriff Charles Kerber represented the law in the Salt War.

JUN 30

1877 The *Black Hills Daily News* reports that there have been more than a dozen stagecoach robberies in Dakota Territory during the month of June alone.

WILD BILL AND CALAMITY JANE

Stories connecting Calamity Jane and Wild Bill Hickok began appearing in print during her lifetime. And for good reason—Martha "Calamity Jane" Cannary was the source of a lot of them. In many minds, Calamity and Wild Bill are forever linked as frontier lovers, yet nothing could be further from the truth. Calamity did love Hickok, but greatly inflated their relationship. They did know each other, as in 1876 both of them arrived in Deadwood, Dakota Territory, in the same party. But beyond that, tales claiming they were intimate and suggesting they actually had married contradict all historical records. Like so much in the annals of the Old West, the truth about their relationship may never be uncovered, but their connection appears to have started in 1876 when a party of gold-seekers organized by Hickok and Colorado Charlie Utter departed Cheyenne on June 27 bound for the Black Hills. At Fort Laramie, an army officer prevailed upon Hickok to take on a new member—Martha Cannary, who was currently installed in the guardhouse sleeping off a big drunk. Miss Cannary was given some clothing, including soldier's undergarments, a buckskin coat, and a wide-brimmed hat. For the rest of the journey, Calamity proved her worth as a competent bullwhacker and storyteller at evening campfires. The party made it to Deadwood about July 12. On their arrival, several members of the group loaned Calamity some money to buy a dress to replace the old buckskins. Hickok threw in twenty dollars with the request that she "wash behind her ears." When Calamity tried to repay Hickok, he refused, saying, "At least she looks like a woman now." Only days later, Hickok would be shot dead, and the tale telling would begin.

▲ The last photograph of Wild Bill Hickok, taken in Cheyenne in 1876.

▶ Calamity Jane, c. 1876.

Calamity

JUL 1

1896 Judge Isaac Parker sentences the Buck Gang to hang in Fort Smith, Arkansas.

DEAD MAN'S HAND

At approximately three o'clock on the afternoon of August 2, 1876, as Wild Bill Hickok sat playing poker in Nuttall & Mann's No. 10 Saloon, he was shot and killed. His assassin was Jack McCall. Just the night before, McCall had lost all of his money playing cards with Hickok, who kindly returned enough for him to get breakfast. When he raised his .45 Colt Single-Action Army revolver, McCall exclaimed, "Damn you, take that!" The bullet crashed into the back of Hickok's head, passed through his brain, and ended up lodged in the wrist of one of the other card players. Hickok, forty-eight years old, fell lifeless to the floor and bled out, giving him the appearance of a wax figure. "I have seen many dead men on the field of battle and in civil life, but Wild Bill was the prettiest corpse I have ever seen," Ellis "Doc" Pierce later recalled. "His long moustache was attractive, even in death, and his long tapering fingers looked like marble." Hickok, who always insisted on sitting with his back to the wall to avoid being shot from behind, had made the fatal mistake of sitting with his back to the bar and had no time to pull his twin Navy Colts. When it was reported that four of the cards in Hickok's final poker hand were two eights and two aces, that combination of pairs was thereafter known as the "Dead Man's Hand" and became part of the Hickok legend. McCall was first tried by a miner's court in Deadwood and found not guilty. But in 1877, a court in Yankton, Dakota Territory, tried him again. This time McCall was found guilty and hanged.

▲ The grave of Wild Bill in Deadwood with its first marker.

▶ To this day, Deadwood regularly reenacts the trial of Jack McCall for tourists.

"WILD BILL"

Plan To See--

Trial of Jack McCall

For The Killing of

WILD BILL HICKOK

Old Town Hall, Deadwood

Monday, Tuesday, Wednesday
Friday and Saturday at 8 p.m.

JUL 2

1872 In Hartford, Connecticut, a patent is issued for the new Colt revolver. This 1873 Single Action Army will come to be known as the "Peacemaker."

CALIFORNIA JOE

Moses Embree Milner was a talented scout known from the Missouri River to the Pacific as "California Joe." He left Kentucky in 1849 to join the exodus to California. After working the goldfields, Milner moved to Oregon and later Montana, where he acquired his nickname. He also killed a claim jumper and in 1862 murdered another man "for kicking my dog." Prodded by pursuing vigilantes, Milner left Montana and roamed the West. In 1867, he was named chief of scouts under George Armstrong Custer, who later described Milner as a full-whiskered man who liked whiskey, preferred riding mules, and constantly puffed a briar pipe while chewing tobacco. Milner had first scouted for Custer in his 1874 Black Hills Expedition that resulted in finding gold in "them thar hills." Milner and six others, including Jack Crawford, killed fifteen Sioux in a May 1876 ambush that took place just weeks before Custer's swan song at Little Bighorn. Later that summer, Milner was in the Deadwood area when his good pal Wild Bill Hickok was shot from behind at a card table. Supposedly, Milner was instrumental in seeing to it that Hickok's assassin, Jack McCall, left town. That October, after scouting for General George Crook, Milner himself was killed. Just as with Hickok, Milner was shot in the back by Tom Newcomb, a man with whom he had constantly feuded. "California Joe" was buried with full military honors at Fort Robinson in Nebraska. A granite headstone furnished by the government bears the simple inscription:

MOSES MILNER
SCOUT

▲ Moses Embree Milner, known as "California Joe."

▶ California Joe (left) with his friend Buffalo Bill Cody (right).

JUL 3

1898 In Pinal, Arizona Territory, Wyatt Earp's former wife Mattie Blaylock commits suicide by overdosing on laudanum.

THE POET SCOUT

John Wallace "Captain Jack" Crawford—soldier, scout, and entertainer—was best known by his admirers as the "Poet Scout." A native of Ireland and son of a hopeless drunk, Captain Jack returned from the Civil War and swore to his dying mother that no strong drink would ever touch his lips. His sobriety—a rare condition among army scouts—prompted Buffalo Bill Cody, a bona fide two-fisted drinker, to remark that Crawford was the only man he knew who could be trusted to deliver an unopened bottle of whiskey without pulling the cork. In the summer of 1876, Crawford replaced Buffalo Bill as chief of scouts for the Fifth Cavalry shortly after Custer's shocking end and only weeks before Wild Bill Hickok's death in Deadwood. Captain Jack composed tribute poems for both Custer and Hickok. He also made some appearances onstage with Cody, but that abruptly ended when Crawford shot himself in the groin during a performance and blamed the accident on Cody's drunkenness.

Did I hear the news from Custer?
Well, I reckon I did, old pard.
It came like a streak o' lightning,
And you bet, it hit me hard.
I ain't no hand to blubber,
And the briny ain't run for years,
But chalk me down for a lubber
If I didn't shed regular tears.

—Captain Jack Crawford, 1876

▲ One of the Poet Scout's many books.

▶ Captain Jack Crawford, scout.

1882 Buffalo Bill Cody presents his Old Glory Blowout show in North Platte, Nebraska.

THE GREAT NORTHFIELD RAID

The most famous bungled bank robbery in Old West history took place in Northfield, a tranquil Minnesota mill town far from the storied frontier. It came on the afternoon of September 7, 1876, when eight horsemen—Jesse and Frank James; Cole, Bob, and Jim Younger; Charlie Pitts; Clell Miller; and Bill Chadwell—rode into town intent on increasing their personal wealth. The outlaws were far from their native Missouri but figured the good folks of Northfield—mostly Scandinavian immigrants—would pose no problems, and they would find easy pickings at the First National Bank. "They're only a bunch of dumb farmers who wouldn't know an outlaw if one bit them in the foot," Chadwell had told Cole Younger. "It will be a walk in the park." He was dead wrong. Citizens' suspicions were raised as soon as they spied the strangers, wearing long linen dusters to conceal their sidearms, riding two by two into town and pulling up near the bank. Jesse (some claim Frank), Bob Younger, and Charlie Pitts strode into the bank and brandished their guns while the others either stood guard or remained mounted. Inside the bank, the robbery quickly fell apart when bookkeeper Joseph Lee Heywood refused to open the vault and was pistol-whipped and shot dead. Out on the street, the best-laid plans of the James-Younger Gang were quickly being blown apart.

"A man modest, true, gentle; diligent in business; conscientious in duty; a citizen benevolent and honorable; towards God reverent and loyal; who, while defending his trust as a bank officer, fearlessly met death at the hands of armed robbers, in Northfield, Sept. 7, 1867."

—memorial plaque for Joseph Lee Heywood, Carlton College, Northfield, Minnesota

▲ Joseph Heywood, the brave cashier of the First National Bank, killed for refusing to open the vault.

▶ An engraving of the James-Younger Gang's escape during the September 1876 robbery of the First National Bank in Northfield (located in front of the horses tied to the railing). This image appeared in *The Northfield Tragedy*, published in 1877.

WHEELER
CLOTHING
BANK
LEE AND HITCHCOCK
H. SCRIVER
BAKER Co

JUL 5

1896 Bill Doolin and "Dynamite Dick" Clifton escape from jail in Guthrie, Oklahoma Territory.

SHOT ALL TO PIECES

The townsfolk of Northfield were not about to stand by as the First National Bank was being robbed. Before the trio of outlaws inside the bank burst through the door, all kinds of hell had broken loose out on the street. "Get your guns, boys; they're robbing the bank," yelled local merchant J. S. Allen. Citizens armed with shotguns, rifles, and pistols rushed to the scene and opened fire. "For God's sake come out," Cole Younger screamed at the gang members inside the bank. "They're shooting us to pieces." The three robbers made their exit and were met with a hail of gunfire. Henry M. Wheeler, a medical student home for the summer, saw what was going on from his father's pharmacy. He made his way to the upper stories of the Dampier Hotel and, with an old army carbine, picked Clell Miller off his horse. Anselm Manning, owner of a hardware store, shot and killed one of the outlaw's mounts. Then, after clearing a jam in his breech-loading rifle, Manning took aim again, wounding Cole Younger and cutting down Bill Chadwell. Charlie Pitts was struck in the ankle, but managed to get on his horse. Jim Younger had half of his upper jaw blown away, and his brother Bob also was badly wounded. Frank James was wounded in a leg, but he and Jesse beat a hasty retreat with the three Youngers and Pitts, leaving behind the slain Miller and Chadwell. An innocent bystander, Nicholas Gustafson, also was killed in the crossfire. The outlaws fled Northfield with only $26.70 of the bank's money. The entire debacle took only twenty minutes and forever changed the lives of the infamous outlaw gang.

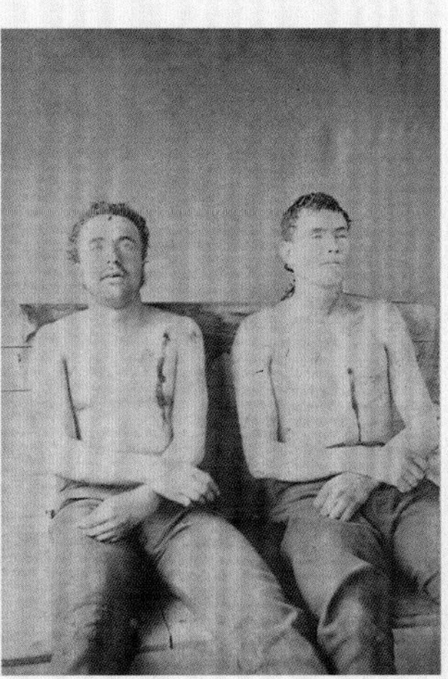

▲ Bill Chadwell and Clell Miller, the two bandits killed in the streets of Northfield by Manning and Wheeler, respectively.

▶ Henry M. Wheeler, a young medical student who picked off Clell Miller as he tried to escape the bungled bank robbery in Northfield.

▶▶ Anselm Manning, a Northfield hardware merchant.

JUL 6

1862 In Virginia City, Nevada, journalist Samuel Langhorne Clemens begins using the pen name Mark Twain.

THE MADELIA SEVEN

The gun smoke had barely cleared in Northfield following the James-Younger Gang fiasco, when posses, vigilantes, Pinkerton agents, and big city detectives spread out across southern Minnesota hunting for the culprits. The James brothers broke off from the rest of the gang and headed west toward Dakota Territory and then south on a circuitous route home. The other gang members had sustained serious wounds and were forced to move more slowly. After two weeks of dodging the massive manhunt, they were recognized by a farm boy who rode to the nearby town of Madelia and alerted the authorities. A posse was organized and on September 21, 1876, they surrounded the Younger brothers and Charlie Pitts tending to their many wounds at Hanska Slough, a low swampy thicket of willows and plum trees. When Sheriff James Glispin and Captain William W. Murphy asked for posse members to help flush out the outlaws, only five brave volunteers stepped forward—Ben Rice, Jim Severson, George Bradford, T. L. Vought, and Charles Pomeroy. A brief but furious gun battle ensued, and Charlie Pitts was shot and killed before the three Youngers surrendered. Pitts's body and the shot-up Youngers were loaded into a hay wagon and carted off. "Boys, this is horrible," Sheriff Glispin told them as the wagon lurched forward, "but you see what lawlessness has brought to you." Each of the Madelia Seven received $246 for their acts of courage and the everlasting gratitude of the community.

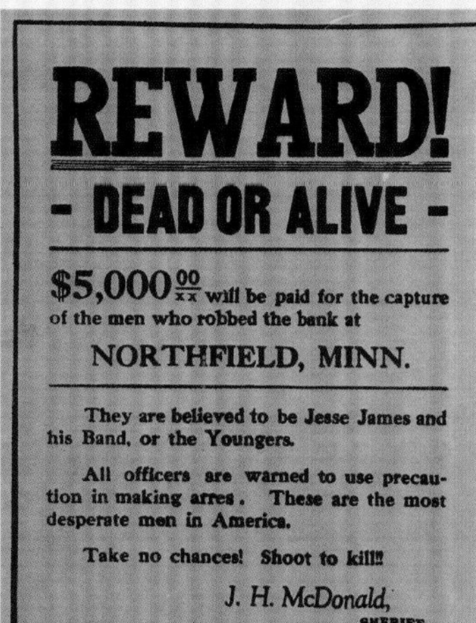

▲ A wanted poster offering a substantial reward spurred a huge manhunt for the fleeing bandits.

▶ The "Madelia Seven" located the Younger brothers and Charlie Pitts in a swampy area near Madelia, Minnesota.

JUL 7

1871 John Wesley Hardin guns down Juan Bideno in a cafe in Bluff City, Kansas, only one day after killing Charles Cougar during a quarrel in Abilene.

MINNESOTA JUSTICE

The three Younger brothers—Cole, Bob, and Jim—captured following the buggered up Northfield bank robbery, were amazed that the posse did not transport them to Madelia and string them up immediately. Instead, they were treated like celebrities. Before being jailed, they were taken to the Flanders Hotel where their many gunshot wounds were treated. When one of the Youngers asked for tobacco, the teenage farm boy who had turned them in fetched a half-cent plug. Photographs were taken of the Youngers and also the dead Charlie Pitts, his eyes still wide open. In a month, more than fifty thousand souvenir photographs of the living and dead gang members were sold to a public that was captivated by the crime and the criminals. While awaiting trial at the city jail, the Youngers received large numbers of visitors, many of them female admirers who brought flowers, cigars, and food. Law enforcement authorities, however, did not let down their guard. Figuring that the James brothers might come back and attempt to break the Youngers out of jail, extra guards were posted. Although Jesse and Frank never appeared, one nervous guard shot and killed a policeman who he thought was going for a gun, but had only opened his coat to show his badge. In November of 1876, the Youngers were scheduled for trial in Faribault, Minnesota. When they learned that according to Minnesota law guilty pleas would save them from a date with the hangman, all three brothers pled guilty to robbery and murder charges and were handed life sentences. "The excitement that followed our sentence to the state prison, which was popularly called 'cheating the gallows,' resulted in the change of law in that respect," Cole Younger later noted.

▲ The three captured Younger brothers—Cole (top), Jim (left), and Bob (right)—all severely wounded.

▶ Charlie Pitts in death, killed by the posse.

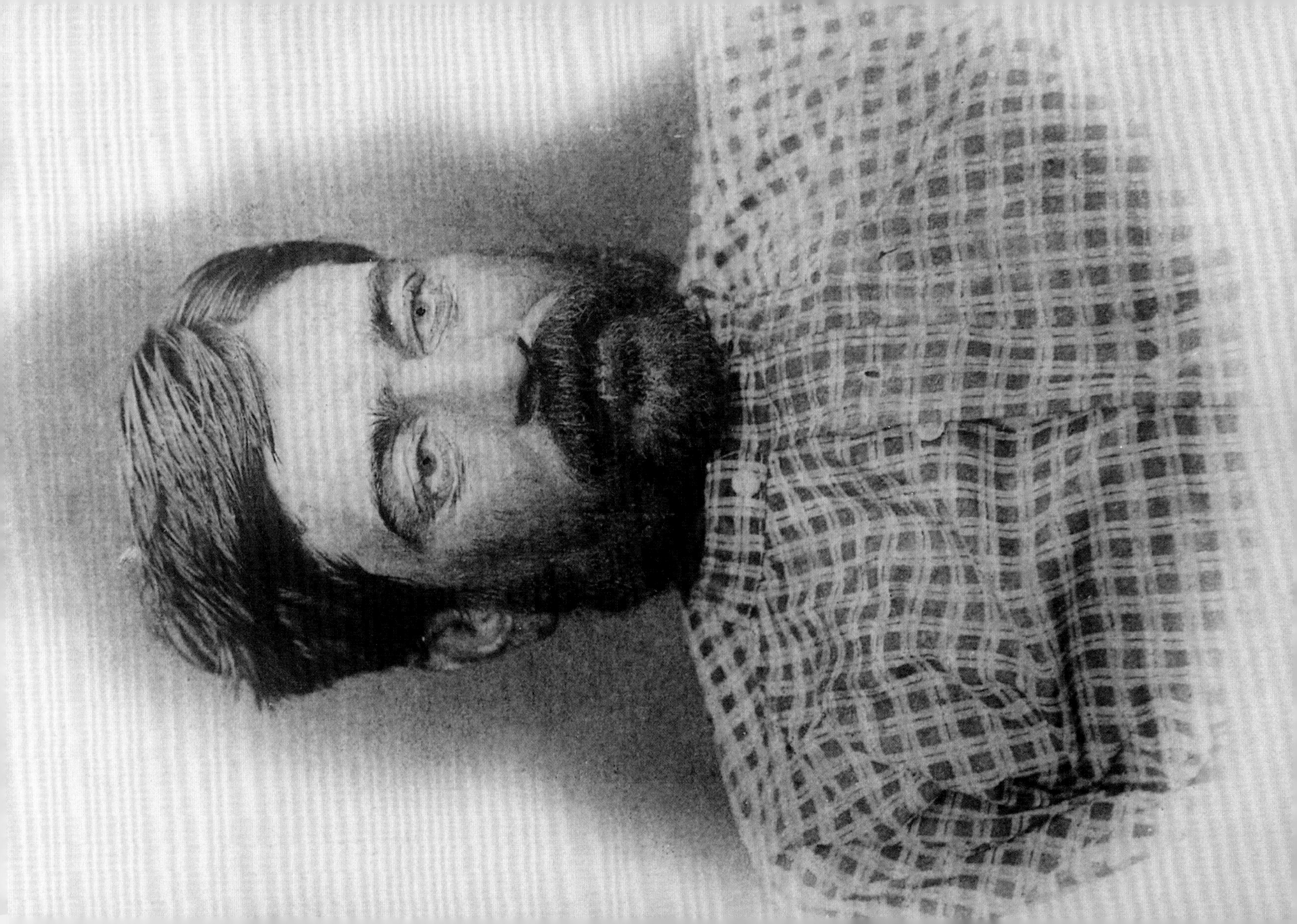

JUL 8

1884 Vigilantes kill five known rustlers during a shootout at Bates Point, Montana Territory. Four other rustlers are also caught and hanged the next day at the mouth of the Musselshell River.

HARD TIME

The Younger brothers entered the Minnesota State Prison in Stillwater on November 26, 1876. Warden John Abbott Reed spoke to them before they were marched to their three adjacent cells. They were considered good prisoners overall, only occasionally breaking any of the strictly enforced regulations. Jim was once written up for entering the dining hall wearing his cap, and Cole was reported for laughing at a guard, staring at visitors, and—twice on the same day—"making signs to visitors and throwing kisses to ladies going up the street." Jim oversaw the extensive prison library containing more than six thousand books, and all of the brothers contributed money to launch *The Prison Mirror*, the inmate newspaper. Cole wrote for the paper and helped with editing. He also spent hours in the prison woodshop and worked as a nurse in the infirmary. Bob Younger became an accounting clerk and used his free time to pore through medical books. He died of consumption in 1889, shortly after the brothers were allowed to don suits and sit for their picture with sister Henrietta (Rheta) visiting from Missouri. In 1876, John Jay Lemon, a journalist who had interviewed the Youngers just after their capture, produced an eighty-nine-page book entitled *The Northfield Tragedy.* It went into several printings—the first of many publications about the Youngers and their activities that appeared over the years, including accounts penned by Cole after he and Jim won their release in 1901.

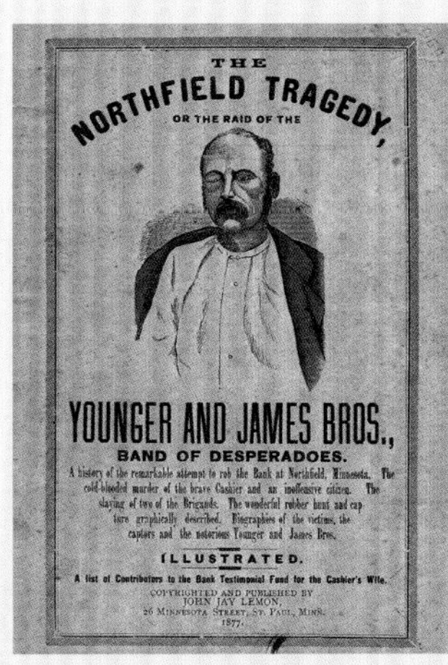
THE
NORTHFIELD TRAGEDY,
OR THE RAID OF THE
YOUNGER AND JAMES BROS.,
BAND OF DESPERADOES.
A history of the remarkable attempt to rob the Bank at Northfield, Minnesota. The cold-blooded murder of the brave Cashier and an inoffensive citizen. The slaying of two of the Brigands. The wonderful robber hunt and capture graphically described. Biographies of the victims, the captors and the notorious Younger and James Bros.
ILLUSTRATED.
A list of Contributors to the Bank Testimonial Fund for the Cashier's Wife.
COPYRIGHTED AND PUBLISHED BY
JOHN JAY LEMON,
26 MINNESOTA STREET, ST. PAUL, MINN.
1877.

▲ John Jay Lemon's *The Northfield Tragedy*, produced following interviews with the captured Younger brothers after the robbery.

▶ The Youngers (left to right: Bob, Jim, and Cole) with their sister Henrietta, who was visiting her brothers in prison after they had been incarcerated for thirteen years.

JUL 9

1881 Before being hanged, Arizona bandit Tom Harper warns "Curly Bill" Brocious to give up the outlaw life. The warning is published the next day in the *Arizona Mining Journal*.

CODE OF THE WEST

By the 1870s, a new unwritten code of behavior governing the principles of violence and honor had become the accepted norm in parts of the nation, especially the American West. The code included a new doctrine of "no duty to retreat," a clear departure from the tradition of medieval British common law that required a person under threat to retreat until his back was to the wall before using deadly force. In 1876, an Ohio court held that a "true man," if attacked, was "not obligated to fly." The following year the Indiana Supreme Court, upholding the legality of no duty to retreat, stated: "The tendency of the American mind seems to be very strongly against the enforcement of any rule which requires a person to flee when assailed." Soon this code of behavior for settling disputes became known as the Code of the West across the cattle ranges of Texas, New Mexico, Arizona, and beyond. This is not to be confused with the saccharine set of commandments governing behavior contrived by those who romanticized the West. That simplistic code, chronicled by Zane Grey, the popular pulp writer of melodramatic and improbable Old West tales, stressed self-reliance, accountability, and integrity while it celebrated the frontier values of the people. Instead, the official Code of the West simply dictated that a man did not have to back away from a fight. It also meant a man could not only fight, but also pursue an adversary until the threat was over, even if that resulted in death. "Stand your ground" was a popular battle cry for many years.

▲ The Code of the West called for self-preservation. The revolver was a great equalizer.

▶ Shootouts had to follow an accepted fairness to satisfy the Code.

& Flour
SALOON
SKINNER & DUNN.
Remington

JUL 10

1889 "Buckskin" Frank Leslie kills his lover, the prostitute Mollie Williams, in Tombstone, Arizona Territory.

SON OF SAM

If there was one thing that Temple Lea Houston disliked, it was being referred to as "Sam's boy." It was not that he disliked his illustrious father, who died when the boy was only three years old. Temple simply wanted to be respected for his own accomplishments. His mother passed away only a year after her husband, leaving the youngster to be raised by her relatives. When barely a teenager, Temple signed on for a cattle drive to Dakota Territory, worked on a Mississippi steamboat, and was appointed as a page in the U.S. Senate. During his time in Washington, D.C., he studied law and developed his talent for oration. Back in Texas, the nineteen-year-old finished up his studies and was admitted to the Texas Bar in 1878. He started out as a brilliant defense attorney and, before he turned twenty-one, was appointed the first district attorney for a court that had jurisdiction over fourteen hundred square miles in the Texas Panhandle. Starting in 1880, Houston worked out of Mobeetie, which he described as "a baldheaded whiskey town with a few virtuous women." As prosecutor, Houston took on gamblers, horse thieves, cattle rustlers, and killers. To back up his work, he wore a pair of Colt six-guns beneath his long frock coat. He went on to serve a couple of terms in the state legislature and then moved to Woodward, Oklahoma Territory, and resumed the practice of law as a defense attorney. Noted for his flamboyant speech, Houston zealously defended killers and harlots, such as Minnie Stacey. A framed copy of his eloquent argument for Minnie, which won her acquittal, was hung in the Library of Congress.

▲ Temple Houston on a hunting trip in Nebraska, c. 1895.

▶ Texas State Senator Temple Houston.

HON. TEMPLE HOUSTON,
When a Member of Texas State Senate, 1885

JUL 11

1901 Brothers Cole and Jim Younger are released from prison in Stillwater, Minnesota, after serving twenty-five years.

TEXAS, BY GOD!

John Wesley Hardin, called by some "the fastest gun in the West," met his match on August 23, 1877, in the smoking car of a passenger train in Florida. On the run for three years for the murder of Deputy Sheriff Charles Webb, the elusive Hardin—using the alias J. H. Swain—figured he was perfectly safe so far away from Texas lawmen. Apparently, he had greatly underestimated the doggedness of the Texas Rangers. It was only a matter of time for Hardin once veteran Ranger John B. Armstrong went on the chase. Armstrong hired Jack Duncan, a Dallas detective, to go undercover among Hardin's wife's family in Texas and pick up any useful information that might reveal the fugitive's hiding place. It was not long before Duncan learned that Hardin was living in Florida and Alabama with others on the run, including Hardin's brother-in-law. Armstrong and Duncan went to Florida, where they were tipped off that Hardin and some associates were aboard a train headed for Alabama. At Pensacola Junction, the Texans and several local lawmen boarded the train and confronted Hardin. When he saw Armstrong with a Colt .45 in hand, Hardin yelled, "Texas, by God!" He went for a gun, but it got tangled in his fancy suspenders, giving Armstrong time to club Hardin over the head with a revolver. Armstrong shot and killed one of Hardin's associates and took two more into custody. The shackled Hardin was spirited back to Texas where a jury in Austin found him guilty in the slaying of Deputy Webb. On October 5, 1878, Hardin entered the prison in Huntsville to serve a twenty-five-year sentence, but was granted early parole sixteen years later.

▲ John B. Armstrong, the Texas Ranger who captured Hardin with the help of local officers.

▶ The capture of John Wesley Hardin on a train in Florida, as illustrated in his autobiography, published posthumously.

THE ARREST AT PENSACOLA.

JUL

12

1861 At Rock Creek Station, Nebraska Territory, Wild Bill Hickok gets into a shootout with the McCanles Gang.
1893 In Chicago, Illinois, Frederick Jackson Turner presents his essay "The Significance of the Frontier in American History" at the World's Fair.

THE MOUTHPIECE

The person most responsible for molding Missouri outlaw Jesse James into a Robin Hood figure was John Newman Edwards, a former Confederate soldier and editor of the *Kansas City Times* throughout the James Gang's heyday. Edwards's unabashed adoration of the outlaw was apparent in 1872 when James and two followers made off with the cash box at the Kansas City Fair. The bold sunset robbery yielded only about one thousand dollars and a stray bullet wounded a young girl. The sheer audacity of the crime brought James much attention, especially from Edwards. The day after the robbery the *Times* ran Edwards's editorial entitled "The Chivalry of Crime," praising the robbery as "a deed so high-handed, so diabolically daring and so utterly in contempt of fear that we are bound to admire it and revere its perpetrators." In later writings, such as a twenty-page supplement devoted entirely to the James Gang, Edwards wrote that Jesse and his accomplices might have sat with King Arthur at his Round Table and ridden into tournaments with Sir Lancelot. Edwards published letters from James in which he defended himself as an innocent party being hounded by the devilish Yankee politicians and lawmen. "Some editors call us thieves," wrote James. "We are not thieves—we are bold robbers. It hurts me to be called a thief." Edwards continued to glorify James until the outlaw's death. In so doing, he helped the brazen killer and thief build a positive image with his adoring public who believed every word that Edwards and James wrote.

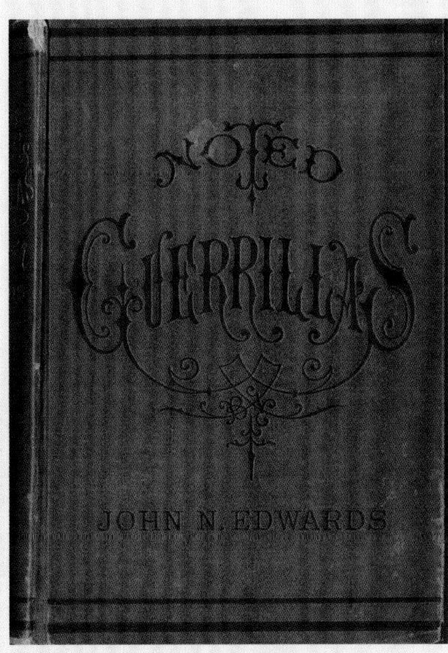

▲ John Newman Edwards's book, *Noted Guerrillas*, published in 1877.

▶ John Newman Edwards, newspaper reporter and stalwart defender of the James Gang.

JUL

13

1852 Wells Fargo Express opens its California office in San Francisco.

CHIEF JOSEPH

There was a time when Chief Joseph, leader of the Nez Perce, could quietly boast that since their first encounter with the Lewis and Clark Expedition in Oregon country, no member of his tribe had ever killed a white man. That changed in 1877, when the Nez Perce were given thirty days to move to a reservation in Idaho. The young warriors resisted. They carried out raids and fought in at least a dozen engagements. Finally, Chief Joseph attempted to lead his people on a seventeen-hundred-mile trek to Canada. Only thirty miles from the border, the fugitive Indians were intercepted by Colonel Nelson Miles and General O. O. Howard. On October 5, 1877, at his surrender in the Bear Paw Mountains, Chief Joseph gave a simple but eloquent speech.

"Tell General Howard I know his heart. What he told me before, I have in my heart. I am tired of fighting. Our chiefs are killed. Looking Glass is dead. Toohoolhoolzote is dead. The old men are all dead. It is the young men who say yes and no. He who led on the young men is dead. It is cold and we have no blankets. The little children are freezing to death. My people, some of them, have run away to the hills, and have no blankets, no food; no one knows where they are—perhaps freezing to death. I want to have time to look for my children and see how many I can find. Maybe I shall find them among the dead. Hear me, my chiefs. I am tired; my heart is sick and sad. From where the sun now stands I will fight no more forever."

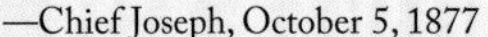

—Chief Joseph, October 5, 1877

▲ Chief Looking Glass of the Nez Perce.

▶ Chief Joseph, leader of the Nez Perce.

JUL 14

1881 At Fort Sumner, New Mexico Territory, Billy the Kid is shot and killed by Pat Garrett.

THE KID

After escaping the Silver City jail in 1875, Henry Antrim hightailed it to Arizona Territory, where he became a saddle tramp, part-time cowhand, and accomplished horse thief. By the autumn of 1876, Henry sported the sobriquet of "Kid," a popular generic name for some youngsters in the West. In 1877, following more scrapes with the law and another jail escape, Kid Antrim was living in the vicinity of Camp Grant. One sweltering August night, Antrim—flush with a pay advance from a local rancher—wandered into a cantina near the army post. In the crowd was Francis Cahill, a blacksmith bully called "Windy" because of his many tall tales. Cahill spied the Kid, a favorite target for verbal and physical abuse, and engaged him in an argument that exploded into violence. Cahill threw the Kid to the ground, pinning him to the floor and slapping his face. The Kid freed an arm and pulled his .45 pistol. There was a deafening roar, and Cahill slumped to the side. Before the smoke cleared, the Kid dashed out the door and jumped on a fleet pony. In a flash, he vanished in the moonlit night. Windy Cahill, gut-shot at close range, died the following morning. Even though many said the bully had it coming, the law saw it otherwise. "He had no choice," one witness said of the Kid. "He had to use his 'equalizer.'" It would not be the Kid's last time.

"Cahill was killed on the [military] *reservation. His murderer, Antrim alias Kid, was allowed to escape and I believe is still at large."*

—Major Charles Compton, August 23, 1877

▲ The earliest published image of Billy the Kid appeared March 5, 1881.

▶ The second circulated image in the second dime novel on his life, published later in 1881.

▶▶ The third published image appeared in Sheriff Pat Garrett's book, put out in 1882, a year after the Kid was killed.

"BILLY THE KID," AS A COW BOY

JUL 15

1862 At Apache Pass, Arizona Territory, Apache warriors battle with California Cavalry units marching to New Mexico Territory.

EYE OF THE STORM

By 1878, Lincoln County in New Mexico Territory had grown in size until it was the largest county in the United States. Its twenty million acres made it about one-fourth of the entire territory and two-thirds the size of England. Lincoln County epitomized the desires of the lawless. Crooked politicians, ruthless cattle lords, and hired gunmen cohabitated there in a milieu of unspeakable cruelty and vindictiveness. Exploitation became the norm, and the distortion of truth was commonplace. By the 1870s, sparsely populated New Mexico Territory accounted for at least 15 percent of all murders in the nation, and by 1880, the homicide rate there was forty-seven times higher than the national average, with gunshot wounds the leading cause of death. Much of that violence occurred in Lincoln County. The area's geographical remoteness and a corrupt legal system worked against law and order. It became the sanctuary of the reckless and brazen and, in so doing, an especially fertile ground for spawning myth. This stronghold of violence and treachery with a backdrop of ethnic hostility, greed, and corruption was fertile ground for the Lincoln County War.

"Lincoln County held within its boundaries all the props, trappings, and paraphernalia needed for staging an out-of-doors theatrical production of huge proportion."

—William A. Keleher, *Violence in Lincoln County*, 1957

▶ The only street in Lincoln, New Mexico Territory, "the deadliest street in America."

JUL 16

1886 Edward Zane Carroll Judson, known as Ned Buntline on the covers of his numerous dime novels, dies in New York.

THE HOUSE

There were no heroes in what became known as the Lincoln County War. Everyone involved was motivated by personal gain. It was not a fence-cutting war or a range war. It was a war of greed and corruption waged by profiteers, charlatans, and hired guns. Before the war officially started in 1878, two main alliances had emerged along with various splinter groups made up of Anglos and Hispanics, and including politicians, ranchers, and merchants. Both sides would employ gangs of mercenaries. Lawrence G. Murphy and later a former clerk-turned-business-partner James Dolan headed up the establishment faction, greatly assisted by corrupt power brokers in Santa Fe. Natives of Ireland, both Murphy and the younger Dolan came to the territory as soldiers before establishing the imposing two-story L. G. Murphy & Co. store that residents called "The House." These two men and their cohorts controlled local politics, law enforcement, and economic life in Lincoln County. As the business grew richer by monopolizing government contracts and charging outrageous prices, Murphy slid deeper into alcoholism. He retired in 1877 and died the next year, leaving Dolan in command.

▶ Murphy's partner and successor, James Dolan.

▶▶ Lawrence G. Murphy.

1881 Mountain man Jim Bridger dies nearly blind and in poor health in West Port, Missouri.

RIVALS

In the summer of 1877, a new alliance formed in the town of Lincoln to challenge the Murphy-Dolan faction and The House. The partners were an unlikely trio—Alexander McSween, a local lawyer known to be argumentative and rigid; John Henry Tunstall, a wealthy twenty-four-year-old English dandy; and John Simpson Chisum, a rough-and-ready rancher whose spread had become prime pickings for every Pecos Valley cattle thief. Tunstall, a polished Londoner, had come to Lincoln County looking for investment opportunities in grazing lands. He immediately aligned himself with McSween and Chisum in their concerted effort to create a ranching-mercantile empire all their own. In spite of many warnings, Tunstall and McSween, with Chisum's support and financial backing, established their own store and banking operation just down the road from The House.

▶ Lawyer Alexander McSween.

▶▶ John Henry Tunstall, a wealthy Englishman.

JUL 18

1857 U.S. Army troops under Colonel Albert Sidney Johnston are dispatched from Fort Leavenworth, Kansas, for Salt Lake City, Utah Territory, to deal with unrest following President James Buchanan's appointment of Alfred Cumming, a non-Mormon, to replace Brigham Young as territorial governor. The conflict becomes known as the Mormon War.

JINGLEBOB

Texan John Simpson Chisum, along with his brother, Pitzer, and their cowboys muscled their way into Lincoln County in the late 1860s and began selling beef to the army. Like other cattle kings, John Chisum was known to steal livestock from the smaller ranchers as he claimed squatter and homestead rights along the Pecos River. The enormous Chisum ranch was known as the Jinglebob (later the Jinglebob Land and Cattle Company), after the distinctive earmark on Chisum cattle, made by cutting two-thirds of each ear so the lower part dropped down like a dewlap. In the late 1870s, Chisum was running a herd of one hundred thousand Longhorns on open range that spanned more than two hundred miles, from Fort Sumner in the north all the way to the Mexican border. This area, the Trans-Pecos, was wide-open, unfenced territory. Scattered among the high plains were mountains with springs and canyons (perfect places for outlaws to hide out), and very little law enforcement. It was a cattle rustler's dream. Cattle roamed free for the taking. The Jinglebob herds were a tempting target for rustlers, and it was often said that every man who lived in those parts stole from Chisum. He reasoned that turnabout was fair play.

▲ Pecos Valley cattle king John Simpson Chisum.

▶ Cowboy Charley Nebo (left), who worked on Chisum's ranch.

JUL 19

1878 The Sam Bass Gang is ambushed by lawmen at Round Rock, Texas, and Bass dies two days later on his twenty-seventh birthday.

THE SANTA FE RING

Miguel Antonio Otero, a two-term governor of New Mexico Territory, best summed up the coalition that sparked the Lincoln County War and begot the undying myth of Billy the Kid that rose from its ashes. Otero wrote of "the all-powerful Santa Fe Ring, political powerhouse of New Mexico and the most lawless machine in the territory's history . . . actively involved in the Lincoln County slaughter, lining up solidly behind the Murphy-Dolan-Riley faction. . . . The allegiance of the Santa Fe Ring gave to the Murphy clan a semblance of legality and lawfulness that only the cold facts belied. The McSween-Chisum party, were, as a logical outcome, declared the desperadoes and law-breakers." Thomas Benton Catron was the undisputed leader of the Santa Fe Ring. Often referred to as Boss Catron, this Missouri native was a true son of the Gilded Age, as was his law and banking partner, Stephen Benton Elkins, also a Missourian and a former teacher of outlaw Cole Younger. Catron and his Santa Fe Ring cohorts were every bit as ruthless and greedy as the robber barons back East. Ring members included political and business figures and law enforcement officers. A charter member was William Rynerson, a district attorney who shot and killed a New Mexico Territory chief justice in 1867 but won an acquittal due to the legal maneuverings of Elkins. Boss Catron became spectacularly wealthy by acquiring valuable New Mexico land grants from their owners through fraud, encroachment, trickery, and violence. He and his political and banking allies further enriched themselves by pushing small ranchers off the open range.

▶ The leader of the Santa Fe Ring, Thomas Benton Catron.

▶▶ Southern New Mexico district attorney William Rynerson, a strong ally of Catron.

"Everything *in New Mexico, that pays off* at all . . . *is worked by a 'ring.'*"

—John Tunstall, letter to his father, April 1877

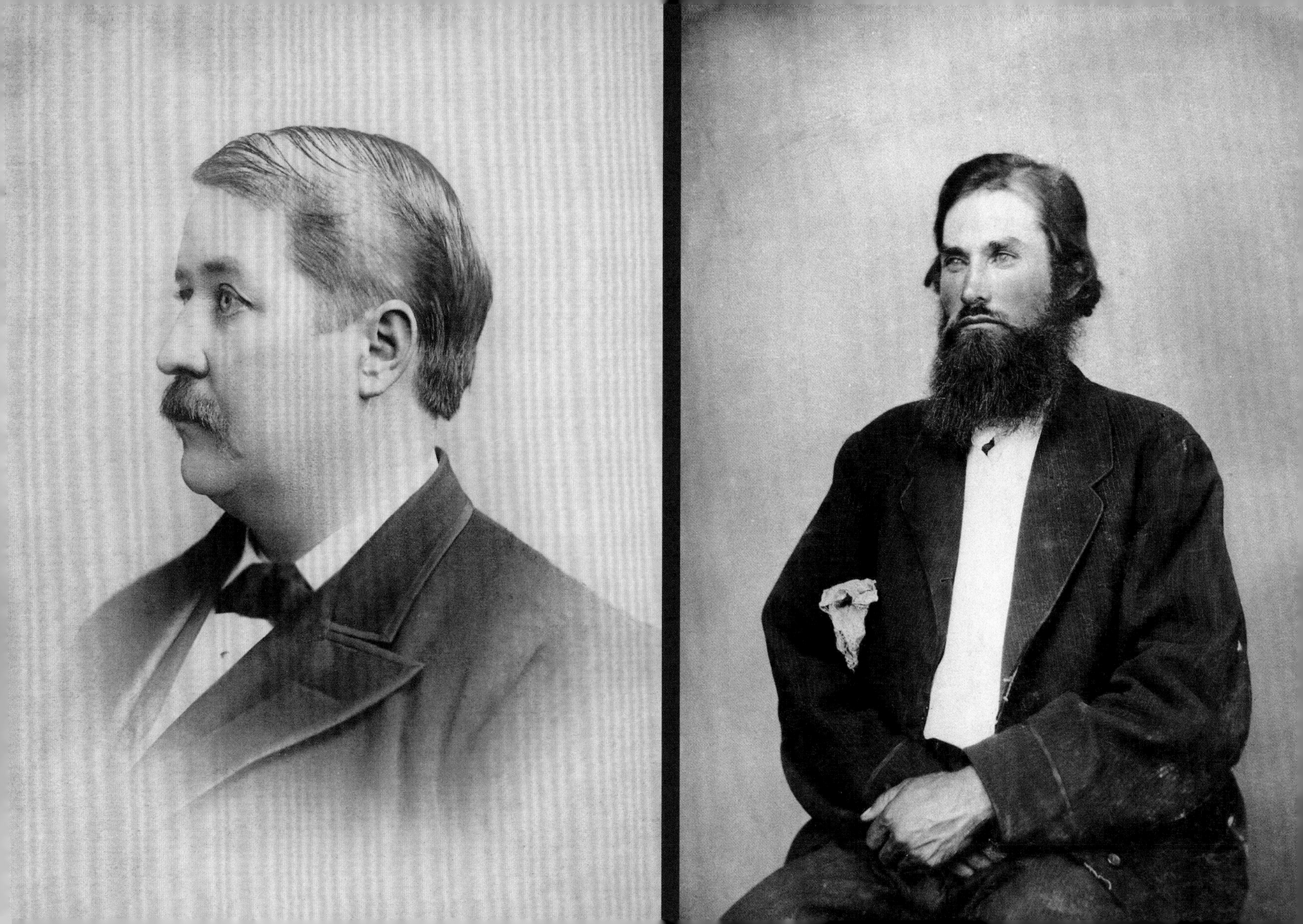

JUL 20

1889 Ella Watson, also known as "Cattle Kate," and James Averell are lynched on suspicion of cattle rustling near Independence Rock, Wyoming Territory.

LINCOLN COUNTY WAR

Henry Antrim or simply the Kid, now using the alias William Bonney, struck up friendships with some hands from the Tunstall ranch, and in late 1877 he hired on as a cowboy and cattle guard. During the ten weeks he worked for the Englishman, the Kid impressed his pals with his skillful handling of firearms. He prized his Winchester '73 rifle, but the compact .41-caliber Colt double-action Thunderer pistol was his favorite. That was fine with Tunstall, as he wanted no one but capable gunmen riding for him. "It cost a lot of money," Tunstall wrote in a letter to his family, "for men expect to be paid well for going on the war path." A few confrontations and threats from Dolan's gang of gunmen had prompted the Tunstall forces to remain on constant alert for raids on their herds. On February 18, 1878, Tunstall and some of his men, including Bonney, set out for Lincoln. At the same time, a posse deputized by Sheriff William Brady and led by Jimmy Dolan, rode out in search of Tunstall. Late in the afternoon, some of the Dolan party caught up with Tunstall's men, who had scattered in pursuit of a flock of turkeys, leaving Tunstall alone. As the riders drew near him, one of them leveled a rifle and shot the Englishman through the chest. Tunstall tumbled to the ground. While he thrashed about, another man shot him point-blank in the head and then killed Tunstall's prized bay horse. The Lincoln County War had officially begun.

▶ A painting of John Tunstall by Bob Boze Bell.

JUL 21

1865 In Springfield, Missouri, Wild Bill Hickok kills Dave Tutt in the Wild West's first recorded shootout.
1873 The James-Younger Gang robs the Rock Island and Pacific train on its way to Adair, Iowa. It is their first train robbery.

THE REGULATORS

News of Tunstall's murder spread quickly throughout Lincoln County and far beyond. In response to the Tunstall killing, Alexander McSween became the leader of those opposed to Jimmy Dolan and his gang from The House. Meanwhile, Dick Brewer, Tunstall's capable and aggressive foreman, formed the Regulators, a handle some said Kid Antrim may have pulled from dime novels. Captain Brewer's newly deputized posse included William Bonney (once Henry Antrim), Charlie Bowdre, Fred Waite, Doc Scurlock, cousins George and Frank Coe, Henry Brown, John Middleton, Jim French, John Scoggins, and other like-minded men opposed to corruption in Lincoln. The number of active Regulators varied from as few as ten to as many as sixty, including local Hispanics sympathetic to the cause. The core group was about a dozen riders, each bound by an oath they called the "Iron-clad." The essence of the oath was that members were never to divulge any information about their activities or bear witness against the other Regulators. For the next five months, operating only with a promise of four dollars a day in pay, the Regulators considered themselves a lawful posse, rather than vigilantes, as they set out to avenge the Tunstall slaying. The Kid was singled out as one of the most loyal Regulators, and the die was cast. William Bonney would emerge as Billy the Kid from the bloodshed that followed, riding a wave of illusion and deception created by the true perpetrators from both sides of the war.

▶ Fred Waite, a Chickasaw Indian and one of the Regulators.

▶▶ Regulator Doc Scurlock.

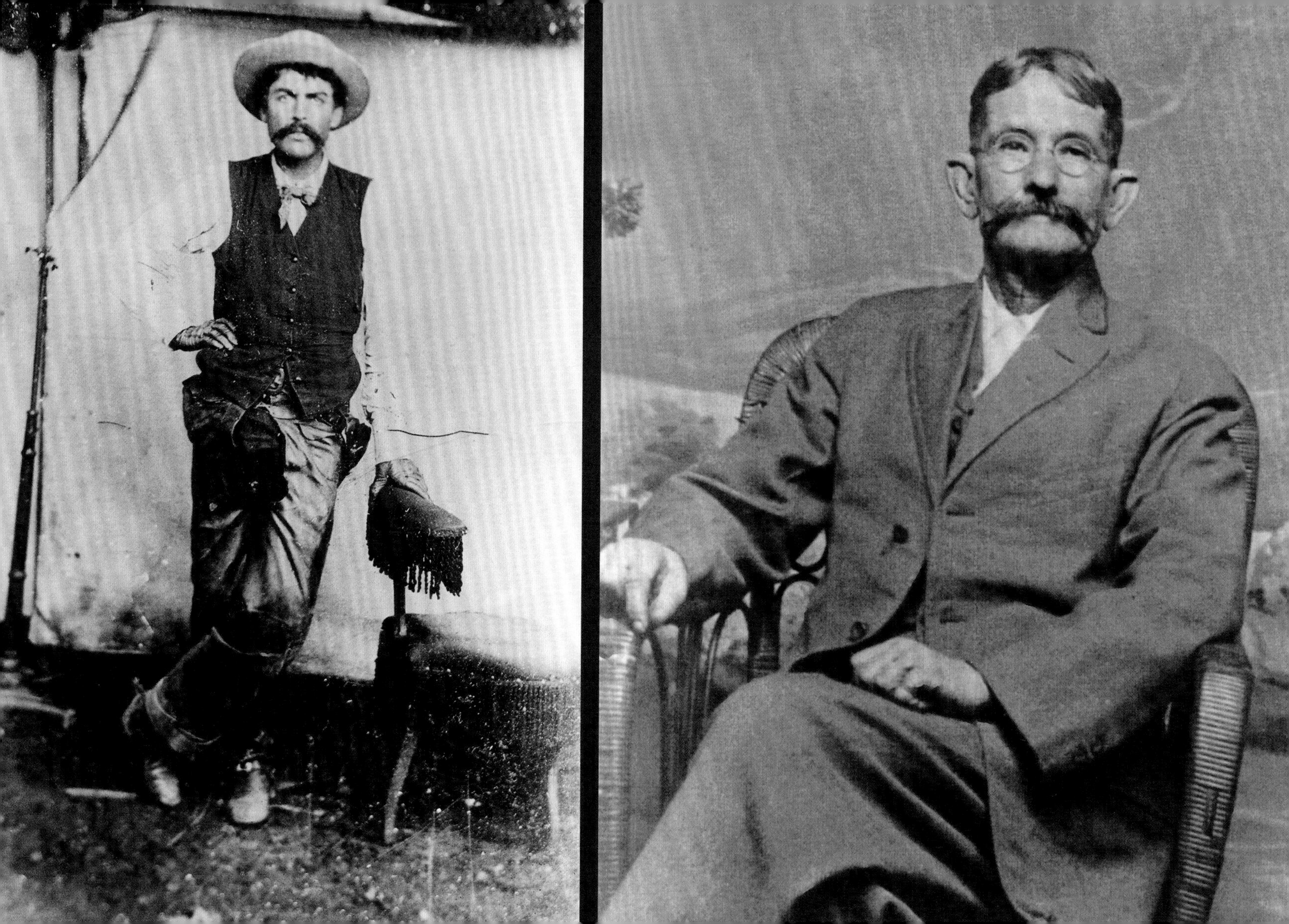

JUL 22

1883 An arson fire destroys much of Miles City, Montana.

A SCORE TO SETTLE

In early 1878, the Regulators began to seek revenge. After tracking down and killing three members of the gang that murdered Tunstall, some Regulators, including the Kid, met at Alexander McSween's home and hatched a plot to take out Sheriff William Brady. Heavily in debt to The House, Brady was bound in allegiance to the Murphy-Dolan faction and rode at the head of the gang responsible for Tunstall's demise. On the night of March 31, Billy Bonney and five other Regulators slipped into Lincoln and took up positions near the Tunstall mercantile store in a corral hidden by an adobe wall. They waited for daybreak. Around nine o'clock on the morning of April 1, Brady and some of his deputies posted some legal notices and were walking up the main street of Lincoln when the Regulators rose as one, poked their Winchesters through gun ports carved in the adobe wall, and cut loose with a steady stream of fire. At least a dozen rounds tore through Brady, the main target. Sitting in the middle of the road, Brady groaned, "Oh, Lord," as he attempted to get to his feet. A second volley struck him dead. One of the deputies was killed as he ran for cover. When the shooting stopped, Bonney and Jim French jumped over the wall and ran to the lifeless Brady. While they bent over the body, a bullet fired by one of the fleeing deputies ripped through the Kid's thigh and struck French in the leg. They hobbled off and escaped with the other Regulators. The killings of Brady and his deputy had a devastating impact on the community. Public opinion shifted, and both sides in the war were now considered equally nefarious and bloodthirsty.

▶ Lincoln County sheriff William Brady.

▶▶ Deputy William Mathews, who survived the gunfire that killed Sheriff Brady.

JUL 23

1875 The first trial of John D. Lee, accused of leading the 1857 Mountain Meadows Massacre, begins. It ends in a hung jury, but a year later Lee is found guilty in a second trial and executed.

BLAZER'S MILL

On April 4, 1878, just three days after the ambush of Sheriff Brady in Lincoln, Dick Brewer led sixteen Regulators, including Billy Bonney alias the Kid and Jim French (both recovering from their gunshot wounds) to the settlement of Blazer's Mill. Soon after arriving, the Regulator Frank Coe encountered Andrew "Buckshot" Roberts, yet another who rode with Brady's posse the day Tunstall was killed. When Coe failed to convince Roberts to peacefully surrender, a fierce gun battle ensued. Although greatly outnumbered, the mortally wounded Roberts held his own. Four Regulators also received wounds, and when Captain Brewer lifted his head above a log barricade, Roberts cut loose with his Springfield rifle and a bullet crashed into Brewer's left eye and blew out the back of his head. Stunned by Brewer's death, the Regulators lost their taste for further battle that day. Roberts, in so much pain that two men had to hold him down, died the following day. In a macabre twist, Brewer and Buckshot were buried in a common grave, some said next to each other in the same coffin. The Blazer's Mill shootout did not endear the McSween faction and his Regulators to the local populace. Despite the death of Brewer, a well-liked and sympathetic figure whom McSween called "nature's nobleman," the public generally disapproved of the circumstances of Buckshot Roberts's death. Many people admired that Roberts put up a gutsy fight against overwhelming odds.

▶ Dick Brewer was the first leader of the Regulators, and the first to die. He was killed at Blazer's Mill by Buckshot Roberts's unerring aim.

▶▶ George Coe was one of the last Regulators to die. He lived until 1941, but without his trigger finger, which he lost at Blazer's Mill.

JUL 24

1897 Members of the Twenty-fifth Infantry Bicycle Corps arrive in St. Louis, Missouri. The all-black unit of infantrymen had set out from Missoula, Montana, forty days earlier on a grueling journey to test the effectiveness of bicycles for military transportation.

FIVE DAYS BATTLE

Following a slew of inconclusive gun battles and more deaths, the Lincoln County War essentially ended in July 1878 in a fiery spectacle known as the Five Days Battle. It started on July 15 when the two opposing factions faced off in Lincoln. A large force of Regulators, including some of the original "Iron-clads," took positions in a store and the residence of Alexander and Susan McSween. At the same time, Jimmy Dolan's hired gunmen gathered at the Wortley Hotel, across the road from The House. Newly appointed sheriff George Peppin, an ardent Dolan supporter, led them. The first four days brought mostly sporadic gunfire, some casualties, and no resolution. On July 19, the stalemate ended when Peppin convinced Lieutenant Colonel Nathan Dudley, an incompetent alcoholic sympathetic to the sheriff, to bring troops from nearby Fort Stanton. With Dudley's backing, Peppin's men moved in for the kill. After surrounding the McSween place, they set the house on fire. When night fell and the flames spread, Susan McSween and the other women were allowed to leave. Finally the remaining defenders were forced to make a desperate break. They ran into an explosion of gunfire. One of those who died was Alex McSween, riddled with five bullets. Peppin's boys broke out fiddles and danced, swilling whiskey and shooting their guns in the air to celebrate. Lieutenant Colonel Dudley shooed away chickens pecking at McSween's lifeless eyes. Other corpses lay bloody and burned. The Kid was not one of them. He had escaped. Billy Bonney danced through the ring of flames and a hail of bullets into the safety of the shadows.

▲ Robert Beckwith, the only casualty on the sheriff's side when the Regulators fled the burning McSween house.

▶ The only known photograph of George W. Peppin, 1905.

JUL 25

1853 California Rangers led by Captain Harry Love kill the infamous leader of the Five Joaquins gang Joaquin Murieta and his lieutenant Three-Fingered Jack.

LEW WALLACE

In the aftermath of the Lincoln County War, heads rolled. The crimes committed, including the illegal use of federal troops by civilians, did not go unnoticed. Although he retained much of his power, Tom Catron was forced to resign as U.S. attorney. Following a federal investigation, President Rutherford B. Hayes removed Governor Samuel Axtell from office. His replacement was Lew Wallace, a noted Civil War general who came home to Indiana to pursue a legal and literary career and in 1873 publish *Fair God*, his first novel. Hayes figured Wallace was just the man to tame the renegades in New Mexico Territory. Once on the scene, Wallace called for an immediate halt to the violence. He issued a proclamation of amnesty for all parties that had taken part in the Lincoln County War, except for those already under criminal indictment. William Bonney failed the amnesty test since he had previously been indicted for the murder of Sheriff Brady and faced a federal indictment in the slaying of Buckshot Roberts. Still, the Kid was hopeful and wrote letters to Wallace, offering his help in exchange for immunity. On March 17, 1879, as he was completing his newest novel, *Ben-Hur: A Tale of the Christ*, Wallace slipped into Lincoln for a secret meeting with the Kid. Wallace promised that the young man would go free if he testified before a grand jury probing a Lincoln County murder. The Kid appeared and told what he knew about the crime that he had witnessed. Although the Kid's testimony helped win indictments, the district attorney disregarded Governor Wallace's order to set Bonney free.

▶ General Lew Wallace during the Civil War.

▶▶ Lew Wallace, governor of New Mexico Territory and author of *Ben-Hur*.

JUL 26

1878 Wyatt Earp kills drunken cowboy George Hoyt, a pal of gunslinger Clay Allison, in Dodge City, Kansas. Hoyt shoots at Earp and misses three times outside the Comique Theater, forcing comedian Eddie Foy to take cover onstage in the midst of his act. Earp returns fire and hits his mark.

NEW MEXICO'S CATTLE QUEEN

Susan McSween was never afraid to speak her mind. Even in the face of danger and death during the Five Days Battle of the Lincoln County War, the feisty lady stood up to the men who later that day made her a widow. Born Susan Ellen Hummer in Pennsylvania in 1845, she married Alex McSween in Kansas in 1873, shortly before moving to New Mexico Territory. Susan never forgave the killers of her husband and she hired lawyer Huston Chapman to bring those men to trial. James Dolan and three of his men murdered Chapman and threatened Susan's life, but she never cowered. She took over her dead husband's property, as well as land owned by John Tunstall and his foremen Dick Brewer. She married George Barber in 1884, but divorced him eleven years later and kept his surname. John Chisum gave her some cattle to start a herd, and eventually she ran upward of eight thousand head on her ranch near Three Rivers, New Mexico Territory. Known as "New Mexico's Cattle Queen," she sold her ranch in 1917 to Albert Bacon Fall, later a key figure in the Teapot Dome Scandal. Susan McSween Barber retired to White Oaks where she died in 1931.

▶ Susan McSween, c. 1873 after her marriage to Alex.

▶▶ Susan McSween Barber, long after the Lincoln County War.

"Billy was not a bad man, that is he was not a murderer who killed wantonly. Most of those he killed deserved what they got. Of course I cannot very well defend his stealing horses and cattle, but when you consider that Murphy, Dolan, and Riley people forced him into such a lawless life through efforts to secure his arrest and conviction, it is hard to blame the poor boy for what he did."

—Susan McSween Barber, reflecting on Billy the Kid, 1881

JUL 27

1867 At Walnut Grove, Arizona Territory, Harvey Twaddle is hit in the ear by an Apache arrow while searching for stray mules. He returns fire, killing two Apaches and wounding another. Twaddle chases two mules back to camp where he relates his story, but dies nine days later.

THAT DAMN PICTURE

In 1880, an itinerant photographer came to the remote frontier town of Fort Sumner, New Mexico Territory, and took what would become one the most famous, valuable, and controversial photographs in the history of the West. The subject—a twenty-year-old cowboy and small-time rustler—was still using the name William H. Bonney, but everyone called him the Kid. More than likely, the photographer used a multilens camera that simultaneously produced four two-by-three ferrotypes, popularly called tintypes. Ferrotypes were easy to prepare. The photographer would have set up the shot, taken the image, developed it, varnished a ferrotype plate, and handed it to the Kid in only minutes at a cost of probably twenty-five cents. The only documented photograph of the Kid was misunderstood and abused. The original, being a tintype, is a mirror image, so for many years it was believed the Kid was left-handed because his pistol appears to be on his left hip. Several people who actually knew the Kid, including his favorite girlfriend Paulita Maxwell, maintained that the photo was distorted and not an accurate portrayal. "I never liked the picture," Paulita said many years later. "I don't think it does Billy justice. It makes him look rough and uncouth. The expression of his face was really boyish and very pleasant." Shortly after the iconic photo was taken, the young man shown with his head slightly tilted and Winchester at his side would be known across the nation by the name journalists gave him—Billy the Kid.

▲ The first publication of the only known photo of Billy the Kid.

▶ In the early 1980s, this original tintype surfaced in the family of descendants of the Dedrick brothers, close associates of the Kid.

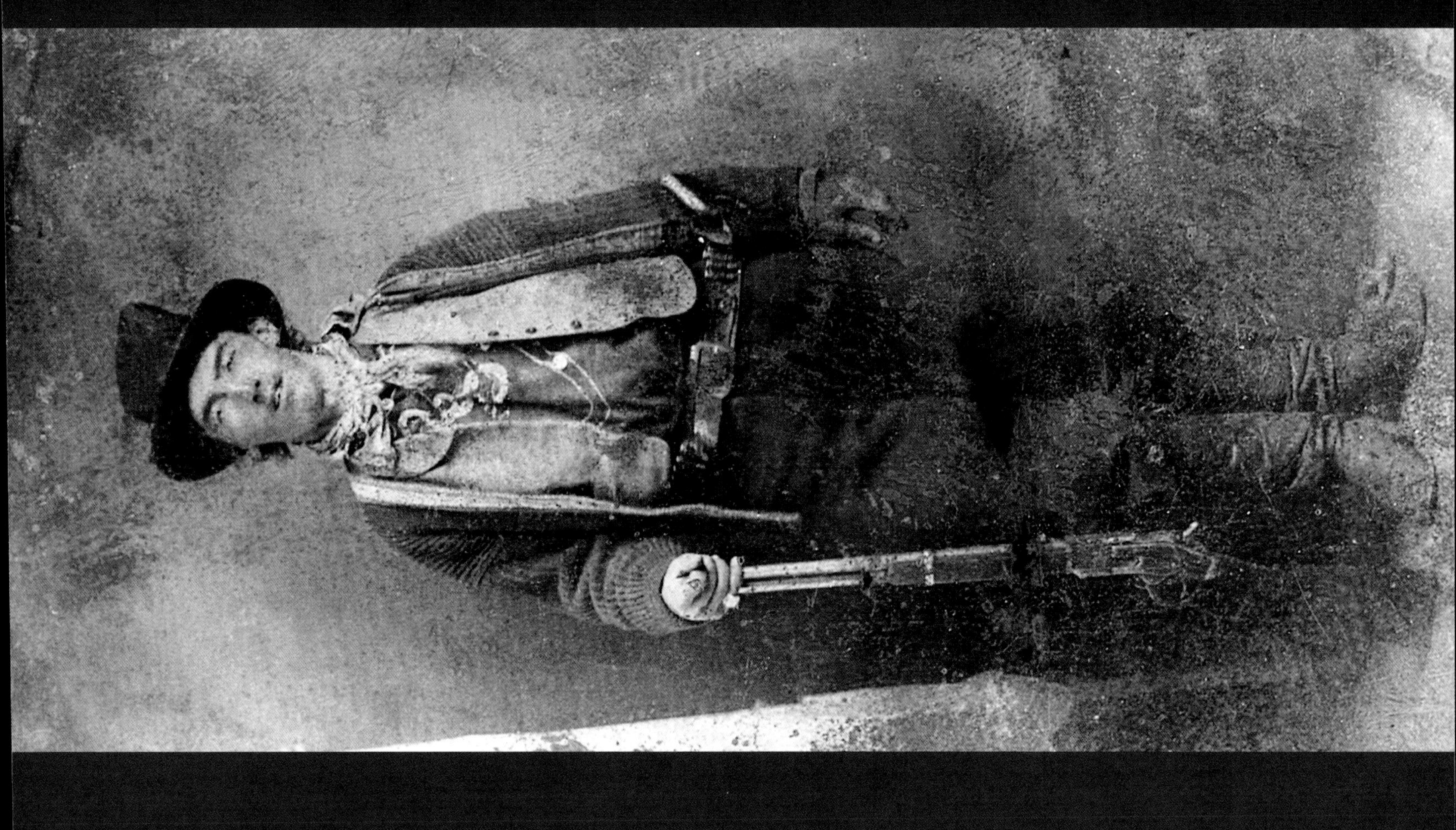

JUL 28

1877 Missouri Governor Thomas Crittenden offers a one-thousand-dollar reward each for Jesse and Frank James.

WANTED

"There's a powerful gang of outlaws harassing the stockmen of the Pecos and Panhandle country, and terrorizing the people of Fort Sumner and vicinity. The gang includes forty or fifty men, all hard characters, the off-scourings of society, fugitives from justice, and desperadoes by profession. . . . The gang is under the leadership of 'Billy the Kid,' a desperate cuss, who is eligible for the post of captain of any crowd, no matter how mean or lawless."

—J. H. Koogler, *Las Vegas Gazette*, December 3, 1880
The first time the name Billy the Kid appeared in print

"I found Billy different from most boys his age. He had been thrown on his own resources from early boyhood. From his own statement to me, he hadn't known what it meant to be a boy; at the age of twelve he was associated with men of twenty-five and older. Billy was eager to learn everything and had a most active and fertile mind. He was small and of frail physique; his hands and feet were more like a woman's than a man's. . . . Billy explained to me how he became proficient in the use of firearms. He said his age and his physique were handicaps in his personal encounters, so he decided to become a good shot with both rifle and six-shooter as a means of protection against bodily harm."

—Regulator Frank Coe, 1923

▲ This high-quality close-up of the Dedrick tintype is perhaps the best available rendering of the real Billy the Kid.

▶ Following the Lincoln County War, Billy the Kid rustled some Chisum cattle and horses and became a wanted outlaw. This reward notice appeared in a Santa Fe newspaper for several weeks.

BILLY THE KID.

$500 REWARD.

I will pay $500 reward to any person or persons who will capture William Bonny, alias The Kid, and deliver him to any sheriff of New Mexico. Satisfactory proofs of identity will be required.

LEW. WALLACE,
Governor of New Mexico.

JUL 29

1849 Stakeholders in the California goldfields meet and pass a resolution banning all blacks, slave or freedmen, from owning claims or working the mines.

EL CHIVATO

While the Anglo establishment and Santa Fe Ring, aided and abetted by sensationalist journalists and dime novelists, propagated the legend of a demonic Billy the Kid, many in the Hispanic community cheered him as their hero. To them, he was not a ruthless killer. He was their *El Chivato*, their little Billy, a champion of the poor and oppressed. As a boy, he had learned the Spanish language and was always attracted to the native culture, as well as to several comely señoritas. His love of dancing and singing came from his spirited Irish mother, and he showed up at countless fandangos and socials to whirl the ladies around the floor. Although she later denied it, there is little doubt that Paulita Maxwell was one of the Kid's favorite girls. For a brief time he was smitten with Sallie Chisum, the pretty niece of cattleman John Chisum. He also was linked romantically to other young women—Nasaria Yerby, Abrana Garcia, and Celsa Gutierrez, a sister of Pat Garrett's second wife—and supposedly fathered children with at least two of them. Yet many who knew the Kid believed it was his love for Paulita that kept him in the Fort Sumner area and ultimately lured him to his death.

"Billy the Kid, I may tell you, fascinated many women. . . . Like a sailor he had a sweetheart in every port of call. In every placita [small plaza] *in the Pecos some little señorita was proud to be known as his* querída [lover]."

—Paulita Maxwell Jaramillo, 1924

▲ Paulita Maxwell, sister of Pete Maxwell and daughter of Lucien Maxwell, of the Maxwell Land Grant.

▶ Sallie Chisum, niece of John Chisum.

JUL 30

1837 Four Bears, a Mandan chief, makes a speech to his tribe condemning the white man for the diseases they have spread to the Indian population.
1878 Black Bart robs the Laporte-to-Oroville stage. When a passenger throws out her purse, he hands it back telling her, "In that respect, I honor only the good office of Wells Fargo."

PAT GARRETT

By 1880, the Kid had encountered Patrick Garrett, a trail driver and buffalo hunter from Texas who had moved to New Mexico Territory. When the Kid was not rustling cattle, dancing, or courting, he liked dealing some monte at Beaver Smith's, a popular drinking and gambling establishment where Garrett worked as a barkeep. Almost six-and-a-half-feet tall, Garrett turned heads wherever he went. Hispanics dubbed him Juan Largo, or Long John. When he first got to Fort Sumner, he worked as a cowhand for Pete Maxwell, big brother of the Kid's girlfriend Paulita. Following a disagreement, Maxwell fired Garrett, so he began serving drinks at the saloon and raising a few hogs on the side. Controversy dogged him. The story that Garrett had killed a fellow buffalo hunter made the rounds as did rumors that he was wanted for another murder and had abandoned a wife and children in Texas. Garrett, who rubbed shoulders with all sorts of lawbreakers at the saloon, undoubtedly knew the Kid, but stories that the pair were bosom pals and rode together are doubtful. No longer content to slop hogs and tend bar, Garrett considered his options. He had caught the attention of the all-powerful cattle interests weary of losing their stock to thieves like the Kid. At their urging, Garrett ran for office, and on November 2, 1880, he was elected sheriff of Lincoln County. As a sworn law officer, Garrett now became a principal player in the ongoing drama of Billy the Kid.

▲ A depiction of Pat Garrett in one of the first books about Billy the Kid, 1881.

▶ Sheriff Pat Garrett shortly after he killed Billy the Kid, 1881.

JUL 31

1878 A lone, masked gunman, most likely Bill Brazelton, robs the Tucson-to-Florence stage in Arizona Territory.

NIGHT RIDERS

Immediately after becoming Lincoln County sheriff, Garrett assembled bands of armed men and went on the hunt for cattle rustlers. The pursuit was only sweetened when Governor Lew Wallace, after paying no mind to the Kid's letters claiming innocence, placed a hefty five-hundred-dollar reward on his head. Garrett pulled together a posse composed of his best men and some Texas stock detectives, and when information gathered by scouts and spies led the posse to Fort Sumner, they took over the old Indian hospital. Living in one of the many rooms was Charlie Bowdre's wife, Manuela, and her mother. Bowdre was a close associate of the Kid and was riding with him. Garrett spread a rumor that he and his men had left, hoping to lure the Kid, Bowdre, and the others to Fort Sumner. Garrett figured they would head directly to Manuela, where his posse now waited. He was right. On the evening of December 19, 1880, lookouts spotted dark figures moving through the fog and snow. Six riders approached, including the Kid. When they drew closer, Garrett yelled, "Halt!" One of the riders, Tom O. Folliard, the Kid's closest friend, went for his sidearm and a barrage of gunfire broke out. The surprised horsemen wheeled about and dashed away into the darkness, but one horse lingered with a man hanging on the saddle. Folliard was shot through the chest and whispered, "Don't shoot, Garrett, I'm killed."

▲ Tom O. Folliard, close companion of Billy the Kid.

▶ Cowboy Jim East, seated on the right, with three more Texas Panhandle cowboys. East joined Garrett's posse in the search for the Kid.

AUG 1

1867 Near Hays City, Kansas, in what has become known as the Victoria Massacre, a group of Cheyenne Indians kill and scalp six men working on the Kansas Pacific Railroad. Thomas Birmingham is the only survivor.

STINKING SPRINGS

When the shooting ceased and smoke cleared at Fort Sumner, Sheriff Garrett's men helped the badly wounded Tom O. Folliard from his horse and carried him inside Charlie Bowdre's home. Folliard muttered a few curses and died. Garrett bought a coffin, and the next day some villagers buried him in the old military cemetery. Garrett waited for a break in the snowstorm and managed to find out through his spies where the Kid and the rest of his gang were hiding. In the early hours of December 23, 1880, the posse surrounded an abandoned one-room stone house at Stinking Springs on Taiban Creek. Garrett told the men that the Kid often wore a Mexican sugarloaf hat and that if they saw him, they should "cut down and kill him." When first light broke, a man wearing a sombrero came outside to feed the tethered horses. Convinced it was the Kid, Garrett ordered his men to fire, and a ring of Winchesters exploded. The man staggered inside, mortally wounded. However, it was not the Kid, but Charlie Bowdre. When Bowdre came back outside, he fell over dead. Garrett later checked the body and found a bloodstained ferrotype of a heavily armed Bowdre with his wife. The four others were trapped inside the cabin with no place to hide or run. For most of the day, the Kid and Garrett bantered back and forth. Finally the aroma of cooked bacon and beans outside did the trick. The Kid and his gang surrendered.

▲ Pat Garrett removed this bloodstained photograph of Charlie Bowdre and his wife from Bowdre's body at Stinking Springs.

▶ Pat Garrett, dressed for a New Mexico winter.

1876 In Deadwood, Dakota Territory, Wild Bill Hickok is assassinated at Nuttall & Mann's No. 10 Saloon by Jack McCall.

BEHIND BARS

After their capture at Stinking Springs, the Kid and his three companions were taken back to Fort Sumner, where the shackled Kid delivered a farewell kiss to Paulita. The prisoners were loaded into a wagon and set out under heavy guard for the New Mexico Territory settlement of Las Vegas. They enjoyed a wild turkey Christmas dinner in Puerto de Luna and arrived at their destination the following day, where the lawmen were treated like celebrities. A local businessman, who wanted "to see the boys go away in style," presented Billy and his friends with new suits of clothes.

"*The lovers embraced, and* [Paulita] *gave* [Billy] *one of those soul kisses the novelists tell us about, till it being time to hit the road to Vegas, we had to pull them apart, much against our wishes, for you know, all the world loves a lover.*"

—Sheriff Deputy Jim East, December 24, 1880

"*I don't blame you for writing of me as you have. You had to believe other stories but then I don't know, as anyone would believe anything good of me anyway. I wasn't the leader of my gang, I was for Billy all the time. . . . I haven't stolen any stock. I made my living by gambling but that was the only way I could live. They wouldn't let me settle down; if they had I wouldn't be here today,' and then he held up his left hand with the bracelet.*"

—Billy the Kid, *Las Vegas Gazette*, December 27, 1880

▲ The Kid bids Paulita Maxwell goodbye in this Bob Boze Bell painting.

▶ This painting by J. N. Marchand depicts the arrival of Garrett's posse in Las Vegas, New Mexico Territory, with the Kid and his gang chained in a wagon.

AUG 3

1876 A miner's court in Deadwood, Dakota Territory, acquits Jack McCall of Wild Bill Hickok's murder. He is later retried in Yankton, found guilty, and hanged.

BIG SPRINGS ROBBERY

The first and the biggest robbery of a Union Pacific train took place on the moonlit night of September 18, 1877, just above the Colorado border near the town of Big Springs, Nebraska. Sam Bass, a Texas lawman-turned-brigand and five hardcase companions had already taken the stationmaster captive and destroyed the telegraph before the eastbound express train stopped to pick up the mail. The outlaws swept through the train and pried open strongboxes containing a total of sixty thousand dollars in currency and shiny twenty-dollar gold coins newly minted in San Francisco. They had to leave behind three hundred thousand dollars in gold bullion because the bars were too heavy to carry away on horseback. They did take the time, however, to collect another thirteen hundred dollars in cash plus many gold watches and rings from the passengers. Then the robbers disappeared into the darkness, stopping to cook supper and divide up the loot at the remains of Lone Tree, a towering cottonwood near the Platte River. For many years, rumor had it that the outlaws buried some of their gold coins near the tree, but none were ever found. Bass and his boys had attracted attention before the train heist when they robbed seven stagecoaches in Dakota Territory. But the Nebraska train robbery was a much more ambitious endeavor. Lawmen were under pressure to find the bandits, who had split into pairs and ridden off in different directions. Within a few weeks, three of them had been killed while resisting arrest. But Bass made it back to Texas unscathed and formed a new outlaw band.

▲ The only authentic photograph of Sam Bass, standing left. Bass and Joel Collins, seated at right holding the gun, were two of the six who pulled off the Big Springs train robbery.

▶ This rare book appeared only weeks after the robbery that netted the bandits over sixty thousand dollars in gold coins.

"HANDS UP!"

OR

THE HISTORY OF A CRIME.

THE GREAT UNION PACIFIC EXPRESS ROBBERY.

BY AL. SORENSON.

ILLUSTRATED.

OMAHA, NEB.:
PUBLISHED BY BARKALOW BROS.,
1877.

AUG 4

1920 Frank "Jelly" Nash, who once rode with the Al Spencer Gang, is convicted of robbery and sentenced to twenty-five years in the Oklahoma State Penitentiary at McAlester.

BAT MASTERSON

He was christened Bartholomew Masterson, and later changed his given name to William Barclay. But everyone called him Bat. Still in his teens when his family settled near Wichita, Kansas, Bat and his brothers Ed and James became hide hunters. In 1874, Bat was one of the twenty-eight buffalo hunters who tangled with warring Comanches at the Battle of Adobe Walls. Later that year, Bat spent time with the U.S. Army as a civilian scout for Nelson Miles in the campaign against the Kiowas and Comanches in the Texas Panhandle. His first gunfight took place at Sweetwater (later Mobeetie), Texas, in 1876, when he killed Sergeant Melvin King in a dispute over the affections of a woman. In the fray, the lady also died, and Bat was wounded in the pelvis. After he recovered, he joined his brothers in Dodge City, Kansas. Older brother Ed had been appointed assistant marshal of Dodge, and Jim later worked as a Dodge policeman. By the spring of 1877, Bat was working at Jim's saloon and also serving as under-sheriff to Charles E. Bassett. In the autumn of 1877, Bat and Bassett joined in the massive manhunt for Sam Bass and his crew following the robbery of the Union Pacific train in Nebraska. The next year, Ed Masterson was killed while trying to disarm two drunken cowboys. Bat succeeded Bassett as sheriff of Ford County and served until January 1880. During that time, Bat became a close friend of Wyatt Earp, and for several years after he left Dodge City, Bat made his living as a gambler and visited Earp in Tombstone, Arizona Territory. He left there just before the famous gunfight at the O.K. Corral.

▲ Bat, standing, with his fellow lawman Wyatt Earp in Dodge City, Kansas. The two would remain lifelong friends.

▶ Bat Masterson, photographed in Dodge City.

AUG 5

1881 During a dispute over his association with the U.S. government, Sioux chief Spotted Tail is killed by Crow Dog, a tribal shaman.

SHOOTOUT AT ROUND ROCK

After the train robbery at Big Springs, Nebraska, in the fall of 1877, outlaw Sam Bass laid low in Texas. The next year, however, he recruited a new gang and planned a string of robberies. In rapid succession, Bass and his cohorts robbed four trains and two stages within twenty-five miles of Dallas. The holdups netted little return, but alerted state authorities that Sam Bass was back in business. The heat on Bass and his boys intensified when the Texas Rangers and Pinkerton agents launched a manhunt. Gang members grew restless when Bass failed to duplicate his earlier successes. Soon most of the outlaws deserted, leaving Bass with only his chief lieutenant Seaborn Barnes, Frank Jackson, and newcomer Jim Murphy, who told the others he had just broken out of jail but was actually a paid informant. On July 19, 1878, the gang rode into Round Rock, Texas, with plans to rob the bank. The town was filled with concealed lawmen, undercover agents, and Texas Rangers who had been tipped off by Murphy. The outlaws gunned down a deputy sheriff when he confronted them, and a fierce battle broke out. Barnes killed two Rangers before he took a bullet in the head; Bass was badly wounded but was able to escape. The next day he was found barely alive in a grove outside of town and taken back to Round Rock. He died the following morning, July 21, on his twenty-seventh birthday.

PRICE FIFTY CENTS

AUTHENTIC HISTORY

OF

SAM BASS

AND

HIS GANG.

By a Citizen of Denton County, Texas.

DENTON, TEXAS:
Monitor Book and Job Printing Establishment.
1878.

▲ One of several rare books on Sam Bass and his gang that appeared immediately after his death, 1878.

▶ Sam Bass, as pictured by artist Bob Boze Bell, based on the only known photo of Bass.

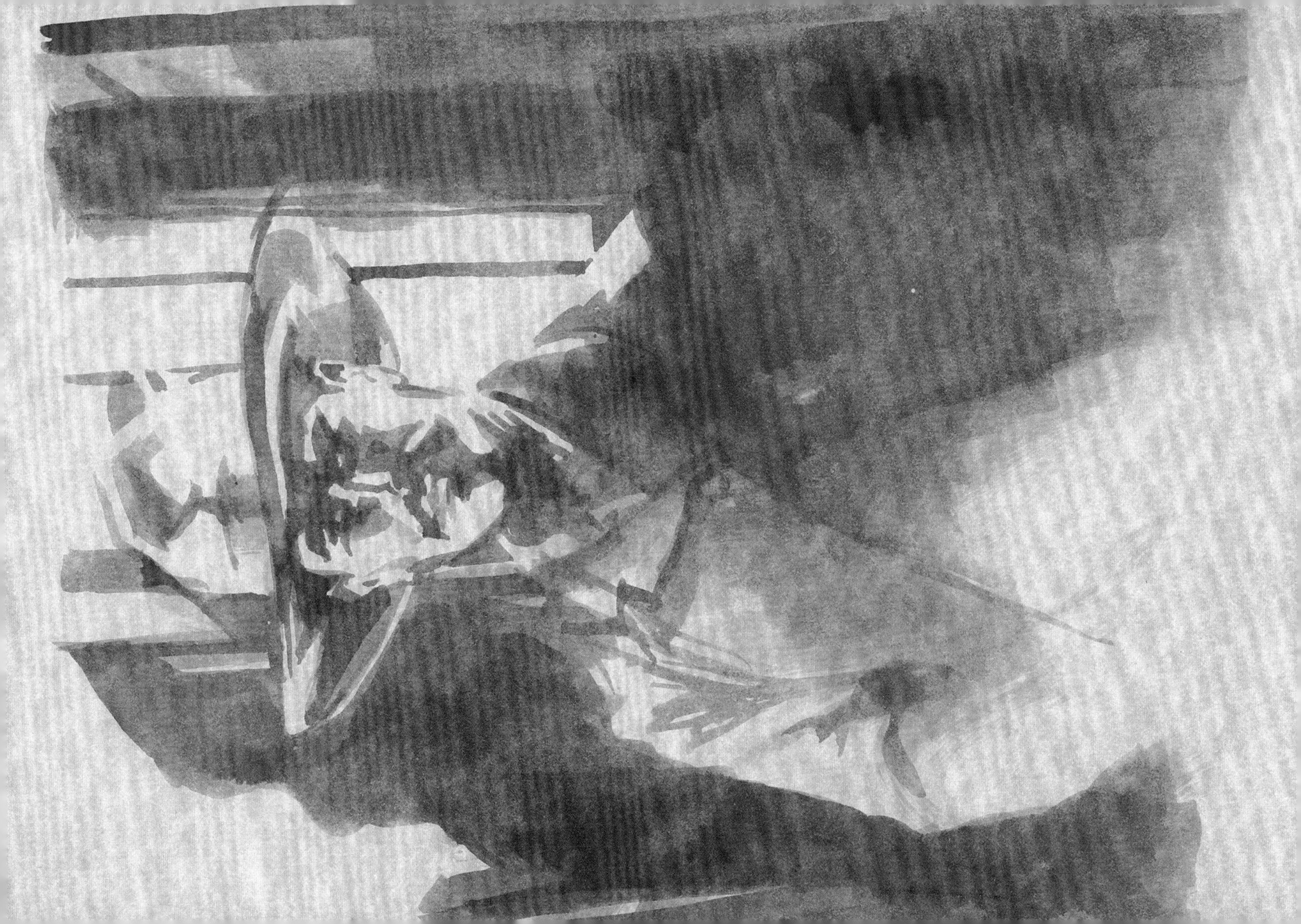

AUG 6

1874 Near Paris, Texas, outlaw Jim Reed is killed by a deputy sheriff. Reed rode with William Clarke Quantrill during the Civil War, ran with the James-Younger and Tom Starr gangs, and was the first husband of the notorious Belle Starr.

JACK SWILLING

John "Jack" Swilling took his final breath on August 12, 1878, in a stifling cell at the Yuma Territorial Prison, where he was serving hard time for a crime he did not commit. Instead of being honored as the founder of Phoenix, Swilling died a reviled outlaw, all because of a joke he told in a saloon and a posed photograph depicting him as one bad hombre. The real Jack Swilling story began with a boy raised on a plantation who fought in the Mexican War and then came west as a teamster. He suffered chronic pain from an old head wound and a bullet lodged in his back—injuries that led to his dependency on alcohol and morphine. Swilling arrived in Arizona Territory in the late 1850s, and went to work building a canal to divert water from the Salt River for a colony that by 1868 was the settlement of Phoenix. Swilling was the first postmaster and justice of the peace and a prominent leader in the fledgling desert town. His legal problem began when he returned from a trip and joked that he would have to rob a stage to recoup his money. The offhanded remark got back to Wells Fargo agents investigating a recent stage robbery, and Swilling suddenly became a suspect. Although there was no real evidence, a photograph showing Swilling and his adopted Indian son posing as outlaws convinced authorities to arrest him for armed robbery. While awaiting trial in Yuma, Swilling wrote an impassioned letter declaring his innocence. Deprived of the morphine he depended on to relieve the constant pain, Swilling died of natural causes. The real culprits who robbed the stage later confessed and Swilling's name was cleared.

▶ Jack Swilling (seated) and his adopted Indian son.

1864 On the Little Blue River near present-day Oak, Nebraska, a raid by Cheyenne Indians leaves forty dead. Lucinda Eubank, her two children, and a nephew are kidnapped, but are later returned by Two Face and Black Foot in a show of goodwill.

MICKEY FREE

The mysterious Mickey Free, one of many capable men serving in the Apache scouts from the 1870s to the 1890s, was not an Apache at all. Born Feliz Tellez in 1847 in Santa Cruz, Sonora, Mexico, to Jesusa Martinez and Santiago Tellez, the boy's reddish-blond hair and gray eyes reflected his Mexican father's Irish blood. When his father died, Feliz and his mother moved to the Sonoita Valley in Arizona Territory. She entered into a relationship with rancher John Ward, who gave his surname to the boy. On January 21, 1861, a band of Apaches raided the ranch and made off with some oxen and the fourteen-year-old Feliz. The Mexican boy's abduction was blamed on the revered Apache leader Cochise, an accusation that quickly escalated into a full-blown war. Meanwhile, Feliz was adopted by the White Mountain Apaches and raised as one of their own. In 1872, the young warrior enlisted in the Apache scouts, and by 1874 he was elevated to first sergeant. He became known among the soldiers and other scouts as Mickey Free, a catchy name taken from a popular Irish novel. Free never returned to the home of his Mexican mother and white stepfather. His ability to speak Apache, Spanish, and English made him a useful interpreter, and his tracking skills proved invaluable. Yet most Apaches generally mistrusted him. They often referred to him as "the coyote whose kidnapping had brought war to the Chiricahuas."

▲ Two Apache Indian scouts and a black scout.

▶ Mickey Free—an Apache captive who became a warrior for the tribe and later an Indian scout for the U.S. Army.

AUG 8

1877 Shoshone chief Washakie entertains President Chester Arthur during negotiations for a larger reservation on Wyoming's Wind River.

I SEE BY YOUR OUTFIT

Of all the trappings associated with cowboys, the most iconic were their hats and boots. Although there were many brands of both, most drovers wore Stetson hats and cowhide Justin boots. The ubiquitous cowboy hat began appearing across the frontier soon after the Civil War when an entrepreneur named John B. Stetson set the standard with the "Hat of the West." The durable beaver-fur hat had a six-inch crown and a seven-inch brim. The inside was waterproof and could double as a bucket, which earned it the moniker "10-gallon hat," even though the originals never held more than a half-gallon. It was said that a Stetson was heavy enough to knock a man down in a fight and kept its shape after being hit by twenty bullets. In less than twenty years, Stetson owned the world's largest hat factory and employed four thousand workers. The most common cowboy boots took their name from Herman Joseph "Daddy Joe" Justin, a cobbler at Spanish Fort, Texas, on the Red River, who started making boots in 1879 for Chisholm Trail cowboys. Justin's custom-fitted boots adorned the feet of cattle barons, Texas Rangers, cowhands, and bandits. One local legend spoke of three cattle thieves strung up from a tree limb near Wichita Falls, Texas. All three died with their boots on—and all of them were wearing Justins.

"I see by your outfit, that you are a cowboy."

—from the "Cowboy's Lament"

▲ Ad for Stetson hats featuring a photograph of a Navajo Indian.

▶ A cowboy and his boots.

AUG 9

1877 On the present-day border of Montana and Idaho, the Battle of Big Hole, a major engagement in the Nez Perce War, pits U.S. troops led by Colonel John Gibbon (known to Indians as "he who limps" due to an old Civil War wound) against a force of Nez Perce warriors. Both sides sustain heavy casualties.

BRAZEN BILL

If William "Brazen Bill" Brazelton was anything, it was ingenious. A better con artist than highwayman, Brazelton first attracted attention in the mid-1870s when he announced to the citizens of Prescott, Arizona Territory, that he was capable of swallowing a wagon wheel and would do so when his traveling show came to town. Ticket sales soared following the outrageous claim. After collecting all the money at the gate, Brazelton told the audience that his assistants for the stupendous wheel act had just arrived and were "making their toilet." When the crowd started to fidget, Brazelton ducked out, saying he would hurry the others along. There's no way of knowing just how long the audience sat before they realized there would be no show that day. Brazelton was long gone. He had more luck with his wagon wheel scam than his later attempts at stagecoach robbery. His first heist on September 27, 1877, went well enough. Wearing a black gauze mask and waving a shotgun and a six-shooter, he stole several thousand dollars in cash, gold dust, and jewelry. After four more stage robberies in Arizona and New Mexico Territory, an expert manhunter realized that Brazelton was putting horseshoes on backward to confuse pursuers. The curtain finally fell on Brazen Bill in 1878, when deputies ambushed him just east of Silver City. As the shots rang out, Brazelton was heard to gasp, "I die brave, my God, I'll pray till I die." They took the slain outlaw to Tucson, tied his bullet-riddled body to a chair, and displayed it at the courthouse.

▶ A photograph of William Brazelton taken after his death.

AUG 10

1867 In an Ellsworth County, Kansas, special election, Ezra Kingsbury beats out Wild Bill Hickok for the position of sheriff.

WILD BILL LONGLEY

It was said that Texas gunslinger William "Wild Bill" Longley roamed far and wide with trouble as his constant companion. A tally of thirty-two murders was mute proof. He was only fifteen in 1867 when he murdered three black men in two encounters. Despite slaying other black men and at least one black woman before his own death in 1878, Longley claimed to be an equal opportunity killer. "The report of my killing negroes for pastime just to see them kick, is an ungodly falsehood," he wrote after becoming one of the most wanted desperados in Texas. However, Longley did not limit his long string of murders to Texas either. While a drover, an army deserter, and a teamster, Longley drifted throughout the West. In his wake, he left the victims from saloon shootings, gun battles with lawmen, arguments turned violent, and revenge killings. In a fit of jealous rage over a woman, Longley shot a preacher to death while the man milked a cow. In June 1877, deputies found Longley hiding out in Louisiana and hauled him back to Texas. After being tried and convicted of murder, Longley was hanged on October 11, 1878, just five days after his twenty-seventh birthday. When the trapdoor was released and Longley dropped, his feet touched the ground, and he had to be hoisted back up. The rope was adjusted, and the second attempt was a success. Eleven minutes later, Wild Bill Longley was dead, and widows and orphans across the West breathed a collective sigh of relief.

▶ William Longley, Texas desperado, photographed shortly before he was hanged.

AUG 11

1875 The Soledad-to-Paso Robles stage is robbed in California by an unknown assailant and is hit again the next day.

DOAN'S STORE

For drovers making the long cattle drive north on the Western Trail from Texas to the cow towns in Kansas, there was no more welcome sight than Doan's Store. Strategically situated where the trail crossed the Red River from Texas into Indian Territory, Doan's Store (also called Doan's Crossing or "the jumping-off place") was the only oasis where cowhands could briefly rest and replenish tobacco pouches and wardrobes. They also could quench parched throats, as cowboy scribe Roscoe Logue pointed out: "Here it was that he could look forward to the foaming schooners or a snort of Old Crow or Sunny Brook. The sluggish herd, on nearing, would seem more sluggish still until the thirsty, trail-worn punchers in their impatience would leave the herd and race to the bar hell-bent for a drink. Doan did not set out the sparkling glasses himself, consequently, the old cowboy saloon through necessity came into existence and was quite a center for the customary transactions of the day." In fact, the building had originally housed a saloon before the coming of Corwin F. Doan and his general merchandise store in 1878. Bullet holes peppered the ceiling above clientele that included trail drivers, buffalo hunters, Indians, ranchers, peddlers, and such famous visitors as Comanche chief Quanah Parker. They came to use the corrals and branding pens as well as to purchase sow bosom, cartridges, Winchesters by the case, flour and bacon in carloads, and even Stetson hats.

▲ Life on the cattle trail was a popular theme for Western novels.

▶ Doan's Store on the Texas side of the Red River on the Western Trail to Dodge City.

DOAN'S STORE

AUG 12

1878 Jack Swilling, one of the founders of Phoenix, Arizona Territory, dies in a prison cell at Yuma.

$20 HORSE, $40 SADDLE

Cowhands and drovers spent so much time astride a horse that they seemed to have been born in the saddle. Some folks even joked that cowboys had lost the ability to walk and had morphed into an altogether different critter. As Alex Sweet and John Armoy explained in their 1883 book, *On a Mexican Mustang Through Texas*: "It is argued that once the cowboy was a human being—a biped with the ordinary powers of locomotion—but that during the course of ages, becoming more and more attached to his horse, and having gradually ceased to use his legs, these important adjuncts have been incapacitated for pedestrian use, and thus the cowboy and his pony have developed into a hybrid union of man and beast—an inferior kind of centaur." Bunkhouse humor aside, every working cowboy knew all too well that a man afoot was no man at all. They also knew that their saddle was of equal importance. Many cowpunchers were provided with mounts by the outfits they worked for and seldom owned their own ponies. They did, however, supply their own saddles. A good saddle cost about a month's wages or more, making it a cowboy's most expensive and prized possession. This led to the familiar saying: "There's the cowboy on his twenty-dollar horse with the forty-dollar saddle."

▲ An example of a cowboy who rode a twenty-dollar horse with a forty-dollar saddle.

▶ A very handsomely outfitted Wyoming cowboy on a fine horse.

"THE COWBOY"

AUG 13

1881 Newman Haynes "Old Man" Clanton is ambushed on the Mexican border at Guadalupe Canyon, Arizona Territory. He and four of his gang are killed because of previous cattle rustling raids into Mexico.

CABIN FEVER

After eighteen-hour days of riding fence lines and tending cattle, cowhands sought out pleasure in a bunkhouse card or dice game. Boredom could set in faster than a Fort Worth whore, and cabin fever was contagious. Stray dogs, skunks, gophers, birds, snakes, and turtles were convenient targets for shooting contests during lulls in the monotonous work schedule. Sometimes a bored cowboy would take a potshot at a fly on the bunkhouse ceiling or set loose packs of hounds to run down predators and varmints. In a pinch, even macho wranglers would bite the bullet and take turns acting as female partners at a Saturday night dance.

"*At Christmas* [1902] *when I was driving the mail we were at Tippett's Ranch and they had a dance there. There were only four women, so they could make a set for a quadrille. I played the harmonica and an old Scotsman played the harmonica also, and we traded off and danced all night.*"

—Raymond Larson, recollection of Tippett's Ranch, Nevada, 1902

"*That Christmas* [1903] *we went back to Tippett's to a dance and this time there were only three women there, so I was the slimmest man. We drew presents under the Christmas tree, and I drew a Mother Hubbard dress and some corsets, so I put them on and danced with the men.*"

—Raymond Larson, recollection of Tippett's Ranch, Nevada, 1903

▲ Cowboys spent their quiet hours playing cards, reading, and just relaxing, or telling stories outside the bunkhouse after a hard day's work.

▶ Men danced with one another when no female partners were available.

AUG 14

1835 During a rendezvous on the Green River in what would become southwestern Wyoming, French-Canadian trapper Joseph Chouinard challenges Kit Carson to a duel after an Arapaho woman named Singing Grass chooses Carson as a suitor over Chouinard. Carson, who emerges unscathed, shoots off Chouinard's thumb.

RIDING THE HOME RANGE

When cowboys were not busy moving cattle to market, there was plenty to be done at the home ranch. New herds had to be gathered, horses broken, fences mended, and cows castrated and branded. "Anyone who's taken part in a gathering, roping, branding, dehorning, castrating, ear notching, wattle clipping, or winching a calf from its mother knows how mean and tough and brutal it can be," observed social critic Edward Abbey. "And if the cowboy's mind and sensibilities have not been permanently deformed by that kind of work, he'll admit it. Brutal work tends to bring out the brutality in all of us." Working cowboys had to be "double-backboned," in the vernacular of that time, and capable of committing larceny and even murder if it would benefit their cattle outfit. They faced inclement weather, tamed mustangs, scared off squatters, and chased cow thieves without giving quarter. Men and boys had to be resilient and resourceful. Small ranchers and big-time cattlemen alike hired only those who had the moxie to ride for their brand.

▲ A cowboy with his fully outfitted horse.

▶ Branding cattle.

Thunder of hoofs on the range as you ride,
Hissing of iron and sizzling of hide,
Bellows of cattle and snort of Cayuse,
Longhorns from Texas as wild as the deuce.
Mid-nite stampedes and milling of herds,
Yells of the Cow-men too angry for words,
Right in the thick of it all would I stay,
Make me a Cowboy again for a day.

—anonymous

AUG 15

1872 A group of Kansas businessmen establish the Dodge City Town Company and begin planning a settlement.

HOME ON THE RANGE

There was very little appeal and certainly nothing at all romantic about a cow-puncher's life. In reality, those who took to the cattle trails and range faced untold dangers, hardships, and challenges. Beyond the stampedes, perilous river crossings, and rustlers on the prowl, cowboys and drovers had to endure drought, torrential rain, hail and snowstorms, stinging sleet, mud and quicksand, tornadoes, range fires, venomous snakes, mosquitoes, and ticks. Nature was a constant torment to man and beast throughout the West, and those in the cattle business unquestionably realized that each season held its own particular terrors. The scorching summer sun, choking clouds of dust, hailstones the size of quail eggs, and violent thunderstorms ranked high on any cowboy's list of miseries. Lightning was one of the most common causes of death for a cowboy in the late 1800s. Still, many of the veteran cowhands argued that winter was the worst time of the year. Icy blizzards struck the plains and prairies with the fury of a scorned woman. When particularly wicked north winds, known as "blue northers" or "blue whistlers," quickly dropped temperatures to below freezing, most men on horseback felt like they were in hell with the heat off.

Oh, give me a home where the buffalo roam.
Where the deer and the antelope play,
Where seldom is heard a discouraging word
And the skies are not cloudy all day.

—"Home on the Range," 1873

▲ Stampedes were always a potential danger when trailing cattle. This artist shows the gruesome reality as a cowboy takes a tumble he will not likely survive.

▶ Casualties on the trail were met with a prairie burial, attended by all the local outfits and those passing through the area.

AUG 16

1861 The *San Francisco Herald* reports that the Pony Express will stop running in October after only eighteen months of operation.

ETHNIC COWPOKES

Though the most popular image of the cowboy was that of a young white male, the work actually drew comers from a variety of ethnic backgrounds and social classes who ranged in age from grizzled old Rebels to awkward adolescents. Some were from Southern stock of Scots-Irish descent, while others were greenhorn immigrant lads, Indians, blacks, Mexicans, and mestizo cowboys, especially from Indian Territory and Texas. The blatant racism of nineteenth-century America caused white Texans and Anglo ranchers to treat cowboys of different races with derision and distain, often giving them the worst jobs on the range, such as breaking outlaw horses, standing extra night watches, or shooting calves born during the night that would slow the herd's movement. But many of these men had an indisputable impact on the trade. Mexican vaqueros, some of the most expert ropers and horsemen ever to ride the plains, made a tremendous contribution to the ranching industry in Texas. So did black cowboys, some of whom had been slaves tending herds before and during the Civil War. On the great cattle drives of the late 1800s when about eight million to ten million Longhorns were trailed north from Texas, approximately one in every six cowboys was black.

▲ Black cowboys were quite numerous in the West.

▶ Many Indians took up the work of a cowboy.

AUG 17

1837 An Arickaree Indian, angry at the whites for spreading smallpox, kills an employee of a local merchant in Fort Clark, Dakota Territory.

THE COWBOY CAPITAL

For its many ardent aficionados, Dodge City defined the "Wild West." Dodge (most folks just dropped the "City") was not only the last of the many Kansas cattle towns; it was hands-down the busiest and most famous. Its location on the historic Santa Fe Trail and, by the early 1870s, as a major stop on the Atchison, Topeka, and Santa Fe Railroad put Dodge City in the catbird's seat. For several years, it was the major center for the booming buffalo trade. Between 1872 and 1874, an estimated 850,000 buffalo hides were shipped from Dodge. It became a busy rendezvous spot for cowboys, hunters and trappers, soldiers, and railroad workers. By 1875, when the buffalo hunters moved on with the diminishing herds, a new breed of critter made the town boom—Longhorns. Soon most of the cattle trails led to Dodge City, christened the "Cowboy Capital" of the world and "Queen of the Cow Towns." From 1875 until 1885, more than five million head of cattle ended up in Dodge. In 1884 alone, Texas drovers brought in 106 herds numbering three hundred thousand head.

"What made Dodge City so famous was that it was the last of the towns of the last frontier of the United States. When this was settled, the frontier was gone, it was the passing of the frontier with the passing of the buffalo, and the Indian question was settled forever."

—Robert M. Wright, founder of Dodge City, 1913

▲▲ This book calls Dodge City the "Cowboy Capital," and others referred to it as the "Queen of the Cow Towns."

▲ Buffalo hides piled up in Dodge City, Kansas, awaiting shipment on the railroad back east.

▶ Dodge City, c. 1874.

THE CARRYING OF
FIRE ARMS strictly
PROHIBITED.
TRY
Prickly Ash
BITTERS

AUG 18

1877 At Fort Grant, Arizona Territory, Billy the Kid kills his first man when he shoots Frank "Windy" Cahill during a scuffle.

FRONTIER BABYLON

From its very beginnings in the early 1870s, Dodge City's status as an important cattle-shipping point made it the perfect setting for gamblers, thieves, and carousers. As the *Kinsley Graphic* noted in an 1878 article entitled "The Beautiful, Bibulous Babylon of the Frontier": "Dodge City is far famed, not for its virtues, but for its wickedness; the glaring phases of its vices stand pre-eminent, and attract the attention of the visitor; and these shadows of Babylon are reproduced in the gossip's corner and in the press." It was commonly said about Dodge that a cowboy could break all the Ten Commandments in a single night, die with his boots on, and be laid to rest on Boot Hill the following morning. Not even the likes of Wyatt Earp, Doc Holliday, Bat Masterson and his brothers, or Bill Tilghman could quite tame the wild and wicked town. That stood to reason, since most of Dodge's lawmen were themselves a bit tainted and tended to walk the shady side of the dusty street. During the summer, the population swelled with the many drovers and cowboys coming off the trails. Scarlet women, dance hall girls, and gamblers followed, anxious to separate them from their newly issued pay. One of the sixteen rowdy drinking establishments in town was the Long Branch Saloon, where a five-piece band played nightly and drinks were chilled with ice cut from the Arkansas River or shipped in from the Colorado Rockies.

▶ The famous Long Branch Saloon of Dodge City, Kansas.

AUG 19

1895 At the Acme Saloon in El Paso, Texas, gunfighter John Wesley Hardin is killed by constable John Selman.

FRONTIER CLOWN

During the late 1800s, a small army of entertainers crisscrossed the frontier performing in the fancy theaters of San Francisco and Denver as well as on the rough boards of makeshift stages in cow towns and mining camps. In Kansas alone between 1870 and 1900, at least seventy-five opera houses opened to stage theatrical companies, musical troupes, traveling lecturers, impersonators, hypnotists, masters of the black arts, puppeteers, and comics. One of the most popular male performers was Eddie Fitzgerald, who started out on the streets and in the saloons of Chicago when he was just six years old to help support his large Irish family. At the age of fifteen, he changed his last name to Foy and traveled throughout the West on the vaudeville circuit, sharing the stage with such luminaries as Edwin Booth and Joseph Jeffers. Foy's comedic skits, operatic burlesques, and dance routines appealed to the mostly male audiences known to lose interest in performances when disputes among drunken spectators turned into brawls or gunfights. While Foy performed at the Comique in Dodge City and the Bird Cage Theatre in Tombstone, Arizona Territory, he encountered some of the more notable Old West figures such as Wyatt Earp, Bat Masterson, Doc Holliday, and Wild Bill Hickok. It was said that when Foy first entered the Bird Cage he remarked that, "It reminds me of a coffin—long and narrow." Foy went on to become one of the leading comic performers of his day, and by 1910 he had formed a family vaudeville act called "Eddie Foy and The Seven Little Foys." He also brought back to eastern audiences the more colorful tales of escapades in the Wild West.

▲ Comedian Eddie Foy.

▶ Eddie Foy wrote of his adventures with Western gunfighters in his book, *Clowning Through Life*.

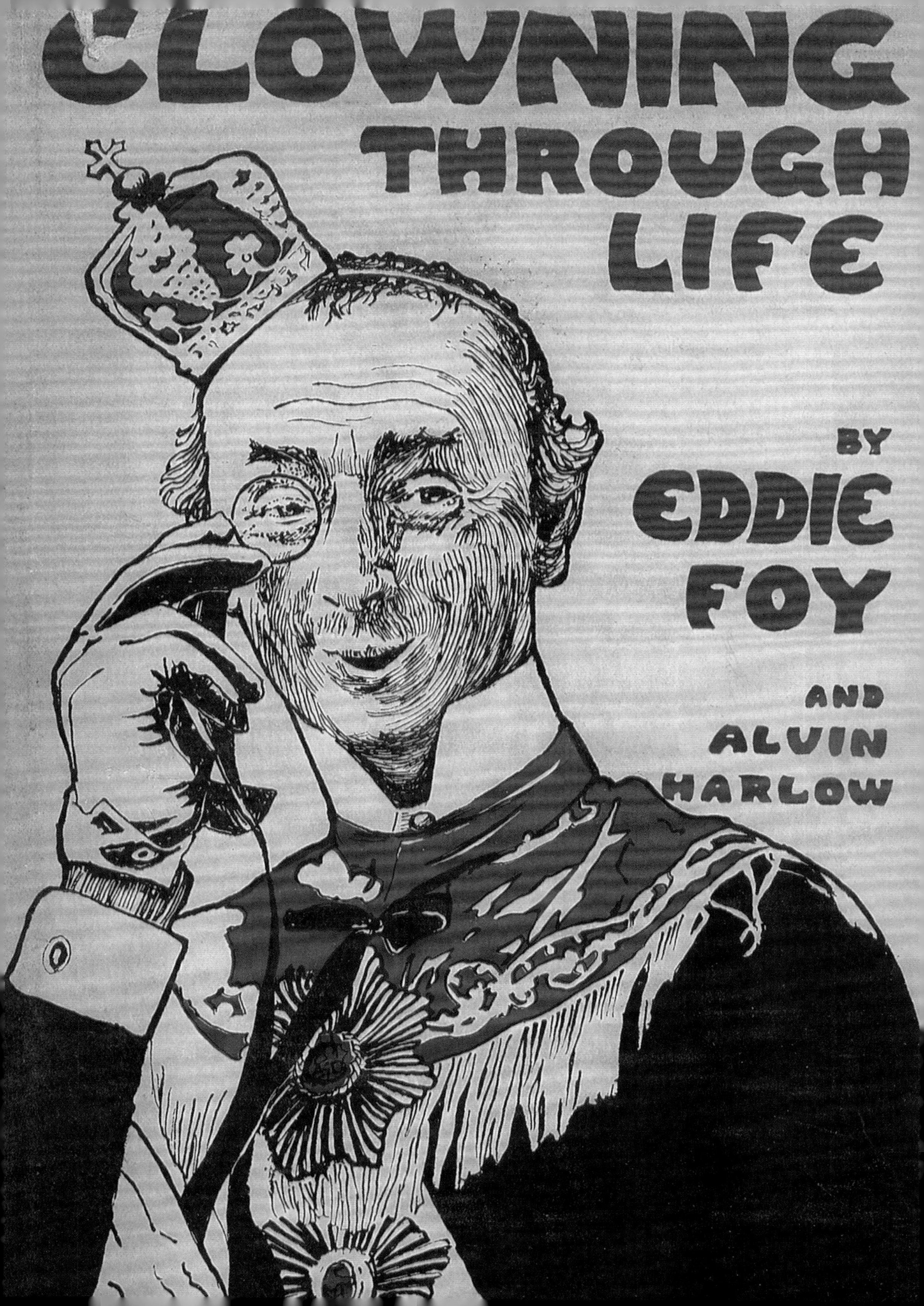

CLOWNING THROUGH LIFE

BY

EDDIE FOY

AND

ALVIN HARLOW

AUG 20

1871 The Newton Massacre, known as the "Gunfight at Hyde Park," takes place in Newton, Kansas. Five men are killed and two wounded in the bloody affair.

DOC HOLLIDAY

John Henry "Doc" Holliday, born to an affluent Georgia family in 1852, graduated from the Pennsylvania College of Dental Surgery at age twenty. Soon after opening a practice in Atlanta, he was diagnosed with tuberculosis, the same disease that took his mother's life. Holliday moved west for his health, but on arriving in Texas, quickly gave up dentistry and turned to gambling, an activity that seemed to come naturally to him. Aware that frontier gamblers often had to defend themselves, Holliday practiced with a six-shooter and knife until he became expert with both weapons. These skills proved useful as he moved from town to town plying his trade and fending off drunken soldiers and disgruntled faro opponents in shootouts and knife fights. Often the encounters were made worse by Holliday's heavy drinking and hair-trigger temper. After drifting through Colorado, Wyoming, and New Mexico, Holliday came back to Texas and met the only woman he ever cared for—Kate Elder, a doctor's daughter from Hungary who worked as a dance hall girl and prostitute and was known as "Big Nose" Kate for her rather prominent feature. About the same time, Holliday also met Wyatt Earp and the two men became fast friends. After bouncing around Dodge City and Las Vegas, New Mexico Territory, Holliday's ties with "Big Nose" Kate eventually ended, but his friendship with Earp remained strong. Bat Masterson later wrote of Holliday's devotion to Earp: "His whole heart and soul were wrapped up in Wyatt Earp and he was always ready to stake his life in defense of any cause in which Wyatt was interested."

DENTISTRY.

J. H. Holliday, Dentist, very respectfully offers his professional services to the citizens of Dodge City and surrounding country during the summer. Office at room No. 24, Dodge House. Where satisfaction is not given money will be refunded.

June 28 '78 Dodge City Times

▲▲ John Henry Holliday when he graduated from dental college, c. 1872.

▲ Doc Holliday's advertisement in the *Dodge City Daily Times*.

▶ Doc's dental office was in the Dodge House Hotel, where he also roomed.

DODGE HOUSE
BILLIARD HALL

AUG **21**

1923 Southwest of Bartlesville, Oklahoma, bandits Al Spencer and Frank "Jelly" Nash perform one of the last train robberies on horseback in American history.

"BUCKSKIN" FRANK LESLIE

When Nashville Franklyn Leslie, known as "Buckskin Frank," was liquored up, he often demonstrated that the combination of gunpowder and whiskey could prove fatal. One of his cronies described Leslie as "a likable damn fellow when he was sober, but when he was tanked up he turned as sour as a barrel of Dago red." Leslie—an army scout in the 1870s—got the "Buckskin" tag from the fringed leather jacket he often wore. He was fast with a six-shooter, aided by a quick-fire rig attached to a slotted plate on his belt, which allowed him to fire his Peacemaker .45 by swiveling it from the hip. Leslie drifted into Tombstone, Arizona Territory, in 1880, sporting his trademark jacket, long mustache, and matched pistols. In no time at all he had as many as a dozen notches on his pistol grip. A notorious ladies' man, Leslie killed Mike Killeen in a dispute over Killeen's wife, Mary. Cleared in the shooting, Leslie had the nerve to marry the widow. She later divorced him when she tired of Leslie taking target practice by shooting around her profile. Leslie was best known in Tombstone for the 1882 killing of Billy Claiborne, a survivor of the famous O.K. Corral gunfight shot down just outside the Oriental Saloon where Leslie worked as barkeep. But in 1889, Leslie got in a bind he couldn't shake. In a drunken rage, he killed a prostitute and wounded the man she was with at the time. The man recovered and testified against Leslie, who was sent to the Yuma Territorial Prison.

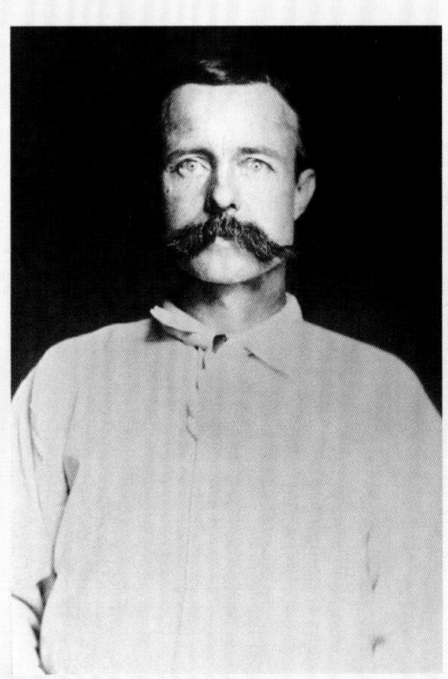

▲ Buckskin Frank Leslie.

▶ A later photo of what was once Tombstone's Oriental Saloon, c. 1935.

Coca-Cola
PRESCRIPTIONS
ORIENTAL SALOON
ICE CREAM

AUG 22

1867 Near Fort Chadbourne, Texas, the Fourth Cavalry encounters a group of hostile Indians. Two enlisted men are killed in the confrontation.

MYSTERIOUS DAVE

Not much is known about David Allen Mather, one of many Old West characters who tiptoed on the thin line separating the law-abiding and the lawless. The little on record about his early life suggests that Mather—the son of a New England sea captain—was descended from the Increase Mather family that yielded Cotton Mather, the Puritan zealot associated with the Salem witch trials. There was nothing puritanical about "Mysterious Dave," a battle-scarred veteran of saloon shootings, knife fights, and blood feuds in the late 1800s in such towns as Dodge City, Kansas, and Las Vegas, New Mexico Territory. It is likely that Mather began as a cattle rustler in Arkansas before trying his hand at buffalo hunting, during which he met Bat Masterson, Wyatt Earp, and Bill Tilghman. It was said that in 1878 Mather and Earp were chased out of Mobeetie, Texas, when they cooked up a scheme to peddle fake gold bricks to naive rubes. A year or so later, Mather moved to Kansas where for some time he alternated between being a gunslinger and wearing a badge. Often while working in some capacity as a law officer or riding with a posse, Mather also ran with vigilantes, took part in cathouse shootouts, stole jewelry, and robbed stagecoaches. In 1885, after being implicated in a couple of high-profile killings, Mather skipped out of Dodge, jumping bail on a murder charge, and vanished. Several accounts of his whereabouts surfaced over time, including one rumor that he had joined the Royal Canadian Mounted Police. None were proven and "Mysterious Dave" Mather stayed true to his name.

▲▲ A street in "Old Town" Las Vegas, New Mexico Territory, c. 1876.

▲ Mysterious Dave Mather.

▶ A view of Las Vegas from the east after the railroad arrived in 1879 and "New Town" had sprung up between the railroad and Old Town.

356

AUG

23

1877 Outlaw John Wesley Hardin is captured by four lawmen aboard a train in Florida.

THE BANDIT QUEEN

The most famous female outlaw of the nineteenth century was born February 5, 1848, in Carthage, Missouri. Her prosperous parents named their little girl Myra Maebelle Shirley. At the Carthage Female Academy she studied literature, Greek, Latin, Hebrew, art, and deportment. She also became an accomplished pianist and was said to have entertained guests with musical interludes at her father's popular hotel on Carthage's main square. Myra adored her older brother John Allison Shirley—better known as Bud—as much as she appreciated good horses. The young lady with Kentucky bloodlines could ride like the wind, and she and her brother roamed the Missouri hills on horseback. Bud also taught his sister how to handle firearms. When she reached her teens, Myra Shirley was both a fearless rider and a crack shot, capable of shooting a bumblebee off of a thistle at thirty yards with her pistol. Despite her classical education and family's hopes to turn out a genteel Southern maiden, Myra had other notions about her future. Instead of a life of comfort and elegance, she was to become a convicted horse thief and a constant companion of killers and renegades. History, with some help from pulp writers, would remember this spirited woman not as Myra Shirley, but by the name she used the last nine years of her troubled life—Belle Starr.

▶ Belle Starr, seated sidesaddle with a revolver strapped around her waist, while she awaits trial for horse theft in Fort Smith, Arkansas. Also pictured is Deputy U.S. Marshal Tyner Hughes. This photo did much to create the popular image of Starr as a "Bandit Queen."

Belle Starr

AUG 24

1866 Near Big Timber, Montana Territory, after getting separated from a wagon train heading for Fort Smith on the Bozeman Trail, Joseph Schultz, William Thomas, and his son Charles are killed by Blackfoot Indians.

"BIG NOSE" GEORGE PARROTT

In 1881, George Manuse—widely known as "Big Nose" George Parrott due to his sizable proboscis—was the most hated man in Wyoming when two hundred vigilante citizens dragged him from the Rawlins jail and strung him up from a telegraph pole. The animosity stemmed from the outlaw's attempt to rob a payroll train east of town that left two pursuing lawmen dead. Manuse's body was left hanging for most of the day, but no one claimed it. The undertaker delivered Big Nose George to Dr. John Osborne to perform an autopsy and study the outlaw's brain in hopes of finding some abnormality. After making a death mask, Osborne sawed off the skullcap and examined the interior. Seeing nothing out of the ordinary, he proceeded to skin the corpse. The doctor sent the skin to a Denver tannery with instructions to "make a pair of shoes and leave the nipples on." When the shoes came back, sans nipples, Osborne was disappointed but loved the shoes and wore them constantly. He also had a medicine bag made from the chest skin. He gave the skullcap to Dr. Lillian Nelson, the first female physician in Wyoming, who used it as an ashtray and doorstop. The rest of Big Nose was sealed in a whiskey barrel and buried. In 1892, when Osborne was elected governor of Wyoming, he proudly wore his special shoes to the inaugural ball. Some years later, he wore them when he went to Congress, and then as first assistant secretary of state under President Woodrow Wilson.

▲ "Big Nose" George Parrott.

▶ Some relics of "Big Nose" George, including a death mask, his shackles, and a photo of the shoes made from his skin.

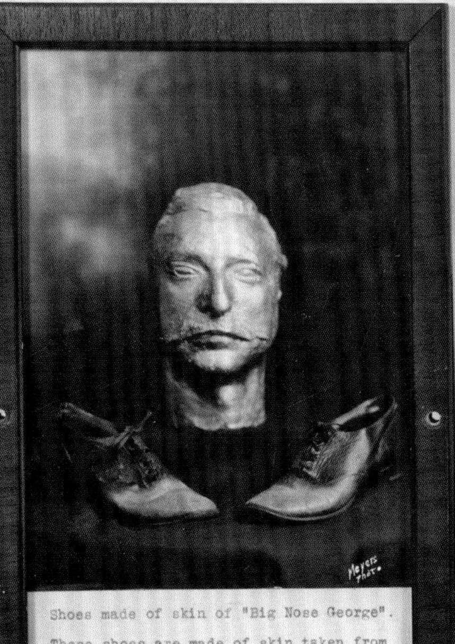

Shoes made of skin of "Big Nose George".

These shoes are made of skin taken from the breast of "Big Nose George" after he was lynched at Rawlins, Wyoming.

Presented by
Dr. J. E. Osborne,
Ex-Governor of Wyoming,
Rawlins, Wyoming

TANNED HUMAN SKIN

This is a piece of skin taken from the chest of "BIG NOSE" George Parrott who was hanged for attempted hold-up of Union Pacific train, the killing of Deputy Sheriffs George Widdowfield and Tip Vincent, and assaulting Jailer Rankin, of the Carbon Co. jail. It was in possession of Professor Reed of the Wyoming University at Laramie for years, then passed to Mr. A. J. Hull, President, Valley Oil Company, who presented it to Mr. E. E. Calvin, Vice President-Operation, Union Pacific System, who is said to have taken the confession of "Big Nose" George, while Agent at Carbon, Wyo

Death Mask of "Big Nose George"

Plaster paris death mask made by Dr. John E. Osborne, immediately after lynching of "Big Nose George."

Presented by
Dr. J. E. OSBORNE,
Ex-Governor of Wyoming,
Rawlins, Wyoming

AUG 25

1877 In Arizona Territory, Ed Schieffelin records his first silver claim and calls it Tombstone.
1926 In Covington, Oklahoma, the Kimes brothers hold up two banks.

THE GREAT ESCAPE

After being found guilty of murder and sentenced to be hanged, Billy the Kid was taken back to Lincoln County, New Mexico Territory, and housed in the jail facilities on the top floor of the county courthouse in Lincoln. Ironically, the building had once been the old Murphy-Dolan store known as "The House," headquarters for many of the Kid's old enemies. On April 28, 1881, while Sheriff Pat Garrett was away on business, deputies James Bell and Bob Olinger were left to guard the Kid and some other prisoners. The Kid, tired of being tormented by Olinger, decided to take advantage of Garrett's absence and attempt an escape. He made his move on Bell while Olinger was taking the other prisoners to a nearby hotel for supper. The Kid asked to be escorted out back to use the privy, and somehow—either before or after they returned to the courthouse—he procured a gun. The Kid turned on Bell and struck him with the heavy handcuffs. The stunned deputy tried to get away, but the Kid fired twice. Bell staggered outside and fell dead. Hearing the gunshots, Olinger bolted from the hotel and rushed to the courthouse. By then, the Kid had armed himself with a shotgun and waited at a second-story window. As the deputy approached, the Kid cut loose, and the bully was dead before his body slammed to the ground. The Kid jumped on a pony and rode away. His escape spawned hundreds of news stories and pulp articles and became the most famous moment of his brief life. As some would later say, the escape is when the Kid was catapulted into folklore. In only a few months, he would be dead.

▲ Robert Olinger, one of the guards killed by Billy the Kid during his escape.

▶ The Lincoln County courthouse from which the Kid escaped. He shot Robert Olinger from the second-story window just to the left of the tree.

AUG 26

1877 Famed brothel owner Kate Fulton departs Denver, Colorado, by stagecoach the day after taking part in the first recorded duel between two women. Fulton and Mattie Silks, another prominent madam, squared off with pistols. Neither hit her target, but Silks's bullet accidentally struck Cortez Thomson, the object of their mutual affection. Nonetheless, Silks came out the victor. She not only got her man, but broke her opponent's nose in an after-duel fistfight.

"¿QUIÉN ES?"

It was almost midnight, July 14, 1881, at Fort Sumner, New Mexico Territory. Pat Garrett and two deputies on the hunt for Billy the Kid were snooping around the family home of Pete Maxwell, brother of the Kid's sweetheart Paulita. Garrett opened a door and stepped into Maxwell's bedroom to ask about the Kid. The deputies hunkered down outside. In only minutes, a figure, fumbling with his trouser buttons and padding on stocking feet, walked toward them through the shadows on his way to get some grub. A freshly butchered yearling hung from the portal, and he carried a knife to slice off some meat for a late meal. As he came closer, the men on the porch stirred. The young man was startled. "*¿Quién es*? [Who is it?]" he hissed. He asked again, then a third time. He backed into the darkness and through a familiar door. Garrett was inside, sitting on Maxwell's bed. *"Pedro, ¿quienes son esos hombres afuera*? [Peter, who are those men outside?]," the young man asked. He sensed the presence of the other man. "*¿Quién es*?" he asked, and then in English, "Who is it?" The only reply was the explosion of a single-action .44 Colt pistol. It was quickly followed by a second blast. The young man, best known as Billy the Kid, crashed to the floor. He gurgled his final breath and lay dead in the shadows—hungry and without his boots on. He died not knowing who had taken his life. How fitting that his last spoken words formed a question with no response. Even then there were so many unanswered questions about the young man who died in a shroud of darkness beneath a full New Mexico moon.

▲ Pat Garrett, seated left, and John W. Poe, seated right. Standing is James Brent, a later sheriff of Lincoln County.

▶ The Maxwell house in Fort Sumner, New Mexico Territory. Billy the Kid was killed in the left corner room.

AUG 27

1926 The infamous brothers George and Matt Kimes, after holding up a pair of banks two days earlier in Covington, Oklahoma, encounter a roadblock just west of Sallisaw and a shootout ensues. The Kimes escape after killing a deputy sheriff and taking the Sallisaw chief of police hostage. He is later released unharmed.

THE KID'S ENDLESS RIDE

As soon as Billy the Kid was laid in his grave, dime novelists and hack journalists began churning out far-fetched accounts of his short and violent life and death. One of the more sensational stories appeared in the *Santa Fe Weekly Democrat*: "No sooner had the floor caught the descending form, which had a pistol in one hand and a knife in the other, than there was a strong odor of brimstone in the air, and a dark figure with the wings of a dragon, claws like a tiger, eyes like balls of fire, and horns like a bison, hovered over the corpse for a moment, and with a fiendish laugh said, 'Ha! Ha! This is my meat!' and then sailed off through the window." At least eight dime novels were published between the Kid's death on July 14, 1881, and April 1882, when Sheriff Pat Garrett's own book about the young man he had killed made its debut. Garrett's book was titled *The Authentic Life of Billy the Kid, the Noted desperado of the Southwest, Whose Deeds of Daring and Blood Made His name a terror in New Mexico, Arizona and Northern Mexico*. The title alone suggested the windy yarns and myths that were to follow. Coauthored—some say ghostwritten—by Connecticut-born Marshall Ashmun Upson, the book was commissioned by Garrett to burnish his image and also make the lawman a bit of money. Garrett's portrayal became the accepted version of events, establishing the Kid as something between hero and villain. It influenced a generation of authors who would retell the story of Billy the Kid.

▲ This five-cent novel was on the market only a month after the Kid was killed, c. 1881.

▶ This longer, more substantial book, only slightly more accurate, appeared a few weeks later.

▶▶ Pat Garrett's book was published in 1882, one year after the Kid's death.

THE TRUE LIFE OF
BILLY THE KID

The NOTED NEW MEXICAN OUTLAW

PUBLISHED BY
THE DENVER PUBLISHING CO.
DENVER COLO.

PRICE 25 CENTS

AN AUTHENTIC
"Life of Billy the Kid"
THE Noted Desperado OF THE Southwest
By PAT F. GARRETT
Sheriff of Lincoln County
AT WHOSE HANDS HE WAS KILLED.

Published by
THE NEW MEXICAN PRINTING & PUBLISHING Co.
SANTA FE N.M.
1882

AUG

28

1872 Wild Bill Hickok appears in a disastrous show called "The Great Buffalo Hunt" at Niagara Falls, New York. When Hickok shoots his pistol in the air, the buffalo stampede into a residential neighborhood, trailed by four Comanche Indians, a pack of stray dogs, and a gang of local boys. The Indians' pet bear breaks loose and attacks an Italian vendor's cart, devouring all his sausages. The buffalo are sold to local butchers to pay for the performers' train fare home.

TOMBSTONE

The story of the town with the morbid name of Tombstone began in 1877, when Ed Schieffelin, a prospector working the hills and dry washes near Camp Huachuca deep in Arizona Territory, came across a vein of high-grade silver ore. He called his claim Tombstone, mindful of a soldier's warning that in Apache country the only rock he could expect to find was one to mark his grave. Fueled by Schieffelin's silver discovery, the mining settlement laid out in early 1879 soon turned into a boomtown. By 1881, Tombstone boasted one thousand residents, and the next year it became the seat of Cochise County. The population later soared to as high as fifteen thousand as Tombstone attracted a broad range of settlers, including European immigrants, Chinese laborers, and every sort of undesirable. They were not only drawn there by the promise of wealth, but also by amenities such as running water, a telegraph, and, later, limited telephone service. There was even refrigeration for drinks, ice cream, and eventually, a skating rink. From 1880 to 1887, C. S. Fly operated a photo studio and boardinghouse. He welcomed all arrivals to drop by and have their picture made in their new hometown. Although Schieffelin had cashed in by 1882 and moved on to Alaska and the Pacific Northwest, when he died in 1897, his wish was that his body be brought back to the town he started. He was buried in the clothing of a prospector with pick, shovel, and canteen not far from that first claim. Later, a huge monument was erected. As the soldier had predicted long before, Schieffelin finally got his tombstone.

▲▶ Four photographs of unidentified citizens of Tombstone taken in C. S. Fly's studio.

AUG 29

1900 The Wild Bunch robs another Union Pacific train near Tipton, Wyoming, but gets away with only fifty dollars.

THE TOWN TOO TOUGH TO DIE

Although Dodge City might try to stake a claim as the toughest town in the West, Tombstone would edge it out for the title. It was, after all, called "the town too tough to die." As in any self-respecting mining town (particularly one as isolated as Tombstone), drinking, gambling, and whoring were the most popular forms of recreation. At one point in Tombstone's early years, an astounding 110 businesses were licensed to dispense hard drink, including the popular Oriental Saloon and Crystal Palace. The many sporting houses, where daughters of Venus plied their age-old trade, stayed busy from noon until dawn every day of the week. Prices varied depending on the establishment and the clientele. But every love-starved miner and cowboy could usually find an affordable harlot. The great abundance of silver wealth kept higher-end professional ladies in demand, which resulted in Tombstone offering some of the best palaces of pleasure in the West. Madams with names such as Crazy Horse Lil, Irish Meg, Dutch Annie, Blonde Marie, and Madame Moustache at one time or another managed brothels elegantly furnished with gilt mirrors, marble tables, and soft feather beds. All soiled doves in Tombstone were required to be certified by the city. In addition, they made weekly visits to Dr. George Goodfellow for a thorough examination. If they were disease-free, each woman had to buy a certificate of health. In Tombstone, the taxes on prostitution and saloons alone completely supported the public school system.

▲ A Tombstone soiled dove.

▶ A Tombstone city license for "the business of House of Ill Fame," issued in the same month as the O.K. Corral gunfight.

KEEP THIS POSTED IN A CONSPICUOUS PLACE.

No 592 Class 14 $4 30

CITY LICENSE.

CITY AUDITOR'S OFFICE,

Tombstone, Cochise Co., A. T., SEP 20 1881 188

Received from Emma Parker Cancelled
Allen St.

the sum of Four 30/100 Dollars, for License on the business of House of Ill Fame

, Class two , for the term of thirteen days from Sept 17 1881

Seward B. Chapin
City Auditor.

EPITAPH PRINT

John P. Clum
Mayor.

AUG 30

1904 Start of the 1904 Cheyenne Frontier Days Celebration in Cheyenne, Wyoming.

THE BIRD CAGE

The Bird Cage Theatre—Tombstone's most popular full-service entertainment center for nine raucous years—was never a respectable place. Decorum, modesty, and high-brow interests were in short supply, which was perfectly fine with the mostly all-male regulars. Some folks thought the building site was cursed. The year before the lot was cleared, on October 30, 1880, the first town marshal, Fred White, was shot by gunman "Curly Bill" Brocious and died two days later, elevating Virgil Earp, brother to Wyatt, to the post of acting marshal. Originally opened as the Elite Theatre on Christmas Day, 1881, the name was soon changed because of the fourteen cage-like compartments suspended from the ceiling, each one with a painted lady inside who entertained randy customers for an exorbitant price. "Access to them is had by means of stairways, one leading thereto from the ground floor and another from the dressing or wine room at the west end of the stage," a reporter for the *Arizona Star* wrote in 1884. "The boxes are all heavily curtained, and in and behind these the girls ply their trade." It was said that the Bird Cage inspired the tearjerker "She's Only a Girl in a Gilded Cage," a popular tune many years later. The combination theater, saloon, gambling parlor, and brothel operated twenty-four hours a day, every day of the year. In 1882, the *New York Times* described it as, "The wildest, wickedest night spot between Basin Street and the Barbary Coast." At least sixteen gun and knife fights took place inside the Bird Cage, accounting for twenty-six dead bodies laid to rest on Boot Hill.

▲ Virgil Earp.

▶ Curly Bill's shooting of city marshal Fred White occurred just outside the Bird Cage Theatre.

BIRD CAGE THEATRE
1881

AUG

31

1843 Showman P. T. Barnum puts on the first Wild West exhibition in Hoboken, New Jersey. Called the "Grand Buffalo Hunt," Barnum's terrified animals break loose and flee to a nearby swamp. During the commotion, one spectator is killed when he falls out of a tree.

THE CLANTONS

In the mythology of Tombstone violence in the early 1880s, more often than not the Clanton family and their associates are cast as diabolical villains. Though they would be best remembered for the gunfight at the O.K. Corral, the Clantons had shared a relatively peaceful family life before this bloody incident. Patriarch Newman Haynes Clanton, usually referred to as Old Man Clanton, ruled the roost until his untimely death. Born in Tennessee in 1816, Clanton settled in Missouri, where three of his five sons were born. He also fathered two daughters. After moving west following the California gold rush, Clanton ran a ranch in Texas, briefly served with the Confederate Home Guard during the Civil War, and ultimately settled in Arizona Territory. By 1877, the brusque widower and his offspring operated a successful ranch on the San Pedro River where they sold beef cattle to the U.S. government for reservation Apaches and also supplied customers in the nearby mining boomtown of Tombstone. As was common of that time and place, the Clantons also did some cattle rustling and raided Mexican herds south of the border. Old Man Clanton's third son, Joseph Isaac (known as Ike), was active in the family cattle business, but also opened the Star Restaurant in Tombstone in 1878, and enjoyed racing fast horses purchased in Texas. He and his brothers lost their father on August 13, 1881, when Old Man Clanton and four others were shot and killed while sleeping in their saddle blankets in Guadalupe Canyon. Though no one was ever charged with the murders, more than likely the killers were Mexicans weary of having their cattle rustled by the Clantons.

▶ Newman H. "Old Man" Clanton.

▶▶ Isaac Clanton.

SEP 1

1893 The Battle of Ingalls in Indian Territory pits the Doolin-Dalton Gang against a posse of lawmen, but results in few casualties.
1904 Johnny Mack Brown, star of the 1930 motion picture *Billy the Kid*, is born in Dothan, Alabama.

THE EARPS

▶ Wyatt Earp, 1885.

The faction that stood in stark contrast to the Clantons was the Earp brothers and their cronies. When Wyatt, Virgil, and James Earp arrived at Tombstone with their families on a windy day in December 1879, the ten-month-old settlement teemed with prospectors, card sharks, merchants, cowboys, con artists, and dance hall floosies. The restless Earps were attracted to Tombstone by the promise of wealth. Eldest brother James was intent on opening a saloon, and Virgil looked to make quick money prospecting for silver. Wyatt had plans of his own. In the past, he had spent time on either side of the law as both an indicted horse thief and a law officer in Kansas cow towns. While assistant marshal in Dodge City, Wyatt doubled his income by moonlighting as a card dealer at the Long Branch. He thought a similar situation would earn him a good living in Tombstone. However, not all of the Earps' dreams came true. When Tombstone's city marshal was shot and killed, Virgil stepped up to take his place. Wyatt, with interests in the Oriental Saloon, also played faro every night at the Eagle Brewery, and became Virgil's assistant. In 1880, Morgan, the fourth Earp brother, joined the others in Tombstone. He rode shotgun on a Wells Fargo stage and occasionally worked on Tombstone's police force. John "Doc" Holliday, the ex-dentist battling consumption and demon rum, fell in love with the Earps. Their old friend also saw an opportunity to improve his lifestyle at the lively gaming tables. Doc Holliday and the Earps would soon find themselves in the center of a deadly confrontation with the Clantons.

SEP 2

1885 During Arizona's Pleasant Valley War between the Tewksbury, Graham, and Blevins families, the shooting at the Tewksbury ranch temporarily ceases while the widow of John Tewksbury shoos hogs away from his corpse. Once Tewksbury is buried, the fighting resumes.

THE MCLAURYS

Brothers Frank and Tom McLaury had a key role in the confrontation that put the town of Tombstone on the map. The McLaurys were known to be hardworking cattlemen who roosted in Arizona Territory in 1877, established a ranch next door to Old Man Clanton, and became good friends with brothers Ike, Phineas, and Billy. The Clantons and McLaurys began to resent the Earps and other Tombstone newcomers who were eager to become the power brokers controlling the economic life of the area. The Earps, especially Wyatt, had no tolerance for cowboys and their wild ways. Wyatt had had his fill of dealing with their breed as a lawman in Kansas and thoroughly despised everything about them. Needless to say, the Clantons and McLaurys were no friends of his. Several incidents between the two factions caused resentment, and tempers flared on both sides. Accusations flew, fingers were pointed, and grudges turned into violence. But much more lurked beneath the surface. The conflict was rooted in two diametrically opposed political and social factions. The Clanton-McLaury side stood for the mostly Democrat, populist cowboys with unreconstructed Confederate roots. They took on the Earp contingency of hired guns from Republican ranks backed by the establishment, trying to control and regulate the personal interests of settlers. It was all part of the ongoing struggle between those who wished to "civilize" the West and those who wanted nothing to change. In the end, there would be no winners, only losers, widows, and orphans.

▶ Tom McLaury.

▶▶ Frank McLaury.

SEP 3

1897 At Folsom, New Mexico Territory, Sam Ketchum, Elza Lay, and others rob a Colorado and Southern Pacific Railroad train.

O.K. CORRAL

The gunfight at the O.K. Corral took place at about three o'clock on Wednesday afternoon, October 26, 1881, in Tombstone, Arizona Territory. Contrary to the name it is remembered by, the conflict did not occur at the O.K. Corral but rather on Fremont Street near C. S. Fly's Lodging House and photographic studio. On one side stood Ike and Billy Clanton, Frank and Tom McLaury, and a young friend who just happened to be in town that day named Billy Claiborne. And on the other side, supposedly representing law enforcement, were Wyatt, Virgil, and Morgan Earp, and their alcoholic pal Doc Holliday. Everyone in the Clanton-McLaury party, except for Ike, was armed. Town marshal Virgil Earp approached with the intention to disarm them with his newly deputized force, packing revolvers and a shotgun. Words were exchanged and instantly drawn guns blazed away. At least thirty shots were fired between the two sides. Morgan and Virgil Earp and Doc Holliday were wounded, but Wyatt emerged unscathed. Both McLaury brothers were dead at the scene, and Billy Clanton died in great agony just a few moments after the dust cleared. Ike Clanton and Billy Claiborne escaped without a wound. The confrontation lasted less than thirty seconds but became the most famous shootout in the annals of the American West.

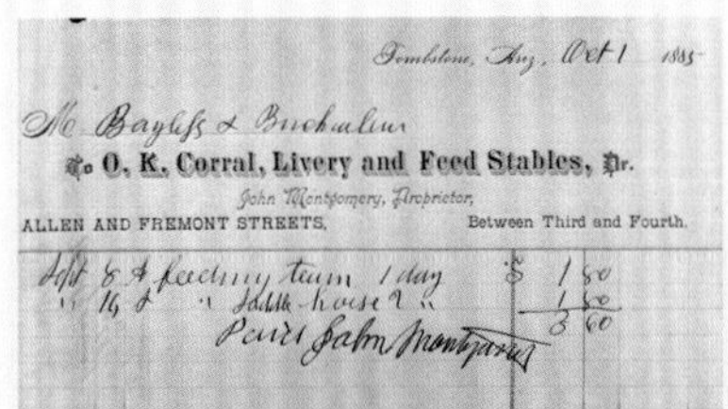

Tombstone, Ariz., Oct 1 1885

M Bayliss & [illegible]

To O. K. Corral, Livery and Feed Stables, Dr.

John Montgomery, Proprietor,

ALLEN AND FREMONT STREETS. Between Third and Fourth.

Sept 8 & feeding team 1 day	$ 1	80
" 16 " " saddle horse 2 "	1	80
	3	60

Paid John Montgomery

▲ A receipt from John Montgomery's O.K. Corral.

▶ The opening moment of the gunfight at the O.K. Corral as painted by Bob Boze Bell. The Earps and Holliday are in black.

SEP 4

1887 Near Holbrook, Arizona Territory, Sheriff Commodore Perry Owens single-handedly squares off against the Blevins Gang, killing three and wounding one.

AFTERMATH

Just moments after the shootout at the O.K. Corral, Tombstone was buzzing with excitement. Whistles sounded at the nearby mines summoning a large party of miners who grabbed weapons and patrolled the streets to preserve order. The Earps and Holliday were nowhere to be seen. They quickly went into hiding in case any friends of the Clantons or McLaurys came seeking revenge. Meanwhile, the bodies of Tom and Frank McLaury and Billy Clanton were taken to the Ritter and Ream Funeral Parlor. Undertakers cleaned the corpses, rouged their cheeks, and dressed them in dark suits and cravats. When all preparations were done, the bodies were placed on view in the window. A large sign hung over the caskets read: MURDERED IN THE STREETS OF TOMBSTONE. On the day of the funeral, two hearses bearing the three dead men slowly creaked toward Boot Hill. The Tombstone Brass Band, three hundred mourners on foot, two-dozen buggies, and a four-horse stagecoach followed. The procession route was lined with silent crowds, and at least three thousand showed up for the burial of Billy next to the grave of Old Man Clanton and the two McLaury brothers, who were laid in a single grave. The joint funerals were the largest ever held in Tombstone history. Although the cowboys had their rowdy times, the merchants appreciated the money they spent in town.

▶ Frank and Tom McLaury and Billy Clanton in their coffins.

1877 At Nebraska's Red Cloud Reservation, Crazy Horse, noted war leader of the Oglala Sioux, is bayoneted by a soldier while being arrested for subversion and subsequently dies.

VIRGIL AND MORGAN

Wyatt Earp and Doc Holliday were arrested on October 29, 1881, and charged with murder, but on November 29, Judge Wells Spicer ruled that the defendants "were fully justified in committing these homicides that it was a necessary act done in the discharge of official duty." Despite two other attempts to try Wyatt Earp and Holliday for the murders of Billy Clanton and the McLaury brothers, no conviction ever occurred. A coroner's inquest came to the anticlimactic conclusion that Billy Clanton and the McLaurys had died from the effects of gunshot wounds. Accusations were made that the Earps and Holliday had not enforced the law but committed cold-blooded murder. As a result, Wyatt and Doc, the only ones not formally employed as lawmen at the time, were charged with murder. At a preliminary hearing there was not enough evidence to bond either one over for trial. A short time later, a grand jury refused to indict either man. Although a judge scolded Virgil for enlisting his brothers and Holliday to arrest the Clantons, all of them were fully exonerated. Only two months after the O.K. Corral shootout, Virgil Earp, suspended as town marshal, had almost fully recovered from his wounds. The evening of December 28, 1881, Virgil was blasted with a shotgun as he walked along a dark Tombstone street. The wound was not fatal, but Virgil's left arm was shattered and he never regained use of it. Only three months later, on March 18, 1882, revenge came for the Earps again. While Wyatt watched Morgan playing billiards at a saloon, two shots were fired through the glass of the back door. Morgan was bent over the table when he was struck and fell to the floor, his spine severed. As Wyatt and others carried him to a coach, Morgan managed to joke, "This is the last game of pool I'll ever play." He died thirty minutes later.

▶ Morgan Earp.

▶▶ Virgil Earp, with one arm hanging useless.

SEP 6

1924 *Billboard* magazine announces that the 101 Ranch Wild West Show will hit the road again.

VENDETTA RIDE

After Tombstone police chief Morgan Earp died in a pool hall ambush, his brother Wyatt was determined to have revenge with help from a band of experienced gunmen. On March 20, 1882, just two days after Morgan's assassination, Wyatt, his brothers Warren and Virgil, Doc Holliday, and others loaded Morgan's coffin onto a train bound for California, where the Earps' parents had settled. At the stop in Tucson, the Earp brothers spied Frank Stilwell, a Clanton friend and one of the main suspects in Morgan's demise. By the time the train moved on, Stilwell lay dead by the tracks with six shots in his body, a killing which marked the beginning of what became known as the "Vendetta Ride." Over the next three weeks, a gang that included Wyatt, Warren, Holliday, Sherman McMasters, and Turkey Creek Jack Johnson claimed more victims. One of them was Florentino Cruz, alleged to have held the horses for the killers the night Morgan died. Cruz was shot and killed at a camp in the Dragoon Mountains on March 22. Some days later, the Earp posse engaged another suspect, William "Curly Bill" Brocious, at Mescal Springs and sent him to his reward. After their bloody rampage, the Earp posse departed Arizona Territory, sure they would not get a fair trial in the slaying of Stilwell. Though the vendetta seemed to have ended, on July 14, 1882, Johnny Ringo, a legendary badman with Clanton ties, was found dead in Arizona Territory with a bullet hole in his temple. Several theories were floated about the cause of death, including suicide. Many years later, however, after Wyatt's death in 1929, Josie Earp, his wife of forty-seven years, credited her husband and Doc Holliday with ending Ringo's criminal career.

▲ Warren Earp, youngest of the Earp brothers, joined Wyatt on his "Vendetta Ride."

▶ Johnny Ringo.

SEP 7

1876 At Northfield, Minnesota, the James-Younger Gang attempts to rob the First National Bank. Only the James brothers manage to escape. The Youngers and other gang members are not so lucky.

1881 At Blue Cut, Missouri, the James Gang robs the Chicago and Alton Railroad and gets away with twelve thousand dollars.

JESSE'S LAST HURRAH

After their escape from the botched Northfield, Minnesota, bank robbery and the demise of the Younger brothers in 1876, Jesse and Frank James laid low for several years, visiting old haunts, including a few in Indian Territory. For a time, they left Missouri and lived quietly with their families in Tennessee under assumed names. Jesse married his cousin Zerelda (Zee) Mimms in 1874 and was proud of their two children born in Nashville. He especially doted on his son, Jesse Edwards James. The lad's middle name honored the Kansas City newspaper editor John Newman Edwards who had written several heroic accounts of Jesse's life. By 1879, even though public sentiment had turned against the James brothers, Jesse and Frank came out of semiretirement and returned to their old outlaw tricks. They formed a new gang and rode out in search of prey. However, the men they recruited were not like the proud ex-Confederate guerrillas who had ridden with them earlier. The new gang members were green and unseasoned and sometimes overcompensated for their inexperience with extreme shows of violence. They were more like hired guns, not emotionally bound to the James brothers or each other through Civil War bloodshed as the Youngers had been. Many of them drank too much, while others liked to swagger and brag about their exploits. Jesse longed for the old days when each member of his gang could be trusted like kinfolk. Over the next few years, more banks and trains were robbed, but because of the large rewards on the heads of Jesse and Frank, a natural tension arose within the outlaw band.

▶ Alexander Franklin James, known as Frank.

▶▶ Jesse James.

SEP 8

1893 In Geuda Springs, Kansas, the violent life of gunfighter Luke Short ends when he dies peacefully of dropsy, the nineteenth-century term for congestive heart failure.

THE ASSASSINATION OF JESSE JAMES

By the late 1870s, Jesse James, using the name Thomas Howard, had become the sole leader of the gang after big brother, Frank, had decided to start supporting his family through an honest living. In 1881, Jesse and his wife and children moved to a comfortable cottage on a hilltop in St. Joseph, Missouri. Gang members, however, were being picked off one by one. Some were killed, while others who were apprehended confessed to their sins and implicated their accomplices. The infamous James Gang was crumbling. On the morning of April 3, 1882, two relatively new gang members, brothers Robert and Charley Ford, decided to claim the staggering ten-thousand-dollar reward offered for James. During a secret meeting in Kansas City, Missouri, Governor Thomas T. Crittenden had already assured the Fords of the substantial bounty. He had dangled full pardons before their eyes if they could deliver the outlaw leader dead or alive. After breakfast with the Ford boys at his home, James, who had just returned from Indian Territory where he had been planning his next bank robbery, walked into the parlor and pulled off his coat and two pistols. When he climbed onto a chair to brush some dust off a picture, Charley winked at Bob, who then drew his gun and fired a shot directly into Jesse's head. Jesse James tumbled headlong to the floor. He was thirty-four years old and stone dead.

▲ The book cover illustrates the assassination of Jesse James.

▶ Huge crowds gathered at Jesse's home in St. Joseph, Missouri, when word of his murder spread.

SEP 9

1876 At the Battle of Slim Buttes in Dakota Territory, U.S. troops under General George Crook fight a band of Sioux warriors under Chief American Horse, who later dies of his wounds. Troopers recover the Seventh Cavalry guidon and other "souvenirs" taken during the Battle of Little Bighorn.

THE FORD BROTHERS

The smoke still hung in the air and Zee James was screaming in horror, when Bob Ford ran from the house yelling, "I have killed Jesse James!" Within hours, the word had spread through the rest of the nation. A banner headline in the *St. Joseph Gazette* shrieked, "JESSE, BY JEHOVAH!" The public wanted all the gory details, shocked that the desperado had been shot from behind in his own home, betrayed by a member of his inner circle. After the assassination, Bob and his older brother Charley wired Governor Crittenden in Missouri to claim the reward. Later, in describing the killing of James to Crittenden, Bob said: "As he stood there, unarmed, with his back to me, it came to me suddenly, 'Now or never is your chance. If you don't get him now, he'll get you tonight.' Without further thought or a moment's delay I pulled my revolver and leveled it as I sat. He heard the hammer click as I cocked it with my thumb and started to turn as I pulled the trigger. The ball struck him just behind the ear, and he fell like a log, dead." The Fords expected to become instant heroes, but instead had to stand trial for James's murder. They were found guilty and sentenced to hang, but within hours the governor pardoned them. The brothers never saw the reward money they had been promised.

▶ Robert Ford.

▶▶ Charley Ford.

SEP 10

1866 Near Fort Kearny, Wyoming Territory, the Eighteenth Infantry encounters a group of hostile Indians and two soldiers are killed.

DEATH WATCH

"*Jesse James was about five feet eight inches in height, of a rather solid, firm and compact build, yet rather on the slender side. His hair was black and not overly long; blue eyes well shaded with dark lashes, and the entire lower portion of the face was covered by a growth of dark brown or sun browned whiskers, which are not long and shaggy, but are trimmed and bear evidence of careful attention. . . . He was neatly clad in a business suit of cashmere, of a dark brown substance, which fit him very neatly. He wore a shirt of spotless whiteness, with collar and cravat, and looked more the picture of a staid and substantial business man than the outlaw and robber that he was.*"

—*Kansas City Times*, April 4, 1882

"*After a short consultation, Messrs. Craig* [police commissioner], *Timberlake* [sheriff], *and the* Times *representative visited the undertaking establishment where the dead body of Jesse James had been placed in a cooler. The officers were, of course, allowed to look at it, and from the calm and peaceful countenance none would imagine the terrible experience its former owner had passed through. Upon the body was the wound through the head, which caused death, two in the right breast near the nipple, received during the war, one in the right leg, received at Northfield, and the first joint of the third finger of the left hand had been shot off. These were the only wounds upon the body.*"

—*Kansas City Times*, April 4, 1882

▶ Jesse James in his coffin.

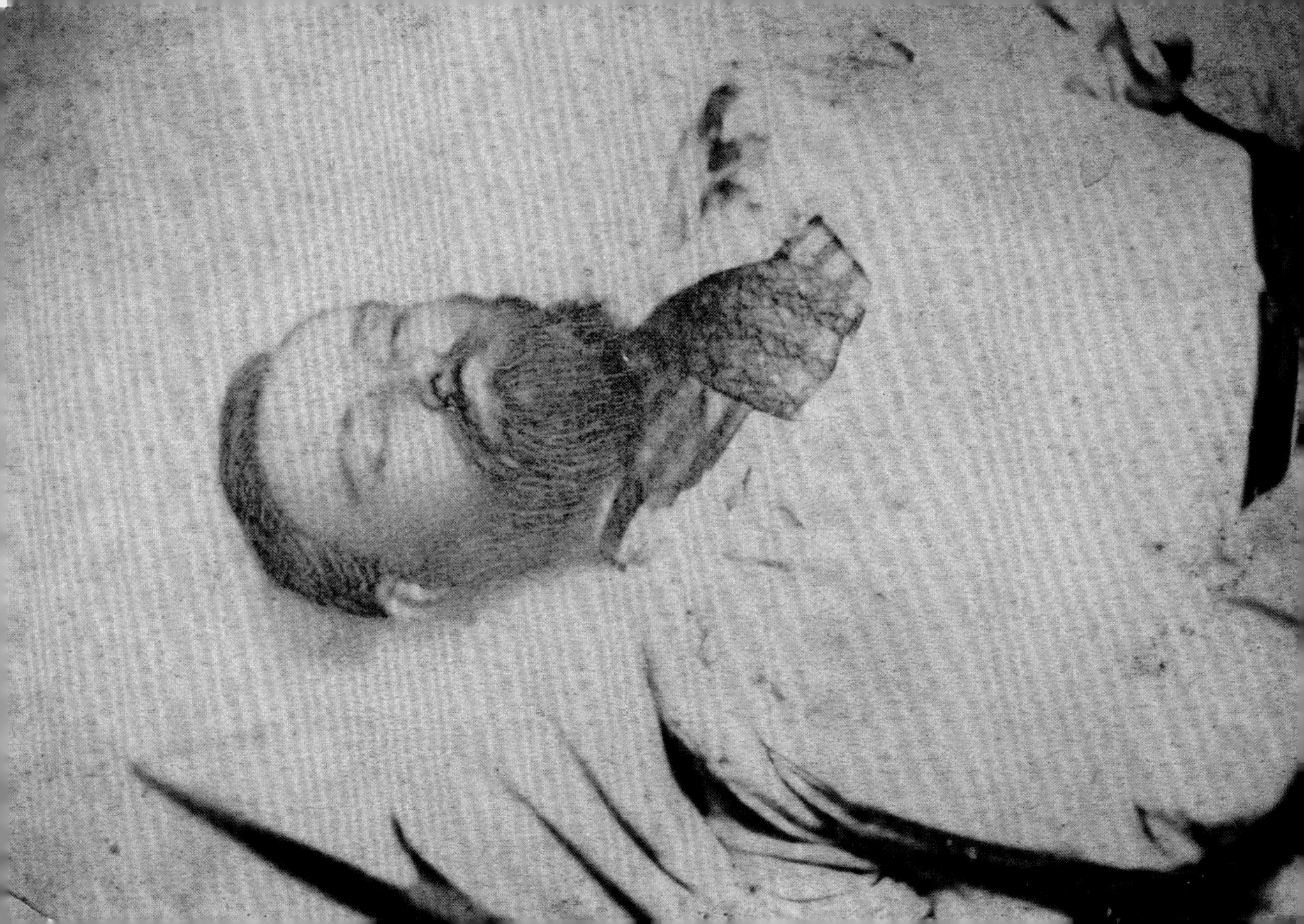

SEP 11

1857 At Mountain Meadows, Utah Territory, Mormons led by John D. Lee attack a wagon train, killing at least 120 men, women, and children. This becomes known as the Mountain Meadows Massacre.

DIRTY LITTLE COWARD

Jesse James was a lad that killed many a man
He robbed the Glendale train;
He stole from the rich and he gave to the poor
He'd a hand and a heart and a brain.

Poor Jesse had a wife to mourn for his life,
Three children, they were brave;
But that dirty little coward that shot Mr. Howard
Has laid poor Jesse in his grave.

It was Robert Ford, that dirty little coward;
I wonder how he does feel
For he ate of Jesse's bread and he slept in Jesse's bed,
Then laid poor Jesse in his grave.

Poor Jesse had a wife to mourn for his life,
Three children, they were brave;
But that dirty little coward that shot Mr. Howard
Has laid poor Jesse in his grave.

—popular folk song, 1882

▶ The "dirty little coward" who shot Jesse James.

SEP 12

1883 In Socorro, New Mexico Territory, rancher and bushwhacker Joe Fowler, who once boasted of killing fourteen men, shoots and kills another victim, demonstrating, in the words of a local newspaper, that for Fowler "homicide had become a habit." The following year, Fowler is hanged by vigilantes after savagely stabbing a friend to death with a Bowie knife.

FRANK JAMES GOES STRAIGHT

After the assassination of his brother, Jesse, a grieving Frank James began negotiations to surrender. Frank had quit his outlaw life some time before, but he still faced charges for crimes in Missouri and also Minnesota stemming from the failed Northfield robbery in 1876. On October 5, 1882—six months after Jesse's death—Frank rode to the Missouri capital at Jefferson City to surrender to Governor Thomas Crittenden, whom Frank considered honorable and trustworthy. John Newman Edwards, the *Kansas City Times* editor who had perpetuated the heroic outlaw image of the James-Younger Gang, escorted Frank into Crittenden's chambers. As he handed over his pistols, Frank spoke: "Governor, I am Frank James. I surrender my arms to you. I have removed the loads from them. They have not been out of my possession since 1864. I now give them to you personally. I deliver myself to you and the law. . . . I have been hunted for twenty-one years. I have literally lived in the saddle. I have never known a day of perfect peace. . . . When I slept it was in the midst of an arsenal." Crittenden refused to deliver James to Minnesota, and eventually all charges against him were dropped. But first, James had to stand trial on one count of murdering a passenger during a train robbery. At the courthouse in Independence, Missouri, Frank was given a hero's welcome. Bankers offered to post his bail, and while in jail, he enjoyed many luxuries. Represented by former Confederate Secretary of War Leroy Pope Walker, Frank was found not guilty by a sympathetic jury in spite of evidence to the contrary. He was released and lived his last thirty years in peace.

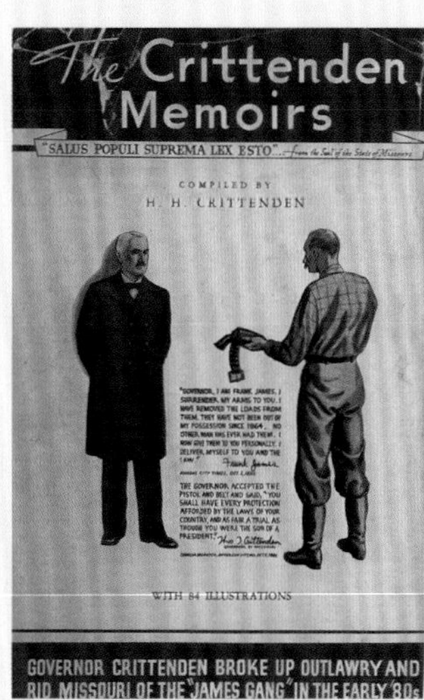

▲ This cover of Missouri governor Crittenden's memoirs features an illustration of the surrender of Frank James.

▶ Frank James as he looked at the time of his surrender in 1882.

SEP 13

1892 Chris Evans and John Sontag ambush a posse in California's Sierra Nevada mountain range and kill two lawmen.
1925 In Sallisaw, Oklahoma, Charles "Pretty Boy" Floyd and Fred Hildebrand are jailed on suspicion of highway robbery.

LAW WEST OF THE PECOS

Judge Roy Bean—a notorious frontiersman, saloonkeeper, and justice of the peace—was tailor-made for Texas. Only that big brash state could support such a colorful figure of Bean's proportions. In 1882, after running a successful saloon in San Antonio for twenty years, Bean sold all he owned, left his wife and children, and moved to west Texas to start fresh. At the junction of the Pecos River and the Rio Grande, Bean opened a combined general store, saloon, and billiard hall at Vinegarroon, a whistle-stop settlement. Named for the nasty whiptail scorpion that emitted a vinegarlike smell when bothered, Vinegarroon was just a collection of shacks perched quite literally along the newly laid tracks. A short time later, the town was abandoned completely as everyone relocated to a new railroad camp that came to be called Langtry, in honor of a railroad engineer. Bean was appointed justice of the peace at the insistence of a handful of Texas Rangers who tried to keep order along the wild Texas border. Bean proclaimed himself the "Law West of the Pecos," and though he was an unabashed racist and greedy swindler, any culprit dragged before him could at least count on a speedy trial. The crusty Bean dispensed his own brand of justice about as fast as he did beer and shots of whiskey at his saloon-courtroom on the banks of the Rio Grande. One story claimed that Bean held an inquest over a dead man found with forty dollars and a pistol in his pockets. Bean promptly fined the corpse forty dollars for carrying a concealed weapon and then bought the house a round of celebratory drinks.

▲ Judge Roy Bean.

▶ Roy Bean's first store and bar in Langtry, Texas, not far from the train tracks. Bean, with white beard, is standing front and center.

HALL
RAIL ROAD STORE.
by Roy Bean
BEER ON ICE

SEP 14

1847 American troops take possession of Mexico City as Santa Anna flees, virtually ensuring that the United States will win the war against Mexico.

BABY DOE

The romance between silver baron Horace Tabor and a flamboyant beauty dubbed "Baby Doe" is one of the classic "rags to riches" stories of the American West. It began when Tabor, a furniture store owner with a seventeen-dollar grubstake, netted millions in the great Colorado silver mining boom. By the early 1880s, Tabor was the richest man in Denver. He also was tired of his longtime wife, Augusta. Tabor obtained a divorce in 1883 and quickly legalized his scandalous relationship with the glamorous Elizabeth "Baby Doe" McCourt, during a Washington, D.C., wedding ceremony attended by President Chester Arthur. Although twenty-five years her senior, Tabor and his beloved Baby Doe seemed to be madly in love. They attended events at Tabor's opera houses in Leadville and Denver, graced the floor of the Windsor Hotel taproom studded with three thousand silver dollars, and supped in the elegant dining room on frog legs, mountain trout, venison, and bear steaks. Tabor—known as "The Bonanza King of Leadville"—dabbled in politics, serving an unexpired term in the U.S. Senate and running unsuccessfully for governor. But a series of poor investments and swindles chipped away at Tabor's wealth. By 1893, the nation was in an economic depression and his mines played out. Tabor died penniless in 1899 after imploring Baby Doe to never give up their Matchless Mine, believing that one day it could be restored to produce silver. A grieving Baby Doe returned to Leadville. Left without a penny, she lived at the worthless mine for the last thirty-six years of her life. In 1935, her frozen corpse was found in the shack where she lived.

▲ Baby Doe Tabor, while a wealthy woman from the Colorado silver boom.

▶ Baby Doe at the door of her shack in Leadville, Colorado, where she would freeze to death.

SEP 15

1858 The Butterfield Overland Mail Service sends its first stagecoaches to deliver U.S. mail from the East to the Pacific.

BLACK BART

His friends called him Charley, but the well-mannered gentleman bandit variously known as Charles Bolton, Charles Earl Boles, and Charles E. Bowles, was best remembered by his ominous nickname—Black Bart, a name pulled from a dime novel. In his mid-forties when he robbed his first stagecoach in 1875, he became one of the most successful outlaws in California history. That first robbery was memorable because Charley politely asked the driver to "Please throw down the box." Occasionally, he left verse at the crime scenes, which gave rise to his reputation as the poet-bandit. On August 3, 1877, he robbed a Wells Fargo stage and scribbled on a strongbox waybill:

I've labored long and hard for bread,
For honor and for riches
But on my corns too long you've tred
You fine-haired Sons of Bitches.

It was signed "Black Bart, the Po-8," standing for poet. In a string of stage robberies over eight years, Black Bart never fired a single gunshot and never robbed any passengers. When not wearing his flour sack mask with holes cut for his eyes and a long linen duster, Black Bart lived a respectable life in a quiet San Francisco neighborhood. On November 3, 1883, his twenty-eighth stage robbery became his last when he was wounded and dropped a handkerchief. Private detective Harry Morse traced the laundry mark and discovered it belonged to Charles E. Bolton. Black Bart was arrested, tried, and sentenced to six years at San Quentin. Thanks to his impeccable behavior, he got out after only four years and was never seen again.

▶ Charles E. Bolton, dressed as a gentleman in San Francisco. In his other persona, he robbed stagecoaches as "Black Bart."

▶▶ Harry Morse, the detective who discovered Black Bart living in San Francisco.

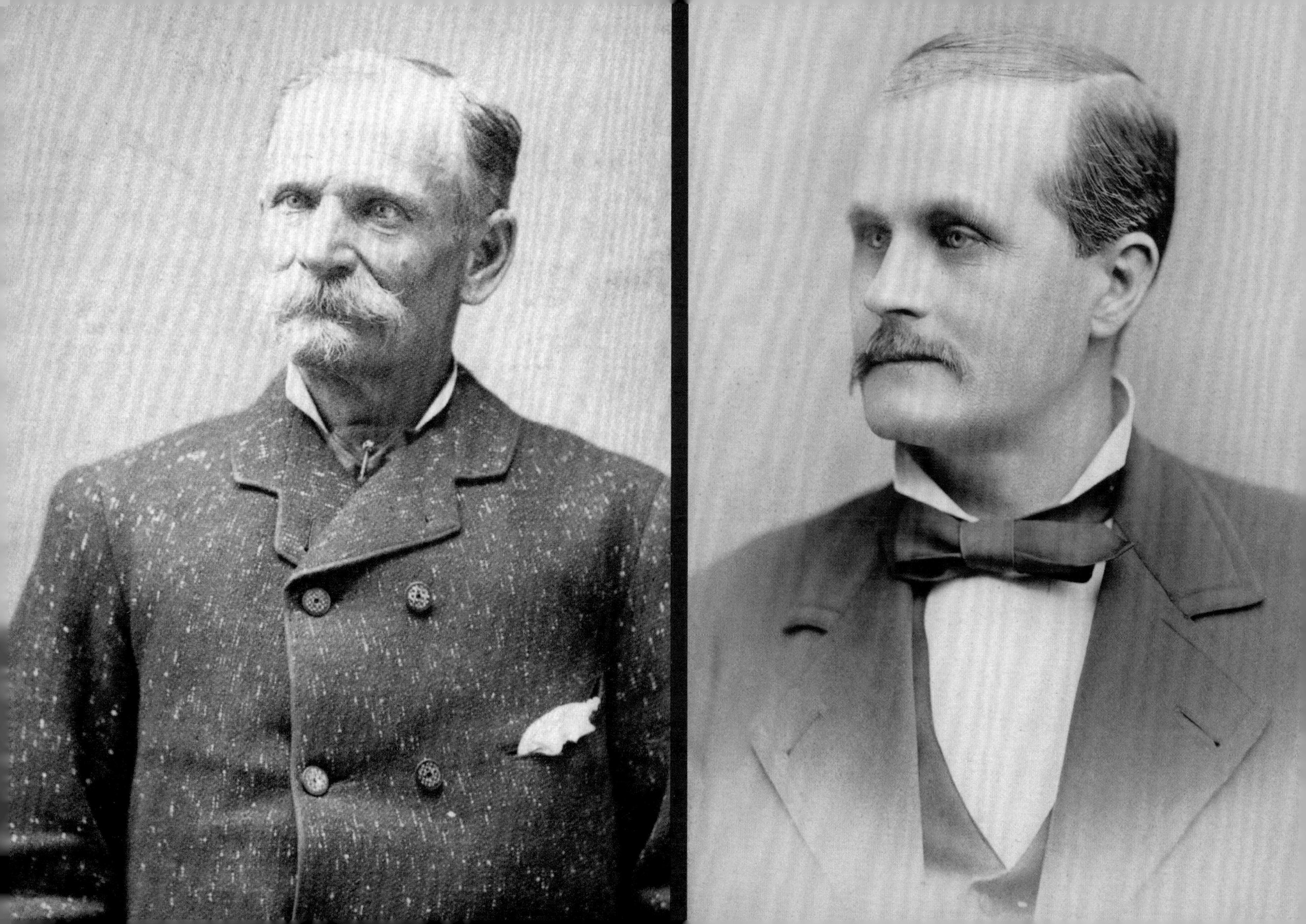

SEP 16

1893 Millions of acres of land in the Cherokee Outlet in what is now Oklahoma are opened to settlers.

THE OLD GLORY BLOWOUT

On Independence Day 1882, William F. "Buffalo Bill" Cody staged the "Old Glory Blowout" in North Platte, Nebraska. Cody, who had established his Scout's Rest Ranch near North Platte in 1877, put on the event in response to townsfolk's pleas for a memorable shindig to mark the Fourth of July. That sweltering afternoon, as many as one thousand cowboys competed for prizes in riding, roping, bronco busting, and shooting. Using blank ammunition, Cody—turned out in his finest frontier outfit—demonstrated the hunting of buffalo from horseback. The Old Glory Blowout was so successful it served as a trial run for a road show that Cody produced the following year on a larger scale. He and partner Doc Carver unveiled "The Wild West, Hon. W. F. Cody and Dr. W. F. Carver's Mountain and Prairie Exhibition" in May 1883, at the state fairgrounds in Omaha. The crowds went wild. The show toured several cities to great acclaim, inspiring Cody to abstain from drinking so as to not miss a single performance.

▲▲ The handsome young William F. Cody when he opened his Buffalo Bill's Wild West.

▲ Doc Carver, sharpshooter and Buffalo Bill's first partner in the show.

▶ A program for the show

BUFFALO BILL'S
WILD
WEST
COL. W. F. CODY.
AND
CONGRESS OF ROUGH RIDERS
OF THE WORLD.
HISTORICAL SKETCHES,
& PROGRAMME.

SEP 17

1868 In the Battle of Beecher Island in Yuma County, Colorado Territory, Major George A. Forsyth and a party of handpicked frontiersmen hold off more than seven hundred Sioux, Cheyenne, and Arapaho warriors. The well-armed troopers are eventually rescued by Buffalo Soldiers of the Tenth Cavalry.

GERONIMO

Just hearing the name Geronimo froze the blood of white settlers and soldiers across the Southwest in the 1880s. A dedicated warrior for many years, Geronimo became an even more significant force following the death of the Chiricahua Apache leader Victorio, considered one of the greatest Indian strategists. After Victorio and his followers fled the San Carlos Reservation in 1877, he began three years of raiding in Texas, New Mexico Territory, and Mexico. On October 15, 1880, Mexican militia surrounded Victorio's mountain camp and massacred all the warriors. The few surviving women and children were taken to Chihuahua City where they were held for several years. After Victorio's death, Geronimo continued the Apache battle against the white invaders. Victorio and Cochise had fought alongside Geronimo in the 1850s, after Mexicans slaughtered his wife and three children. Named Goyathlay, *One Who Yawns*, the bereaved warrior fought so fiercely that his Mexican enemies cried out, "Geronimo!" calling for the help of San Geronimo (Saint Jerome), patron saint of the Mexican army. For the first several years of the 1880s, Geronimo battled the U.S. Army with a ferocity reflected in the earliest known photograph of him, taken in 1884 when he was sixty years old.

▲ The only image of the great Apache chief, Victorio.

▶ The earliest photograph of Apache chief Geronimo.

SEP 18

1877 At Big Springs, Nebraska, Sam Bass and others rob a Union Pacific Train and get away with more than sixty thousand dollars.

LUKE SHORT

At about five feet, five inches tall, the diminutive Luke Short measured up to his name. Said to have killed as many as fourteen men, Short was also known as "The Undertaker's Friend," because he always aimed for the chest and never the head, making the mortician's job much easier. A skilled gambler and always nattily dressed, Short made the rounds of cow towns and mining camps plying his trade. He supplemented his income peddling rotgut whiskey to Indians, several of whom he killed when they became disorderly. By 1880, Short had shown up in Tombstone, Arizona Territory. He felt at home with the Earps, Doc Holliday, and Bat Masterson—all good friends who cheered Short's acquittal in the February 25, 1881, shooting death of Charlie Storms over a gambling disagreement at the Oriental Saloon. Short left Tombstone before the famous shootout at the O.K. Corral. He settled in Dodge City and in 1883 purchased a half-interest in the Long Branch Saloon, the popular and oftentimes violent establishment on Front Street. Short quickly wore out his welcome in the trail town even though he was trying to erase a disreputable image. Just two days after a new ordinance banning prostitution took effect, the police arrested three Long Branch "entertainers" accused of doing more than singing. The evening after the trio was jailed as prostitutes, Short came to bust them out and exchanged gunfire with the city clerk on Front Street. Although there were no injuries, Short was arrested. Told that his presence was no longer welcomed in Dodge, Short was put on a train bound for Kansas City with orders to never return.

▲ Luke Short.

▶ Dodge City's Front Street, 1879.

DODGE HOUSE
BILLIARD HALL.
J. MUELLER

SEP 19

1900 At Winnemucca, Nevada, Butch Cassidy, the Sundance Kid, and some of the Wild Bunch rob the First National Bank.

THE DODGE CITY PEACE COMMISSION

After his banishment from Dodge City, Luke Short spent every waking moment calling in political chits and seeking the support of old friends. He was not about to be driven out by business rivals and do-gooders with reform on their minds. In the spring of 1883, a dozen Dodge citizens sent letters to Kansas Governor George Glick protesting Short's forcible removal. Then, the defiant Short was joined in Kansas City by some of his gunfighter pals, including Wyatt Earp and Bat Masterson. They made no secret of their plan to return to Dodge City. "Yesterday a new man arrived on the scene who is destined to play a part in a great tragedy," warned the *Daily Kansas City Journal*, on May 13, 1883. "This man is Bat Masterson . . . one of the most dangerous men the West has ever produced. . . . Wyatt Earp is equally famous in the cheerful business of depopulating the country." The inflated news reports made Dodge City fathers nervous, and they prepared for the worst. But when Short and his well-armed allies returned to town, both sides reached a compromise without a single shot fired. What was hailed as the "Dodge City War" ended quietly before it really began. Assurances were made that if Short lived within the law, he would be welcomed back. Eight of Short's friends, calling themselves the Dodge City Peace Commission, sat for a historic photograph and departed. Short remained to get his affairs in order. In November 1883, he sold his interest in the Long Branch Saloon and quit Dodge on his own terms.

▶ The Dodge City Peace Commission. Back row, from left: W. H. Harris, Luke Short, Bat Masterson, W. F. Petillon; front row, from left: Charles Bassett, Wyatt Earp, Frank McLean, Neil Brown.

SEP 20

1923 In Oklahoma, just below the Kansas border on the Osage-Washington County Line, outlaw Al Spencer is found by lawmen and killed.

BEN THOMPSON

Born in England in 1842, Ben Thompson—known as one of the most deadly accurate gunman of the West—died in Texas forty-one years later. Whether drawing his weapon in self-defense, out of revenge, while collecting a gambling debt, or as a peace officer, Thompson remained cool under fire and seldom missed his mark. A career gambler, in his early years he did a two-year stretch in the Texas penitentiary for killing his brother-in-law after learning he had physically abused Thompson's sister. After that he moved around the West, but returned to Texas and became the Austin city marshal in the early 1880s. After a few years on the job, Thompson shot and killed a San Antonio theater owner during an argument. He was eventually acquitted, but resigned as marshal and never returned to law enforcement. An aging Bat Masterson, when pondering his own checkered past, singled out Thompson as one of the best gunmen of the late nineteenth century. "Ben Thompson was a remarkable man in many ways and it is very doubtful if in his time there was another man living who equaled him with the pistol in a life and death struggle," Masterson wrote in 1908. "Thompson in the first place possessed a much higher order of intelligence than the average 'gun fighter' or man killer of his time. . . . He was more resourceful and a better general under trying conditions than any of that great army of desperate men who flourished on our frontier thirty years ago. He was absolutely without fear and his nerves were those of the finest steel. . . . Thompson killed many men during his career, but always in an open and manly way."

▲ A book on the life of Ben Thompson, published in 1884.

▶ Ben Thompson.

SEP

21

1904 At Washington State's Colville Reservation, Nez Perce Chief Joseph dies. The reservation doctor claims he died of a broken heart.

KING FISHER

Like his friend Ben Thompson, and many others on the frontier of the 1880s, Texas gunslinger King Fisher built his reputation by working both sides of the law. In the final analysis, it seemed he usually favored the criminal side. His full name was John King Fisher, but he went by King even as a child. He grew up tough, in and out of trouble for horse theft and other transgressions that netted him a brief prison sentence. After his release and still in his teens, Fisher rode with a gang of rustlers and honed his shooting skills. He cut a handsome figure dressed in a broad sombrero, embroidered vests, silk shirts, crimson sashes, and his trademark Bengal tiger–skin chaps made from an animal killed when his gang held up a traveling circus. During a dispute over dividing up loot, Fisher shot and killed as many as ten of the Mexican bandits he rode with and took control of the gang. When asked about his shooting victims, Fisher only admitted to killing seven men, "not counting Mexicans." Continually pursued by Texas Rangers, Fisher was indicted for murder and other crimes, but managed to avoid prosecution. After being cleared of a murder charge in 1881, he became a deputy sheriff in Uvalde County, Texas, and went on to serve as acting sheriff. In 1883, Sheriff Fisher shot and killed one of two brothers he had arrested for robbing a stagecoach. After King died, the boys' mother visited his grave each year on the anniversary of her son's death. She would gather kindling, build a fire on King's grave, and dance on it while the flames crackled.

▲ King Fisher (left) with an unknown companion.

► John King Fisher.

SEP 22

1887 John Graham and Charlie Blevins are killed by a posse led by Sheriff William Mulvenon of Yavapi County, Arizona Territory, during the Pleasant Valley War between sheepherders and cattlemen.

FATAL CORNER

On March 11, 1884, a twin killing occurred in downtown San Antonio at Soledad Street and West Commerce, popularly called the "Fatal Corner" owing to the violence that transpired at this site over the years. The victims were old friends Ben Thompson and King Fisher. They had bumped into each other and decided to enjoy themselves at the Vaudeville Variety Theater, where, just two years before, Thompson had shot and killed theater owner Jack Harris during an argument. Thompson had been acquitted, but resigned as city marshal of Austin. In hopes of putting the matter to rest, when Thompson and Fisher arrived at the theater, they asked to speak to the proprietor Joe Foster and his new partner Billy Simms. The four men met in a theater box and were joined by Jacob Coy, a local law officer. At some point, the discussion turned to the death of Harris, and tempers flared. Simms and the others stepped outside the box, leaving Thompson and Fisher alone just as a burst of gunfire erupted from an adjacent theater box. The two men targeted did not have a chance. Thompson was shot multiple times and died almost instantly. Fisher was struck by thirteen rounds before he died, but managed to squeeze off one shot. Coy was hit and crippled for life, and Foster, the mastermind of the assassination, accidentally shot himself in the leg and died a short time later. A bloodstained photograph of Thompson was found on Fisher's body inscribed, "To my friend King Fisher," and signed by Thompson that very same day. There was a public outcry, but the prosecutor had little interest in the matter and no action was ever taken.

▲ Billy Simms—gambler, sportsman, and owner of the Vaudeville Variety Theater in San Antonio.

▶ The Vaudeville Variety Theater, which came to be known as the "Fatal Corner."

TOBACCONIST
SMOKE
HART'S
CIGAR
HART'S
5¢
GENUINE
TOBACCO
CIGARETTES
HART

1903 Near Portland, Oregon, bandit Bill Miner and his gang rob an express train.

MEDICINE LODGE ROBBERY

During a driving rainstorm on the morning of April 30, 1884, four men rode into Medicine Lodge, Kansas, and hitched their horses to the coal shed of the Medicine Valley Bank. At just a few minutes past nine o'clock, the quartet entered the bank with guns drawn and ordered the two men inside—bank president Wiley Payne and cashier George Geppert—to throw up their hands. Instead, Payne went for a revolver, and the bandits opened fire, killing both men. Bystanders heard the shots, and the alarm went out. As the thwarted robbers broke for their horses, the town marshal and others returned gunfire, and within minutes a well-mounted posse was in hot pursuit. Just a few miles outside of town, the outlaws were surrounded in a canyon and surrendered. The possemen were shocked when they confronted their captives, especially the leader—Henry Newton Brown, the respected marshal of Caldwell, Kansas. Brown's accomplices were his assistant Ben Wheeler and two well-known area cowboys, John Wesley and Billy Smith. Known to have ridden in Lincoln County with Billy the Kid, Brown had given up his outlaw ways in order to serve as a deputy sheriff in Tascosa, Texas, before becoming a peacekeeper in Caldwell in 1882. The next year, after Brown killed two outlaws, the citizens presented him with an engraved Winchester rifle. Now the lapsed Brown and the others were taken to the Medicine Lodge jail. That evening a lynch mob rushed in, and as the prisoners broke for freedom, Brown was gunned down. Wheeler was wounded and, along with the two hapless cowboys, dragged to an elm tree and hanged.

▶ The four Medicine Lodge, Kansas, bank robbers shortly before they were dealt with by the citizen vigilantes. Ben Wheeler, far right, and Henry Brown, with the white bandanna second from the left, were both lawmen in nearby Caldwell, Kansas, at the time they robbed the bank.

1913 In Canon City, Colorado, famed bank robber Henry Starr is paroled from prison for good behavior.

THE LEGEND OF ELFEGO BACA

Elfego Baca, a spunky nineteen-year-old Mexican boy, fought a pitched thirty-six-hour gun battle against eighty well-armed Texas cowboys in Frisco, New Mexico Territory, and lived to tell about it. The encounter began innocently enough in late 1884, when Baca, acting as deputy sheriff, apprehended a drunken cowboy who had shot up a saloon on the Frisco plaza. The notion of a Mexican kid arresting a white cowboy did not sit well with some of the other wranglers, and soon the town was crowded with armed and angry men, who, in the words of a bystander, were "full of zeal and whiskey." In the commotion, a cowboy was crushed by his horse and later died. Baca was forced to flee for his life and take cover in a ramshackle adobe building. During the siege, another cowboy was shot and killed by Baca, as estimates of as many as four thousand rounds poured into his flimsy sanctuary, causing part of the shack to collapse. Finally, after intense negotiations, Baca surrendered. He stood trial on two counts of murder, won acquittals, and was so impressed with his lawyers that he became one himself. Later, Baca was elected sheriff of Socorro County for a term and then resumed his law practice. In 1940, five years before his death, the citizens of Socorro presented Baca with the key and the door to the jail cell he occupied in 1884.

"I will show the Texans there is at least one Mexican in the county who is not afraid of an American cowboy."

—Elfego Baca, 1884

Attorney and Counsellor at Law
Albuquerque, N. M.
My dear Judge:
Very truly yours,

▲ Elfego Baca, an attorney in later life, 1918.

▶ Elfego Baca.

SEP 25

1872 Troopers from the Fifth Cavalry kill forty Indian hostiles during a skirmish on the Santa Maria River in Arizona Territory.

QUEEN OF THE RED LIGHTS

For twenty years, the notorious Mattie Silks reigned as "Queen of the Red Lights" in Denver. By the mid-1880s, she had become one of the most successful brothel-keepers in the American West. Mattie, whose true name was Martha Ready, boasted that she had never worked as a prostitute, only as a madam. She was only nineteen years old when she started operating her first house of ill repute in Springfield, Illinois, and soon traveled west to stake her claim in bustling Denver. Mattie was known for lending her most popular girls to her other brothel operations in Leadville and Georgetown, Colorado, and as far away as Dawson City, Alaska. Mattie, who always carried a pistol and was a crack shot, was also a participant in the first recorded duel in Denver between two women. Her opponent was Kate Fulton, another top-notch madam who competed with Mattie for male clientele and also for the affections of Cortez Thomson, a famous foot racer, gambler, and dashing man-about-town. The duel was staged on the banks of the South Platte River, and both women appeared topless and swore to kill the other. Neither one hit the intended target, but it was Mattie's shot that reportedly struck poor Thomson in his neck. He survived and, despite the unfortunate results of the duel, the couple briefly wed. The official union came to an end when Mattie tired of his infidelities and penchant for spending her money. Mattie ran three cathouses in Denver and eventually took control of Jennie Rogers's impressive House of Mirrors, a three-story brick mansion with sixteen bedrooms, a mirrored ballroom, and an all-black orchestra. After her death in 1929, Mattie was buried as Martha Ready beside her one-time husband and lover, Cortez Thomson.

▲ Mattie's calling card.

▶ Denver madam Mattie Silks.

SEP 26

1879 Fire destroys the entire business district of Deadwood, Dakota Territory.

LITTLE SURE SHOT

In 1885, Buffalo Bill Cody's touring Wild West extravaganza got a real boost when the showman landed an amazing sharpshooter, Phoebe Ann Moses, whom the entire world came to know as Annie Oakley. One of America's first female celebrities, Oakley—born in Ohio in 1860—was only fifteen when she took part in her first shooting contest, pitted against the famous marksman Frank Butler. Despite the odds, Oakley won the prize money when Butler missed his final shot. He did, however, win the heart of his charming opponent, and the couple eventually wed. For several years, Oakley accompanied her husband while he toured the country as an exhibition shooter. When Butler's partner became ill and had to drop out, Oakley stepped in as his replacement. She took the stage name of Annie Oakley, performing on the vaudeville circuit with Butler, who subsequently became her manager and assistant. "She outclassed me," Butler said when asked why he gave up shooting. Starting in 1885 with only a verbal contract, Oakley and Butler toured with Buffalo Bill for sixteen seasons. Sitting Bull, who also toured with Cody in 1885, was so impressed with the young woman's marksmanship he dubbed her "Little Sure Shot." Always competitive, Oakley became concerned when the younger female shooter Lillian Smith, known as the "California Girl," joined the show in 1886. Oakley immediately cut six years off her age and told everyone she was born in 1866. Both women performed before Queen Victoria and other crowned heads of Europe in 1887, but two years later Lillian Smith left Cody's employ. She went on to fame and glory as Princess Wenona with the Miller Brothers' 101 Wild West Show, letting Oakley keep the limelight in Buffalo Bill's show.

▲ Annie's husband Frank Butler, also a sharpshooter.

▶ Annie Oakley while on tour with Buffalo Bill.

SEP 27

1864 Prior to the Battle of Centralia in Missouri, pro-Confederate guerrillas led by "Bloody Bill" Anderson slaughter twenty-three unarmed Union soldiers taken from a train. Future outlaws Jesse and Frank James reportedly take part in the raid and ensuing battle.

COWBOY DETECTIVE

When city folks gobbled up the words of writer Charlie Siringo, they got their first taste of how a young drover earned his thirty-dollars-a-month wages moving stubborn Longhorns up an unforgiving trail. Born and raised in south Texas, the son of an Italian immigrant father and an Irish immigrant mother, Charles Angelo Siringo was a working cowboy and cattle driver by his mid-teens. In 1884, he left the cowboy life and wrote *A Texas Cowboy; or, Fifteen Years on the Hurricane Deck of a Spanish Pony*, a book that established his fame and contributed to the myth of the cowboy as an archetypal Western hero. As writer J. Frank Dobie later pointed out, Siringo was "the first authentic cowboy to publish an autobiography." Will Rogers called the book "the Cowboy's Bible when I was growing up." In 1886, Siringo went on to put in twenty-two years of service with the Pinkertons, where he became known as the "Cowboy Detective," working undercover and tracking the likes of Butch Cassidy's Wild Bunch, Tom Horn, and other outlaws from Alaska to Mexico City. In later years, Siringo wrote more books based on his adventures and consulted with cowboy moviemakers in Hollywood, where he died in 1928.

"Our outfit consisted of twenty-five hundred head of old mossy-horn steers, a cook and twenty-five riders, with six head of good horses to the man. . . . Everything went on lovely with the exception of swimming swollen streams, fighting now and then among ourselves and a stampede every stormy night."

—Charles Siringo, *A Texas Cowboy*, 1885

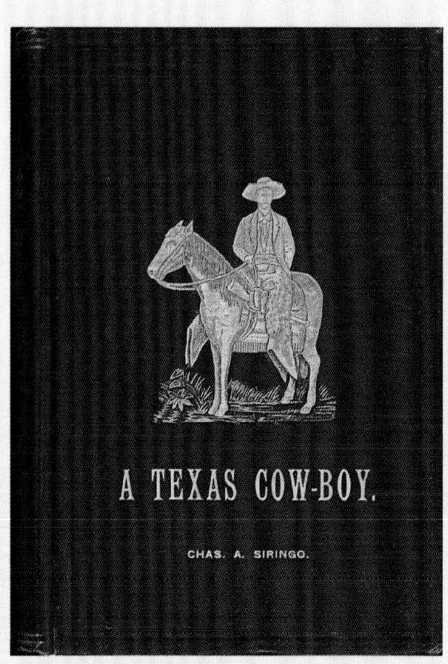

▲ The first cowboy autobiography, published in 1885.

▶ Charles Angelo Siringo during his stint as a Pinkerton detective during the late 1800s.

SEP 28

1874 In the Texas Panhandle, Colonel Ranald S. Mackenzie defeats a large force of Indians at Palo Duro Canyon. This battle helps end the 1874 Red River War between the U.S. Army and warriors from the Comanche, Kiowa, and Southern Cheyenne tribes.

GEORGE CROOK

George Crook—more than any other general of his time—had a deep and abiding respect for his Indian adversaries that was evident both on and off the field of battle. That respect was mutual on the part of some of Crook's fiercest enemies, such as the Oglala Sioux leader Red Cloud who said that Crook "never lied to us. His words gave the people hope." Like most of his fellow generals, Crook came up through the U.S. Army as an officer in the Civil War before taking part in the long series of Indian Wars of the late 1800s. An unorthodox commander and seasoned outdoorsman, Crook preferred mules to horses when in the field. He often was seen riding a mule with a shotgun across the pommel to fend off an attack or bring down some game to feed his troops. Crook disliked uniforms. He opted to wear a weather-beaten canvas suit and either a straw hat or a pith helmet. This manner of dress and his curious forked beard inspired the Indians to call him the Gray Fox. In the mid-1870s, after leading a successful campaign against the Apaches in Arizona Territory, Crook played a key role in operations against the Sioux and Cheyenne. In 1882, he received orders to return to Arizona Territory, where the Apaches had fled their reservation. Over the next four years, Crook engaged in a rigorous quest to quell the guerrilla attacks of Apache warriors led by the emboldened Chiricahua leader, Geronimo. It would be the final campaign of Crook's long and distinguished career.

▲ General George Crook.

▶ Crook on his favorite mount, a mule, with two Apache scouts.

SEP

29

1879 Near Milk Creek, Colorado, Ute Indians besiege troops under Major Thomas Thornburgh. Several days later, thirty-five Buffalo Soldiers from Fort Lewis, Colorado, arrive as reinforcements. A relief expedition of 350 soldiers from Fort Russell, Wyoming, ends the siege and rounds up surviving Indian hostiles.

CHIEF OF SCOUTS

Much of the credit for the U.S. Army's successful Apache campaign culminating with the third and final surrender of Geronimo in 1886 should go to the loyal scout Albert Sieber. Born in Germany in 1843, Sieber came to America as a boy and enlisted in the Union army when the Civil War broke out. He fought in several major battles, including Gettysburg where he was severely wounded. By the late 1860s, Sieber had gone west and found work cutting railroad ties and as a teamster and wagon guard. He spent some time as a cowboy in Arizona Territory before becoming a cavalry scout in the early 1870s. When George Crook took command of the Department of Arizona for the first time in 1871, the general quickly saw the value of utilizing scouts against the hostile Apaches. Crook employed many Indians as scouts, because he believed that familiarity with Apaches would make them best able to track the enemy. Sieber was named chief of scouts in charge of two hundred friendly Apaches. From the start, Sieber and his Tonto Apaches met with great success, chasing hostiles into Mexico and forcing large numbers of renegades to surrender. When Crook returned to Arizona Territory for the final push to subdue the Apaches, Sieber led the way with his stealthy scouts.

▲ Al Sieber.

▶ Al Sieber (seated, center), Chief of Scouts for Crook, with four Apache scouts and a visitor from the East.

447

SEP 30

1859 In Brownsville, Texas, Mexican folk hero and social activist Juan Cortina demands American authorities release his friend Tomás Cabrera. Although Cortina threatens to burn the town if his mandate is not met, Cabrera is hanged the next day.

HOSTILES

After Geronimo and some of his followers broke away from the San Carlos Indian Reservation, General George Crook and his Indian scouts hunted high and low for the elusive Apache shaman. They finally captured Geronimo in 1883 in the Sierra Madre of Mexico and returned him to the reservation in Arizona Territory. For the next two years, it seemed that Geronimo and his people would accept reservation life, but that was not the case. In the spring of 1885, Geronimo and some followers once again fled the reservation and headed south to Mexico. Two troops of cavalry and some Indian scouts rode in pursuit, but were unable to find the Apaches. "People who have been in this rugged country can well understand how easily the Apaches, with their superior speed and endurance, and their willingness to take to the rocks and the mountains tops, were able to evade their pursuers," explained Jason Betinez, Geronimo's cousin, many years later. "Another habit of the Apaches contributed largely to their success in keeping out of reach. . . . It was a mysterious manner of vanishing completely when the soldiers and scouts had just caught up with them or were about to attack their camp. . . . The scouts, who were experienced warriors themselves, had a hard time tracking down the hostiles, as they were forced to follow the many diverging trails, most of which disappeared into the rocks anyway."

▶ Geronimo with some of his Apaches before their surrender.

OCT 1

1878 In Santa Fe, former Union General Lew Wallace is sworn in as governor of New Mexico Territory. Wallace will attempt to quell the Lincoln County War and, in so doing, establishes a relationship with Billy the Kid.

THE FOX AND THE WHIRLWIND

George Crook, under growing pressure from his superiors, mounted another expedition into Mexico in search of Geronimo and other wayward Chiricahuas. In early 1886, some of Crook's troopers, commanded by Captain Emmet Crawford, located the Apache camp and overpowered the Chiricahuas. Both sides were discussing terms of surrender when Mexican troops suddenly appeared. They mistook the Apache scouts for hostiles and in the confusion opened fire, killing Captain Crawford. Despite this incident, talks continued, and Geronimo agreed to meet with Crook and discuss surrender. Geronimo selected Canyon de los Embudos, only twenty miles south of the border, for the parley that started March 25 and ended two days later. C. S. Fly, the Tombstone photographer, was on hand to capture the historic meeting on film. Geronimo, accompanied by a few warriors, appeared wearing a bandanna and traditional Apache garb. He squatted not far from General Crook, in pith helmet and riding gloves, sitting on the ground with some of his troopers. Weary of pursuit by both Mexican and American forces, Geronimo was ready to consider returning to the reservation. During the two days of negotiations, Crook made it clear that if Geronimo did not comply he would be hunted down and killed. Finally, they seemed to come to an agreement. "Do with me what you please," Geronimo told Crook. "I surrender. Once I moved like the wind. Now I surrender to you and that is all." The two men shook hands, and Crook left believing that at last the Apache wars were over. He was almost right.

▶ Geronimo in conference with General Crook at Canyon de los Embudos in Mexico, 1886.

COPYRIGHT 1886 BY
C. S. FLY

OCT 2

1867 At Medicine Lodge Creek in southern Kansas, the Cheyenne, Arapaho, Kiowa, Comanche, and Apache leaders establish the council with Kansas Governor Samuel J. Crawford and other officials that will lead to the Medicine Lodge Treaty.

PRISONERS OF WAR

Following Geronimo's surrender, General George Crook wired the good news to Philip Henry Sheridan, commanding general of the army. But Sheridan—who had wanted an unconditional surrender—rejected Crook's generous agreement. To make matters worse, as the soldiers prepared to escort the Apaches back to Arizona, a fearful Geronimo and his followers, still not convinced that surrender was their best option, slipped away into the Sierra Madre. When Sheridan questioned the integrity of the Apache scouts who claimed they had no prior knowledge of the escape, Crook was offended and requested to be relieved of his command. Sheridan obliged, and chose General Nelson Miles as a replacement. After five months of chasing Geronimo and the last Apache holdouts, Miles arranged a conference on September 3, 1886, at Skeleton Canyon in Arizona Territory. There, Miles induced Geronimo to surrender by promising him that after an indefinite exile in Florida, he and his followers could return to their homeland. This oath would not be kept. On September 8, Geronimo and Naiche, the son of Cochise, were loaded on a train with their bedraggled followers and shipped to a squalid prison camp in Florida. Years passed before they were moved to Fort Sill, Oklahoma Territory. Geronimo, a prisoner of war until his death in 1909, was never allowed to return to Arizona. Naiche, a prisoner until 1913, spent his final years on a New Mexico reservation where he died in 1919. "There is no more disgraceful page in the history of our relations with the American Indians than that which conceals the treachery visited upon the Chiricahuas who remained faithful in their allegiance to our people," wrote John G. Bourke, a former army officer under Crook.

▶ Geronimo and Naiche at Arizona's Fort Bowie after they surrendered and awaiting transport to a Florida prison.

3 OCT

1873 At Fort Klamath, Oregon, Captain Jack, Indian leader of the Modoc War, is tried and summarily hanged.

TEXAS JOHN SLAUGHTER

In 1886, John Horton Slaughter, the newly elected Cochise County sheriff in Arizona Territory, split his time between upholding the law in Tombstone and helping the U.S. Cavalry track Geronimo's Apaches. Slaughter, a veteran of the Confederate army and the Texas Rangers, was never without a sawed-off ten-gauge shotgun he called his "equalizer," along with the pearl-handled .44 pistol he toted for good measure. "Unlike squalid old badge wearers such as John Selman and Wild Bill Hickok, John Slaughter was basically a very reserved sort of man," said Judge Clayton Baird, a longtime Slaughter friend. "Nobody who wished to keep on calling terms with him overstepped that boundary." He proved so successful as a lawman that he was easily reelected to another term in 1888. Slaughter and his second wife, Viola—just sixteen years old when they married in 1878—also maintained their 66,000-acre San Bernardino Ranch, south of Douglas. After the Civil War, Slaughter had learned how to cowboy from the Mexican vaqueros in Texas and was one of the first cattlemen to drive Longhorns up the Chisholm Trail. Unfortunately, he also had a passion for poker and became so addicted to gambling that Viola threatened to leave him. Luckily, Slaughter had a talent for making wise investments that earned him a great deal of money, and he even loaned some to other ranchers for a tidy profit. In 1890, when the once wild and violent Cochise County was somewhat tamed, Slaughter retired from law enforcement, oversaw his ranch, and died an old, contented man in 1922.

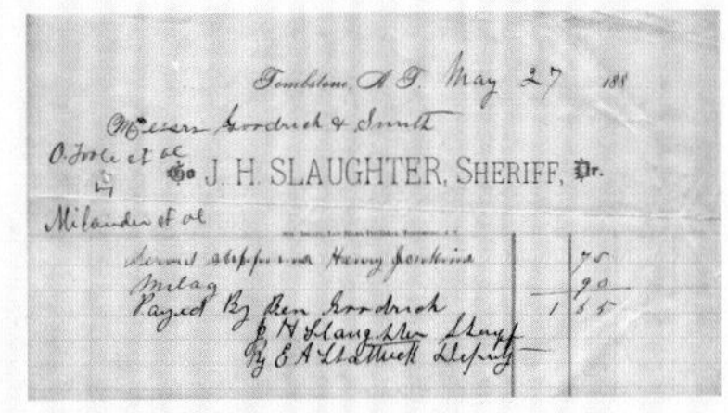
Tombstone, A.T. May 27 188

Messrs Goodrich & Smith

To J. H. SLAUGHTER, SHERIFF, Dr.

Milage 90

Payed By Ben Goodrich 1 65

J H Slaughter Sheriff

▲ A receipt from one of Slaughter's Tombstone deputies.

▶ John Horton Slaughter.

OCT 4

1856 Near the Merced River in California, outlaw Thomas Hodges (sometimes called Tom Bell or Outlaw Doc) is captured and lynched by an angry mob.

THE BIG DIE-UP

In the winter of 1886–87, an unrelenting succession of stinging winter blasts descended on cow country across the American West. This devastating season brought a series of blizzards that swept the Great Plains like a serial killer from the Canadian border to Texas and left millions of head of livestock dead and the entire cattle industry forever changed. Because of the enormous losses, especially on the northern cattle ranges, that long winter—starting with the New Year's blizzard of 1886—came to be called the "Great Die-Up," or the "Big Die-Up." Ten thousand cattle lay dead on the Kansas prairie between Garden City and Punished Woman Creek. Entire families of sodbusters froze to death, huddled in their dugouts and wooden huts. Most of the victims had run out of fuel and had burned all their furniture and possessions for warmth before the cold killed them. The smell of death overwhelmed the aroma of spring flowers on the prairies and plains. After the Big Die-Up, the range was never the same. It was the end of an era.

▶ Charles M. Russell's classic painting illustrates the consequence of the blizzards across the cattle ranges of the Great Plains.

OCT 5

1892 In Coffeyville, Kansas, the Dalton Gang attempts to rob two banks simultaneously. Grat and Bob Dalton are among those killed. Brother Emmett survives despite being shot multiple times.

SHOWDOWN AT THE WHITE ELEPHANT

In the early 1880s, Luke Short—known for his role in the so-called Dodge City Peace Commission—surfaced in Fort Worth, Texas, bringing with him a tarnished reputation. He had killed another gambler in Tombstone and engaged in a shoot-out in Dodge City while being run out of town. In Fort Worth, Short struck up a relationship with William Ward, owner of the White Elephant Saloon, a twenty-four-hour operation that housed a sizable full-service gambling concession offering roulette, monte, keno, faro, and poker. Looking for some big-name partners, Ward found two ideal choices: Jacob "Jake" Johnson, owner of a string of racehorses and one of the wealthiest men in Fort Worth, and the dapper Mister Short, a high-profile draw among the gambling fraternity. Trouble started in early 1887, however, after Short became embroiled in a bitter feud with Timothy "Longhaired Jim" Courtright, a former Fort Worth marshal implicated but never charged in several questionable killings. The evening of February 8, the drunken Courtright, hungry for a fight and packing two six-guns, strode into the White Elephant and challenged Short. They stepped outside the saloon and walked a short ways down the boardwalk. During a brief exchange of words, both men went for their guns. Short's first shot took off Courtright's thumb, which prevented him from returning fire. Short then pumped four more rounds into Courtright to finish the job. He was not charged for the murder and later that year sold out his interest in the White Elephant and moved on.

▶ Saloon owner and gunfighter Luke Short.

▶▶ Fort Worth lawman and gunfighter Jim Courtright.

OCT 6

1866 The Reno Gang commits the first train robbery in North America, stealing ten thousand dollars from an Ohio & Mississippi train in Indiana.

THE BEAUTIFUL ALICE ABBOTT

By 1886, prostitution was big business in the old Texas border town of El Paso, with a wide range of services for weary passengers on the Southern Pacific railroad varying from crib girls and streetwalkers to the ladies of the night in high-dollar parlors. Owen White, an El Paso newspaper columnist, eulogized the passing of the frontier and reveled in El Paso's bawdy past when he wrote: "Prostitutes were recruited in the East and Middle West and shipped in by the carload. . . . Life in El Paso became indeed alluring. A wonderful prosperity . . . was on the way, and so the Sinners, knowing that plucking the Christians would be easy and profitable, garbed themselves becomingly for the harvest. It was a gorgeous display. The calcimined women, both in the humble cribs, and in the big parlor houses which were the pride of the town, donned beautiful gowns." For many years, El Paso was the domain of Alice Abbott. This six-foot-tall, two-hundred-pound madam arrived in 1880 and built the first brothel on Utah Street, El Paso's vice district, variously called the Utah Street Reservation, the Tenderloin, and the Zone of Tolerance. Abbott's satisfied clientele and the painted cats who serviced them sometimes called her "Fat Alice," though never to her face. She saw herself in a different light—in her photographic album she scribbled above her picture "The Beautiful Alice Abbott" and gave herself the title of "Best House Keeper U.S.A."

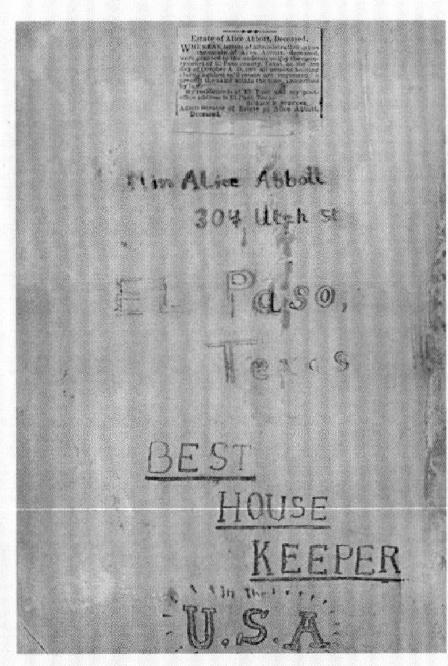

▲ Inside the front cover of Alice's album, she calls herself the "Best House Keeper U.S.A."

▶ "The Beautiful Alice Abbott," as labeled by herself in her photo album.

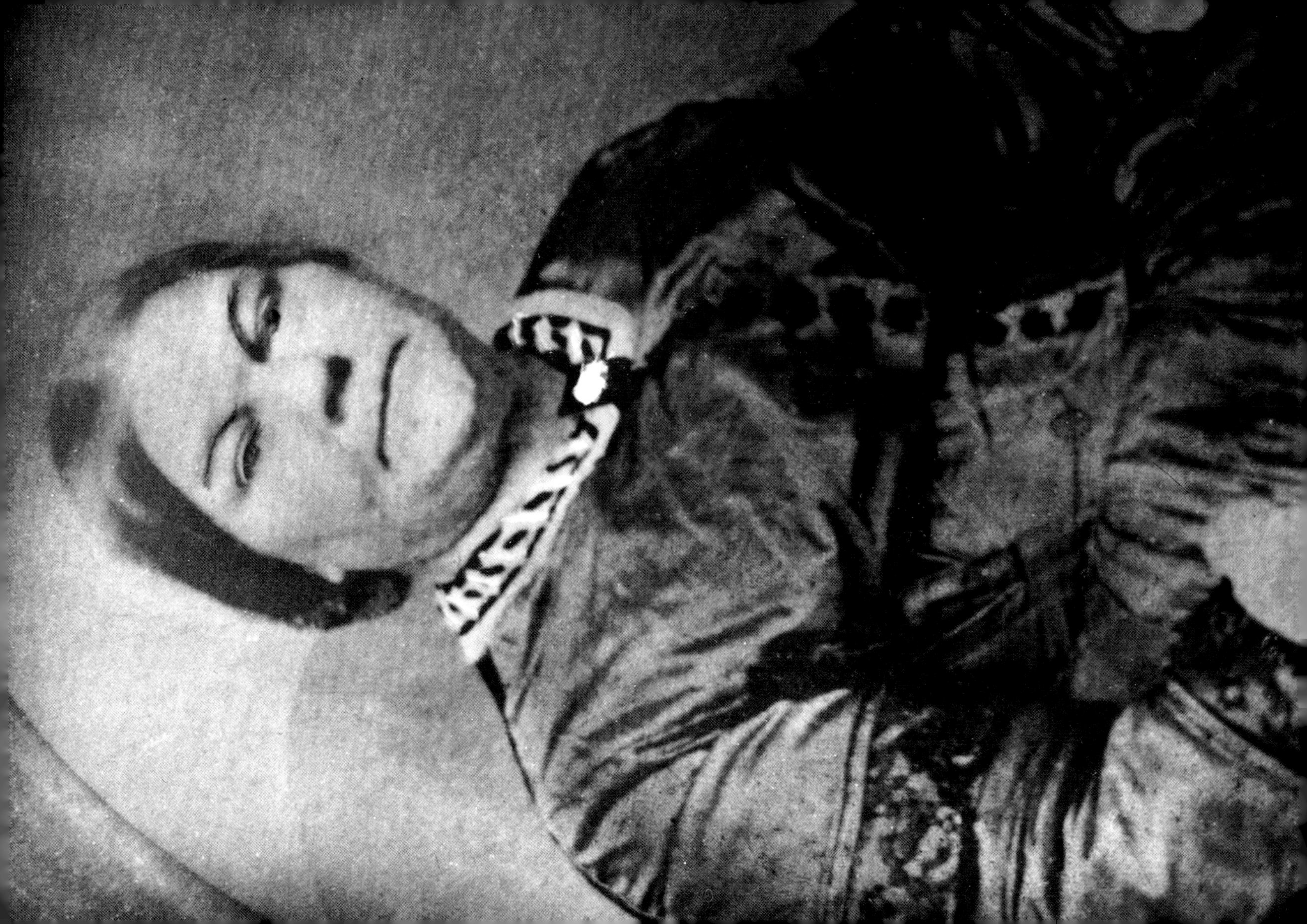

OCT 7

1870 In Elizabethtown, New Mexico Territory, Clay Allison leads an angry mob to the jail where they drag criminal Charles Kennedy from his cell and lynch him. Allison cuts off Kennedy's head and impales it on a pole in front of Henry Lambert's Saloon in Cimarron.

THE PUBLIC ARCH

"Fat Alice" Abbott may have been the pioneering madam who opened El Paso's first "resort," but she had plenty of competition. Just across the street from Alice's lively bordello, a fiery madam named Etta Clark did her best to lure gentlemen callers into her parlor filled with wayward sisters. Etta was a petite five feet tall and weighed less than a hundred pounds, but she packed a mean temper and was a shrewd businesswoman. Alice and Etta detested each other. On April 18, 1886, the tension between the two madams reached a boiling point when one of Alice's more popular working girls, Bessie Colvin, announced she was leaving to work for Etta. An enraged Alice started after Bessie, and the frightened harlot raced to the safety of Etta's place with Alice in hot pursuit. Etta tried to hold off Alice, striking her with a lamplighter and knocking her to the floor. Alice was still able to drag the screaming Bessie toward the door, but Etta retrieved her revolver and ordered Alice to leave. Instead, she advanced on Etta who sent a bullet into Alice's pubic arch. A doctor rushed to the wounded madam and found that the round penetrated to the right of her pubic arch and passed cleanly through her body. No vital organs were hit, and she eventually recovered. The next day the *El Paso Herald* ran a story that became part of southwestern folklore. When describing the altercation, a simple typo changed *pubic* to *public* arch, an irony that put a grin on the faces of even the most straitlaced citizens.

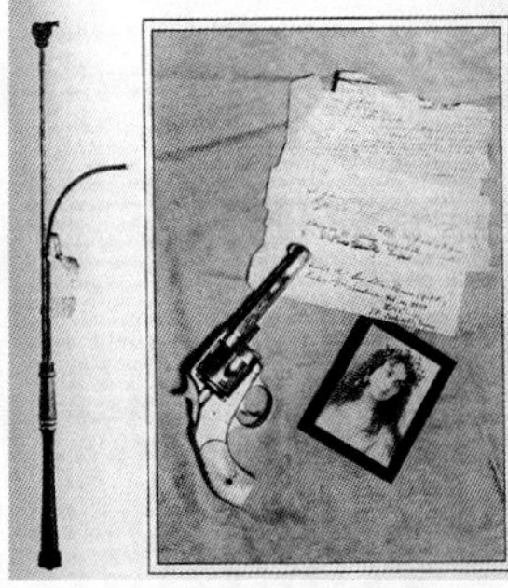

▲ The lamplighter and the pistol used by Etta Clark against Alice Abbott.

▶ Bessie Colvin, the popular working girl who sparked the conflict between Alice Abbott and rival madam Etta Clark.

▶▶ Alice drew this large "X" across Etta's photo in her album.

OCT 8

1878 Dodge City saloon singer Dora Hand is shot and killed by James Kennedy when the drunken cowboy mistakenly thinks his lover is in bed with Mayor James Kelley. In truth, Kelley is in the post hospital at Fort Dodge, and Dora and her friend Fannie Garretson are sleeping in his bed. A posse, including Wyatt Earp, Bat Masterson, and Bill Tilghman, capture a contrite Kennedy, who is later acquitted mostly due to his remorse. Dora is given one of the grandest funerals Dodge has ever seen.

HOG RANCHES

Life was excruciatingly hard and often monotonous for soldiers serving at frontier outposts. The pay was poor, as was the food. Desertion was common. The men spent most of their time in manual labor. When they were in garrison and not on patrol or on the parade field, boredom took its toll on off-duty soldiers. Troopers were more than willing to part with their pay for a game of chance, some strong drink, or a wildcat whore. Just outside the boundaries of military reservations would be a scattering of gambling and drinking dens as well as low-class brothels called hog ranches. A slang term popularized by frontier soldiers, hog ranches operated near the fringes of virtually every military fort and camp in the West. They pretended to be working hog farms, but they actually supplied cheap whiskey, harlots, and other diversions to soldiers, cowhands, and miners in the area. Captain John G. Bourke, a Congressional Medal of Honor recipient and aide-de-camp to General George Crook in Arizona Territory, described one "nest of ranches" as "tenanted by as hardened and depraved a set of wretches as could be found on the face of the globe. Each of these establishments was equipped with a rum-mill of the worst kind and each contained from three to half a dozen Cyprians [sic], virgins whose lamps were always burning brightly in expectancy of the upcoming bridegroom and who lured to destruction soldiers of the garrison. In all my experience, I have never seen a lower, more beastly set of people of both sexes."

▲ A brothel madam.

▶ Two of the prettier hog ranch residents.

OCT 9

1868 Clara Blinn and her two-year-old son, Willie, are taken captive by Cheyenne warriors in Colorado Territory during an attack on a wagon train. The mother and son perish on November 27 when Lieutenant Colonel George Armstrong Custer's Seventh Cavalry troopers kill Cheyenne chief Black Kettle and massacre many of his followers at their winter camp along the Washita River in present-day Oklahoma.

CATTLE KATE

In the late 1880s, the big cattle interests in Wyoming ruled the roost with backing from the kowtowing newspapers and politicians. Perhaps this is why hooded goons hired by the large ranchers were able to get away scot-free with lynching an innocent man and woman on trumped up charges. The victims—Ella Watson and James Averell—had made the mistake of speaking out against wealthy landowners. Ellen Dean Watson, or Ella as her family called her, was a native of Canada who grew up on a Kansas homestead, and in 1886 moved to Rawlins, Wyoming, where she worked as a boardinghouse cook. Some historians have mistakenly suggested that Ella was a prostitute, based on the erroneous report that her place of employment was a brothel. Ella met James Averell, also a Canadian, later in 1886, and joined him at his homestead on the Sweetwater River after filing for her own homestead next to his land. The couple was able to build up a small herd of cattle until they attracted the attention of cattle baron Albert Bothwell, who loathed small-scale ranchers. When Averell wrote letters to newspapers accusing Bothwell and his friends of intimidation and other misdeeds, the die was cast. Ella Watson was thought to be "Cattle Kate," an outlaw who rustled cattle with her lover. A Cheyenne newspaper, aligned with the cattlemen, wrote that she "was as desperate as a man, a daredevil in the saddle." On July 20, 1889, a gang of vigilantes took Watson and Averell into custody and hanged them. The couple's possessions were sold at auction, the cattlemen's association took their property, and life in Wyoming went on without any consequences for the perpetrators.

▶ Ella "Cattle Kate" Watson.

▶▶ James Averell, Kate's paramour.

OCT 10

1867 On the road between the settlements of Linden and Boston in Cass County, Texas, outlaw Cullen Baker holds up a government supply wagon and kills the driver.

COMMODORE PERRY OWENS

Born landlocked in Tennessee and named for a famous naval hero, Commodore Perry Owens single-handedly surpassed the feats of the Earp brothers and Doc Holliday. At the famous O.K. Corral shootout, the Earp band had gunned down three out of five opponents in about thirty seconds, but at his gun battle with the Blevins Gang near Holbrook, Arizona Territory, Owens killed three and wounded one in less than sixty seconds. He used only five bullets to get the job done and rode away unscathed. This legendary altercation began on the afternoon of September 4, 1887, when Owens rode out of Holbrook to serve an arrest warrant on Andy Blevins, a ruthless criminal wanted for murder in Texas and horse theft in Arizona. Owens knew that Blevins was holed up at his mother's house, along with his outlaw brothers and some hard-nosed associates. Undaunted but cautious, Owens cradled a Winchester rifle in his arm when he knocked on the door. Andy Blevins came out with pistol in hand, and when he learned about the warrant, the wanted man turned to go back inside. Owens lowered the rifle and shot Andy through the door just as his half-brother, John Blevins, took a shot at Owens. John's shot missed, but killed a tethered horse. Owens returned fire, striking John in the arm. Then Owens stepped back just as Mose Roberts leaped out a window. Owens brought him down with a single shot and turned in time to kill fifteen-year-old Samuel Blevins coming out the front door with a Colt pistol. Commodore Perry Owens rode back to Holbrook and became an instant legend.

▲ The man seated on the right has been identified as John Blevins.

▶ Commodore Perry Owens.

OCT 11

1878 William "Wild Bill" Longley, gunfighter and gambler, is hanged for murder in Giddings, Texas. Reputed to have killed thirty-two men, Longley writes before his execution, "Hanging is my favorite way of dying." The rope slips when the trapdoor is opened, and Longley's knees drag on the ground. The hangman pulls the rope taut, and it takes eleven minutes for the condemned man to slowly choke to death.

PAWNEE BILL AND THE PRINCESS OF THE PRAIRIE

As a puny youngster in Kansas, Gordon William Lillie, better known as "Pawnee Bill," was rumored to have improved his health by drinking fresh cow's blood from the local butcher. A few years later, Lillie moved to Indian Territory, where he hunted buffalo, rode as a cowboy, and worked as a teamster in the Cherokee Outlet. He befriended some Pawnee Indians and, while living with the tribe, became proficient in their language. He also came by his colorful name, a sobriquet he would keep to his dying day. In 1883, Lillie encountered his boyhood idol, Buffalo Bill, and went on the road with Cody working as an interpreter in charge of the Pawnees who appeared in the show. When they played Philadelphia, Lillie met May Manning, a fifteen-year-old schoolgirl who stole his heart. The daughter of a prominent Philadelphia physician, Manning had been raised as a Quaker and was a student at Smith College. Despite their different backgrounds, Pawnee Bill was determined to win her hand. On August 31, 1886, the socialite and Lillie wed. May quickly adapted to her husband's entertainment career. She learned to ride, rope, and, "cultivated a taste for the rifle" by hunting prairie chickens. In the spring of 1888, Pawnee Bill's Historic Wild West show was launched. The press notices for May were stunning. She was hailed as the "Princess of the Prairie," the "World's Champion Woman Rifle Shot," and the "New Rifle Queen." Their show eventually went bust, but their fifty-year marriage fared better.

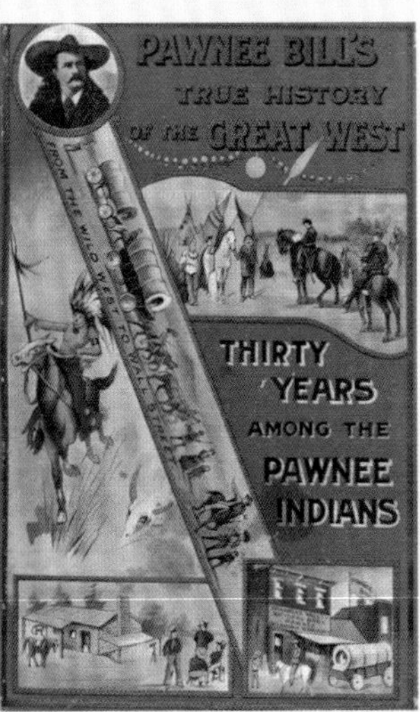

▲ A colorful promotional book of Pawnee Bill's, with the unexpected subtitle, "From the Wild West to Wall Street."

▶ May Lillie and husband Pawnee Bill.

OCT 12

1877 A sheriff in Holbrook, Arizona Territory, deputizes a posse, known as the Outlaw Exterminators, to pursue John Allman, who has left behind nine victims during a recent killing spree. Clay Calhoun finds Allman hiding in old Indian cliff dwelling, shoots him on sight, and brings his body to Holbrook.

YOUNGER'S BEND

Contrary to popular belief, "Bandit Queen" Belle Starr never robbed a train or bank and probably never killed anyone. She did, however, have a lust for adventure and a soft spot for desperate men, such as Jim Reed, Cole Younger, July Johnson, and Sam Starr. As Belle once said: "I am a friend to any brave and gallant outlaw." The only crime she was ever convicted of was horse theft. As punishment, Judge Isaac Parker, the "Hanging Judge" of Fort Smith, Arkansas, sent her to the house of corrections in Detroit, Michigan, for six months. Belle's harsh life ended in 1889 when she was shot from behind with a charge of buckshot not far from her Indian Territory home at Younger's Bend on the Canadian River where she hosted her lawless pals. It was two days before her forty-first birthday. After her death, dime novelists told the Belle Starr story as they saw it. Belle's daughter, Pearl, a notorious Fort Smith prostitute, hired a stonecutter to carve an image of Belle's favorite horse, Venus, on her grave with this inscription:

SHED NOT FOR HER THE BITTER TEAR
NOR GIVE THE HEART TO VAIN REGRET,
TIS BUT THE CASKET THAT LIES HERE,
THE GEM THAT FILLED IT SPARKLES YET.

▲ Belle's tombstone.

▶ Belle Starr with Blue Duck, a fellow prisoner in Fort Smith, not a lover.

OCT 13

1878 Thomas Jefferson "Duck" Goodale is arrested in Iowa for the September 26 robbery of the Monitor treasure coach along the Cheyenne-Redwood route. After authorities put Goodale on a train to Cheyenne, Wyoming Territory, for his trial, he escapes and is never recaptured.

BELLE'S PEARL

From the 1890s until World War I, Pearl Starr—the daughter of "Bandit Queen" Belle Starr—operated a successful bordello in Fort Smith, Arkansas, that claimed to have the best piano player and sipping whiskey in town, as well as the "most beautiful girls west of the Mississippi." Born in Missouri in 1867, Pearl was rumored to be the love child of Belle and outlaw Cole Younger, who never acknowledged fathering the child. Belle named the girl Rosie Lee "Pearl" Reed, after Jim Reed, her common-law husband. Pearl grew up fast and wild, around the desperate men her mother preferred to keep company with at Younger's Bend, her outlaw haven on the Canadian River in Indian Territory. In 1887, when Belle's "Canadian Lily"—another name of endearment for Pearl—turned up pregnant, she was sent away to relatives to give birth to an illegitimate daughter named Flossie. The baby was later put up for adoption. After Belle's murder in 1889, Pearl briefly married, the first of many relationships that produced three more children. By then, Pearl had become a prostitute in Fort Smith. She wisely stashed her income and, in 1891, opened her own house in Fort Smith's red-light district, known as The Row. She changed her name to Pearl Starr, billed herself as the daughter of Belle, and called her brothel Pearl's Place. For twenty years, Pearl operated one of the most prosperous parlors of pleasure in the region. In 1916, financially secure and facing a rise in moral indignation, she moved to Arizona where she died peacefully in 1925.

▶ Belle Starr's daughter, Pearl, on the right. Her companions are unknown.

OCT 14

1832 William Henry Vanderburgh, a prominent official in the American Fur Company, is ambushed and killed by Indians in the vicinity of Alder Gulch, Montana.

BOOMER SOONER

By the late 1880s, the regions surrounding Oklahoma's borders had filled with fidgety white settlers casting covetous eyes on the broad ranges and open spaces of Indian Territory. A systematic movement, or "booming," started for the opening of some of the lands. Kansan David L. Payne and other nervy trespassers known as Boomers began the invasion. Army troops forced squatters to leave, but each time the soldiers escorted the tenacious nesters back across the Kansas line, more of them slipped over the border. The Indians protested, but little more was done to discourage the violators. Finally, the federal government succumbed to the Boomers' demands and purchased an absolute title to nearly two million acres of Indian land. Congress then passed the Dawes Severalty Act, providing that all Indians except members of the Five Tribes should be made to accept individual allotments of land and that the rest of the reservations should be opened to white homesteaders. On April 22, 1889, tens of thousands of white settlers gathered on the borders of Indian Territory ready to grab a parcel of unclaimed land. Soldiers tried to hold back the anxious masses, but gangs of rogues called "Sooners" sneaked across the line ahead of the official starting signal. At high noon, bugle calls and gunfire triggered a wild land grab. Tent towns sprang up within hours. By sunset, the newly created Oklahoma City had a population of ten thousand. Within the next few years there would be four more land runs as white immigrants took over even more tribal land.

▲ Captain David L. Payne, the leader of the Oklahoma Boomers.

▶ The land run into Oklahoma Territory as depicted in a sketch.

OCT 15

1879 Bandits rob an express train leaving Las Vegas, New Mexico Territory, and take two thousand dollars in currency and checks.

BONELAND

Just as the U.S. government had planned, with the extermination of the great buffalo herds came the subjugation of the Plains Indians. The continuous buffalo slaughter by hide hunters had taken its toll. Across the West, only a few buffalo remained. In many areas not a single living specimen could be seen—only bleached skulls and bones blanketing the grasslands where millions once grazed. The Great Plains had turned into a bone field. Bone hunters scoured the land, picking up wagonloads of skeletal remains, hooves, and horns from the Monarchs of the Plains. They sold them to be made into fertilizer, buttons, combs, corset stays, knife handles, and glue. Supposedly, the last buffalo killed in Kansas was in 1879 along the old Santa Fe Trail west of Dodge City. The vanishing herds went south, where most of them met their end. In Texas, fifty-two buffalo were killed not far from Tascosa in 1887. Four more were shot at Buffalo Springs in 1889. They were believed to be the last survivors of the southern herd. General Nelson Miles summed it up in his memoirs published in 1896: "Within a few years millions of buffalo were killed for their hides, and thousands of white men, the best rifle-shots in the world, were engaged in the business. The buffalo, like the Indian, was in the pathway of civilization. Now the same territory is occupied by innumerable numbers of domestic animals that contribute untold wealth to our entire country."

"A cold wind blew across the prairie when the last buffalo fell . . . a death wind for my people."

—Sitting Bull, n.d.

▶ The photo is labeled as the site of the killing of the last buffalo in Kansas.

OCT 16

1880 After the Battle of Tres Castillos in which Apache war chief Victorio dies, Mexican forces led by Lieutenant Colonel Joaquin Terrazas, known as the "Scourge of the Indians," celebrate on both sides of the border. Terrazas reportedly was paid almost thirty thousand dollars for Indian scalps and captive women and children sold into slavery.

POST OFFICE PARLEY

This card-mounted albumen print was taken in June 1889 by an unknown photographer as representatives of the U.S. government and the Indian nations gathered to address the opening of the frontier. Posing in front of the new Oklahoma City post office, these men formed a joint Cheyenne-Arapaho delegation including Southern Cheyenne leader Cloud Chief; George Bent, the half-Cheyenne son of frontier trade William Bent and Owl Woman; and Leonard Tyler, a noted Cheyenne educated at Carlisle Institute. Others in the portrait include former Kansas Governor Samuel J. Crawford; Indian agent John D. Miles; G. A. Beidler, Oklahoma City postmaster; William Couch, the city's first mayor who only a year later would be murdered in a homestead dispute; and Deputy U.S. Marshal George Thornton, who would be killed within two years by the notorious mixed-blood outlaw Captain Willie. Only weeks before the parley to discuss future land openings, the first of the land runs had taken place. Perhaps the Indian delegates saw the writing on the wall, and knew they would not be able to stem the tide of land-hungry pioneers. On April 19, 1892, the Cheyenne-Arapaho Land Run began allowing thousands of white settlers to stake their 160-acre tracts on reservation land. By the end of 1883, there were more than one hundred homes in a new town named Arapahoe.

▶ The joint Cheyenne-Arapaho delegation, meeting in Oklahoma City to determine the future of the Cherokee Outlet, also known as the Cherokee Strip. George Bent, son of William Bent, is seated second from right.

"Quite a number of cattlemen are looking over the allotted lands with a view to leasing them from Indians. These lands offer a splendid opening for stockmen and farmers wanting valuable leases. . . . There are fifty to seventy-five Indians in town every day and they are proving valuable patrons of our merchants."

—*Arapahoe Arrow*, April 29, 1892

POST OFFICE.
Scheyenne & Arrapahoe. Delegates. Counciling. For
Cherokee Outlet

OCT 17

1873 At the Slag Saloon in Akron, Colorado, attorney Henry Farris is shot dead after attempting to collect an overdue bill.

DEATH OF RUBE BURROW

From 1886 to 1890, Reuben Houston Burrow, familiarly called Rube, robbed trains across the South and the Southwest. Chased by hundreds of lawmen and Pinkerton detectives, he became the most hunted outlaw since Jesse James. Burrow was shot and killed on October 9, 1890, during a manhunt in Alabama. Of the many dime novels about him, the most accurate was published by George W. Agee soon after Burrow's death.

"A coroner's inquest was held. . . . After treating the body with preservatives . . . hundreds of people assembled to view the remains of the great bandit. On arrival at Birmingham, at three o'clock on the morning of the 9th of October, fully one thousand people were in waiting to get a glimpse at the body. . . . Special officers were employed to keep the morbid crowd at bay. Photographs of the body were taken, and at seven o'clock A. M. the train leaving Birmingham for Memphis conveyed the remains to Sulligent, Ala. . . . The father was there to receive it. A representative of the Southern Express Company said to him: 'We are sorry to bring your boy back in this shape, but it was the best we could do.' 'I have no doubt,' answered Allen Burrow, 'that he was mobbed.' The weapons were on exhibition for several days, during all of which time the influx of visitors never ceased. Rich and poor, male and female, black and white, all were possessed of the same curiosity, and the deeds of the outlaw were discussed by some with admiration for his courage, by others with an expression of detestation of his crimes—by all with a feeling of relief that he was dead."

—George W. Agee, *Rube Burrow, King of the Outlaws*, 1890

▲ A book on the crimes and the death of Rube Burrow, 1890.

▶ Outlaw Rube Burrow fit tightly in his coffin, with his hat and his firearms.

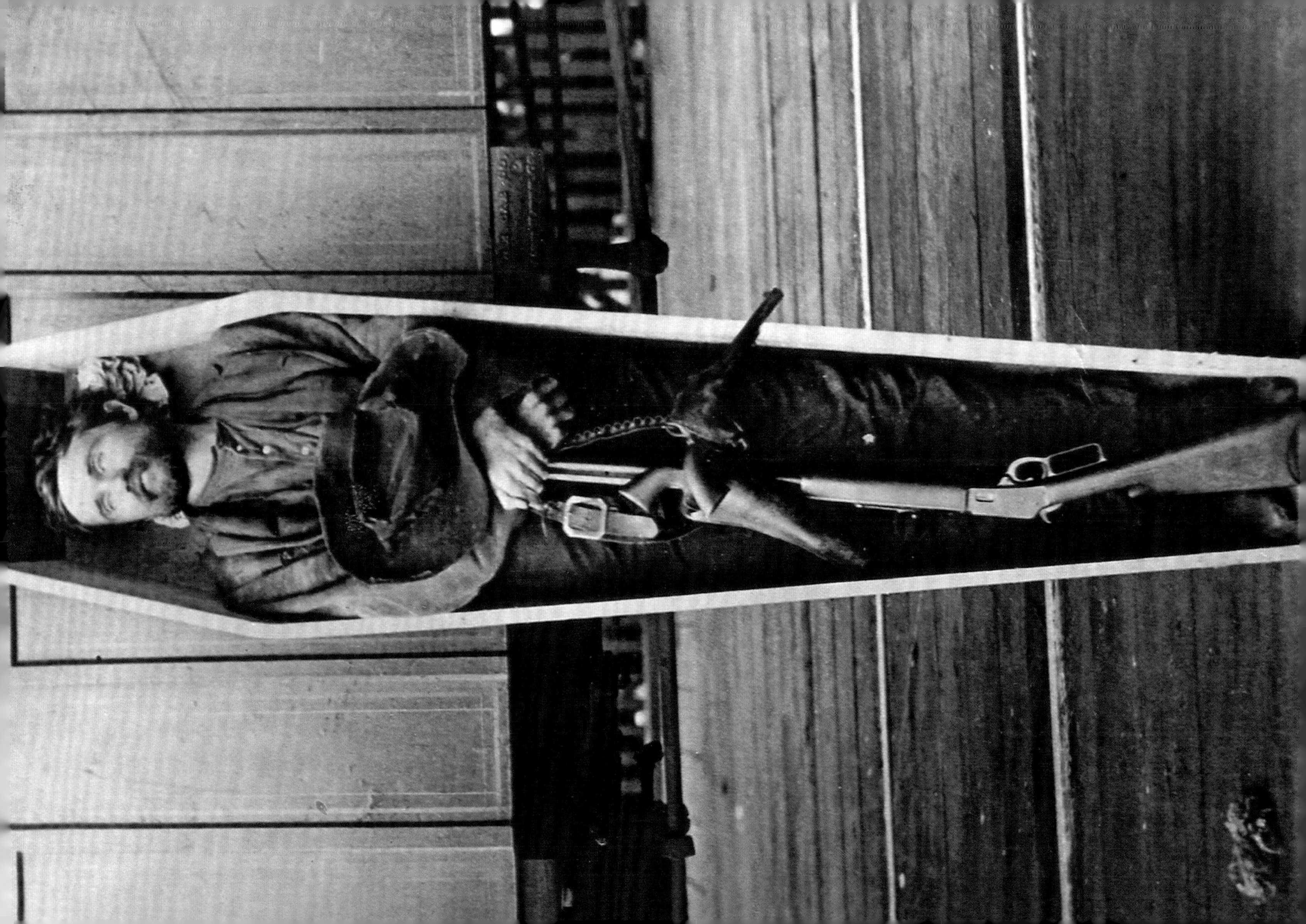

OCT 18

1884 On Black Canyon Road, running from Phoenix to Prescott, Arizona Territory, road agents hold up back-to-back stages. A favorite target of robbers, stages on this route have been robbed four times this year alone.

DEATH OF SITTING BULL

Before dawn on December 15, 1890, a party of Indian police officers and white soldiers shot and killed Sitting Bull, the revered Sioux holy man, outside his reservation cabin in South Dakota. They acted on orders from James McLaughlin, the U.S. Indian agent at Fort Yates, who feared Sitting Bull was preparing to flee the reservation. After bursting into his quarters, soldiers ordered Sitting Bull to mount a horse. When he did not comply, other Sioux appeared and were enraged by the treatment of their leader. A struggle ensued, gunfire rang out, and Sitting Bull was shot point-blank and killed, along with several others on both sides. General Leonard Colby, commander of the Nebraska National Guard, called the death a political assassination by the U.S. government. Colby wrote there was an "understanding between the officers of the Indian and military departments that it would be impossible to bring Sitting Bull to Standing Rock alive . . . there was a tacit arrangement between the commanding officers and the Indian police, that the death of the famous old medicine man was much preferred to his capture." Newspapers showed that many did not share Colby's sentiments. The press spewed out chilling editorials such as one in the *St. Louis Republic* describing Sitting Bull as "a greasy savage, who rarely bathed" and who "entertained the remarkable delusion that he was a free-born American with some rights in the country of his ancestors. . . . So died Sitting Bull. So was removed one of the last obstacles in the path of progress. He will now make excellent manure for the crops, which will grow over him when his reservation is civilized."

▲ Sitting Bull.

▶ A reenactment of the death of Sitting Bull at the site where it occurred, c. 1890.

OCT 19

1902 After failing as a tombstone and insurance salesman, recently paroled outlaw Jim Younger takes his own life with a gun in a St. Paul, Minnesota, hotel room. His body is later exhumed and reburied at Lee's Summit, Missouri.

THE APACHE KID

Almost nothing is known about the early life of the Apache Kid. Born on the San Carlos Reservation in Arizona Territory in the 1860s, he picked up the name Apache Kid when white folks had trouble pronouncing his Apache name Haskay-bay-nay-natyl, meaning "brave and tall will come to a mysterious end." His early years were spent around the mining town of Globe, where he befriended the noted army scout Al Sieber who inspired him to enlist in the Apache scouts in the early 1880s. The Apache Kid made sergeant and accompanied General George Crook on his expeditions into the Sierra Madre, including the Geronimo campaigns of 1885–86. His only transgression an alcohol-fueled riot in Mexico, the Kid's clean record led to his promotion to first sergeant in 1887. Later that year, however, he killed the man responsible for the death of his father. When the Apache Kid and some friends were ordered to turn over their weapons, a scuffle turned to gunplay, and Sieber was wounded in the ankle, leaving him with a permanent limp. The Apache Kid fled and was branded an outlaw. He surrendered, was court-martialed, and found guilty of mutiny and desertion. His death sentence was reduced to a ten-year prison term at Alcatraz. In 1888, the conviction of the Apache Kid was overturned, but a second trial ended in another conviction and sentencing to a seven-year stay at the territorial prison in Yuma. En route, the Kid and others overpowered the guards and escaped. For years to come, stories about the crimes of the Apache Kid were widely known in the Southwest. The Kid was said to move like a desert ghost, preying on ranchers and prospectors. A huge bounty was put on his head, but it was never collected. Several people swore they killed him, but his death was never confirmed.

▶ The Apache Kid, center, while still a scout for the U.S. Army.

OCT 20

1902 First Sergeant Tom Mix, who would become famous for his roles in early Western films, goes AWOL from the U.S. Army.

HELL HOLE

Beginning in 1876, and for the next thirty-three years, the Yuma Territorial Prison housed a total of 3,069 inmates, including twenty-nine women, for crimes ranging from murder to polygamy. From the day it opened and the first seven prisoners were locked into cells that they had built themselves, the Yuma Pen was known as the "Hell Hole." Yuma was the most isolated settlement in Arizona Territory, situated in the scorching desert where temperatures routinely stayed in triple digits. A heat of 110 degrees in the summer was considered normal in the tiny cells. Only twenty-six prisoners managed to escape the Hell Hole, and eight were shot and killed. Of the 111 inmates who perished there, the main cause of death was tuberculosis. There were no executions on the premises since that was the duty of county sheriffs, but punishment at Yuma for breaking prison rules was severe. Prisoners who erred in their ways were chained to the stone floor in a totally dark cell. Mercifully, the overcrowded penitentiary closed in 1909 after inmates built a new prison.

▶ The Yuma Territorial Prison, overlooking the Colorado River.

OCT 21

1872 The Wyoming Territorial Prison opens in Laramie. For many years, the forty-two-cell facility is sparsely populated due to the one-dollar-per-day charge for each prisoner. A federal inspection of the Laramie prison in 1884 finds only ten inmates, some of whom are permitted to go into town on Saturday night.

WOUNDED KNEE MASSACRE

After the murder of Sitting Bull, Sioux chief Spotted Elk—later given the derogatory name Big Foot by soldiers—led his band of 350 followers, mostly widows of the Plains Indian Wars and their children, toward the protection of the Pine Ridge Reservation in South Dakota. While en route, they encountered troops of the Seventh Cavalry and were told to camp on the edge of Wounded Knee Creek. Rations and tents were provided, and a doctor tended to Spotted Elk, dying from pneumonia. During the night more troopers arrived and joined those surrounding the Sioux camp. Just after dawn on December 29, 1890, the soldiers, under the command of Colonel James W. Forsyth, gathered any remaining weapons from the Sioux. During this process, a young Sioux—who was deaf and did not understand what was going on—was reluctant to surrender his brand-new rifle. A scuffle quickly escalated, and when a shot rang out, the killing began. Several Hotchkiss guns positioned around the camp opened fire, raking the lodges with grapeshot. Cavalrymen fired volley after volley at unarmed men, women, and children and chased down the fleeing Sioux. When the madness finally ended, at least 153 Sioux lay dead in the snow, including Spotted Elk. One estimate placed the final death count at 350 Sioux and 25 soldiers, most killed by their own gunfire. The Seventh Cavalry had finally gotten revenge for Custer's Folly. Twenty-three Medals of Honor were awarded at Wounded Knee, more than for any other engagement in the young nation's history.

▲▶ Images of the aftermath of the massacre at Wounded Knee.

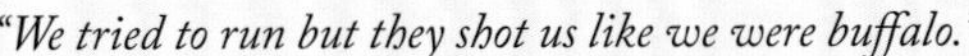

"We tried to run but they shot us like we were buffalo."

—Louise Weasel Bear, survivor of the Wounded Knee Massacre, 1890

Gathering up the Dead of the
Battle Field at Wounded Knee S.D.
Copy Righted by the North Western Photo Co
Jan 1st 1891 Chadron Neb

OCT 22

1902 Cowboy-turned-train robber Camillo Orlando Hanks, called "Deaf Charley," is killed by lawman Pink Taylor after a saloon brawl in San Antonio, Texas.

"MOST REPREHENSIBLE"

Commanding General Nelson A. Miles was outraged when he learned of the Wounded Knee Massacre. He considered what happened "a useless slaughter of Indian women and children" and accused Colonel James Forsyth of "blind stupidity or criminal indifference." Forsyth was immediately relieved of his command, and a Court of Inquiry was formed to probe the matter. The secretary of war, however, wanted to depict the final confrontation of the Indian Wars in a heroic light, so he halted the investigation and reinstated Forsyth to his post at head of the Seventh Cavalry. Miles, however, continued to criticize Forsyth for deliberately disobeying orders. "The action of the Commanding officer, in my judgment at the time, and so I reported, was most reprehensible," Miles wrote in a letter to the Commissioner of Indian Affairs in 1917. "The disposition of his troops was such that in firing upon the warriors they fired directly towards their own lines and also into the camp of the women and children, and I have regarded the whole affair as most unjustifiable and worthy of the severest condemnation."

"When I look back now from this high hill of my old age, I can still see the butchered women and children lying heaped and scattered all along the crooked gulch as plain as when I saw them with eyes still young. And I can see something else died there in the bloody mud, and was buried in the blizzard. A people's dream died there. It was a beautiful dream . . . the nation's hoop is broken and scattered. There is no center any longer, and the sacred tree is dead."

—Black Elk, survivor of Wounded Knee, 1932

▶ General Miles and his staff viewing one of the last hostile Indian camps near Pine Ridge, South Dakota, shortly after the Wounded Knee Massacre.

OCT

23

1862 At Wichita Agency, Oklahoma Territory, a group of Shawnee and Delaware Indians attack and massacre a band of Tonkawas.

POKER ALICE

Anyone who ever sat across from her at a poker table knew the odds were good that Alice Ivers Tubbs, famously known as Poker Alice, was the best female gambler in the Old West. Born in England, the daughter of a conservative schoolmaster, Alice was a little girl when her family moved to the United States and settled in Virginia, where she attended a fancy boarding school. While Alice was in her teens, her family moved to the silver boomtown of Leadville, Colorado. There, at age twenty, Alice met and married Frank Duffield, a mining engineer well known at the local gambling halls. Instead of staying at home while Frank made the rounds, Alice tagged along. She was a quick study, and it was not long before she showed her aptitude for faro and poker. When Frank was killed in a mine explosion, Alice found herself with no means of support, so she decided to make a living at the gambling tables. The petite lady in elegant dresses traveled between mining camps, smoking cigars, packing a pistol, and winning huge pots at the tables. Other skilled gamblers were anxious to challenge her, but few who tried ever won. She played some in New Mexico Territory, worked a spell for Bob Ford (the killer of Jesse James) at Ford's saloon in Creede, Colorado, and made her way to Deadwood. There she met a man named Warren Tubbs. They wed and had seven children. Poker Alice kept right on laying bets until she died at almost eighty years old. Near the end of her life, Alice pointed out, "At my age I suppose I should be knitting. But I would rather play poker with five or six 'experts' than eat."

▲ Poker Alice Tubbs with her ever-present cigar.

▶ Poker Alice dealing in a posed photograph.

POKER (ALICE (TUBBS) (DEALING)

OCT 24

1859 Near Brownsville, Texas, bandit Juan Cortina and his gang defeat a large contingent of American soldiers sent to capture him.

TEXAS JACK

In 1950, Nathaniel Reed, known as "Texas Jack," a crusty old man bearing the scars of fourteen bullet wounds as mementos of his life as a desperado, died peacefully at his home in Tulsa, Oklahoma—with his high-topped boots off. His long hard ride of eighty-seven years was over. To the end, the former robber of banks, stagecoaches, and trains wore his hair to his shoulders in the fashion of the scouts of the plains. For many years after he quit his outlaw ways, Reed made a living giving lectures against the criminal life and peddling for two-bits a pamphlet about both his years as a criminal and those spent "trusting in God." The curious pamphlet is a valuable inside look into the formation and operation of the old bandit gangs. Reed described how he became one of the "47 most notorious bandits of Indian Territory days," starting with the summer of 1888 when he took part in his first train robbery—the Santa Fe Express at La Junta, Colorado. "I stood on the platform of the rear coach, kicked the door and fired my pistol in the air to keep the passengers from coming out of the cars," wrote Reed. He stayed on the scout as an outlaw for eight years. "Seven fights with the marshals and got wounded four different times," he wrote of the summer of 1894. "They killed my horse, left me afoot and shot me under the jaw. There were six or eight marshals after me. I kept my senses and showed that I could shoot as well as they."

▶ The cover of "Texas Jack" Reed's first book, with Reed posed as a train robber with a gun.

▶▶ Thirty years later, Texas Jack has switched from a gun to the gospel.

The Story of Texas Jack

WRITTEN BY HIMSELF.

NATHANIEL REED, "TEXAS JACK"

A REFORMED TRAIN ROBBER.

THE LIFE OF

TEXAS JACK

EIGHT YEARS A CRIMINAL — 41 YEARS TRUSTING IN GOD

25c per Copy

1921 In New York City, famed gunfighter and lawman Bat Masterson dies of a heart attack after writing his final newspaper column.

"THE MAN WHO SHOT JESSE JAMES"

Robert Ford never received the adulation he had expected as the assassin of Jesse James. After the 1882 killing of James, both Bob and his brother Charley laid low, fearing retribution from Frank James or one of the admirers of the slain Jesse. Charley changed his name several times as he moved from town to town, always looking over his shoulder. Bob also stayed on the move in an attempt to capitalize on his deed. He earned money posing for photographs as "the man who killed Jesse James," and also created an act called "Outlaw of Missouri," appearing onstage with Charley in a melodramatic reenactment of the James killing. When audiences began shouting catcalls, jeers, and even challenges, the Fords stopped the stage performances. After two years of running scared and suffering from tuberculosis, Charley committed suicide. Bob operated a saloon in Las Vegas, New Mexico Territory, for a short time and, by 1890, resided in Colorado, first running a gambling house in Walsenburg and then moving to Creede to open a saloon. In 1892, during a drunken rampage, Ford and a gunman pal shot out windows and street lamps, and were banished from town. Ford was later allowed to return and built a new establishment, which burned down just six days after it opened. While rebuilding, Ford set up a tent saloon, where on June 8, 1892, Edward O. Kelly (often erroneously called O'Kelley) entered and immediately emptied both barrels of a shotgun into Ford, killing him instantly. Kelly, touted as "the man who killed the man who killed Jesse James," was convicted of murder and kept in prison until 1902. Two years after his release, he was shot dead in a gunfight with an Oklahoma City policeman.

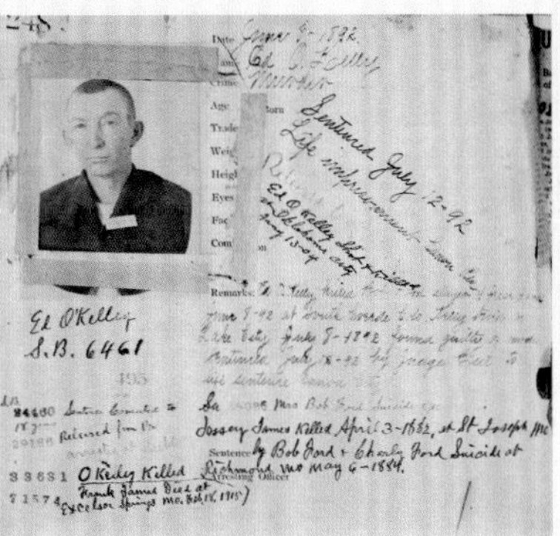

▲ The blotter for Bob Ford's assassin, Edward O. Kelly.

▶ Bob Ford's funeral in the mountains near Creede, Colorado.

OCT 26

1881 In a gunfight near the O.K. Corral in Tombstone, Arizona Territory, the Earps (Wyatt, Virgil, and Morgan) accompanied by Doc Holliday tangle with Frank and Tom McLaury, Billy Claiborne, and Ike and Billy Clanton. Both McLaury brothers and Bill Clanton are killed. Ike Clanton and Billy Claiborne escape. Morgan, Virgil, and Doc are wounded while Wyatt emerges unscathed.

THE CHEYENNE CLUB

From the 1880s until the early 1900s, a cabal of Wyoming power brokers operated with impunity from the Cheyenne Club, an impressive two-story brick building in the heart of downtown Cheyenne. Constructed in 1880, this inner sanctum of the elite was the equal of the finest gentlemen's clubs back East. It featured a pair of grand staircases, wine vaults, tennis courts, and private sleeping rooms. In this male domain, members and their guests retired to lavishly furnished, oak-paneled rooms reserved for reading newspapers from New York and Boston and smoking only the best Havana cheroots. A European-trained chef offered such treats as imported olives, iced oysters, fine cheeses, and Swiss chocolates. The membership, limited to two hundred, included prominent businessmen, politicians from every level of government, and cattlemen who owned the largest ranching operations in Wyoming. Although the club's articles of incorporation plainly spelled out that the organization was strictly social, other activities took place there that remained confidential. In the private third-floor rooms, some members played high-stakes poker and also made decisions that impacted the state's economic and political future. And it was here in 1892 that plans were formulated that would ignite the Johnson County War, a brutal conflict over cattle and land rights.

▲ The Cheyenne Club, c. 1900.

▶ The cattlemen and their hired guns from Texas after they were escorted back to Cheyenne by soldiers.

54

OCT 27

1838 Lilburn Boggs, governor of Missouri, decrees that Mormons must be "exterminated or driven from the state."

THE JOHNSON COUNTY WAR

The puppet masters calling the shots in Wyoming from their headquarters at the Cheyenne Club included members of the powerful Wyoming Stock Growers Association. Made up of the largest cattle ranchers in the state, this group wielded great influence in Wyoming and throughout the American West. The cattle barons were plagued by rustlers and frustrated with overgrazing caused by encroaching sheep herds and upstart small ranchers. In April 1892, they hired some Texas gunmen and cattle detectives to take care of the problems. Sheriff Frank Canton turned in his resignation so he could lead the punitive expedition. "The Invaders," as they were called, rode out to Johnson County, stopping to cut the telegraph wires at Buffalo, a small rancher stronghold. Their first target was the modest KC Ranch, owned by Nate Champion, an activist trying to organize the small ranch owners. Two of the three men with Champion were captured when they emerged from his cabin. The third man, Nick Ray, was shot and died within a few hours. The cattlemen's posse continued "shelling the house like hail," Champion noted in a journal he kept during the siege. Finally, the building was set on fire, and when Champion dashed out the back door, he was mowed down. Some friends tried to ride to his rescue, but arrived days later and found him riddled with twenty-four bullet wounds and most of his corpse eaten by coyotes. In the meantime, the Invaders advanced on Buffalo, but were warned that armed men were lying in wait. They took cover at the TY Ranch on Crazy Woman Creek and were besieged by two hundred Johnson County defenders. Finally, the army stepped in to bring the Johnson County War to an end.

▲ The bullet-riddled barn at the TY Ranch where the Invaders were pinned down by the enraged citizens of Johnson County.

▶ The cabin on the KC Ranch where the Invaders killed accused rustlers Nick Ray and Nate Champion.

OCT 28

1880 In Tombstone, Arizona Territory, Marshal Fred White is accidentally shot while disarming "Curly Bill" Brocious. White dies two days later and charges against Brocious are dismissed.

ALIAS FRANK CANTON

Frank Canton is another notorious example of one of the many who rode on both sides of the law. He was born Joseph Horner in 1849, the son of a Virginia doctor who moved to Texas after the Civil War. During the 1870s, Horner went on a crime spree, robbing banks, rustling cattle, and killing a Buffalo Soldier in a gunfight. He slipped away from some Texas Rangers following his 1877 arrest for bank robbery and joined a trail herd headed to Nebraska. That was when he officially changed his name to the alias Frank Canton and swore that his outlaw days were over. He surfaced in Wyoming, hired on as a range detective, and was even elected sheriff of Johnson County. During the Johnson County War, Canton rode with a vigilante outfit and took part in various gunfights and lynchings. Then, weary of dispensing punishment on behalf of the cattle barons, Canton moved to Oklahoma Territory. He served as under-sheriff in Pawnee County and rode as a deputy U.S. marshal. After helping wipe out Bill Doolin's gang and taking down other desperados, Canton followed the gold rush to Alaska and put in a stint as a law officer in the wild town of Dawson. When Oklahoma became a state in 1907, Canton returned to become the adjutant general for the Oklahoma National Guard, a post he held for many years. In 1927, he died at age seventy-eight, and his true identity became known for the first time. U.S. Marshal E. D. Nix said of his friend, "Frank Canton established a reputation as a fearless officer that gave him an honored place in the regard of Oklahoma citizens."

▲ As Frank Canton, he became a lawman across the country from Oklahoma Territory to Wyoming to Alaska. In this photograph, he has attained the position of the first adjutant general of the new state of Oklahoma.

▶ Frank Canton, who started life as an outlaw in Texas using his real name, Joe Horner.

OCT 29

1926 In Oklahoma, William K. Hale and John Ramsey are found guilty of participating in the murder of Henry Roan. Although sentenced to ninety-nine years, neither man serves more than twenty-three. Numerous unsolved murders in the area come to be known as the Osage Reign of Terror.

TOM HORN

A misfit for most of his life, Tom Horn wrangled mules, scouted for the army, worked as a cowboy, and rode on both sides of the law. What he was best at, however, was committing cold-blooded murder. Born and raised on a Missouri farm, Horn was only fourteen when he ran away to the West. He worked a number of jobs until he signed on as an army scout in 1876 and served through most of the Apache wars. In the late 1880s, he put in time as a deputy sheriff while working a gold claim in Arizona Territory. Horn also was a natural born roper and won a few rodeo steer-roping contests at Globe and Phoenix. While serving as a deputy, Horn came to the attention of the Pinkerton Detective Agency. The agency saw his potential as a man-hunter based on his scouting experience for the army. Hired by Pinkerton in 1890, Horn worked out of the Denver office, carrying out criminal investigations mostly in Colorado and Wyoming. Known for staying calm and cool in any circumstances, Horn could find anyone he was told to locate. He left Pinkerton in 1892 to take a better-paying job as a range detective with the Wyoming Stock Growers Association. Two years later, Horn joined the Swan Land and Cattle Company, a Wyoming corporate cattle operation larger than Connecticut. Hired officially as a horse breaker, Horn was actually paid to kill any rustlers and homesteaders who proved troublesome. As a hired gun, there was none more capable. Horn explained, "Killing is my specialty. I look at it as a business proposition, and I think I have a corner on the market."

▲ Tom Horn had a checkered life as a scout, a Pinkerton operative, and a livestock detective, from Arizona to Wyoming and points between.

▶ Tom Horn, seated far left in a white shirt, as a scout and teamster for Al Sieber, standing far right, and General Crook, seated second from right in a white hat, during the Apache Wars in Arizona Territory.

OCT 30

1838 At Haun's Mill, Missouri, just three days after the governor issues a decree to exterminate Mormons, seventeen members of the sect are massacred by Missouri militia.

THE DALTON GANG

▲ Bob Dalton.

► Grat Dalton.

►► Emmett Dalton.

The Dalton brothers seemed predestined to turn outlaw since their mother, Adeline Dalton, was born a Younger in the outlaw state of Missouri. Her brother Henry Younger fathered the famed Younger brothers, train and bank robbers of the James-Younger Gang who got their comeuppance at Northfield, Minnesota. Yet, most people who knew the Daltons were surprised when they took to the outlaw trail. Frank, Grattan, Robert, and Emmett had served as lawmen, and brother William was a state assemblyman in California. In 1887, Frank—a deputy U.S. marshal for the federal court in Fort Smith—died in a gun battle while tracking a horse thief and whiskey peddler. After Frank's death, Grat took his place as a deputy marshal and was wounded in the line of duty. Bob also served briefly as deputy marshal and a policeman in the Osage Nation. The youngest brother, Emmett, rode with several of his brothers' posses, but mostly made a living as a working cowboy, where he met several future gang members. But by 1890, the Daltons were fed up with low wages for risking their lives and looked for ways to supplement their income. In March 1890, Bob was charged with selling whiskey in Indian Territory, and a few months later Grat was accused of horse theft but managed to get the charges dropped. Discredited as lawmen, the Daltons headed west as outlaws. They robbed a gambling house in Silver City, New Mexico Territory, and joined brother Bill in California, where, in 1891, they were accused of train robbery and beat a hasty retreat to Indian Territory. Their outlaw careers were off to a good start.

Photo by
DENVER
Colo
EMMIT DALTON
FOR

OCT 31

1838 Mormon leader Joseph Smith surrenders to authorities in Missouri, and the Mormons agree to disarm and leave the state.

COFFEYVILLE

The Dalton Gang consisted of the four brothers and some hard-edged recruits, such as George "Bitter Creek" Newcomb, Dick Broadwell, Bill Powers (alias Tim Evans), and later Bill Doolin. Though they robbed four trains between May 1891 and July 1892, they had little to show for their efforts. At what turned out to be their final train robbery, they were surprised by eleven guards who engaged them in a gun battle. Two hundred shots were fired, three guards were wounded, and a stray bullet killed a doctor. No one in the Dalton Gang was hit, but they knew it was time to change tactics. They turned to bank robbery, planning to make history by hitting two banks at the same time in broad daylight, a feat not even Jesse James or the Younger boys had pulled off. On October 5, 1892, five gang members—Bob, Grat, and Emmett Dalton along with Bill Powers and Dick Broadwell—rode to Coffeyville, Kansas, where the Dalton family had farmed for several years. With that in mind, the Daltons wore fake beards so they would not be recognized. They tied their horses in an alley across from the town's two banks—the C. M. Condon Bank and the First National Bank. As they walked across the plaza, they split into two groups—Grat, Powers, and Broadwell went to the Condon Bank and Bob and Emmett to the First National. Their disguises didn't do much good. A man sitting on his wagon recognized the brothers and yelled, "The Daltons! The Daltons! They're robbin' the banks!" Gunfire erupted. The Daltons' Waterloo had begun.

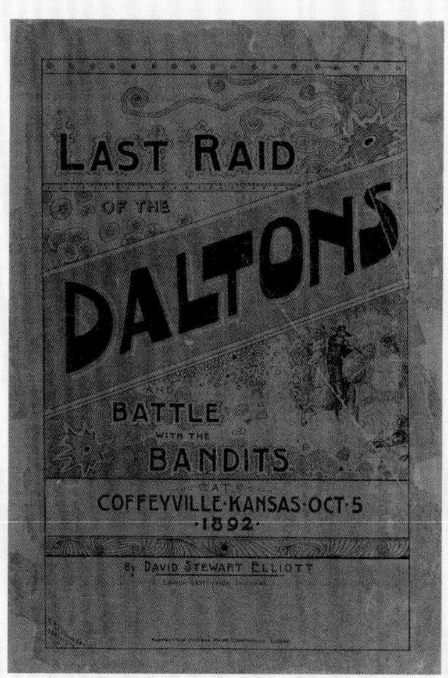

▲ This booklet appeared within a month of the attempted robberies in Coffeyville.

▶ The Dalton Gang planned to rob two banks at the same time in Coffeyville, Kansas, including the C. M. Condon Bank. It proved to be their last raid.

BANK
C. M. CONDON & CO.
BLOCK
1890
Wm McCOY
BANK
BANK

NOV 1

1924 After becoming town marshal of Cromwell, Oklahoma, veteran lawman Bill Tilghman, seventy years old, is shot and killed by corrupt prohibition agent Wiley Lynn. His body lies in state in the capitol rotunda in Oklahoma City for three days as thousands of mourners pay their respects.

DIED WITH THEIR BOOTS ON

The citizens of Coffeyville, Kansas, had no intention of allowing the Dalton Gang to escape with a single dime of their hard-earned money. When the cry went up that the gang was robbing the banks, townspeople raced to the hardware stores and took every rifle, pistol, and shotgun available. In only a few minutes, the banks were ringed with armed men. When Emmett and Bob tried to exit the First National, a hail of gunfire met them. They dove back inside and raced out the back door, killing a clerk in the process. At the Condon Bank, a clever employee had convinced Grat that the vault, unlocked since early morning, was on a time lock and could not be opened for several more minutes. The outlaws dawdled, hoping to get at the money, but finally lost patience and made a break for it. Grat, Broadwell, and Powers (also called Evans) charged out the front door into withering gunfire. All three were wounded as they ran to their horses in the alley. Bob and Emmett, who had killed two more citizens, joined them in the alley at about the same time. "Defying this fire, the two outlaws made another sortie up the alley to give Grat, Powers, and Broadwell what help they could," E. D. Nix, a U.S. marshal in the 1890s, later wrote of the scene. "The trio wheeled and backed toward the alley, firing at each center of resistance on the plaza. It was a magnificent fighting retreat, worthy of a better cause. Broadwell kept gamely pumping his rifle with one arm. The other was dripping blood." There was nowhere to run. Four townspeople died that morning, including the town marshal, Charles Connelly. Of the outlaws, only Emmett Dalton, riddled with twenty-three gunshot wounds, survived.

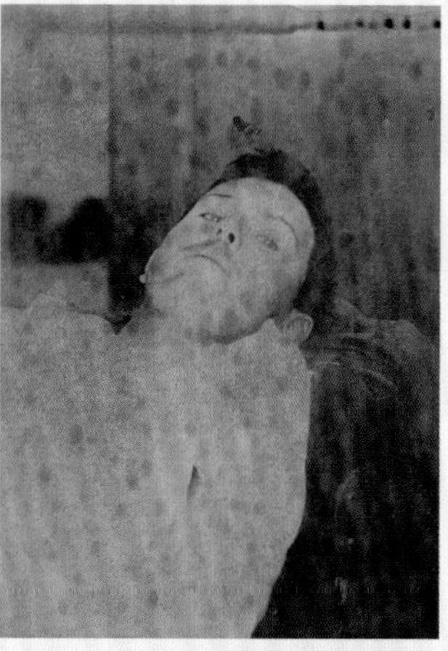

▲▲ The wounded Emmett Dalton, awaiting his fate.

▲The outraged Coffeyville citizens, who lost four of their own in the gunfire, stacked the dead outlaws in a pile.

▶ From left to right, Bill Powers (alias Tim Evans), Bob Dalton, Grat Dalton, and Dick Broadwell, laid out neatly for the photographer.

Tim Evens
Bob Dalton
Grat Dalton
Dick Broadwel
yrighed by Tackett
The Daltons of the Coffeyville raid 1892.

NOV 2

1846 The Donner Party is stranded high in the Sierra Nevada Mountains as they travel west toward San Francisco. When food rations run out, some members of the group resort to cannibalism for survival. Forty of the original eighty-seven travelers die.

DEATH ALLEY

As soon as the shooting stopped at Coffeyville, Emmett Dalton, the only gang member to survive, held up his uninjured hand and surrendered. Some men carried him to a nearby doctor. The corpses of the slain outlaws were heaped in what came to be known as Death Alley. A crowd of curious citizens milled around the scene, looking for a souvenir or memento such as the dead men's personal items, spent cartridge shells, and bloodstained stones. A hayrack was positioned against the stable wall on the south side of the alley, and some boards from the lumberyard were laid on the rack. There, the bodies of Grat and Bob Dalton, Dick Broadwell, and Bill Powers were displayed. After a long recovery, Emmett went to trial and was convicted of murder. Sentenced to life at the Kansas penitentiary, he was a model prisoner and was pardoned after fourteen years.

"The smoke of Wednesday's terrific battle with the bandits has blown aside, but the excitement occasioned by the wonderful event has increased until it has gained a fever heat. The trains have brought hundreds of visitors to the scene of the bloody conflict between a desperate and notorious gang of experienced highwaymen and a brave and determined lot of citizens who had the nerve to preserve their rights and protect their property under the most trying circumstances. The Dalton gang is no more, and travelers through the Indian Territory can go right along without fear now. The country, and the railroads and express companies especially, can breathe easier now that the Daltons are wiped out. The country is rid of the desperate gang, but the riddance cost Coffeyville some of its best blood."

—*The Coffeyville Journal*, October 7, 1892

▲ The cover of this pulp book illustrates the Dalton Gang tying their horses in what would become Death Alley.

▶ The dead bandits were placed in coffins and propped against the wall of a barn in Death Alley for more photographs.

NOV 3

1892 In Adair County, Oklahoma Territory, outlaw Ned Christie dies during a shootout while trying to escape from sixteen lawmen.

SHAPE-SHIFTER

Born in Indian Territory, Ned Christie worked as a blacksmith and gunsmith and served a term on the Cherokee National Council. A staunch advocate for tribal independence, he opposed the railroads entering Cherokee lands. On May 5, 1887, Christie was in Tahlequah, the Cherokee Nation capital, when Deputy U.S. Marshal Dan Maples was shot and killed just outside town as he tried to arrest outlaw Bill Pigeon. Although he adamantly denied any involvement in the Maples killing, the crime was pinned on Christie. When Judge Isaac Parker issued an arrest warrant, Christie refused to surrender, fearing that as a Cherokee he would not be given a fair trial. Christie stayed on the dodge from the law for the next five years, despite the efforts of many officers, including Bass Reeves and Heck Thomas. During one siege, a posse burned down his cabin and badly wounded Christie in the head, leaving him blind in one eye. Still, he remained at large, thanks to a vast network of family and friends who never doubted his innocence. According to Cherokee lore, Christie became a shape-shifter and could elude the white men by transforming himself into an owl or razorback hog. In 1892, however, he met his end. Deputy U.S. Marshal Paden Tolbert and a sixteen-man posse surrounded Christie's reinforced stronghold. After a small cannon failed to dislodge Christie, his pursuers resorted to dynamite. Forced out of his hiding place, Christie was gunned down. His body was tied to a plank door and placed on display in Fayetteville, Arkansas, and later in Fort Smith with a rifle propped in his arms. In 1922, new evidence came to light fully exonerating him in the murder of Maples—thirty years too late.

▶ Cherokee Ned Christie, photographed in death after finally being brought down by Judge Parker's deputies.

NOV 4

1879 Kansas City newspapers erroneously report that Jesse James has been killed by a member of his gang. Ironically, this comes to pass three years later.

STONE CORRAL SHOOTOUT

Chris Evans, a Civil War veteran and army scout, tried his luck at prospecting in California's Tulare County where he met George Contant Sontag and John Sontag, brothers living near his land. On a trip to the Midwest, the Sontags—who operated a quartz mine near the town of Visalia—pulled a couple of train holdups. When they returned to California, Evans learned of their success as highwaymen and decided to join them. From 1889 to 1892, the trio robbed four trains in California, leaving dead and wounded victims in their wake. In August 1892, lawmen captured George, who was sent to prison, but his brother and Evans were able to make a getaway. Tulare County Sheriff Oscar Beaver was shot and killed in pursuit, and the outlaws escaped. Only weeks later, Sontag and Evans killed two posse members at Sampson's Flats. Evans later described killing one of the men, a former friend. "I shot him in the left temple; the gun dropped from his hands; he quivered one instant, and Andy McGinnis climbed the Golden Stairs." Nine months later, on June 11, 1893, during another shootout at Stone Corral, two more deputies were killed, but this time Sontag was mortally wounded and died on July 3. Evans was badly wounded and lost his right eye and part of an arm. He was convicted of murder and sentenced to life in Folsom Prison. After serving seventeen years, he was paroled in 1911 and died seven years later, denying that he had ever robbed a train.

▶ California highwayman Chris Evans after his capture.

▶▶ John Sontag, lying in a haystack fatally wounded.

NOV 5

1870 Near Verdi, Nevada, a band of outlaws led by "Gentleman Jack" Davis robs the Central Pacific Railroad of forty-one thousand dollars in gold coins. The band is later captured and thirty-eight thousand dollars is recovered.

THE THREE GUARDSMEN

Three deputy marshals were best known for keeping the peace in Oklahoma and Indian Territories in the 1890s: Bill Tilghman, a former buffalo hunter and Dodge City marshal; Heck Thomas, a Confederate veteran who was twelve when he fought under Robert E. Lee; and Chris Madsen, a Dane who claimed to have served with the French Foreign Legion in Africa and the U.S. Cavalry in the West. This intrepid trio became known as the "Three Guardsmen." Of the famous threesome, Henry "Heck" Thomas was the only one to ride for Judge Isaac Parker. Thomas was a crackerjack fugitive hunter and law enforcement officer, especially noted for his bravery and integrity. During the 1890s, Tilghman—hide hunter, scout, saloon operator, and city marshal—served as a deputy U.S. marshal and ended the careers of many outlaws. Although Madsen received high praise as a marshal, some historians claim he inflated accounts of his exploits before coming to the United States in 1876. Nonetheless, these three lawmen undoubtedly did their part to put Bill Doolin, the Daltons, and others out of the outlaw business.

"My father was wounded six times during the course of his thirty-year career of helping bring law and order to a crime infested region. . . . My father consistently brought in more prisoners than any other deputy. Once he astounded everyone by arriving with forty-one prisoners handcuffed to his wagon. Nine of these prisoners were later executed."

—Beth Thomas Meeks, *Heck Thomas, My Papa*, 1988

▲ Heck Thomas.

▶ Bill Tilghman.

▶▶ Chris Madsen.

NOV 6

1908 Butch Cassidy and the Sundance Kid are reportedly killed in a shootout in San Vicente, Bolivia. Some believe the pair did not actually die, but returned to the United States and lived for many years under false identities.

WHITE CITY

In 1893, the city of Chicago put on an extraordinary show, which captured the national imagination and offered glimpses of the future. The World's Columbian Exposition celebrated the quadricentennial of Christopher Columbus's arrival in the Americas. Throughout the year, spectators rode the world's first Ferris wheel, munched a new treat called Crackerjack, gawked at imposing Sioux chieftains on display, and roamed the 633-acre fairground site, transformed from swampland into the magnificent "White City." Two significant voices of the American West made their presence known at the Columbian Exposition—Frederick Jackson Turner, a young history professor from the University of Wisconsin; and William F. "Buffalo Bill" Cody, the flamboyant showman and quintessential westerner. On the muggy evening of July 12, Turner read his academic essay "The Significance of the Frontier in American History" to an audience of historians. In his thesis, Turner claimed that the frontier was closed, citing details from an 1890 census. Turner's speech was in effect a eulogy for the single most important factor in molding American character and history. According to him, the westward advance of settlement had shaped the nation's development far more than any European influence. Turner's monumental argument inspired a shift in the focus of the study of American history, from New England and the Atlantic seaboard to the West. His landmark speech revolutionized the teaching of American history and influenced the profession for more than a half-century.

▲ A rare first edition of a Cody biography by John M. Burke, 1893.

▶ Memorabilia saved by Wild Bill Hickok's sister, Lydia, after visiting the Columbian Exposition in Chicago. Her souvenirs include a complimentary pass to Buffalo Bill's Wild West.

Worlds Fair
June 1st 893
Thursday
Called on Buffalo
Bill he gave us
tickets for Wild West
Show, and Worlds fair
went in fair had
dinner at Sweedish
Resturaunt then
Illinois State building
then the Wild West at
three thirty, called in
after the performance
bid him good by
Started for boarding
house Took cars at
61st street change at

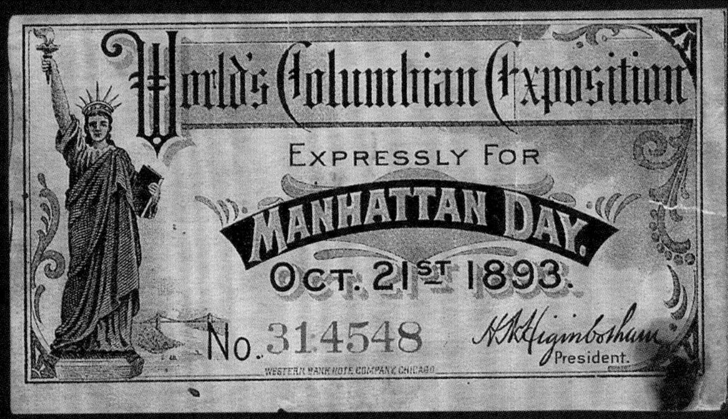

Buffalo Bill's
WILD WEST
COMPLIMENTARY
GRAND STAND
COUPON

SIXTY-THIRD-ST.—Opposite World's Fair
NOW OPEN.
EVERY DAY, RAIN OR SHINE
(Sundays included), at 3 and 8 p. m.
Buffalo Bill's Wild West
AND CONGRESS OF ROUGH RIDERS OF THE WORLD.

THE  TO ALL.

VOTED A WORLD-BEATER.
18,000 Seats. Covered Grand Stand. Herds of Buffalo, Wild Steers, and Bucking Bronchos.
Alley L. Illinois Central, Grip, Electric and Horse Cars all stop at 63d-st. entrance.
Admission, 50 Cents. Children under 10 years, 25 Cents.

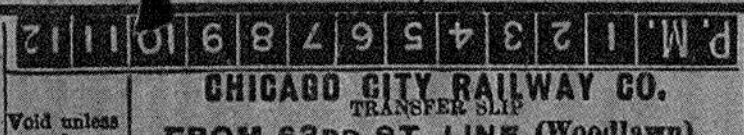

P.M. 1 2 3 4 5 6 7 8 9 10 11 12
CHICAGO CITY RAILWAY CO.
TRANSFER SLIP
Void unless used on JUNE 3 1893 as indicated hereon.
FROM 63RD ST. LINE (Woodlawn).
North or South on Cottage Grove, State, Wentworth Halsted or Ashland Ave., at intersection with 61st and 63rd St. line; or South on 69th St. line at State & 64th.
This slip will not be honored unless presented at transfer points named, for a continuous passage within 60 minutes from hour punched in margin.
G. H. Wheeler Pres't.
A. M. 5 6 7 8 9 10 11 12

C. C. Ry. Co.
TRANSFER COUPON.
WEST ON 61st STREET.
FROM WOODLAWN LINE.
Not good if detached.
Must be presented at
61st and State Sts.
within 60 minutes from hour punched in margin.

NOV 7

1881 Near Sonora, California, Bill Miner and his gang rob a stagecoach. Miner and two others are captured and sent to prison in San Quentin.

CONGRESS OF ROUGH RIDERS

Although both Frederick Jackson Turner and William F. Cody made appearances at the 1893 Columbian Exposition, neither man ever met the other. Turner declined an invitation to see Buffalo Bill's arena antics, and Cody did not attend Turner's lengthy frontier manifesto at the Art Institute building near the lakefront. The buckskinned Cody was too busy leading his Indians and daredevil entertainers, advertised as "Buffalo Bill's Wild West and Congress of Rough Riders of the World." Turner had been invited to make his presentation, but Cody and his colorful bunch were not even official Exposition participants. That did not bother the old buffalo hunter, whose troupe performed twice daily just outside the walls of the Exposition grounds, in front of a covered grandstand that could hold eighteen thousand spectators. As Turner sanctified the American West of myth, Cody—a master of commercial exploitation—did everything he could to keep the frontier alive. Not ready to hear a eulogy for the dying frontier, Cody realized that by marketing the romantic visions of the Old West in the performance arena, he could perpetuate his illustrious career. The showman continued his effort for the next twenty-four years.

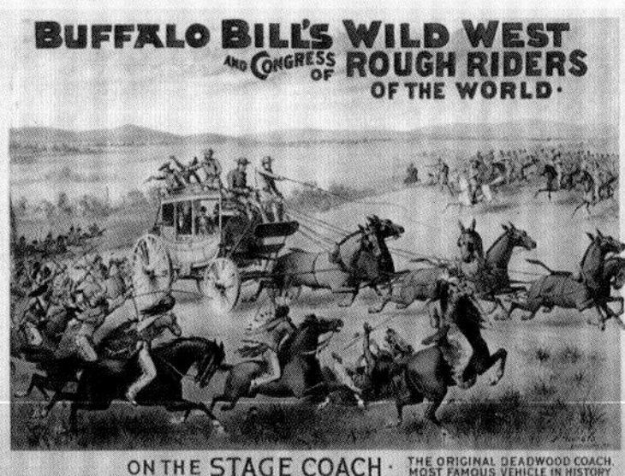

▲▲ Buffalo Bill as he appeared in his show.

▲▶ Posters for Buffalo Bill's "Congress of Rough Riders of the World."

BUFFALO BILL'S WILD WEST AND CONGRESS OF ROUGHRIDERS OF THE WORLD

PERILS OF THE COWBOY

NOV 8

1887 At Glenwood Springs, Colorado, famed shootist Doc Holliday dies of tuberculosis. His last words are, "This is funny."

THE BATTLE OF INGALLS

On the morning of September 1, 1893, a fierce and severely lopsided gunfight took place at a small Oklahoma Territory settlement named Ingalls. Over time, the town had become a safe haven for the Doolin-Dalton Gang, also known as the "Oklahombres," co-led by Bill Doolin and Bill Dalton. Two wagons filled with more than two dozen men, including fourteen deputy U.S. marshals, camped outside of Ingalls the night before the raid. At first light, the lawmen crept up on the town, and gunfire broke out when Doolin Gang member George "Bitter Creek" Newcomb walked out of a saloon. Legend has it that Rose Dunn, a teenage girl called the "Rose of Cimarron," raced from a hotel to her wounded lover's side with ammunition and a Winchester. She fired the rifle at lawmen while Newcomb reloaded his pistols and made his getaway. Although that incident was never verified, what is known is that as a result of the ensuing gunfight between twenty-four lawmen and seven outlaws, three federal peace officers died, two innocent bystanders were killed, and two other citizens were badly wounded. Although some of the outlaws were wounded, all of them except one escaped. The lone exception was Roy Daugherty, known as "Arkansas Tom Jones." He kept the posse at bay by laying down a constant stream of rifle fire from his sickroom on the top floor of the O.K. Hotel, allowing his cohorts to escape. After a lengthy siege, Arkansas Tom surrendered and was taken into custody. Although the Oklahombres may have won that battle, they ultimately lost the war. Eventually every outlaw who had escaped from Ingalls would be killed.

▶ Rose Dunn, who became known as the "Rose of Cimarron." Legend says she carried a rifle to her stranded lover, Bitter Creek, during the height of battle.

▶▶ Arkansas Tom Jones was captured after holding off the posse from the second floor of the O.K. Hotel. He was the only outlaw captured that day in Ingalls, and none were killed.

NOV 9

1876 Cole, Bob, and Jim Younger plead guilty for the robbery at Northfield, Minnesota. They are sentenced to life in prison in the Minnesota State Prison in Stillwater.
1929 The third film reprisal of Owen Wister's classic Western novel *The Virginian*, featuring the then-unknown actor Gary Cooper, is released by Paramount Pictures.

CHEROKEE OUTLET

The great Oklahoma land runs changed forever the lives of veteran cattlemen, who were more comfortable on old cow trails guzzling creek-water coffee than at home with their families. The time of the drover had come to an abrupt and rather unceremonious conclusion. They all knew that the enormous wave of anxious sodbusters, Boomers, and homesteaders could not be stemmed. The largest of all the land runs came on September 16, 1893, when the government opened up to settlers more than six million acres of deluxe grazing land created decades before to provide the Cherokee tribe with hunting grounds in the West following their removal to Indian Territory. This land was called the Cherokee Outlet, but was popularly known as the Cherokee Strip. Between 100,000 and 150,000 people turned up to grab a piece of land. Like the first run of 1889, this, too, was a spectacle to be remembered. People came from all over and made the run on horseback; in wagons, carts, and buggies; and on bicycles. Some walked. By nightfall, it was certain that Oklahoma—named for the Choctaw phrase meaning the "red people"—now belonged to the white man.

▶ The spectacular race for a homestead when the Cherokee Strip was opened to settlers in 1893.

NOV 10

1861 In Independence, Missouri, while riding with William Quantrill during a skirmish with Union troops, Cole Younger kills his first man.
1865 While en route to Virginia City, Nevada, following a lecture appearance, Mark Twain is the victim of a sham robbery staged by several friends as a joke. Twain's goods are later returned.

ANOTHER DALTON BITES THE DUST

"*Bill Dalton, the notorious desperado and bandit, met his death . . . at Elk, I.T.* [Indian Territory]. *C. L. Hart, a deputy marshal of the Paris district, fired the shot that sent the spirit of the outlaw to its home. . . . Hart was less than thirty yards from the house and called on him to halt. Dalton half turned around, tried to take aim while running, and just then the officer shot. Two jumps in the air were the only motions made. His pistol fell from his hand, and with a groan he sank to the ground, and Hart ran up and asked him what he was doing there, but he was too near dead to reply. . . . The remains were taken to Ardmore, where they were viewed by thousands of people. . . . Considerable money was found in the house, besides $275 on the body of Dalton. This was given to his wife. . . . The black hair of the corpse at first led to doubts as to whether Dalton had been killed. These doubts were removed during the process of embalming, where it was discovered that the hair had been dyed.*"

—*The Weekly Elevator*, Fort Smith, Arkansas, June 15, 1894

▶ Bill Dalton.

▶▶ Bill Dalton, killed by lawmen in Indian Territory.

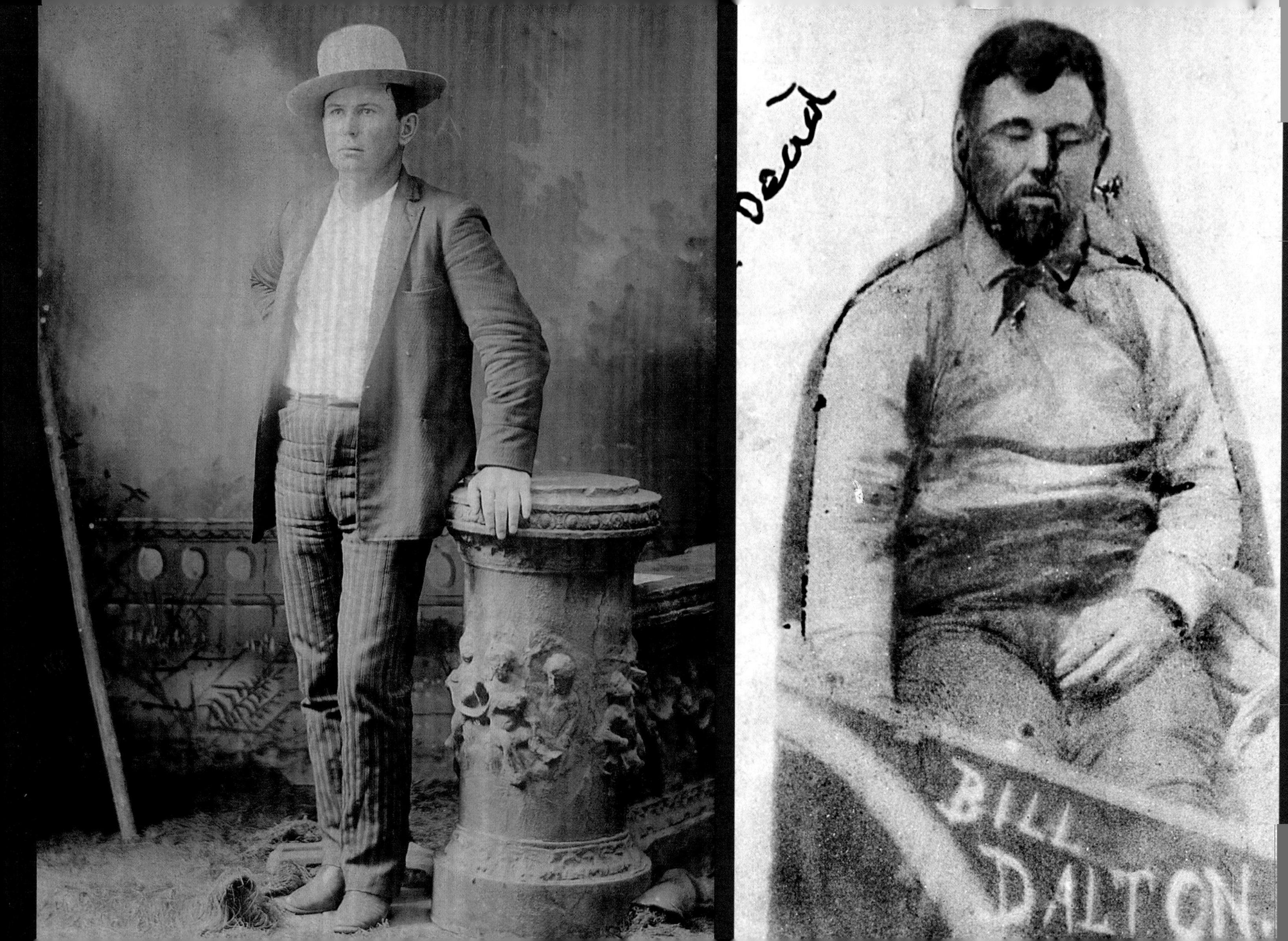

BILL
DALTON.

NOV 11

1916 In Portsmouth, Virginia, an ailing Buffalo Bill Cody makes his final public appearance while riding with the Miller Brothers' Wild West Show. Two months later Cody will die.

DONE IN BY THE DUNNS

As the 1890s progressed, several Oklahoma outlaws from the one-sided gunfight at Ingalls were killed, imprisoned, or simply vanished. George "Bitter Creek" Newcomb and Charley Pierce, another seasoned bank and train robber, had both survived wounds received at Ingalls and continued pursuing their life's work. By 1895, however, they each had a five-thousand-dollar bounty, dead or alive, on their heads. On May 2, 1895, Newcomb and Pierce rode up to the Dunn family's ranch house, not far from Ingalls. This was the home of Rose Dunn and her brothers, Bill, Calvin, Dal, George, and Jim. Whether the wanted outlaws went there to get fresh horses, collect a debt, or for Newcomb to see his sweetheart Rose, was never known. But both outlaws ended up shot dead by Rose's bounty hunter brothers. The next morning the bodies were loaded into a wagon to be taken to Guthrie so the rewards could be collected. Newcomb, though mortally injured, had lived through the night. When he begged for water, the Dunns stopped the wagon and put another bullet in him to finish the job. Some people who saw the corpses believed the outlaws had been killed while they slept because of wounds in the soles of their feet. The following year, Sheriff Frank Canton, who knew the Dunns as cattle rustlers and thieves, killed Bill Dunn in Pawnee. He was buried with other family members in a Guthrie cemetery, where Newcomb and Pierce had been interred. For many years, on the anniversary of the outlaws' death, Pierce's kin placed flowers on the graves of Pierce and Newcomb and threw hog guts on the graves of the Dunns who killed them.

▶ Doolin Gang members Bitter Creek Newcomb (left) and Charley Pierce (right), were gunned down by the Dunn brothers, who seemed to play both sides of the law.

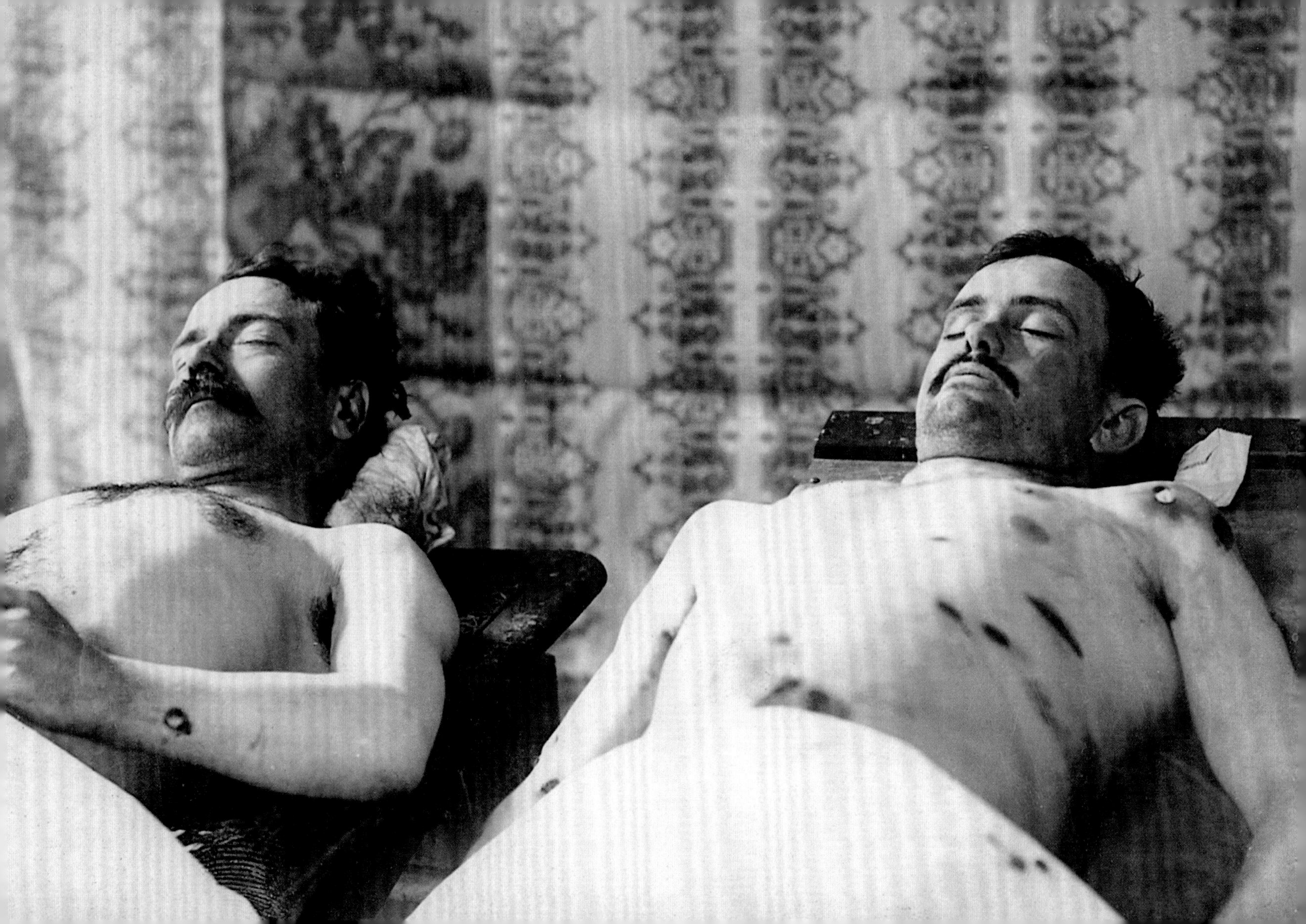

NOV 12

1877 In Deadwood, Dakota Territory, Sheriff Seth Bullock and deputies attempt to apprehend thirty armed miners holed up in a mine they have illegally seized. U.S. Cavalry units are summoned, but before they reach the mine, Bullock lowers burning sulfur into the shaft, causing the miners to surrender.

BORDER BOSS

John Reynolds Hughes paid his dues at an early age working as a cowboy and trail driver before his recruitment by the Texas Rangers in 1887. It was the start of a twenty-eight-year career, the longest term of service of any Ranger. Hughes spent most of that time with the famed Company D of the Frontier Battalion, the unit responsible for creating the Ranger traditions and mythology. In only a few years, Hughes rose from lowly private to sergeant, earning the name "Border Boss" and a reputation as a relentless pursuer of fugitives from justice. After Ranger Captain Frank Jones was killed in an ambush, Hughes led the Rangers in a hunt for the bandits responsible. Eventually, the Rangers shot or hung each of the eighteen suspects. When the Frontier Battalion was abolished in 1900, Hughes was made the captain in command of Company D in the new Ranger force and later was appointed senior captain. After he left the Rangers, Hughes—who never married, smoked, drank, or gambled—traveled, did a bit of prospecting, and became chairman of the board and the largest stockholder in an Austin bank. After spending time with Hughes, the notable Western writer Zane Grey felt compelled to write *The Lone Star Ranger*, a novel said to have inspired the book and later popular radio show, *The Lone Ranger*. In his final years living in Austin with his health declining, the old Ranger, at age ninety-two, ended his life with his well-worn Colt .45 pistol.

▶ Some men of Company D of the Texas Ranger Frontier Battalion. Captain John R. Hughes is seated on the right, and a Mexican prisoner in shackles is seated on the left.

NOV 13

1914 Henry Starr withdraws $2,400 during a robbery of the Farmers State Bank at Glencoe, Oklahoma. The holdup is one of fourteen daring daylight bank robberies carried out by Starr between September 8, 1914, and January 13, 1915.

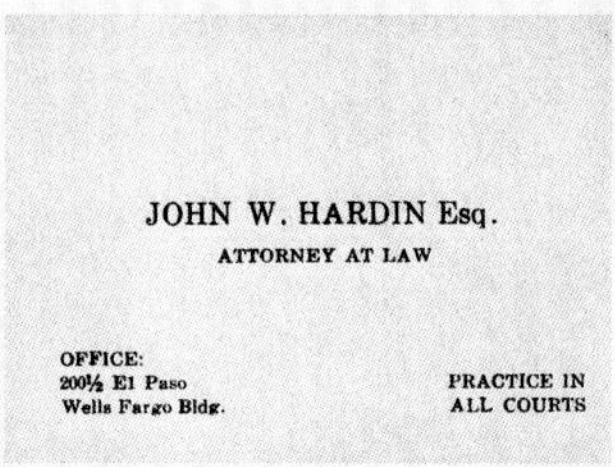
JOHN W. HARDIN Esq.
ATTORNEY AT LAW

OFFICE:
200½ El Paso
Wells Fargo Bldg.

PRACTICE IN
ALL COURTS

THE KILLING OF JOHN WESLEY HARDIN

On the sweltering evening of August 19, 1895, in El Paso, John Wesley Hardin, the infamous gunmen-turned-lawyer and part owner of the Wigwam Saloon, met his match. Constable John Selman, who himself would be shot and killed in El Paso the following year, sent a bullet crashing through Hardin's brain after the two exchanged harsh words at the Acme Saloon.

"John Wesley Hardin, the noted Texas desperado, is no more. He was shot and instantly killed to-night about 11:30 o'clock in the Acme saloon by Constable John Sellman [Selman]. *Hardin threatened Sellman's life several times during the evening but on meeting, Sellman was too quick for him. Hardin fell dead with his boots on before he could get a shot at Sellman. . . . Wes Hardin, as he was familiarly known over Southwest Texas, was especially the most noted of the living Texas desperadoes. Hardin's early career was spent in DeWitt County, and he was a terror in that section in the '70s, or until he was sent to the penitentiary. Hardin during his incarceration concluded that upon his release he would take up the practice of law, and so spent the latter part of the period of his confinement in studying the intricacies of jurisprudence. . . . As an expert shot he was the peer of either King Fisher or Ben Thompson in their palmist days. . . . It was almost sure death for anyone who was in front of his gun when Hardin drew a bead. Seventeen scalps are said to have dangled from his belt and it is likely that the number of human lives that he has taken will exceed that number."*

—The *San Antonio Express*, August 19, 1895

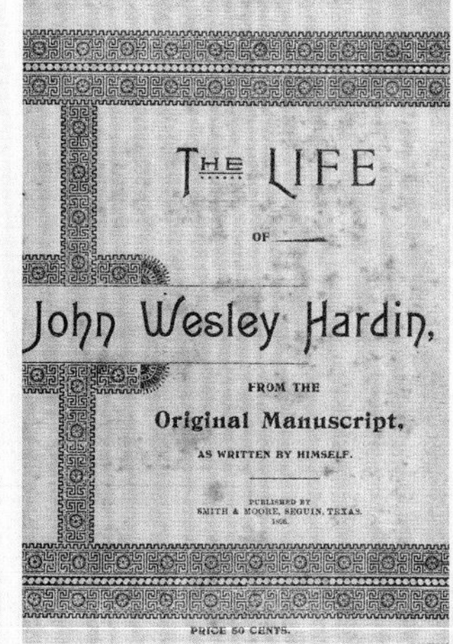

▲▲ John Wesley Hardin's business card.

▲ Hardin was writing his autobiography at the time of his death. It was finished by his son and published a year later.

▶ John Wesley Hardin in death, El Paso, 1895.

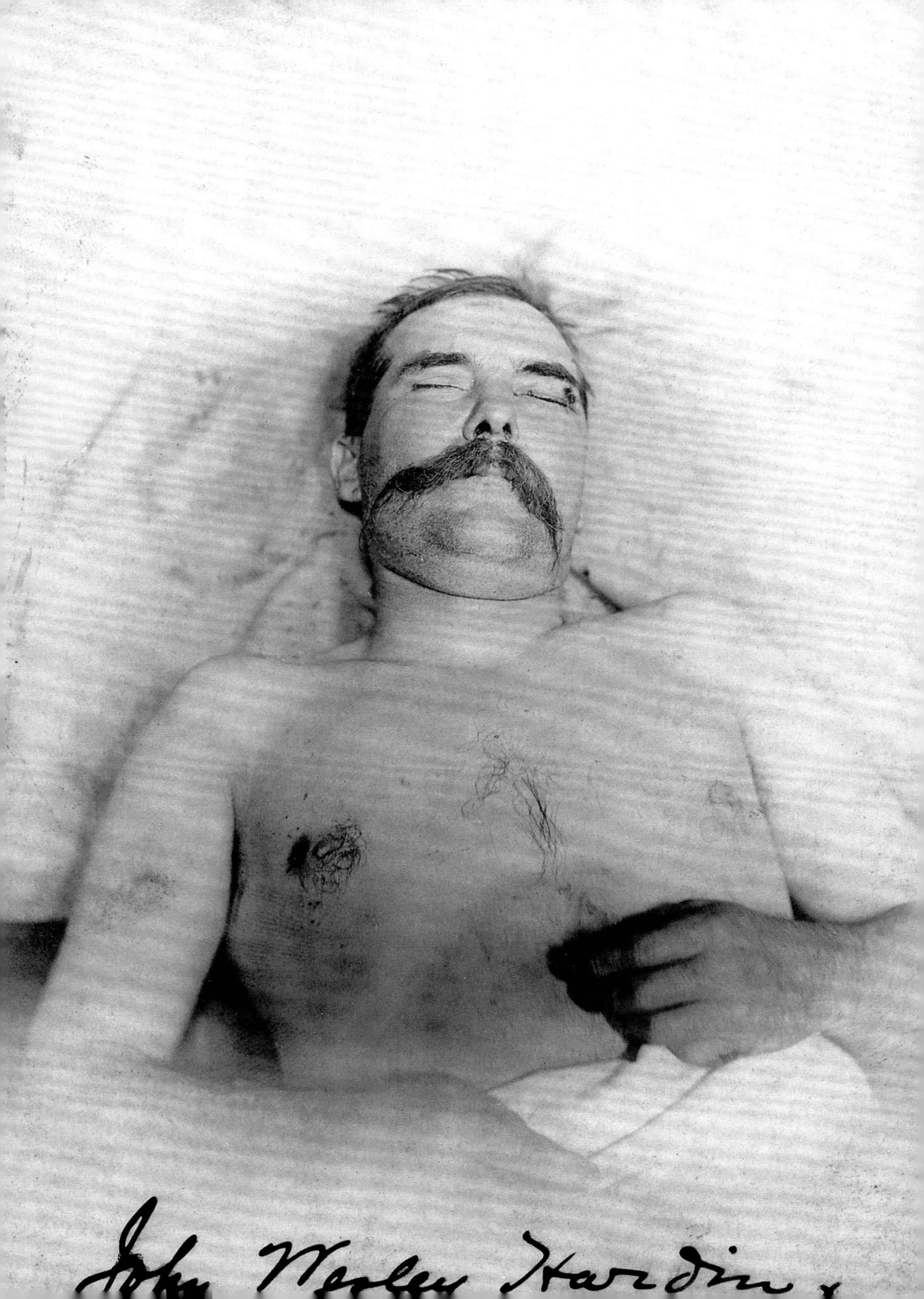
John Wesley Hardin

NOV 14

1879 In Las Vegas, New Mexico Territory, Hoodoo Brown, serving at various times as justice of the peace, coroner, and mayor, appoints "Dirty Dave" Rudabaugh a city policeman. He is one of several Kansas gunfighters whom Hoodoo recruits as peace officers, known as the Dodge City Gang.

RUFUS BUCK GANG

"Rufus Buck and his gang of outlaws, except one, are in limbo at Fort Smith, and are glad to be within its protecting walls. Hundreds of men, whites, Indians and Negroes . . . turned out to hunt them. Every hill, every bottom and every trail for miles around was being critically searched, and there was hardly a hope of escape of the brutal young men who had suddenly made such a fiendish record of crime. . . . The gang was trailed by their week of crime. Women were raped, men shot, stores burglarized, horses stolen, people robbed on the highways. All kinds of crimes were perpetrated against people."

—The *Muskogee Phoenix*, August 15, 1895

▶ The ruthless Rufus Buck Gang got what they deserved from Judge Parker's court. This illustrated lobby card was used with a movie about Oklahoma outlaws.

"Rufus Buck, Louis Davis, Lucky Davis, Maomi July and Sam Sampson comprising what is known as the Buck gang, were executed here today. President Cleveland refusing to interfere in the carrying out of the sentence in Judge Parker's court. . . . It was seven minutes past 1 o'clock when the doors of the jail opened for the egress of the condemned men. When the prisoners entered the gallows enclosure they took a glance at its hideous paraphernalia and then ascended the steps without the least sign of emotion. . . . The trap dropped with its horrible 'chug' at 1:28 o'clock. . . . This, we believe, is the first time in the history of this country that five men have been sentenced by one court and executed by one gallows for this hideous crime. . . . For downright dare deviltry and complete abandon they stand at the head of all the dissolute characters who have been swung into eternity on the gallows at the federal jail."

—*Cherokee Advocate*, July 11, 1896

BUCK GANG

All Hung at Ft. Smith, Ark. July 1st 1896

31

NOV 15

1901 In St. Louis, Missouri, Ben "The Tall Texan" Kilpatrick, member of the Wild Bunch, admits his true identity after authorities mistake him for Harry Longabaugh, also known as the Sundance Kid.

THE FIGHT OF THE CENTURY

When the 1896 World Championship boxing match slated to be held in Texas was in peril of being canceled because of a ban on professional prizefighting, none other than Judge Roy Bean rode to the rescue. The wily scalawag, known as the "Law West of the Pecos," schemed up a solution. Bean presented his idea to Dan Stuart, the promoter who had planned to stage the fight in Dallas, pitting "The Freckled Wonder" Bob Fitzsimmons against the Irish fighter Peter Maher. Bean explained that while boxing might be outlawed in Texas and neighboring Mexico, he had a neutral venue where a big-time slugfest was perfectly legal—a sandbar in the middle of the Rio Grande. Stuart jumped at the solution. On February 21, 1896, two hundred fans and sportswriters boarded a special train in El Paso and journeyed to Langtry to see the fight. A party of Texas Rangers had caught wind of Bean's enterprise and was originally intent on stopping it. But once they saw the ring was on an island out of their jurisdiction, they joined the others crossing the makeshift wooden bridge and became spectators. The fight went by in the blink of an eye. Fitzsimmons knocked out his opponent in ninety-six seconds. The disappointed fans made their way back to the waiting train only to find there would be a delay of several hours. Bean had cut a deal with the engineer to fake mechanical problems. Since his Jersey Lilly saloon-courtroom was nearby, Bean invited the crowd to sample some of his beverages, which he sold at inflated prices all afternoon until the train whistle blew and everyone left.

▲ The Fitzsimmons-Maher championship prizefight ring and spectators on a Rio Grande sandbar just below Judge Roy Bean's town of Langtry, Texas.

▶ Roy Bean standing on a hillside with Langtry and the Rio Grande behind him.

NOV 16

1881 Wyatt Earp takes the stand in Tombstone, Arizona Territory, and testifies that he fired in self-defense at the O.K. Corral shootout.

1907 Oklahoma becomes the forty-sixth state when the Indian and Oklahoma territories are unified.

THE HANGING OF CHEROKEE BILL

On March 17, 1896, after being convicted of murder in Judge Isaac Parker's Fort Smith courtroom and declared a "most ferocious monster," Crawford Goldsby, alias Cherokee Bill, met his maker. Between two thousand and three thousand sightseers surrounded hangman George Maledon's gallows that afternoon. A nearby storage shed collapsed under the weight of those perched on the roof. Cherokee Bill's fall of six feet went much easier, and death came quickly.

"Well, boys, try and shun this place where I am going. . . . I want you to keep in mind there is a judgment day to come for all. I know from a revelation which came to me last night. The doors were opened for me to gaze in the pits of hell; and I am praying for you all to reform before it is too late, and there is a hereafter. . . . You think I have been quite a hero. I killed three men while I was on the scout, and one in jail while trying to get my freedom, but did not make my escape then. I want you to know it was God's will that I did not get the keys, and it was God's power that caused the spring of that six-shooter to break and it was my sister that brought me my gun in a jug of buttermilk. . . . As I walk to the scaffold, I leave you all behind, for I have to die for the crime I did on this earth. I bid farewell to all of you. It won't be long until God will call you all home. Good-bye, I must die like a man."

—Cherokee Bill, 1896

▲ Indian Territory badman Cherokee Bill awaiting hanging on George Maledon's gallows.

▶ An artist's sketch of the hanging of Cherokee Bill.

NOV 17

1871 Due to the rising popularity of guns, two Union army veterans from New York—George W. Wingate and William C. Church—found the National Rifle Association (NRA) to make firearms training available, improve shooting skills, and promote the use of firearms and the gun industry.

OKLAHOMBRES

In the 1890s, as the various runs opened surplus Indian lands to white settlement, Congress created the Twin Territories from what had been called Indian Territory. The eastern half kept the name Indian Territory, while the western portion became Oklahoma Territory. The border between the two became known as Hell's Fringe. Most newcomers settling these lands were dirt poor. Many had lost their land in Texas or Kansas. Some were out-of-work laborers or blacklisted miners. Though tough as cowhide and resilient as coyotes, few of them were the prim and righteous pioneer types. Lawlessness in both territories increased due to the Panic of 1893 and the four years of severe nationwide economic depression that followed. During the 1890s, the Twin Territories accounted for most of the shooting deaths in the West, yielding plenty of killers and thieves who became folk heroes to the downtrodden. Settlers distrusted authority figures. They remembered that during the land rushes some U.S. deputies used their office to secure prime lands. Outlaws, on the other hand, often shared some of their booty. They were welcomed to country dances and church socials. In many instances, the Oklahombres killed or captured during the turbulent 1890s were mourned like members of an extended family.

"The outlaws of that day were not hijackers or petty thieves, and some of them had hearts, even though they were outlaws. . . . While they would stand up and shoot it out with men, when women were around, they were the first to take off their Stetsons and act like real men."

—Lon Stansbery, friend of Bill Doolin, c. 1930

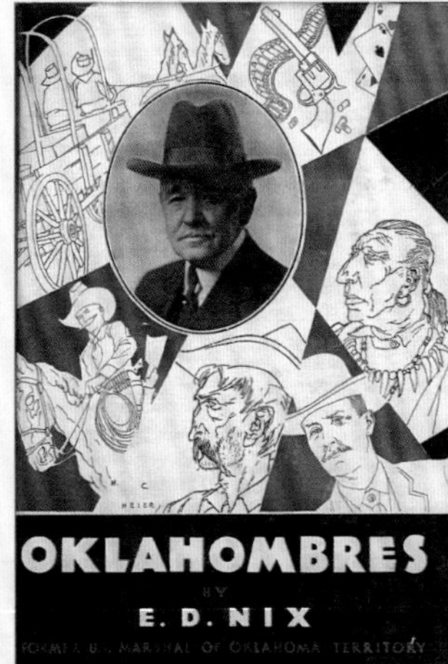

▲ Former U. S. Marshal E. D. Nix coined the name "Oklahombres" to describe the lawless elements in Oklahoma Territory.

▶ A photo montage of dead or captured Oklahoma outlaws created by a Guthrie photographer, c. 1898.

captured or killed
Bill Powers
Grat Dalton
Tackett, Coffeyville, Kansas.
Bob Dalton
Dick Broadwell
Dick Broadwell
Charlie Pierce
Bill Doolin
Swearingen,
Guthrie, O. T.
Bill Dalton Dead
BILL DALTON.
Bill Dalton in Life
Tulsa Jack
Jennie Metcalf
Bill Cook
Cherokee Bill
P. Rich,
Zip Wyatt
Black train robber killed near Canton Woods Co. Okla. Aug 1st, 95. while resisting arrest.
Copied by Swearingen Guthrie O.T.

NOV 18

1923 Silent movie *Wild Bill Hickok* premieres in New York City, starring steely-eyed William S. Hart—famous for his screen portrayals of Western heroes—in the title role.

ADIOS DYNAMITE DICK AND TULSA JACK

William "Tulsa Jack" Blake had been a Kansas cowboy during the 1880s before he drifted south into Oklahoma Territory and hooked up with outlaw Bill Doolin. As a member in good standing of Doolin's gang, the Oklahombres, Blake participated in numerous train and bank robberies and was in attendance at the big shootout in Ingalls. Like his mentor Doolin, the wily Blake was tracked to his hideout by a posse led by Deputy U.S. Marshal Will Banks. During a fierce gun battle on April 4, 1895, Blake held off the lawmen for forty-five minutes until he bolted from his cover to escape and was gunned down. The following year, another outlaw veteran of the Ingalls fight, Dan Clifton, or as he preferred "Dynamite Dick," was shot and killed by Deputy U.S. Marshal Chris Madsen near Blackwell, Oklahoma Territory. Clifton began his life as a criminal before joining the Doolin Gang in 1892. At Ingalls, three of his fingers were shot off. Bounty hunters and posses frequently turned in corpses said to be Clifton, but with all the digits in place. In some instances three fingers were randomly cut off the dead man, but invariably the wrong ones. So many people tried unsuccessfully to collect Clifton's bounty that he became known as the "most killed outlaw in America." Madsen had more luck—he knew Clifton personally and also verified the correct fingers were missing. In any case, Dynamite Dick was never heard from again.

▲ Tulsa Jack Blake, another Doolin Gang member killed by deputy U.S. marshals.

▶ Doolin Gang member Charles "Dynamite Dick" Clifton in death.

Charles Clifton - Dalton

NOV 19

1924 After celebrating his forty-second birthday, pioneer filmmaker Thomas Ince dies mysteriously at his Benedict Canyon home in California. Ince shot early Western epics at the 101 Ranch in Oklahoma and at a sprawling locale in the Santa Monica Mountains known as Inceville.

BILL DOOLIN'S DEMISE

The dangerous outlaw Bill Doolin, cohort of the Dalton brothers and the leader of the gang known as the Oklahombres, took his last breath on August 24, 1896, in Lawson, Oklahoma Territory. He was outgunned by a posse led by famed Deputy U.S. Marshal Heck Thomas, as the bullet wounds dotting Doolin's torso attest to in the post-ambush photograph. Thomas received a reward of five hundred dollars from Wells Fargo Express Company, five hundred dollars from the state of Missouri, and three hundred dollars from one of the railroad companies that Doolin pestered. Of that total, Thomas pocketed four hundred dollars and gave the rest to his posse. While far short of the five-thousand-dollar reward promised for Doolin, dead or alive, the compensation was still a far sight more than the meager two hundred fifty dollars mentioned in Doolin's very succinct obituary in the Fort Smith newspaper.

"Bill Doolin, the outlaw who broke jail at Guthrie a short time ago, was killed Monday night by Deputy Marshal Heck Thomas and his posse. Doolin was one of the hardest cases that ever afflicted a country. He operated for a time with the Bill Dalton gang, and for a time was thought to be the manager of the Cook gang. He was one of the crowd upon whose heads the government once placed rewards of $250. Heck and his posse did a praise-worthy act when they put out his light."

—*The Weekly Elevator*, Fort Smith, Arkansas, August 28, 1896

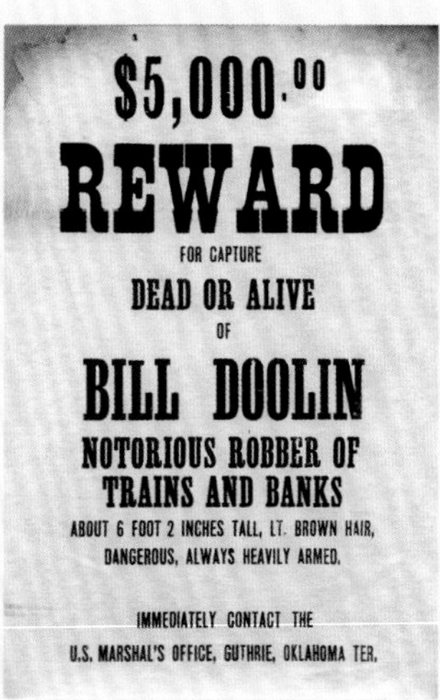

▲ A wanted poster offering a reward of five thousand dollars for Bill Doolin, dead or alive.

▶ Heck Thomas and his posse put two loads of buckshot in Doolin.

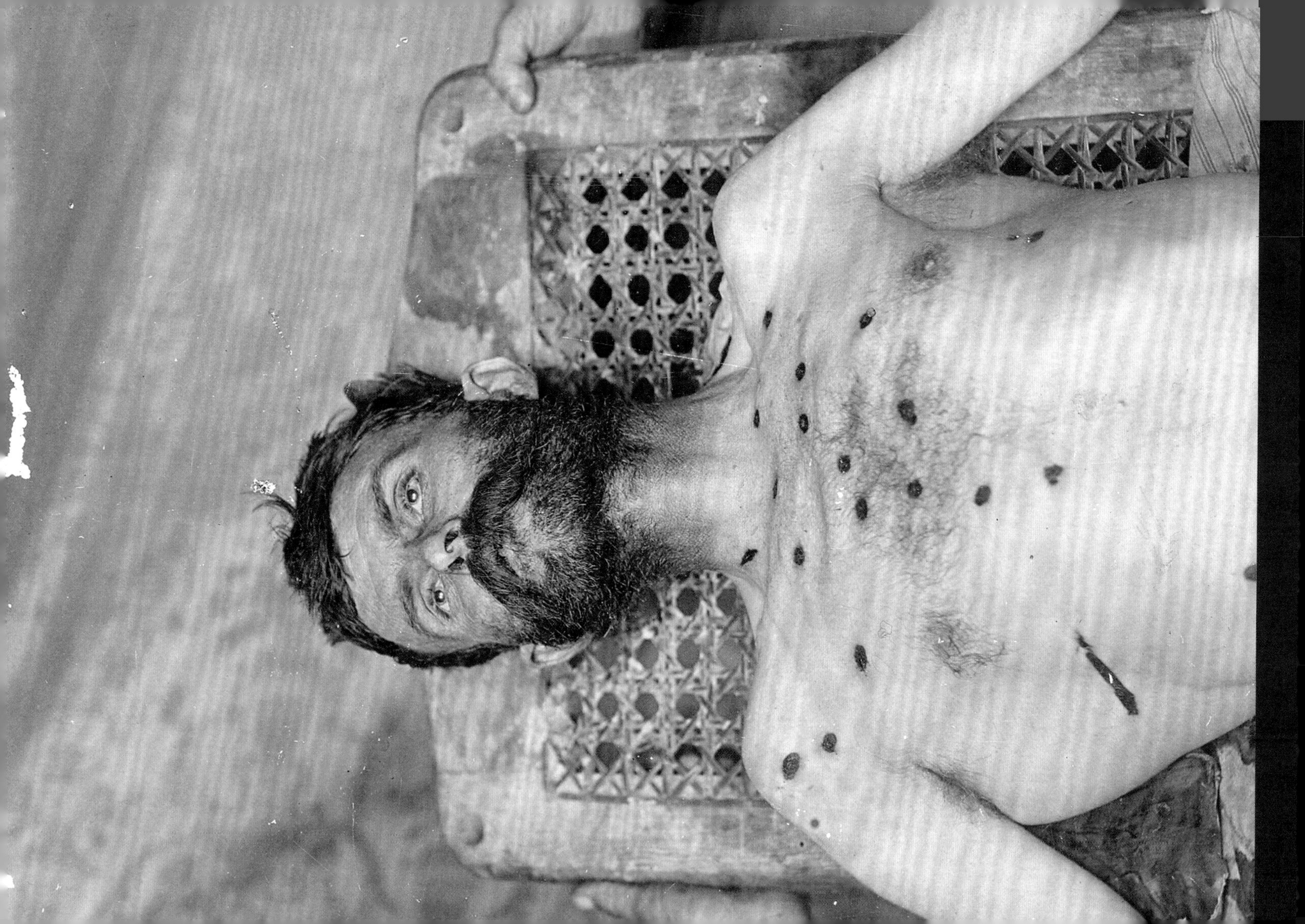

NOV 20

1903 In Cheyenne, Wyoming, hired gunman Tom Horn is hanged one day before his forty-third birthday.

PEARL HART

Canadian-born Pearl Hart gained her share of the Wild West limelight for her participation in one of the last recorded stagecoach robberies in the United States. Hart became totally infatuated with the lifestyle of the West at the 1893 World's Fair in Chicago when she saw a performance of Buffalo Bill's Wild West. She left her husband and took a train bound for Colorado. "I was only twenty-two years old," she later explained. "I was good-looking, desperate, discouraged, and ready for anything that might come." Over the years, Hart had a few reconciliations with her husband, gave birth to a son and daughter fathered by a gambler, and worked as a mining camp cook. In Globe, Arizona, she took up with a prospector named Joe Boot, likely an alias. When she learned that her children were sick in the care of her dying mother, Hart schemed up the stage robbery with Boot. In 1898, the two road agents waited at a watering point thirty miles southeast of Globe. They stopped the coach and took $431 from the passengers, but before riding off, Hart gave each of them a dollar to get some grub. Both bandits were caught, tried and convicted, and sent to the hellish prison at Yuma. Boot was given thirty-five years, but soon escaped. Hart had a five-year hitch to do. The warden was taken with his lone female inmate, and because of her crime and gender, newspaper reporters flocked to the prison to interview the celebrity outlaw. Hart was pardoned in 1902 and, with few exceptions, was not seen again. Her story, however, lived on and became a staple of pulp fiction Westerns.

▲ Pearl Hart as a prisoner, c. 1900.

▶ Pearl Hart as a lady, n.d.

▶▶ Pearl Hart as a bandit, c. 1898.

NOV 21

1900 In Fort Worth, Texas, Butch Cassidy, the Sundance Kid, and three other members of the Wild Bunch sit for a portrait photograph. This classic image will be used by Pinkerton agents in wanted posters.

THE KILLINGEST OUTLAW

One of the most prolific and vicious killers in the American West, Augustine Chacón was known to have taken the lives of at least fifteen Americans and thirty-seven Mexicans on both sides of the border. The darkly handsome mustachioed outlaw was called "The Hairy One," but the title that fit him the best was "The Killingest Outlaw." When terrorizing Tombstone in Arizona Territory, Chacón managed to escape the clutches of John B. Slaughter, one of the toughest lawmen of the day. In 1897, the elusive Chacón was finally captured and jailed at Solomonville where authorities scheduled his hanging. Just ten days before the execution, Chacón burrowed his way to freedom and dashed back to his native Sonora, Mexico. He eluded capture for another five years until Slaughter's protégé—Captain Burton Mossman of the Arizona Rangers—came up with a scheme to apprehend the relentless Chacón. Mossman recruited two former lawmen turned outlaw to find Chacón. The three men went to Mexico, posed as escaped outlaws, and arranged for a parley with Chacón. At the meeting, Mossman pulled his gun and took the killer into custody. On the ride back to Arizona Territory, the Ranger captain made Chacón ride in handcuffs with a rope around his neck. This time there would be no escape. On November 22, 1903, Chacón was hanged at Solomonville. Just before the trap was sprung, he announced, "I consider this to be the greatest day of my life."

▲ Augustine Chacón, Arizona badman, in shackles on the right.

▶ Chacón, dressed as a southwestern desperado.

NOV 22

1880 In Leadville, Colorado, ex-marshal Martin Duggan kills Louis Lamb in a street fight when Lamb pulls his revolver and Duggan shoots him in the mouth.

BUTCH CASSIDY

Butch Cassidy was the outlaw everyone loved. From his first major crime—a bank robbery in Telluride, Colorado, in 1889—until his mysterious disappearance in Bolivia in 1908, Cassidy was generally respected by anyone who met him, with the understandable exception of some bankers and railroad paymasters. Although he was a crack shot, it was said Cassidy never killed anyone in the commission of a crime. Even the wanted posters calling for his capture, described him as "cheery and affable." Born Robert LeRoy Parker in Beaver, Utah, in 1866 to devout Mormon parents, he was the first of thirteen children. He left home in his early teens, and became acquainted with Mike Cassidy, a cattle rustler and horse thief who briefly took the youngster under his wing. Later, while working in a butcher shop in Rock Springs, Wyoming, he picked up the nickname Butch, then added the surname of Cassidy, in tribute to the old bandit who befriended him. It's also likely that he changed his name to avoid bringing any shame on his family when he turned outlaw. Using his cut of the money from the Telluride bank job as his grubstake, Cassidy was hired on at ranches in Wyoming and Utah while cattle rustling on the side. After a few run-ins with the law, he was convicted of horse theft and given a two-year sentence. In 1894, Cassidy entered the Wyoming State Penitentiary in Laramie, but was pardoned six months early on his pledge to steal no more livestock or horses in Wyoming. Cassidy walked out of prison in January of 1896 and kept his word. He stopped stealing horses and cattle in Wyoming and instead became a successful bank and train robber.

▶ Robert LeRoy Parker, alias Butch Cassidy, in prison pants, later to be the leader of the Wild Bunch.

▶▶ Lawman Joe Lefors with a posse traveling by rail to the site of a Wild Bunch train holdup. Their horses are loaded in a stock car.

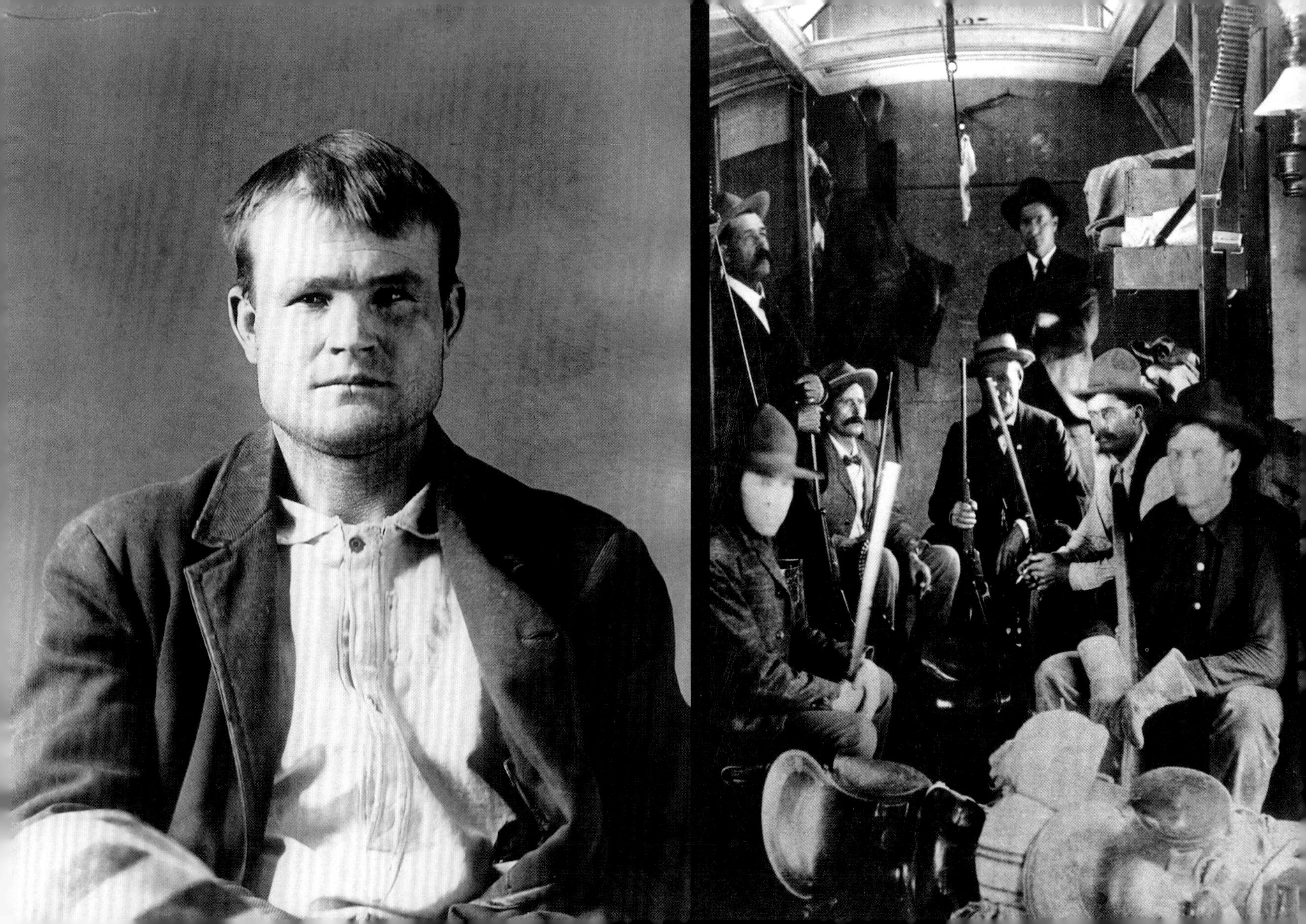

NOV

23

1869 The first of Ned Buntline's stories about William F. Cody, "Buffalo Bill, the King of the Border Men," is published in installments in the *New York Weekly*.

THE WILD BUNCH

After his release from prison in Wyoming, Butch Cassidy rode to an outlaw lair in Colorado, formed a gang, and went on the scout for likely cash targets. He found one on August 13, 1896, at the bank in Montpelier, Idaho, and left with enough money to pay for the defense of some pals being tried for murder. Cassidy's Gang—dubbed the Wild Bunch—included several well-known outlaws such as Harry Longabaugh, known as the Sundance Kid; Ben "The Tall Texan" Kilpatrick; Harvey Logan, alias Kid Curry; and Harry Tracy. More holdups followed, including a coal company payroll in Utah in the spring of 1897. Cassidy and the Wild Bunch roamed far and wide, robbing banks and Union Pacific trains in Wyoming, Utah, Nevada, and Montana. For several years during the late 1890s and into the first decade of the twentieth century, Pinkerton agents and railroad detectives devoted every waking hour to tracking down Butch, Sundance, and the rest of the boys. Perhaps one of the biggest mistakes the gang ever made was when the core members of the Wild Bunch sat dressed to the nines for a group portrait in Fort Worth in 1900. They had just robbed a bank in Winnemucca, Nevada, and went to Texas to relax and buy some new duds. They liked the portrait so much, a copy of it was sent to the Nevada bank with a note that said, "Thanks for the donation." The Pinkertons also obtained a copy of the photograph and began using it for their wanted posters.

▶ The Wild Bunch garbed in new duds in Fort Worth, Texas, for a group photograph, 1900. From left to right: Harry Longabaugh, alias The Sundance Kid; Bill Carver; Ben Kilpatrick, alias The Tall Texan; Harvey Logan, alias Kid Curry; and Robert LeRoy Parker, alias Butch Cassidy.

FORT WORTH, TEX.

NOV 24

1835 A corps of Texas Rangers, consisting of twenty-five men under the command of Silas M. Parker, is created to guard the frontier in the Mexican province of Texas against hostile Indians.

"WHO *ARE* THOSE GUYS?"

Legendary manhunter Joe Lefors, immortalized long after his death in the 1969 film *Butch Cassidy and the Sundance Kid*, in reality never quite lived up to his romanticized big screen portrayal. In the movie, he was presented as an intrepid tracker who always wore a white straw hat and doggedly pursued the famous outlaw pair after a train robbery, causing the frustrated Butch to ask, "Who *are* those guys?" In truth, Lefors and his posse chased and apprehended many members of the Wild Bunch with two notable exceptions—Butch and Sundance. Despite all of his bragging about his expertise at tracking felons, most of the posses Lefors led returned empty-handed. Lefors became best known for obtaining a controversial murder confession from gunman Tom Horn in 1903, by first getting him drunk. After Horn was hanged, Lefors's exaggerated self-worth and allegations of falsifying evidence damaged his reputation. Famed lawman and Pinkerton agent Charlie Siringo labeled Lefors incompetent as a lawman. Another contemporary said of Lefors: "He was not a standup guy. He was all hat and no cattle. He had the manners of an organ grinder and the morals of a monkey." Perhaps instead of white, Lefors should have worn a gray hat.

▲ The posse that trailed the Wild Bunch, with Joe Lefors (No. 3), "the guy in the white hat."

▶ Bob Boze Bell's 2007 painting of Butch and Sundance contemplating the relentless posse with the phrase "Who *are* those guys?" that was made famous in the 1969 movie *Butch Cassidy and the Sundance Kid.*

NOV 25

1876 In the wake of the Battle of Little Bighorn, Colonel Ranald S. Mackenzie's troops attack Cheyenne chief Dull Knife's sleeping winter village in the Bighorn Mountains near the Red Fork of the Powder River in present-day Wyoming. Many Cheyenne flee or surrender as the soldiers burn more than two hundred lodges and take five hundred ponies.

BLACK JACK KETCHUM

Thomas Edward "Black Jack" Ketchum left his native San Saba County, Texas, about 1890, most likely because of a crime, and went to New Mexico Territory to work as a cowboy in the Pecos River Valley. A few years later, his older brother, Sam Ketchum, left his wife and children and joined him. In between working as cowboys on various ranches, the Ketchums began taking part in train and stage robberies in New Mexico and Arizona territories. Black Jack also was implicated in a killing back in Texas. During the late 1890s, the brothers rode with Kid Curry and others from the Wild Bunch. In the summer of 1899, however, things went sour for the brothers when Sam was seriously wounded in a gun battle with a posse. He was arrested and died of blood poisoning in the Santa Fe Territorial Prison on July 24, 1899. Less than a month later, Tom, unaware of his brother's death, attempted to rob a train by himself near Folsom, New Mexico Territory, and was hit by a shotgun blast fired by the conductor. The next day, a posse found Ketchum lying wounded beside the tracks. He was transported to Trinidad, Colorado, where his right arm was amputated. After being nursed back to health, the failed train robber was sent to the town of Clayton where in 1901 he stood trial.

"I wanted to hit the bandit in the heart, but in the dim light I misjudged. It had to be done quickly. I knew that as I opened the door my appearance would be noted by the robber, who faced me. I aimed as best as I could."

—train conductor Frank E. Harrington, 1901

▲ A photograph of Tom "Black Jack" Ketchum taken a short time before he was hanged.

▶ Black Jack was shot and badly wounded by the conductor while attempting a single-handed train robbery.

NOV

26

1864 In Hutchinson County, Texas, near Adobe Walls, a large party of Kiowa and Comanche Indians led by Dohasan and Satanta encounter a small U.S. Cavalry unit led by Kit Carson. In what becomes known as the First Battle of Adobe Walls, the soldiers sustain few casualties, and Carson emerges as a hero.

HEADLESS IN CLAYTON

While Tom "Black Jack" Ketchum was in custody in New Mexico Territory, Arizona Territory authorities tried their best to extradite him to their jurisdiction for the slayings of two shopkeepers in Camp Verde. But New Mexico Territorial Governor Miguel Otero refused to hand over Ketchum, who was to be tried under a new territorial law that called for the death penalty if found guilty of "molesting a train." At the trial in Clayton, there was not an empty seat when the one-armed Ketchum entered a plea of not guilty to the train robbery charge. The unconvinced jury found the opposite, and Judge William J. Mills sentenced Ketchum to hang. The new law that allowed the execution was later found to be unconstitutional, but it was too late for Black Jack. On April 26, 1901, a crowd gathered around the gallows to witness the town's first official hanging. Observers later reported that Ketchum ran to the gallows in the jail yard as if he was ready and eager to die. A noose was placed around his neck and a hood pulled over his head. When Sheriff Salome Garcia asked if he had any last words, Ketchum replied, "Good-bye. Please dig my grave deep. Alright, hurry up." With that, the trapdoor was released and Ketchum's body dropped. When a large amount of blood began seeping from the dead man's hood, everyone knew something had gone wrong. A novice hangman had miscalculated Ketchum's weight and the length of the rope. When the hood was removed, the sheriff found that Ketchum had been decapitated. Before the head was sewn back on for public viewing, a photographer recorded the grisly scene and produced a popular postcard of the headless train molester.

▲ A miscalculation of the length of the drop resulted in Ketchum's head coming to rest a foot or two from his body.

▶ Black Jack having the hanging rope adjusted around his neck, 1901.

NOV 27

1868 On the Washita River near present-day Cheyenne, Oklahoma, Lieutenant Colonel George Armstrong Custer's Seventh Cavalry attacks Black Kettle's Cheyenne camp, killing Black Kettle and his wife, a large number of Cheyenne men, women, and children, and 675 Indian ponies.

CALAMITY'S LAST WISH

For years before her death in 1903, the woman best known as Calamity Jane wandered through the West, frequently wearing out her welcome by getting drunk and shooting up a saloon or brothel. Still, she was generally liked and, when sober and well behaved, was regarded as a celebrity. During her 1895 visit to Deadwood, after more than a fifteen-year absence, she sat for photographs to be sold during tours of eastern cities. Briefly married at various times, Jane had at least one child—a daughter who was taken from her and placed in a convent in Sturgis, South Dakota, to be raised by nuns. Jane aged quickly and was once described as looking like "a busted bale of hay." New Mexico Territorial Governor Miguel Otero wrote his own description: "Calamity Jane, one of the frontier's most notorious characters . . . dressed in a buckskin suit like a man, and was regarded by the community as a camp follower, since she preferred to ply her well-known profession among the soldiers. . . . She was a fearless and excellent horsewoman, and a good shot with either pistol or rifle. Money seemed to mean little to her; she spent it recklessly in saloons or at the gambling table." On August 1, 1903, Calamity Jane died at Deadwood of "inflammation of the bowels." Her last words were of her long-lost daughter. In appreciation of Jane's nursing efforts during an earlier smallpox epidemic, some businessmen made sure she received a proper burial in the Mount Moriah Cemetery. Her final resting place was next to the grave of Wild Bill Hickok. Just as she wanted, for all eternity Calamity Jane would be close to the man she always loved.

▲ Honoring Calamity's request, she was buried in Deadwood next to Wild Bill Hickok.

▶ Calamity Jane dressed in buckskins, 1895.

▶▶ Photographer L. A. Huffman convinced Calamity to pose dressed as a lady.

NOV 28

1869 After robbing the post office at Separ, New Mexico Territory, a gang of outlaws, including Samuel Hassells (alias Bob Hays), is cornered by a large posse at the Diamond A ranch, sixty miles south of town. In the wild gun battle that follows, Hassells is shot and killed.

BAD MEN GONE GOOD

In 1901, the two surviving Younger brothers—Cole and Jim—were paroled from the Stillwater State Prison in Minnesota after serving twenty-five years of their life sentences. Their release, however, came with the stipulation that before getting a full pardon they must reside in the state for two years under strict supervision. Both brothers found employment as traveling salesmen for a tombstone company, an ironic occupation given their past deeds. Cole adjusted to life on the outside more quickly than his younger brother, who was anxious to return to Missouri. When the Board of Pardons turned down Jim's request to marry the daughter of a state legislator, he became so despondent that he took his life with a gun in a St. Paul hotel. In 1903, Cole was granted a full pardon and immediately took a train to Missouri. He quickly reacquainted himself with Frank James, his old ally from days with Quantrill and on the outlaw trail. James, who had been pardoned many years earlier, had worked at a variety of jobs such as doorman at a burlesque house, shoe salesman, and as a celebrity starter at horse races. Together, the aging ex-outlaws developed a plan to earn money without having to rob banks. In 1903, they formed "The Great Cole Younger & Frank James Historical Wild West Show," with used equipment from the defunct "Buckskin Bill Wild West Show." They put their new outfit on the road, playing at county fairs and other venues throughout much of the same territory they once roamed as outlaws. The show barely made it through a season before shutting down. The resilient Frank and Cole turned to other pursuits and lived out the balance of their lives in peace.

THE GREAT
Cole Younger
and Frank James
HISTORICAL
Wild West Show
NOW EN ROUTE
The Finest Exhibition of its Class in History

The Charge of the Rough Riders,
The Frontier as It Was,
Indian Warfare, Illustrated by Real Red-Skins,
Dare-Devil Horsemanship,
Marvelous Marksmanship,
The Perils of the Plains.

FRANK JAMES, the Scout, will personally direct every performance.

The whole under the general supervision of COLE YOUNGER.

H. E. ALLOTT, Manager.

▲ As seen in this advertisement, neither Cole nor Frank performed in the show. They only directed and supervised.

▶ Frank James, early 1900s.

▶▶ Cole Younger, after his release from prison in 1903.

NOV 29

1864 At Sand Creek, Colorado Territory, U.S. soldiers led by Colonel John M. Chivington attack Black Kettle's peaceful camp of Cheyenne Indians. Troops massacre and scalp at least two hundred Cheyenne, mostly women and children.

THAT DAMNED COWBOY

After President William McKinley was assassinated in 1901, an exasperated Senator Mark Hanna declared: "Now look! That damned cowboy is president of the United States!" When he heard Hanna's remark, Roosevelt, the consummate "Rough Rider," broke into his famous toothy grin. To be called a cowboy was a compliment and suited Teddy to a tee. Roosevelt was drawn to the West in 1883, when he journeyed to the Dakota Territory Badlands to hunt buffalo before the herds disappeared and to acquire some ranchlands. The following year, his immense spread became a place of refuge when Roosevelt's wife and mother both died on Valentine's Day. Both before and after his presidency, Roosevelt did all he could to preserve the American West that he loved.

▶ Theodore Roosevelt dressed in buckskins as a western frontiersman, 1886.

"It was still the Wild West in those days, the far West, the west of Owen Wister's stories and Frederic Remington's drawings, the West of the Indian and the buffalo-hunter, the soldier and the cow-puncher. That land of the West has gone now, 'gone, gone with lost Atlantis,' gone to the isle of ghosts and of strange dead memories. It was a land of vast silent spaces, of lonely rivers, and of plains where the wild game stared at the passing horseman. It was a land of scattered ranches, of herds of long-horned cattle, and of reckless riders who unmoved looked in the eyes of life or death."

—*Theodore Roosevelt: An Autobiography*, 1913

NOV 30

1902 Wanted for murder and robbery, Harvey "Kid Curry" Logan—"the wildest of the Wild Bunch"—is captured by authorities in a Knoxville, Tennessee, pool hall.

KID CURRY

When it came to cold-blooded murder, nobody could hold a candle to Kid Curry. His real name was Harvey Logan, and as a lad he had met the infamous Jesse James, an encounter that helped Logan decide on a career path. During his many years as a train and bank robber both alone or with Butch Cassidy's Wild Bunch, Logan is known to have killed at least fifteen men, although it was estimated that he probably killed twice that number. By far, most of his victims were peace officers, an occupation he particularly detested. William Pinkerton, of Pinkerton Detective Agency fame, considered Kid Curry the most vicious outlaw in America. "He has not one single redeeming feature," wrote Pinkerton. "He is the only criminal I know of who does not have one single good point." Those who knew Kid Curry—mainly ladies—disagreed. One of his female admirers called him "a gentleman, clean through," and a Utah schoolteacher described him as "a fine man who never said a bad or cross word to me." After years spent killing and robbing across the West, Kid Curry tried to hide out in Tennessee, but just got into more trouble and ended up in jail. He made a daring escape and tried to join Cassidy and the Sundance Kid in South America, but literally missed the boat. Following a train robbery gone awry near Parachute, Colorado, in June 1904, Kid Curry was wounded by a sheriff's posse and on the run when he shot himself with his .45 pistol. A controversy ensued over the true identity of the body, but most reliable sources agree that instead of faking his death and going to South America as some fantasized, Harvey Logan, alias Kid Curry, took his own life.

▲ Harvey Logan, photographed in death.

▶ Harvey Logan, alias Kid Curry, was said to be the most dangerous and deadly member of the Wild Bunch.

$5,000 REWARD.

PHOTOGRAPH OF HARVEY LOGAN.

Captured at Jefferson Tenn. Dec 15th 1901
20 miles from Knoxville

Arrested in Knoxville Tenn. Dec 15th 1901.

The above is the aggregate amount of reward offered by the GREAT NORTHERN EXPRESS CO. for the arrest and identification of the four men implicated in the robbery of the Great Northern Railway Express train No. 3 near Wagner, Mont., July 3, 1901. A proportionate amount will be paid for one, two or more, and **$500 Additional for each Conviction.**

Under date of Aug. 5th, 1901, we issued a circular bearing a picture of **HARVEY LOGAN** showing him with a full beard, making it difficult to identify. We herewith present a later and better picture of him which has been identified in Nashville, Tenn., as a good likeness of the companion of a woman arrested there for attempting to exchange some of the stolen currency.

DESCRIPTION.

Name, HARVEY LOGAN.

Alias Harvey Curry, "Kid" Curry, Bob Jones, Tom Jones, Bob Nevilles, Robert Nelson and **R. T. Whalen.**

Residence, last known, Landusky and Harlem, Montana.

Nativity, Dodson, Mo.

Color, white.

Occupation, cowboy, rustler.

Criminal Occupation, Bank robber, train robber, horse and cattle thief, rustler, "hold up" and murderer.

Age, 36 years (1901).

Eyes, dark.

Height, 5 feet, 7½ inches,

Weight, 145 to 160 lbs.

Build, medium.

Complexion, dark, swarthy,

Nose, prominent, large, long and straight.

Color of Hair, dark brown, darker than mustache.

Style of Beard, can raise heavy beard and mustache, color somewhat lighter than hair.

Marks, has gun-shot wound on wrist, talks slowly, is of quiet reserved manner.

On Oct. 27th, 1901, a man believed to be GEORGE PARKER, alias Butch Cassidy, whose photograph and description appeared in our circular of Aug, 5th, 1901, attempted to pass one of the $20 bills of the stolen currency at a Nashville store. He escaped from officers after a severe struggle.

On the night of Nov. 5th, 1901, the St. Louis Police arrested Harry Longbaugh, alias Harry Alonzo, one of the train robbers, after he had passed four of the stolen bills at a PAWNSHOP. A female companion was also arrested. They had in their possession about $7,000 of the stolen notes,

Officers attempting to arrest these men are warned that they are desperadoes, always carry firearms and do not hesitate to use them when their liberty is endangered.

Send all information promptly to the undersigned to the nearest office listed at the head of circular, using telegraph if necessary.

PINKERTON'S NATIONAL DETECTIVE AGENCY.

OR WM. A. PINKERTON, 199-201 Fifth Avenue, Chicago, Ills.

CHICAGO, ILL., NOVEMBER 8, 1901.

DEC 1

1903 A silent film called *The Great Train Robbery* is released by Edison Manufacturing Company. It not only becomes a classic Western film, but is also considered one of the most influential early motion pictures.

DOS AMIGOS

With the dawn of the twentieth century, the old-time outlaws' days were numbered. Some die-hards, especially the lone wolves, held fast and stayed on the scout until death took them. Others chose retirement or a career change. A few looked for greener pastures. That was the case for Butch Cassidy and his sidekick the Sundance Kid, the romantic handle of Harry Longabaugh that dated back to his younger days as a rustler around Sundance, Wyoming. After riding off with $65,000 from a train robbery near Wagner, Montana, in July 1901, the Wild Bunch disbanded. Butch and Sundance decided to start new lives in South America. They took along a third party—Etta Place, Sundance's schoolmarm lover. The trio went to New York City and took rooms in a boardinghouse. Sundance bought Etta a lapel watch and stick-pin at Tiffany's before they posed for a portrait at a Broadway photography studio. On February 29, 1902, the happy couple and Butch, traveling under assumed names, boarded the freighter *Soldier Prince* bound for Argentina. They purchased land near the Andes in Chubut Province and devoted a few years to ranching. Eventually, when funds ran low, they sold the ranch and returned to what they did best—robbery. Etta opted to leave, and Sundance escorted her back to the United States. Back in South America, between 1905 and 1909, Sundance and Butch held up banks, trains, and mine payroll offices in several countries. Although their deaths have always been the subject of heated debate, both men were reportedly killed at San Vicente in 1908 while battling a large force of Bolivian soldiers.

▲ Butch (on horseback) and Sundance (tending to his horse) in Bolivia.

▶ The Sundance Kid and the mysterious Etta Place. This photograph was taken in New York, just before they departed with Butch Cassidy to South America.

DEC 2

1896 While refereeing a boxing match in San Francisco, Wyatt Earp is accused of purposefully misjudging the fight between Bob Fitzsimmons and Tom Sharkey.

NO JAIL COULD HOLD HIM

Desperado Harry Tracy proved many times that no jail built could hold him. Whether county calaboose or the walled Oregon State Penitentiary, Tracy always found a way to escape. And whenever this killer and thief, who at times rode with remnants of the old Wild Bunch, was on the loose, no one's life was safe. According to the July 3, 1902, *Seattle Daily Times*: "In all the criminal lore of the country there is no record equal to that of Harry Tracy for cold-blooded nerve, desperation and thirst for crime. Jesse James, compared with Tracy, is a Sunday school teacher." In gunfights and jailbreaks, Tracy created countless widows and orphans while taking the lives of possemen, corrections officers, sheriff deputies, and others who happened to get in his line of fire. When robbing stores and banks, Tracy was known to tell those he held at gunpoint: "I'm Tracy. I don't want to hurt anybody but those who get in my way, but when I say put your hands up, put them up." Tracy terrorized much of the Pacific Northwest until August 6, 1902. On that date, a posse near Creston, Washington, ambushed him. Badly wounded, he crawled into a field and took his own life before he could be taken into custody. He was twenty-seven years old. By the time the coffin carrying his body arrived in Salem, Oregon, all of his clothing and much of his skin had been stripped away by souvenir hunters.

▲ Tracy committed suicide in a field near Creston, Washington, rather than go back to prison.

▶ Mug shots of Harry Tracy.

H. Tracy
4088

DEC 3

1881 Sentenced to hang for the killing of a deputy sheriff, "Dirty Dave" Rudabaugh and six others dig through the walls of the jail in Las Vegas, New Mexico Territory, and escape.

STARR WINS PARDON

On January 16, 1903, President Theodore Roosevelt issued a presidential pardon for Henry Starr, one of the most prolific bank robbers in the nation's history. At the time, Starr resided far from his Cherokee Nation homeland inside the federal penitentiary at Columbus, Ohio, serving a fifteen-year stretch for manslaughter and robbery. Starr had already beaten the hangman twice. His legal problems started in 1892, after he murdered Deputy U.S. Marshal Floyd Wilson (the only man Starr ever killed) during a shootout. His crime spree increased, and throughout 1893, Starr robbed banks and a train in Indian Territory, Kansas, and Arkansas. He was arrested in Colorado, returned to Fort Smith, and indicted on fifteen charges. Starr claimed he killed Wilson in self-defense, but Judge Isaac Parker had a different opinion. Starr was found guilty and sentenced to hang. On appeal to the U.S. Supreme Court, he won a new trial, was again judged guilty, and had a new date with the gallows. Starr's attorney appealed and won a third trial, where Starr pleaded guilty to manslaughter and was sent to the federal pen. In 1901, Starr's mother and the Cherokee National Council applied for a pardon. President Roosevelt was impressed with Starr's bravery when he read an account of how Starr intervened during the Cherokee Kid's attempted jailbreak at Fort Smith and talked his friend into surrendering his firearm. The president commuted the sentence, and Starr was released in 1903. He married and named his first child Theodore Roosevelt Starr. However, within a few years, Starr had forgotten his promise to stop robbing banks and was back on the outlaw trail.

▶ Mug shots of Henry Starr.

DEC 4

1876 In Yankton, Dakota Territory, the second trial begins for Jack McCall for the murder of Wild Bill Hickok in Deadwood. When asked why he didn't challenge Wild Bill to a fair fight, he replies, "I didn't want to commit suicide." McCall is found guilty and hanged on March 1, 1877.

THE JERSEY LILY

Less than a year after the death of Judge Roy Bean in 1903, his beloved Lillie Langtry, the English actress called the Jersey Lily, finally arrived in the dusty Texas border town that bore her name. Although she and Bean never met, Langtry wanted to honor the old man who had loved her from afar. Locals presented her with one of Bean's six-shooters and a plaque that read: "It aided him in finding some of his famous decisions and keeping order West of the Pecos River. It also kept order in the Jersey Lilly [sic] Saloon. Kindly accept this as a small token of our regards." Wiping a tear from her eye, Miss Langtry graciously accepted the mementos, ordered a round of drinks for everyone in the saloon, and avoided having to adopt Bean's pet bear when Bruno broke his tether and sent everyone running.

▲▲ English beauty queen Lillie Langtry, known as "The Jersey Lily."

▲ Judge Roy Bean dreamed of meeting Lillie. He called his saloon "The Jersey Lilly" in her honor.

▶ Langtry visited the town that bore her name only after Roy Bean's death.

JUDGE ROY BEAN NOTARY PUBLIC
JUSTICE OF THE PEACE
LAW WEST OF THE PECOS
ICE BEER.
THE JERSEY LILLY

DEC 5

1873 George Armstrong Custer completes his book *My Life on the Plains* at Fort Abraham Lincoln, Dakota Territory, as he celebrates his thirty-fourth birthday with his wife, Elizabeth.

THE VIRGINIAN

Just after the twentieth century began, a towering bestseller appeared that spawned the myth of the archetypal cowboy hero and became the most influential Western novel ever written. Published in 1902, *The Virginian* by Owen Wister, a native of Philadelphia who went West for his health before studying law at Harvard, was an instant success. In the five decades after it first appeared, more than 1.8 million copies of the novel sold. Dedicated to the author's old friend, Theodore Roosevelt, the book not only glamorized the "Wild West," but also gave it relevancy. *The Virginian* made the cowboy a stalwart heroic figure and put him center stage in the nation's consciousness. Wister helped shape an image of the American West that would endure for all time. Wister's Virginian, described by J. Frank Dobie as a "cowboy without cows," emerged as a chivalrous champion best remembered for uttering one line. When Trampas, the book's vicious villain, sneered, "You bet, you son-of-a-_____," over a saloon poker game, the Virginian calmly replied, "When you call me that, *smile*."

▲ Owen Wister's highly successful Western novel *The Virginian*.

▶ This illustration in the first edition of *The Virginian* captures the poker game where the hero utters his unforgettable line, "When you call me that, *smile*."

DEC 6

1875 A deadline of January 31, 1876, is set by the Indian Bureau in Washington, D.C., for all Indians to be on reservations or be considered hostile and treated accordingly.

THE GREY FOX

During a life of crime spanning a half-century, Bill Miner stole more than $250,000, pulled the first train robbery in Canada, and was cheered by an adoring crowd following one of his many prison escapes. Miner was the last of the old-time bandits. He was just fourteen in 1866 when he was convicted of horse thieving in California and served a four-year hitch in San Quentin. Only a few months after his release, Miner was captured when he and two accomplices robbed a Wells Fargo coach. Sentenced to ten years, he won a new trial on appeal, only to have three more years tacked on. Miner served nine, and after he got out in 1880, he went back to robbing stagecoaches and trains. He picked up the nickname the Grey Fox in the latter part of his criminal career after the turn of the twentieth century. In 1901, he robbed a train in Oregon and then headed north into Canada and robbed two more trains. Miner was captured by the Royal Mounted Police and given a life sentence. In 1907, the Grey Fox slipped over the prison wall and bolted back to the United States. After robbing a train in Georgia in 1911, he was once more apprehended and sent to the state pen for twenty years. Miner tried and failed to escape several times before dying in prison in 1913. He was sixty-six, had never killed anyone, and, according to lore, originated the command, "Hands up!"

▲ A tintype of Old Bill Miner while he was still young.

▶ This lengthy Pinkerton reward notice details the many crimes of Old Bill Miner.

PINKERTON'S BANK & BANKERS' PROTECTION

BY

PINKERTON'S NATIONAL DETECTIVE AGENCY.

FOUNDED BY ALLAN PINKERTON 1850.

WM. A. PINKERTON, CHICAGO.
ALLAN PINKERTON, NEW YORK. } Principals.

GEO. D. BANGS, GENERAL MANAGER, New York.

—OFFICES.—

NEW YORK	92 Liberty Street.	CHICAGO	131-137 South Fifth Avenue.	DENVER	Foster Building.
BOSTON	30 Court Street.	PITTSBURGH	Machesney Building.	KANSAS CITY	Gloyd Building.
PHILADELPHIA	112-116 North Broad St.	CLEVELAND	Hippodrome Building.	HOUSTON	Chronicle Building.
BALTIMORE	Continental Building.	DETROIT	Ford Building.	SALT LAKE CITY	Kearns Building.
ATLANTA	Candler Building.	CINCINNATI	Mercantile Library Building.	SPOKANE	Paulsen Building.
BUFFALO	Fidelity Building.	ST. PAUL	Capital Bank Building.	SEATTLE	Alaska Building.
MONTREAL	Merchants Bank Building.	ST. LOUIS	Wainwright Building.	PORTLAND, ORE	Marquam Block.
TORONTO	Colonial Building.	NEW ORLEANS	Hibernia Bank Building.	LOS ANGELES	Wilcox Building.
WINNIPEG	McArthur Building.			SAN FRANCISCO	Flood Building.

$300.00 REWARD

To Police Officials, Sheriffs, Peace Officers, etc.

Shortly after midnight, Tuesday, October 16th, 1911, GEORGE ANDERSON, alias GEORGE BUDD, alias A. E. MINER, alias A. E. MINOR, alias "BILL" MINER, alias "OLD BILL" MINER, Train Robber, Stage Hold-up and Safe Burglar, escaped from the Georgia State Convict Farm at Milledgeville, Georgia, with John B. Watts and Thomas H. Moore, two other convicts, after overpowering the guards.

Photograph of GEO. ANDERSON alias "BILL" MINER

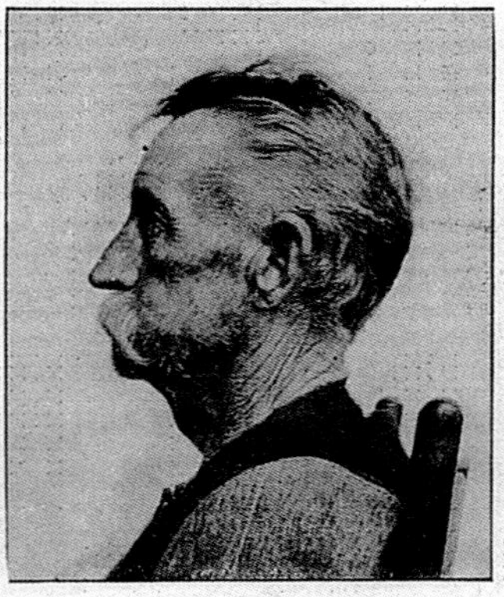

TAKEN FEB. 28th, 1911

DESCRIPTION

NAME........George Anderson
ALIAS. George Budd, A. E. Miner, A. E. Minor, "Bill" Miner, "Old Bill" Miner.
COLOR........White
NATIVITY........American
OCCUPATION........Miner
CRIMINAL OCCUPATION........Train Robber, Safe Burglar and Stage Hold-up.
AGE........69 Years
HEIGHT........5 ft. 8½ inches
WEIGHT........130 pounds
BUILD........Slender
COMPLEXION........Medium Fair
COLOR OF HAIR. Light Chestnut
EYES........Light Blue
STYLE OF BEARD........Mustache
COLOR OF SAME..Sandy Mixed with Gray.

BERTILLION: 74.0, 74, 89.0, 18.7, 14.6, 13.0, 6.9, 25.7, 12.2, 9.5, 47.4.

I. Tattoo heart pierced by arrow (surcharged) at 3 c, above 1st joint index rear. Small round scalloped tattoo on base of thumb rear and inner. Scar of 1.4 oblique outer on base of thumb front.
II. Tattoo, female, short skirt, legs crossed, hands over head holding wreath, below elbow front. Tattoo steering wheel, five spokes at 2 c. above wrist joint.
III. Small mole at 1 c. below left eye, inner. Scar sinuous of 6 horz. at 2 c. below larynx. Small mole on left side of nose at 2 c. below root.
IV. Brown mole on front of right shoulder. Mole at 2 c. to left of median 11 c. below nipple.
V. Tattoo of star at 12 c. below left knee outer.

Thomas H. Moore's description is: White, 21 years of age, height 5 ft. 8 in.; weight 147 pounds; light hair and blue eyes; scar on left side of face above ear, caused by burn.

John B. Watts; white; 41 years of age; height 5 ft. 8 in.; weight 128 pounds; dark hair; brown eyes; small scar on back of right thumb; small scar on knuckle of right index finger; small scar on right side of chin.

George Anderson, alias "Bill" Miner, etc., together with Charley Hunter, alias Charles A. Smith, alias C. E. Black, and Charlie Hanford Couch, alias Jim Hanford, held up Southern Railway train No. 36 on the night of February 18th, 1911. These men were arrested on February 25th, 1911, and convicted on March 3rd, 1911. Lawrence was sentenced to 20 years, Hanford and Hunter 15 years each to the Georgia State Convict Camp, of Hall County, Georgia. During the early part of October, Anderson, alias Miner was transferred to the Georgia State Convict Farm at Milledgeville, Georgia, from where he made his escape.

The Southern Express Company, of Atlanta, Georgia, offers the above reward (expiring on Oct. 17th, 1912), for the arrest, detention, and surrender of George Anderson, alias "Bill" Miner, etc., to the proper authorities of the State of Georgia.

Under its rules, this Agency, or its employees is not permitted to accept any reward or part thereof.

Should Anderson, alias Miner, etc., be located, place under arrest, and notify by telephone, telegraph or otherwise the nearest of the above listed offices, or

PINKERTON'S NATIONAL DETECTIVE AGENCY,

No. 606-607 Candler Building, ATLANTA, GA.

Atlanta, October 17th, 1911.

Bell Telephone, Ivy 629

DEC 7

1869 Frank and Jesse James and Cole Younger rob The Daviess County Savings Bank of Gallatin, Missouri. Jesse poses as a customer and kills cashier John W. Sheets, with whom the brothers have had a grudge since the Civil War. Bank clerk William McDowell is wounded, and the gang gets away with only five hundred dollars.

GERONIMO'S WISH

In 1906, the year after he caused a sensation by appearing in President Theodore Roosevelt's inaugural parade, Geronimo dictated his memoirs:

"There is no climate or soil which, to my mind, is equal to that of Arizona. We could have plenty of good cultivating land, plenty of grass, plenty of timber and plenty of minerals in that land which the Almighty created for the Apaches. It is my land, my home, my fathers' land, to which I now ask to be allowed to return. I want to spend my last days there, and be buried among those mountains. If this could be I might die in peace, feeling that my people, placed in their native homes, would increase in numbers, rather than diminish as at present, and that our name would not become extinct. I know that if my people were placed in that mountainous region lying around the head waters of the Gila River they would live in peace and act according to the will of the President. They would be prosperous and happy in tilling the soil and learning the civilization of the white men, whom they now respect. Could I but see this accomplished, I think I could forget all the wrongs that I have ever received, and die a contented and happy old man. But we can do nothing in this matter ourselves—we must wait until those in authority choose to act. If this cannot be done during my lifetime—if I must die in bondage—I hope that the remnant of the Apache tribe may, when I am gone, be granted the one privilege which they request—to return to Arizona."

—*Geronimo's Story of His Life*, 1906

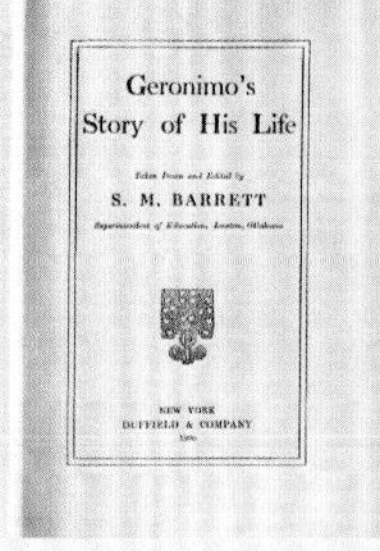

Geronimo's
Story of His Life

S. M. BARRETT

NEW YORK
DUFFIELD & COMPANY

▲ Geronimo, through an interpreter, told the story of his life.

▶ Geronimo at Fort Sill in Indian Territory following his confinement in Florida.

DEC 8

1883 Five men attempt to hold up the Goldwater & Castaneda Store in Bisbee, Arizona Territory, but unbeknownst to the outlaws, the payroll they expected to seize had not yet arrived. While making their getaway, the brigands shoot and kill four citizens, including a New Mexico peace officer and a pregnant woman.

OKLAHOMA'S GALA DAY

On June 11, 1905, the three Miller brothers—Joe, George, and Zack—hosted a one-of-a-kind celebration on their sprawling 101 Ranch, just south of Ponca City, Indian Territory. By best estimates, at least sixty-five thousand men, women, and children showed up at the ranch, making it the largest gathering of its kind in the history of the Twin Territories (Oklahoma Territory/Indian Territory). The Miller brothers called it "Oklahoma's Gala Day." Several thousand of the guests were editors and publishers from across the nation who arrived on special trains. Thousands of visitors showed up in wagons or buggies or on horseback. Pickpockets, purse cutters, and watch stealers known as super twisters stayed busy all day and into the night. Cowboys hauling fresh drinking water drained two ponds. There were rodeo contests, a buffalo chase, trick shooters, and a simulated Indian attack on a wagon train that appeared so real, people watching swooned. One highlight was the appearance of Geronimo, brought to the ranch in chains by soldiers from Fort Sill. Spectators watched wide-eyed when the old Apache warrior dropped a buffalo with his Winchester rifle. Later Geronimo donned a top hat and posed for pictures behind the wheel of an automobile. The spectacular event at the 101 Ranch was a complete success and served as a springboard for the entry of the Millers into the world of big-time show business.

▲ Geronimo became a big attraction at fairs, parades, and other public events.

▶ In this illustration, Geronimo wears a top hat and drives a car.

INDIANS UP TO DATE. APACHE CHIEF GERONIMO AND THREE BRAVES, OKLAHOMA.

DEC 9

1866 Nelson Story and his gnarly drovers arrive in Virginia City, Montana Territory, after trailing one thousand head of Longhorns from Texas. This completes one of the first and longest cattle drives in history.

DUSKY DEMON

There never was another cowboy quite like Bill Pickett. This black wrangler, who endured extreme racial prejudice, invented bulldogging—the only rodeo event ever originated by an individual. Pickett's style for bringing down a steer was unusual. He would leap from his pony, Spradley, onto the steer's back, grab a horn in each hand, and dig his boot heels into the ground. After twisting the critter's head to bring up its nose, he chomped his teeth on the cow's tender lip and fell backward causing the beast to fall down. With flair, Pickett threw his hands into the air to show the audience that he no longer needed to hold the horns. Billed as the "Dusky Demon," Pickett signed on with the Miller Brothers' 101 Ranch in 1905. He rode with them as both a performer and cowhand until his death at age sixty after he was kicked in the head while taming an unbroken chestnut gelding. Will Rogers spoke of his passing on national radio. More than one thousand people gathered on the ranch for Pickett's funeral. He was laid to rest on a windswept hill, not far from where his beloved Spradley was buried. For the rest of his own life, Zack Miller looked folks straight in the eye and told them, "Bill Pickett was the greatest sweat-and-dirt cowhand that ever lived—bar none."

▲ One of the 101 Ranch's most popular attractions was Bill Pickett, later featured in a film as advertised in this poster.

▶ Oklahoma's 101 Ranch used their resources to start their own Wild West show.

DEC 10

1852 The first legal public hanging in San Francisco takes place before a crowd of ten thousand when accused murderer José Forner y Brugada, a native of Valencia, Spain, is executed on the gallows on Russian Hill. The condemned man dies proclaiming his innocence.

AMERICA'S COWGIRL

Just before the Miller Brothers' Gala Day extravaganza in 1905, they acquired the services of a bona fide world-champion rodeo performer—the spirited nineteen-year-old Lucille Mulhall. The ranch already boasted many skilled bronco-fighters and rope-tossers, but most of the hired hands were rough saddle tramps and unpolished working cowboys. The Millers believed a few rousing specialty acts were needed as crowd pleasers, and Lucille fit that bill perfectly. Weighing less than a pair of fancy Mexican saddles, Lucille not only threw steers and busted broncs, but also stalked prairie wolves, branded cattle, and roped as many as eight running range horses at once. She was an absolute showstopper. Earlier in her life, while riding with her father's Wild West troupe, Lucille became acquainted with a lariat artist billed as the Cherokee Kid, the first one to call Miss Mulhall "America's First Cowgirl." The young part-Cherokee cowboy ended up not doing too bad for himself. Thanks to his spinning rope and natural wit, he eventually became known and loved around the world by his real name—Will Rogers.

▲ The 101 Ranch's "Real Wild West" show thrived.

▶ Lucille Mulhall (left) was a popular performer in the Miller Brothers' show.

DEC 11

1881 El Paso, Texas, city marshal Dallas Stoudenmire celebrates his thirty-sixth birthday with James B. Gillett, his newly hired assistant. Two days later, Stoudenmire receives a belated gift when he captures accused killer Chris Moesner, returns him to New Mexico authorities, and gains a five-hundred-dollar bounty.

TILL THE REAPER COMES ALONG

Tom Horn, who for so long made his living as a hired killer in the employ of big cattlemen, met his own fate at the end of a noose for a murder he may or may not have committed. Horn's date with the hangman did not come about until 1903, a few years after he served as a mule skinner in the Spanish-American War, managing to survive malaria but never setting foot on Cuban soil. Back in Wyoming, Horn returned to bronco busting and working as a hitman, taking out rustlers who plagued the large ranchers. In 1900, after Horn ambushed several suspected thieves in Brown's Hole, a notorious haunt for Wyoming outlaws, he boasted, "I stopped cow stealing there in one summer." Then on July 18, 1901, fourteen-year-old Willie Nickell was shot twice in the back at his family's homestead. The intended target was the boy's father, Kels Nickell, but in the dim light the attacker mistakenly killed the youngster. Deputy U.S. Marshal Joe Lefors suspected Horn and, in January 1903, convinced him to meet to discuss taking care of some Montana rustlers. At the meeting, Lefors claimed that Horn admitted killing the boy. Later at his murder trial, Horn complained that he was drunk and Lefors twisted his words to get the so-called confession. Horn was found guilty. One year later, on November 20, 1903, just one day shy of his forty-third birthday, Tom Horn was hanged.

▶ Tom Horn with horsehair ropes, which he made while in a Cheyenne, Wyoming, jail waiting to be hanged.

▶▶ Horn maintained that Joe Lefors (pictured) tricked him into a confession of shooting a young boy. Nonetheless, Horn was found guilty of the crime and hanged.

DEC 12

1872 Buffalo Bill Cody and Texas Jack Omohundro arrive by train in Chicago, Illinois, to prepare for the debut of their Wild West stage show, *The Scouts of the Prairie*.

BROADWAY BAT

In 1902, Bat Masterson turned his back on the American West he had helped mythologize and moved to New York City. After spending most of his life bouncing around cow towns and frontier hot spots as a buffalo hunter, saloon keeper, and lawman, Masterson decided to use his talent as a writer in the city that never sleeps. He was captivated by New York and enjoyed living and working in the heart of the sporting and theatrical district, a far cry from the dusty streets of Dodge City. Masterson became the subject of countless newspaper and magazine articles, and also pursued his own work as a journalist. In 1905, President Theodore Roosevelt appointed him a deputy federal marshal for the southern district of New York, a post that he kept only two years. He concentrated instead on his writing. Masterson was persuaded to write "Famous Gunfighters of the Western Frontier," a series of sketches about his old pals, including Wyatt Earp, Luke Short, Bill Tilghman, Doc Holliday, and Buffalo Bill Cody. In New York, Bat ran with a much different crowd, including John Barrymore, Louella Parsons, Stuart Lake, and Damon Runyon, who used him as inspiration for Sky Masterson in *Guys and Dolls*. For twenty years, Masterson wrote a regular sports column for the *Morning Telegraph*, mostly reporting on two of his passions—boxing and horse racing. His close friend, William S. Hart, the top Western movie star of the day, admitted, "I play the hero that Bat Masterson inspired." On October 25, 1921, after writing his final column, Masterson quietly died of a heart attack at his desk.

▶ Bat Masterson moved to New York City and became a sportswriter in 1902.

DEC 13

1894 Deputy Marshal Newton LeForce dies of bullet wounds the day after being shot while he and a posse searched for two train robbers near Broken Arrow, Indian Territory. As the posse approached a haystack where the outlaws were sleeping, several dogs began barking, awakening one of the suspects and his wife. Gunfire broke out, and LeForce was mortally wounded.

DEATH BY URINATION

Pat Garrett, the lawman who shot Billy the Kid, died on February 29, 1908, while urinating alongside a road not far from Las Cruces, New Mexico Territory. Like the legendary outlaw he killed in 1881, Garrett never knew what hit him when a bullet slammed into the back of his head. His unceremonious killing, humorously called "death by urination" by some cowboys, closed out a lifetime of lost dreams and broken promises. After he killed the Kid, Garrett basked in a short-lived limelight. He lost several sheriffs' elections and also a seat in the New Mexico Senate. By the late 1890s, Garrett once again served as a sheriff and, in 1901, was appointed customs collector in El Paso by Theodore Roosevelt. After five years of service, Garrett was not reappointed because he embarrassed Roosevelt by allowing a notorious gambler to pose in a photograph with the president at a Rough Riders reunion. At the time of his murder, Garrett resided on his ranch, trying to find a way to pay off taxes and impatient creditors. The day he died, Garrett was in a buggy with Carl Adamson, a prospective buyer for some of Garrett's land. Just east of Las Cruces, they happened upon Wayne Brazel, a cowboy who leased land from Garrett for grazing goats. Brazel refused to break his lease to allow sale of the land unless Adamson also bought Brazel's goat herd. The deal was on the verge of collapse. The men were arguing when they stopped to relieve themselves. In only minutes, Garrett was dead. Brazel confessed to the crime. He was tried for murder and acquitted after telling the jury he shot Garrett in self-defense. No one else was ever brought to justice for the slaying of the man who killed Billy the Kid.

▲ Wayne Brazel confessed to shooting Pat Garrett on the trail near Las Cruces, New Mexico Territory. Many did not believe he did it and Garrett's death is still a mystery.

▶ Pat Garrett, after being appointed customs collector in El Paso, Texas, by President Roosevelt, achieved a level of success and recognition and was included in the book *Men of Texas*.

Men of Texas

DEC 14

1878 A Texas newspaper supports a law that would make it illegal to kill buffalo for their hide alone. General Philip Henry Sheridan opposes the law, pointing out that buffalo hunting has done more to control Indians than the entire U.S. Army.

OLD WARRIORS DEPART

Two of the most capable and at one time feared Indian leaders died in 1909. On February 17, the old Chiricahua Apache guerrilla fighter Geronimo succumbed to pneumonia while still confined as a prisoner of war at Fort Sill, Oklahoma. A week before his passing, Geronimo rode to a store in Lawton and paid a soldier to buy some illegal whiskey. The following morning, an unconscious Geronimo was found lying in a shallow creek. He had become intoxicated and fallen from his horse the night before. Pneumonia set in, and he quickly declined. Geronimo hung on hoping to see his son and daughter, who had been summoned from school, but they arrived too late. Later it was found that the army officer had mailed a letter to the school instead of sending a telegram. Surrounded by old warriors, Geronimo died with his greatest wish unfulfilled—to once more see his beloved Arizona homeland. On November 10, 1909—ten months after Geronimo's passing—Red Cloud, former chief and war leader of the Oglala Sioux, died at the age of eighty-seven on the Pine Ridge Reservation. Nearly blind in his last years, Red Cloud still remained an important symbol of strength to his tribe, although, unlike the steadfast Geronimo, he had converted to Christianity and allowed the Jesuits to educate future generations of reservation children.

▶ Red Cloud at a very advanced age, c. 1905.

▶▶ Geronimo, not long before his death in Oklahoma in 1909.

DEC 15

1890 At the Standing Rock Indian Reservation in South Dakota, Sioux holy man Sitting Bull is killed by Indian Affairs authorities who claim he is resisting arrest.

KILLIN' JIM MILLER

Despite the acquittal of Wayne Brazel in Pat Garrett's murder, there was plenty of speculation about who might have been the real triggerman. Even though Brazel had confessed to the crime, he was acquitted after a jury deliberated for less than thirty minutes. Many alternative theories arose as to what really transpired that day. Some thought that the goat controversy was a ruse and Brazel intentionally took the blame for Garrett's murder, confident he would never be punished. Fingers pointed at Jim "Killer" Miller, a psychopath and hired assassin credited with at least fourteen killings, although the actual number may have been closer to fifty. The first man Miller killed was his sister's husband, blasted with a shotgun while he napped. It was said that Miller was addicted to killing and had no compunction about murdering anyone for money, including law officers. Whether or not Killin' Jim Miller really was paid ten thousand dollars to slay Garrett was never proved. Only weeks after Garrett was shot, Miller's life ended after he was taken into custody and charged with accepting money from three Oklahoma Territory ranchers to kill former Deputy U.S. Marshal Augustus Bobbitt. The ranchers wanted Bobbitt dead as the result of a disagreement over land and money. The morning of April 19, 1909, in the town of Ada, a lynch mob of about fifty angry Oklahomans dragged Miller and the three ranchers from the jail to an old livery stable. After binding the foursome's hands with wire cables, the vigilantes hanged them from the rafters. The bodies were left there for hours, resulting in this famous photograph. Eighty-eight years later, a monument was erected near the site of the livery stable commemorating "The End of the Old West."

▲ Killin' Jim Miller, c. 1906.

▶ Miller, at the left, and his three confederates hanging from the rafters of a barn in Ada, Oklahoma, left there by a lynching party.

A.A. BOBBIT

DEC 16

1853 At Chino Pond, New Mexico Territory, James Magoffin and a posse attack a wagon train returning from the salt beds with a load of salt and a herd of oxen. Magoffin originally denies the theft, but later apologizes and returns the stolen goods.

WILD WEST SHOWS

During the early 1900s, any number of Wild West shows, using the successes of pioneer showmen Buffalo Bill Cody and Pawnee Bill Lillie as models, toured the nation and the world. The long roster of new shows barnstorming the countryside came in all sizes, but few were as large as Cody's operation. Most troupes that popped up vanished from sight just as quickly. From 1883 to the mid-1930s, more than one hundred Wild West shows came and went. One of the most popular and long-lasting was the Miller Brothers' 101 Ranch Real Wild West. During the first three decades of the twentieth century, the Millers' show was known halfway around the globe. It featured as many as one thousand performers—cowboys and cowgirls, Indian warriors in bright paint and flowing feathers, clowns, sharpshooters, Russian Cossacks, equestrian acrobats, brave bull riders, and much more. In 1929, *Time* magazine wrote: "To thousands of U.S. citizens the 101 Ranch Wild West Show represented the embodiment, the incarnation of that vanished West in which cowboys had not become associated with drugstores and Indians were not graduates of Carlisle." Kings and queens, millionaires, and hundreds of thousands of ordinary working folks cheered themselves hoarse when the 101 Ranch riders performed at rodeo grounds, stadiums, and exhibition halls in the United States, Europe, Mexico, and Canada.

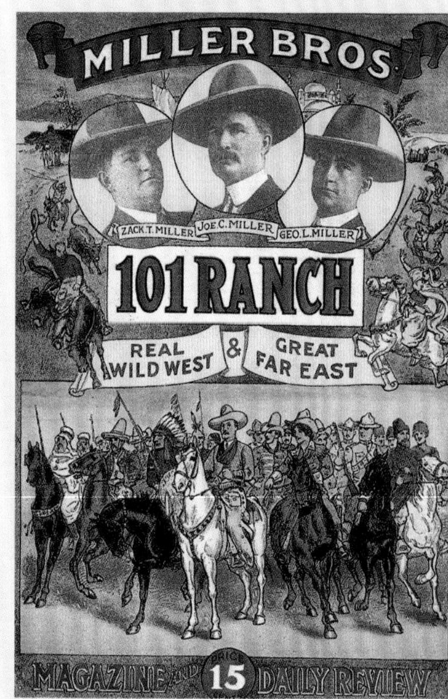

▲▶ Posters and programs for the three leading Wild West shows at the beginning of the twentieth century.

REALISTIC SCENES FROM
EARLY FRONTIER DAYS
TRUTHFULLY DEPICTED BY
REAL COWBOYS AND INDIANS
IN CONJUNCTION WITH
PAWNEE BILL'S PIONEER DAYS

DEC 17

1866 General Patrick Connor, known as a ruthless Indian fighter, orders that any Indians living north of the Platte River "must be hunted like wolves." Connor's troops are told, "Attack and kill every male Indian over twelve years of age."

TWO BILLS

In the summer of 1908, Major Gordon W. "Pawnee Bill" Lillie settled his touring Wild West show for an entire season at Boston's Wonderland Park. While his show played in Boston, Pawnee Bill went to New York and met with the administrator of the estate of James Bailey of Barnum & Bailey fame, who had died in 1906. Bailey's executors, anxious to sell the Bailey interest in the Buffalo Bill Wild West, offered the deal to Lillie. After a parley with Cody at Keene, New Hampshire, where his Wild West was playing, Lillie purchased the Bailey interest. He and Cody agreed to call their combined shows "Buffalo Bill's Wild West and Pawnee Bill's Great Far East," popularly known as the "Two Bills" show. The combined endeavor would not make its first major public appearance until the 1909 season opener at New York's Madison Square Garden. From the start, Lillie's wife, May, vehemently opposed the merger. Keenly aware of Buffalo Bill's reputation as a womanizer, hard drinker, and poor business partner, May reminded her husband that they had finally made their own show profitable and had nothing to gain from partnering with Cody. She vowed to never travel with the Two Bills, but retire instead to their ranch at Pawnee, Oklahoma. It was a promise that Miss May—"Champion Girl Shot of the West"—kept, to the lasting regret of her husband and her many fans. The Two Bills show lasted less than five years. By 1913, Cody's poor management and his proclivity for reckless investment had taken a toll. Pawnee Bill and Buffalo Bill finally closed shop, and the two old showmen declared bankruptcy.

▲ A program for the combined show.

▶ Pawnee Bill (left) and Buffalo Bill (right) sign an agreement to merge their two shows in 1908.

DEC 18

1876 Just west of unruly Fort Griffin, Texas (a haven for buffalo skinners known as "Hide Town"), vigilantes hang eleven horse thieves. This prompts the Austin *Weekly Statesman* to report: "No wonder the highwaymen are seeking security east of the Colorado [River]."

THE LAST COMANCHE CHIEF

For the last thirty years of his life, Comanche chief Quanah Parker, son of a white woman and Indian warrior father, embraced some of the white man's culture without giving up his Comanche way of life. Parker refused to become a Christian, remained polygamous, and advocated the use of peyote in religious practices. He also hunted wolves with President Theodore Roosevelt, established a ranching industry on the reservation, and built a solid relationship with the U.S. government that he had once fought. In December 1910, shortly after bringing the remains of his beloved mother and baby sister from Texas to Oklahoma, Parker's heart weakened, and he began a rapid decline. In early 1911, while attending a Cheyenne medicine feast, he became ill and was taken by train back to Oklahoma. Surrounded by his many wives at his home called Star House, the warrior priest realized his end was near. He refused to see a white physician but allowed a tribal medicine man to minister to him. After the holy man prayed, he placed his arms around the chief's body, flapped his hands, and made the call of an eagle, the messenger of the Great Father. Parker sipped some water and died. They dressed Parker in the regalia of a Comanche warrior. His funeral attracted two thousand people from across the nation. Four years after his death, grave robbers desecrated his resting place. Parker's bones were ritually washed and placed in a new coffin. Many years later the remains of Parker, his mother, and sister were moved to the Fort Sill Cemetery—the final resting place for the last chief of the Comanches.

▶ Quanah Parker in 1911, toward the end of his life.

DEC 19

1880 At Fort Sumner, New Mexico Territory, Billy the Kid barely escapes a midnight ambush.
1905 In Villa Mercedes, Argentina, Butch Cassidy, the Sundance Kid, Etta Place, and an unknown accomplice rob the Banco de la Nación and flee with twelve thousand pesos.

THE TALL TEXAN

Not every outlaw died of gunshot wounds or twitching from the end of a hangman's hemp necktie. Case in point was desperado Ben Kilpatrick, a long and lanky Lone Star State native whose running mates called him the "Tall Texan." Kilpatrick, described as being "absolutely fearless" and a crack shot, quit cowboying and took up train and bank robbery. As a member of Butch Cassidy's Wild Bunch, Kilpatrick participated in some high-profile heists and was sitting dead center in the famous group photograph taken in 1901 at Fort Worth. That same year, he was back in Texas where his partner William Carver was killed in an ambush. Kilpatrick comforted Carver's grieving outlaw girlfriend, Laura Bullion. The couple was arrested and sent to prison at Jefferson City, Missouri. Miss Bullion got out after serving five years, but Kilpatrick remained behind bars until 1911 when he immediately returned to a life of crime. On March 12, 1912, Kilpatrick and his former cellmate Ole Hobek tried to pull off the last train robbery in Texas. They had everything carefully planned, including having a boy waiting with getaway horses that had been shod with their shoes backward to throw off pursuing lawmen. The robbers never got that far. In the course of the holdup, a rookie Wells Fargo messenger distracted Kilpatrick and fatally struck him in the back of the neck and on the head with a wooden ice mallet. When Hobek entered the train car, he was shot dead with Kilpatrick's rifle. The slain outlaws were taken to nearby Sanderson, where townsfolk posed with the corpses as though they were hunting trophies. Then the bodies were wrapped in sheets and buried in one coffin—making the pair partners forever.

▲ This wooden ice mallet was the weapon used by the Wells Fargo messenger to kill Ben Kilpatrick.

▶ The bodies of former Wild Bunch member Ben Kilpatrick (left) and his partner Ole Hobek (right) are being held up after their failed attempt to rob a train's express car.

TRAIN ROBBERS KILLED NEA
NDERSON TEX MAR 13 1912
PHOTO BY NOGLE

DEC **20**

1878 In the Cherokee Hills of Oklahoma Territory, famed Deputy U.S. Marshal Bass Reeves—the first black marshal west of the Mississippi—kills outlaw Bob Dozier when he refuses to surrender.

AL JENNINGS

The mold was broken after the making of Alphonso "Al" Jennings, an attorney who robbed banks, ran for governor of Oklahoma, and ended up in the movie business in California. During the 1890s, Jennings served as a prosecuting attorney in Oklahoma Territory. He joined brothers Ed and John in a law practice in Woodward, where in 1895 Ed was killed and John wounded in a shootout with rival lawyer Temple Houston. After Houston's acquittal, Al moved to the Creek Nation in Indian Territory and called together some outlaws that eventually became known as the Jennings Gang. One notable member was Richard "Little Dick" West, who formerly rode with Bill Doolin's bunch and was killed by a posse led by Deputy U.S. Marshal Chris Madsen in 1898. About that same time, Jennings, never successful as a criminal, was captured after a bungled train robbery. In 1899, he was convicted and given a life sentence. Thanks to the efforts of his brother John, Al's prison time was reduced to five years. He was freed on technicalities in 1902, and received a full presidential pardon in 1907. A contrite Jennings returned to Oklahoma, opened a law practice, and started his profession as a movie actor, appearing in several early Westerns filmed in the new state. He published his biography in 1913 and made it into a movie. The next year, Jennings ran for governor, pledging, "If elected I promise to be honest for a year—if I can hold out that long." He made a strong third place finish on a slate of six, garnering 24 percent of the vote. Jennings retired to California and worked in the motion picture industry as an actor and consultant. A movie on his life came out in 1951, ten years before Jennings quietly passed away.

▶ Oklahoma's Al Jennings.

▶▶ "Little Dick" West was killed just outside of Guthrie. He rode for a short time with Jennings.

DEC 21

1876 Gunfighter Clay Allison kills town marshal Charles Faber in the Olympic Dance Hall of Las Animas, Colorado. Clay's brother John is also shot during the fracas. Although seriously wounded, John recovers, and Clay is released when no witnesses are willing to testify.

RIDERS OF THE PURPLE SAGE

In 1912, Zane Grey, regarded as the greatest storyteller of the American West, published *Riders of the Purple Sage*, his first bestselling novel of the scores he would write over the next quarter of a century. The book has never been out of print, and for many years some Old West buffs considered it the best Western ever written. Grey had been a semiprofessional baseball player and later a dentist, before taking up the pen and following his dream of becoming an author of Western fiction. Following his breakthrough success in 1910 with the publication of *Heritage of the Desert*, Grey built a family home in California and established a hunting lodge on the Mogollon Rim in Arizona. After submitting *Riders of the Purple Sage* to Harper and Brothers, Grey was told the book was too controversial because of the way Mormons were portrayed. There was serious talk of rejecting the book until Grey threatened to self-publish. Harper and Brothers relented and printed the novel. The book was an instant success, except in the state of Utah. During Grey's life and since his death in 1939, at least 113 movies have been made from his stories.

▲ *Riders of the Purple Sage*, Zane Grey's bestselling Western.

▶ An illustration of romance on the trail in *Riders of the Purple Sage*.

DOUGLAS DUER-

DEC

22

1879 In the dining room of the Stratford Hotel in Shakespeare, New Mexico Territory, Ross Wood is shot and killed by "Bean Belly" Smith during an argument over the last egg in the kitchen.

SATURDAY'S HEROES

During the first three decades of the twentieth century, the Miller brothers of 101 Ranch fame kept alive the memory of the Old West through their touring shows. But their efforts stretched beyond the Wild West shows, which played to live crowds around the world. Most of the earliest Western motion pictures were filmed at the 101 Ranch, allowing the Millers to reach an even broader audience. Outlaws, ex-lawmen, Indians, rugged cowboys, and cowgirls were used as extras and principals in some of the earliest Westerns shot on the ranch and in California, where the show entertainers wintered. The timing was impeccable. It was a chance for the real Old West figures to become big-screen heroes and heroines at Saturday matinees. Although early cowboy star William S. Hart never appeared in one of their productions, he visited the 101 Ranch and worked with several of the Millers' top hands. More than a few of the authentic cowboys and cowgirls who worked for the Millers made the leap to film. Tom Mix, Hoot Gibson, Buck Jones, Ken Maynard, Yakima Canutt, and many others saddled cow ponies and drew wages on the ranch long before becoming famous film stars. During the ranch's glory years from about 1905 through 1925, movie crews moved freely around the property among the working cowhands. On the 101 Ranch, the West of myth collided and merged with the West of reality—a spectacle that could never be duplicated.

▶ Tom Mix was a genuine cowboy before becoming a big success in Western films.

▶▶ Cowboy William S. Hart acting in a Western film.

WILLIAM FOX
PRESENTS
TOM MIX
IN
CUPID'S ROUND UP
A THRILLING STORY OF THE GOLDEN WEST
By GEORGE SCARBOROUGH
SCENARIO BY
CHARLES KENYON
FOX FILM
CORPORATION
STAGED BY
EDWARD J. LeSAINT

DEC 23

1880 At Stinking Springs, New Mexico Territory, Billy the Kid and three pals—trapped inside a rock cabin—surrender after Pat Garrett's posse shoots and kills Charlie Bowdre.

THE PASSING OF THE OKLAHOMA OUTLAWS

While the Miller brothers kept film crews busy shooting Western movies at their 101 Ranch and out in California, other film companies were hard at work churning out "shoot-'em-up" films in Oklahoma. One of the most notable was *The Passing of the Oklahoma Outlaws*, subtitled *Picturization of Early Days in Oklahoma*. A silent movie produced by the Eagle Film Company in 1915, this six-part film re-created the high crimes and subsequent demise of several of Oklahoma's most notorious desperados, including Al Jennings, Henry Starr, and Bill Doolin. Bill Tilghman, one of the most famous Western law officers, directed the movie, filmed by Bennie Kent, a noted early photographer. Tilghman established the film company because he was so incensed by other films made by Jennings and Starr that depicted outlaws as victims driven to crime. Tilghman recruited his old running mates, former deputy U.S. marshals Chris Madsen, Bud Ledbetter, and E. D. Nix to take starring roles in his film, and he managed to convince the lone survivor of the Doolin Gang—Roy Daugherty, alias "Arkansas Tom Jones"—to play himself. The movie previewed in a special showing in Tilghman's hometown of Chandler and premiered in Oklahoma City to an audience peppered with equal parts lawmen and outlaws.

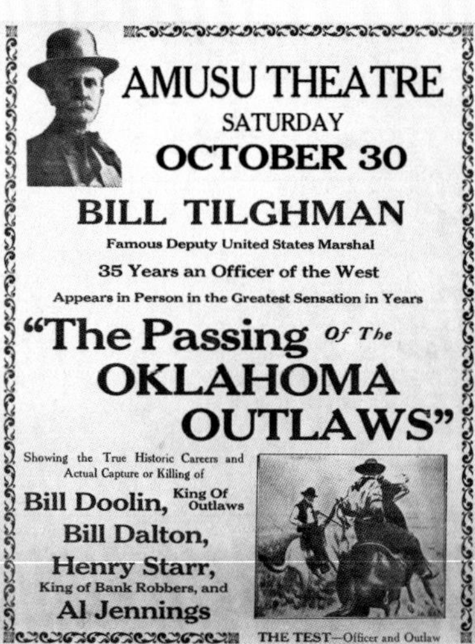

▲ Bill Tilghman directed and Chris Madsen and E. D. Nix starred in a 1915 movie called *The Passing of the Oklahoma Outlaws*.

▶ Sold at the movie showings was this small red book titled *Oklahoma Outlaws*, written by a reporter with help from Tilghman.

OKLAHOMA OUTLAWS
BILL DOOLAN
KING of OUTLAWS

DEC 24

1894 In Landusky, Montana, town founder and deputy sheriff Pike Landusky is killed by Kid Curry (Harvey Logan) in Jew Jake's Saloon. Kid, seeking some Christmas cheer, is confronted by Landusky for flirting with one of his stepdaughters.

LAST OF THEIR KIND

"It wasn't an easy thing to find six men to act as pallbearers for the body of Frank James, the former Quantrell [sic] *man and erstwhile bandit, funeral services for whom are to take place at the James farm near Kearney, Mo. at 2:30 o'clock this afternoon. . . . It was the request of the former bandit that no religious services be held at the funeral. He had a religion all his own, which involved a belief in the existence of a supreme being, but which did not coincide with a formulated creed. . . . 'When I die cremate me and put the ashes in a safety deposit vault,' he said. As was his wont, he made no explanation."*

—*Kansas City Journal*, February 20, 1915

"Cole Younger, one time famous bandit and member of the Jesse James gang, died at 8:45 o'clock tonight at the home of his niece, Miss Nora Hall. He had resided here since his return from Minnesota after serving a term of twenty-five years in prison for the participation in the attempted robbery of the Northfield State Bank. . . . Virtually everyone in this community was the former bandit's friend. Many children knew him as 'Uncle Cole,' and he was never too busy or too sick to greet them pleasantly. . . . Life in the open air always was a tonic to him. Like a fighting bulldog he was covered with scars. There were twenty bullet wounds in his body and yet he stood up under a long prison sentence in fair condition and soon after liberated was able to go on a lecture tour."

—*Kansas City Journal*, March 22, 1916

▶ Frank James, in his old age.

▶▶ Cole Younger "got religion" and enjoyed smoking his pipe in his old age.

DEC 25

1881 The toughest town in the West—Tombstone, Arizona Territory—proudly reports a quiet Christmas.

BUFFALO BILL'S LAST STAND

After several bumpy years on the entertainment circuit, Buffalo Bill Cody finally managed to clear his debts and in 1916 cut a deal with the Miller Brothers of Oklahoma, the only ones still operating a major Wild West show. It would be Cody's last stand. Failing to gain any share of ownership in the Millers' show, Cody settled for a performance fee of one hundred dollars a day and a percentage of the daily profits. In light of the coming World War, the new show was billed as "Buffalo Bill (Himself) and 101 Ranch Wild West Combined, with the Military Pageant [of] Preparedness." To give the production even more authenticity, Cody and the Millers convinced the U.S. War Department to lend some regular army troops to the spectacle. The new production had a strong start, but then a series of problems, including illness and inclement weather, plagued the show and audiences shrank. Cody's own health was failing, and the old showman had to be hoisted into the saddle, eventually riding into the arena in a buggy pulled by matched steeds. He still delighted audiences by shooting glass balls tossed in the air. Cody hung on until the final performance of the season on November 11, 1916. Thoroughly exhausted, Cody headed to Colorado to regain his health and do some writing. His condition continued to deteriorate. Just after high noon on January 10, 1917, the old scout—one of the prime creators of the mythical Wild West—died, six weeks before his seventy-fourth birthday.

▲ The program for Buffalo Bill's last show.

▶ One of the last photographs taken of Buffalo Bill Cody, 1913.

DEC 26

1862 In Mankato, Minnesota, thirty-eight Indians who took part in the Great Sioux Uprising are hanged by the U.S. Army—the single largest execution to date in American history.

A DEBTOR TO THE LAW

In 1919, celebrated Oklahoma bank robber Henry Starr was paroled from the penitentiary after serving only four years of a twenty-five-year sentence for bank robbery. For the next two years, Starr led an exemplary life and encouraged others to do so. He produced and starred in *A Debtor to the Law*, a film depicting Starr's ill-fated 1915 bank robbery in Stroud, Oklahoma, and even cast the young man who had shot Starr from his horse to play himself. Starr went on to appear in other silent movies, but in time he found himself back on the outlaw trail.

▲ After his release from prison and between robberies, Henry Starr starred in a movie about his life.

▶ Al Jennings, on the horse, had more success in Hollywood than he had robbing trains in Oklahoma.

HOTEL

DEC 27

1900 Carry Nation launches her campaign against the consumption of alcohol by attacking the bar in the Carey Hotel at Wichita, Kansas. The zealous Nation shatters a large mirror and throws rocks at a provocative painting of Cleopatra bathing.

▲▲ Paul Curry after he shot and wounded Henry Starr in Stroud, Oklahoma, in 1915.

▲ Henry Starr's book about his life.

▶ Starr in *A Debtor to the Law.*

SPICE OF DANGER

On February 18, 1921, Henry Starr and three companions drove into Harrison, Arkansas. It was the first time any outlaw had ever showed up to a bank job in an automobile. They strolled into People's National Bank with their .45-caliber pistols drawn. Starr wore a stylish dark pin-striped suit and silk cravat. As the armed men terrorized customers and ordered tellers about, former bank president W. J. Meyers, who happened to be there, remembered that twelve years earlier he had hidden a .38-40 Winchester Model 1873 rifle in the vault. While the robbers collected six thousand dollars in cash, Meyers slipped into the vault, grabbed the weapon, and opened fire. A slug slammed into Starr, severing his spine. He crashed to the floor, and his accomplices fled empty-handed. All of them were soon captured. On February 22, Starr died on a jail cot. At his side were his mother and his new wife. It was George Washington's birthday and the couple's first wedding anniversary. Also at the deathwatch was Theodore Roosevelt Starr, a son from an earlier marriage, named for the cowboy president who had granted Starr pardon years before. "I have robbed more banks than any man in the United States," Starr had told his doctor the day before he died. "It doesn't pay. I was in debt two thousand dollars and had to have money, so I turned bank robber again. I am sorry the deed is done." Like so many others, Starr's life and death instantly became entwined in myth and legend. He had made the transition from the days when outlaws rode horses to a time when they arrived at banks in swift motorcars and wore tailored suits.

DEC 28

1881 In Tombstone, Arizona Territory, after leaving the Oriental Saloon, Virgil Earp is wounded by shotgun blasts as he walks to the Cosmopolitan Hotel. He survives, but loses the use of an arm.

THE LAST SHOOTOUTS

After Bill Tilghman released his film *Passing of the Oklahoma Outlaws* in 1915, he devoted the next eight years to busily traveling with his morality flicker and lecturing on the folly of a life of crime. Then in 1924, the seventy-year-old lawman once more responded to a call to arms when a delegation of worried citizens from Cromwell, Oklahoma, asked him to clean up their oil boomtown, reputed to be the most wicked community in the state. It was in Cromwell that oil field roustabouts went to work each morning with a lunch pail in one hand and a club in the other. "If I don't get killed in a gunfight, I'll have to go to bed some day and die like a woman," Tilghman laughed. He got his wish. One November evening, a drunken prohibition officer shot him down in a confrontation in Cromwell. Tilghman's body was taken to the state capitol in Oklahoma City, where it lay in state for three days. Tilghman had outlived one of the star players in his outlaw movie. In January 1924, the dangerous Roy "Arkansas Tom" Daugherty died a violent death. After deciding that robbing banks was more enjoyable than making movies, Arkansas Tom, using an automobile instead of a horse, successfully robbed several Missouri banks until he was shot and killed in Joplin. Thousands of spectators filed past his open coffin in a funeral home to get a glimpse of one of the last links to the Wild West.

▶ Lawman Bill Tilghman (left) and outlaw Arkansas Tom Daugherty (right) shortly before their deaths in 1924.

DEC 29

1890 Near Wounded Knee Creek in South Dakota, the Seventh Cavalry attacks a group of Sioux. In the process of disarming them, some three hundred men, women, and children are massacred.

THE SAGA OF BILLY THE KID

In the Roaring Twenties, the American public rediscovered Billy the Kid. The Kid's dramatic reappearance in the culture of that decade seemed spawned by the disparity between the rich and poor of the time. Additional legends were propagated by Doubleday's 1926 publication of *The Saga of Billy the Kid*, written by Walter Noble Burns, a Chicago journalist. Thin on research but strong on fable, *The Saga* presented the Kid as a Robin Hood figure, a "quixotic, romantic idealist who symbolized a lost pastoral world." The book sold well and became the first selection of the Book-of-the-Month Club. This book as much as any work of its time confirmed and romanticized the youth's status as a mainstay of popular culture for decades to come.

▲▶ Two editions of Walter Noble Burns's book that started Billy the Kid on the path to becoming the most famous Wild West outlaw.

"That a boy in a brief life-span of twenty-one years should have attained his sinister preeminence on a lawless and turbulent frontier would seem proof of a unique and extraordinary personality. He was born for his career."

—Walter Noble Burns, *The Saga of Billy the Kid*, 1926

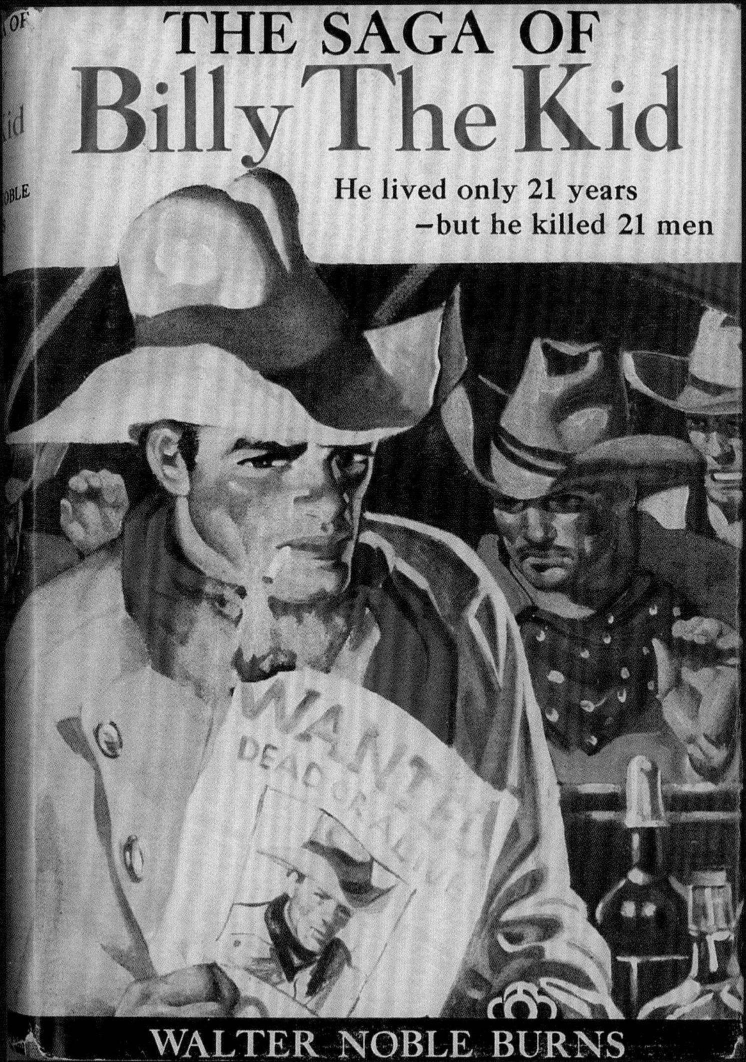

THE SAGA OF

Billy The Kid

He lived only 21 years
—but he killed 21 men

WALTER NOBLE BURNS

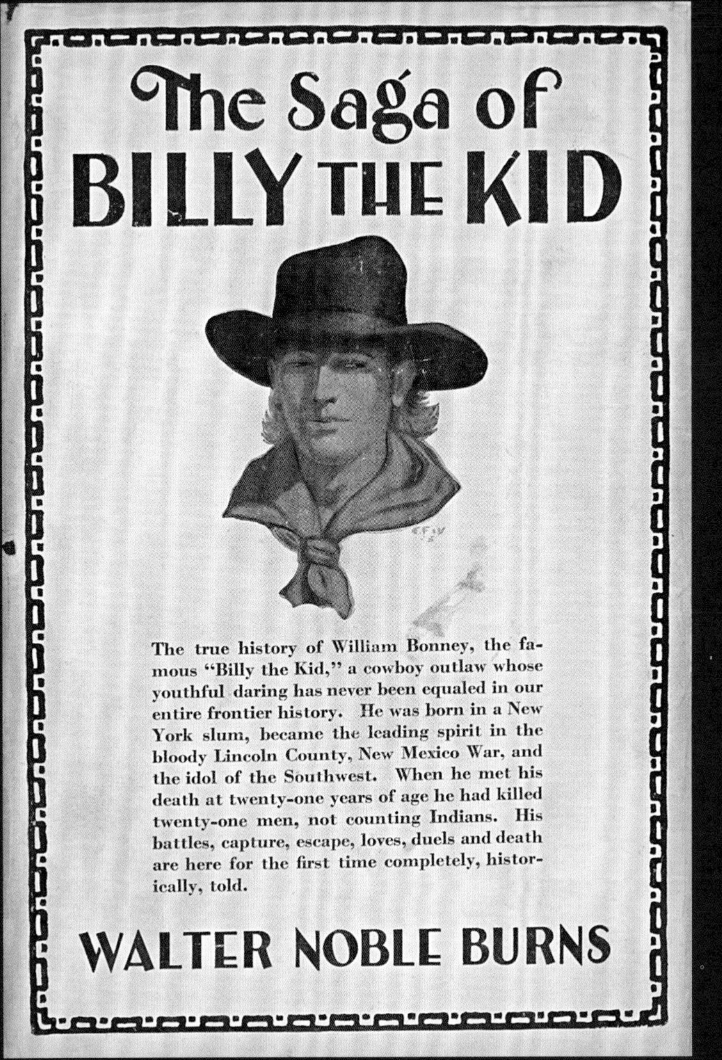

The Saga of

BILLY THE KID

The true history of William Bonney, the famous "Billy the Kid," a cowboy outlaw whose youthful daring has never been equaled in our entire frontier history. He was born in a New York slum, became the leading spirit in the bloody Lincoln County, New Mexico War, and the idol of the Southwest. When he met his death at twenty-one years of age he had killed twenty-one men, not counting Indians. His battles, capture, escape, loves, duels and death are here for the first time completely, historically, told.

WALTER NOBLE BURNS

DEC 30

1853 The U.S. government approves the Gadsden Purchase, acquiring Arizona and New Mexico Territories from Mexico for ten million dollars.

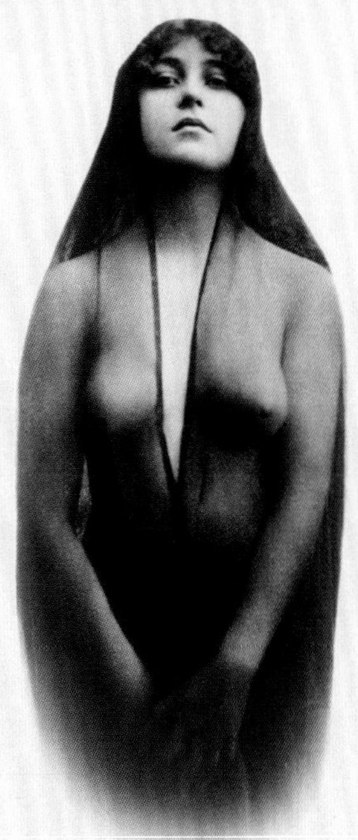

ADIOS WYATT

Wyatt Earp and Josephine Sarah Marcus, a girl from a prominent Jewish family in San Francisco, lived as husband and wife for nearly fifty years. The couple was a classic case of opposite temperaments complementing each other. Earp was quiet and reserved, while his wife was fiery. Still, Josie and Wyatt remained devoted to each other to the end. For Earp, that end came in Los Angeles, just a few minutes past eight in the morning on January 13, 1929. The old lawman died quietly. As Josie later wrote in her published recollections, "My darling had breathed his last, dying peacefully, without a struggle, like a baby going to sleep. I don't know how long I continued to hold him in my arms; I wouldn't let him go. They finally had to drag me away. I had gone with him on every trail he had ever taken since those days at Tombstone so long ago." Included among Earp's honorary pallbearers were cowboy movie heroes William S. Hart and Tom Mix. Wyatt's ashes were buried in a Jewish cemetery in Colma, just south of San Francisco. When Josie died in 1944, she was laid to rest with her husband. Cowboys often come to pay their respects. They doff their hats and stand on the manicured grass, surrounded by tombstones topped with menorahs and Stars of David, a world away from the blood and smoke of the O.K. Corral.

▲ A pinup photo from around 1915 that many wrongfully believed was of a young Josephine Sarah Marcus.

▶ An elderly Wyatt Earp.

▶▶ The real Josephine Earp, at about age sixty.

DEC **31**

1852 In California, the most prosperous year of the gold rush ends, with $81.3 million in gold mined.

GUN THAT KILLED THE KID

At the witching hour of July 14, 1881, Lincoln County Sheriff Pat Garrett shot and killed the young man known as Billy the Kid. The weapon Garrett used to dispatch the legendary young man was a blued-steel Colt Frontier Model, single-action, 44.40-caliber pistol. Garrett acquired the revolver, as well as an 1873 Winchester rifle, from outlaw Billy Wilson in December 1880 when Garrett and his posse captured Wilson, the Kid, and others at Stinking Springs. The handgun had been shipped from the Colt factory in 1880 to a store in Las Vegas, New Mexico Territory, where Wilson bought it. Garrett liked Wilson's weapons because both could conveniently fire the same ammunition, and he used them until 1900. Six years later, Garrett either loaned or sold the guns to Tom Powers, a gambler and owner of the Coney Island Saloon in El Paso. Powers wanted to include the pistol used to kill the Kid in a collection of historically important guns displayed over the bar at his saloon. Many years after Garrett's violent death, his widow Apolinaria wanted the guns returned, but Powers refused. When Powers died in 1930, the Garrett family sued his estate and three years later was awarded possession of the guns. The Colt pistol, along with other weapons, badges, engraved watches, and personal items that belonged to Garrett remained with the family for many years. Ultimately, Jarvis Garrett, who was only two years old when his famous father died, sold many of the items. The Colt revolver Garrett used to write history in 1881 today resides in a private collection in Texas.

▲ Apolinaria Garrett, the widow of Pat, proudly holding the gun her husband used to kill Billy the Kid.

▶ The Colt .44 single-action that killed the Kid.

UNITED STATES OF AMERICA.
THE STATE OF TEXAS,
ND, GOVERNOR.
of the State of Texas.
Know Ye, That I JOHN IRELAND, Governor
In Testimony Whereof,
BY THE GOVERNOR
Secretary of State.
Governor of Texas.
Adjutant-General.

INDEX

Page numbers in *italics* refer to illustrations.

All images are from the Robert G. McCubbin Collection, excluding those noted below.

Courtesy of Bob Boze Bell: pages 407, 439, 497, 661

Courtesy of the Buffalo Bill Historical Center, Cody, Wyoming; Vincent Mercaldo Collection: pages 73 (left), Neg. P.71.136; 184, Neg. P.71.168; 233, Neg. P.71.460; 294, Neg. 71.314; 311, Neg. P.71.839; 519, Neg. P.71.1030; 546, Neg. P.71.218; 585, Neg. P.71.112; 629 (right), Neg. P.71.1189

Courtesy of the Chuck Parsons Collection: page 388

Courtesy of Cowan Auctions: pages 107, 175, 178, 193, 244, 245, 263, 323, 340, 341, 349, 359, 542, 543, 688

Courtesy of the Craig Fouts Collection: pages 166, 493

Courtesy of Dorothy Sloan Books: page 37

Courtesy of James and Theresa Earle: pages 429, 465, 501 (right), 502, 735

Courtesy of the James D. Horan Collection: pages 7–11, 15, 18, 21, 23, 25, 28–31, 36, 39, 46, 51, 57, 59 (left), 62, 63, 65–67, 77, 81, 87, 90, 91, 93, 98–101, 103 (left), 108 (top), 109, 114, 115, 120, 121, 125, 126 (bottom), 128, 129, 133, 137–141, 145, 147, 149, 155, 159 (left), 168, 170–172, 176, 181, 185, 187, 189, 190, 194, 195, 197, 200, 201, 203, 208, 214, 215, 218, 220, 227–231, 235, 237, 239, 247, 251, 252, 262, 274, 275, 277 (left), 281, 292 (bottom), 295–297, 299, 303, 307, 314, 315, 324, 325, 332, 333 (left), 339 (right), 343, 345 (left), 353 (right), 374, 377, 379, 386, 387, 391, 392, 433, 436, 443, 447, 451, 452, 455, 458, 459, 462 (bottom), 463, 466, 469, 470, 472 (bottom), 476, 477, 491 (right), 495, 499, 527, 532, 533, 535, 559, 569, 570, 573–575, 577, 579, 581, 592, 593, 600, 601, 604, 605, 626 (bottom), 627, 643, 645, 652, 654, 657 (left), 663, 671, 674, 676, 695, 701 (left), 704 (top), 705, 718, 721 (right), 726 (top), 729

Courtesy of the John McWilliams Collection: page 131

Courtesy of the Len Gratteri Collection: page 672

Courtesy of the Palace of the Governors Photo Archives (NMHM/DCA): pages 80 (top), Neg. #7004; 153 (left), Neg. #133930; 285, Ben Wittick, Neg. #15855; 524, Clarence Batchelor, Neg. #2109

Courtesy of the Richard Ignarski Collection: pages 345 (right), 653, 662

Courtesy of John and Karen Tanner: page 591

Courtesy of the Woolaroc Museum, Bartlesville, Oklahoma: page 49

Michael Wallis is a bestselling author and has published sixteen books, most of which focus on aspects of the American West. His works include *Billy the Kid: The Endless Ride* (2008), *David Crockett: The Lion of the West* (2011), and *Route 66: The Mother Road* (1990). His books have garnered many honors, including awards from the Western Writers of America and the National Cowboy Hall & Western Heritage Museum.

Suzanne Fitzgerald Wallis owned and operated a large public relations firm in Tulsa, Oklahoma, for twenty-five years. She has collaborated on three books with her husband, Michael, and has been published in a variety of magazines and newspapers.

Most of the images in the book are from the **Robert G. McCubbin** Collection, one of the premier private collections of American Old West photographs. McCubbin is publisher emeritus of *True West* magazine and a founder of the Wild West History Association.

Project Manager: Deborah Aaronson
Editor: Caitlin Kenney
Designer: Darilyn Lowe Carnes
Production Manager: Anet Sirna-Bruder
Photo Editor: Robert G. McCubbin

Library of Congress Cataloging-in-Publication Data

Wallis, Michael, 1945-
The Wild West—365 days / by Michael Wallis; with Suzanne Fitzgerald Wallis, Robert G. McCubbin.
p. cm.
ISBN 978-0-8109-9689-2 (alk. paper)
1. West (U.S.)—History. 2. Frontier and pioneer life—West (U.S.) 3. West (U.S.)—Biography. I. Wallis, Suzanne Fitzgerald, 1943- II. McCubbin, Robert G. III. Title.
F591.W2574 2011
978--dc22
2010031064

Printed and bound in China

10 9 8 7 6 5 4 3 2 1

115 West 18th Street
New York, NY 10011
www.abramsbooks.com